Statistical Decision Theory and Related Topics

substantive field is the study of evolution conducted on the level of moleucles, or on the level of genes. While it appears most attractive, it has the drawback that, in order to get a glimpse of the variety of chance mechanisms contemplated, it is unavoidable to struggle through a great multitude of concepts and through an arsenal of terminology developed by molecular biologists, not to speak of a mass of facts and of their varying interpretations. My own status with these obstacles is that of a beginner, and the source of thoughts described below is limited to what I found, and thought I understood, in just four articles. The first two articles, [1] and [2], appeared in the August 1969 issue of the *Proceedings of the National Academy of Sciences*. The other two papers, [3] and [4], are published in a very interesting volume, *Evolving Genes and Proteins*, which I highly recommend.

2. *Background*. The idea that inheritance is carried by genes, located in chromosomes, is a very familiar one and many of us like to use in our lectures the consequences of the Mendelian laws as illustrations of elementary sections of probability. Thus, the difference, say, between Whale and Man is determined by some genes. However, the organism of a whale and that of a man have some characteristics in common. For example, both organisms depend on blood. Thus, among the genes of these two species there must be some, probably quite a few, carrying "messages" that demand the manufacture of blood cells. Furthermore, it is plausible that the blood cells of the two species, performing comparable functions, depend upon molecules, which, if not exactly identical, at least exhibit a substantial similarity. If a species A and another species B stem from a common

MOLECULAR STUDIES OF EVOLUTION: A SOURCE OF NOVEL STATISTICAL PROBLEMS*

By Jerzy Neyman

Statistical Laboratory, University of California, Berkeley

Abstract. The recently opened and rapidly developing field of evolution research, conducted on the level of molecules, is a novel source of interesting statistical and probabilistic problems. The biological studies are concerned with macromolecules which, in organisms as diverse as Man, Monkey, Carp, Whale and Yeast, perform similar functions and have similar structures. The apparently inconsequential differences among such homologous macromolecules, their sites and their frequencies, are at the base of current efforts to establish lineages linking the species studied to a common ancestor. The nature of statistical problems originating from such biological studies is illustrated on two tentative stochastic models of "inconsequential" substitutions in the macromolecules.

1. *Introduction.* The purpose of this paper is to bring to the attention of the community of mathematical statisticians a relatively novel, but rapidly developing. domain of substantive study which promises to generate a number of interesting problems of statistical theory. This new

*This investigation was supported in part by research grant GM 10525-08 from the National Institutes of Health, Public Health Service.

Statistical Decision Theory and Related Topics

particularly want to thank S. Zacks, D. Gilliland, David Moore, P. R. Krishnaiah, K. Alam, David Root, George McCabe, P. Puri, W. J. Studden, Y. L. Tong, Gary McDonald, James Arvesen, S. Panchapakesan, E. J. Dudewicz, and Eugene Klimko for their assistance. The tireless persistence of our typist, Mrs. Dorothy Penner, has produced a manuscript for photocopy which we feel to be of top quality, and we want to thank her for her devotion to this project.

Facilities for the formal meetings of the symposium were provided by the Krannert School of Industrial Management at Purdue University. The Conference Bureau at Purdue provided their counsel on many of the details necessary to arrange an organized meeting of this size. Thus it is apparent that these proceedings represent the culmination of efforts by many people with whom it has been a privilege to work.

Shanti S. Gupta
James Yackel

PREFACE

For nearly a decade there has been research activity in statistical decision theory at Purdue University. The area of multiple decision theory (selection and ranking procedures) has received particular attention. Since the year 1970-1971 was a special year in statistics and probability at Purdue University, and since the last Conference on Decision Processes was held here in 1961, it was felt that a conference to bring together research workers in decision theory and related topics would be quite timely.

The year 1970-1971 was designated by the Office of Naval Research as a special year in statistics and probability at Purdue University; the symposium was the main event of our special year. We unfortunately had to limit invitations to people in the United States due to the shortage of travel funds and the scheduling of the symposium in mid school year. Nevertheless, about one hundred participants from all areas of the country attended the sessions and showed a great deal of enthusiasm for the topics which were discussed both in the formal sessions and in informal gatherings during the time provided for such interchange.

This volume is a collection of the papers presented at the Symposium which was held November 23-25, 1970. There are twenty papers contained in the volume. An invited paper which was presented at the symposium by Herman Chernoff does not appear. The invited paper by R. E. Bechhofer and B. Turnbull, which is included here, was not presented at the symposium.

Professor Felix Haas, Dean of the School of Science of Purdue University, deserves particular thanks for his welcoming address and for the financial support of the symposium which was received from his office. The symposium was also sponsored partly under contract N00014-67-A-0226-00014 at Purdue University and we wish to thank the Office of Naval Research for this financial assistance.

We received cooperation and assistance from many colleagues in the profession in making the symposium a success. In particular, we wish to thank E. Lukacs, L. Katz, J. Wolfowitz, R. R. Bahadur, M. Sobel, P. R. Krishnaiah, M. L. Puri, W. J. Studden, E. Klimko, and H. Rubin for presiding over the various formal sessions of the conference.

The editorial work on this volume could not have been accomplished without the aid of colleagues who were willing to serve as referees. We are indebted to them for their careful reading of the various manuscripts. We

CONTRIBUTORS TO THE SYMPOSIUM

Shanti S. Gupta, Purdue University, Lafayette, Indiana (79)

J. Kiefer, Cornell University, Ithaca, New York (109)

E. M. Klimko, Purdue University, Lafayette, Indiana (225)

S. Kumar, University of Wisconsin, Milwaukee, Wisconsin (119)

Gary C. McDonald, General Motors Research Laboratories, Warren, Michigan (299)

Klaus Nagel, Purdue University, Lafayette, Indiana (79)

Jerzy Neyman, University of California, Berkeley, California (1)

S. Panchapakesan, University of Southern Illinois, Carbondale, Illinois (275)

Bernard Rosner, Harvard University, Cambridge, Massachusetts (161), (239)

Herman Rubin, Purdue University, Lafayette, Indiana (103)

Milton Sobel, University of Minnesota, Minneapolis, Minnesota (119), (255)

Yung Liang Tong, University of Nebraska, Lincoln, Nebraska (363)

Bruce Turnbull, Cornell University, Ithaca, New York (41)

J. Van Ryzin, University of Wisconsin, Madison, Wisconsin, (181)

L. Weiss, Cornell University, Ithaca, New York (29)

Robert Wijsman, University of Illinois, Urbana, Illinois (217)

J. Wolfowitz, University of Illinois, Urbana, Illinois (29)

James Yackel, Purdue University, Lafayette, Indiana (225)

Nicholas Zaino, Jr., University of Rochester, Rochester, New York (347)

CONTRIBUTORS TO THE SYMPOSIUM

Numbers in parentheses indicate the pages on which the authors' contributions begin.

James N. Arvesen, Purdue University, Lafayette, Indiana (239)

Robert Bechhofer, Cornell University, Ithaca, New York (41)

P. J. Bickel, University of California, Berkeley, California (207)

S. Blumenthal, New York University, New York, New York (119)

Thomas Bratcher, University of Southwestern Louisiana, Lafayette, Louisiana*

Herman Chernoff, Stanford University, Palo Alto, California*

A. P. Dempster, Harvard University, Cambridge, Massachusetts (161)

M. M. Desu, State University of New York at Buffalo, Buffalo, New York (255)

Edward J. Dudewicz, The University of Rochester, Rochester, New York (347), (363)

Bennett Eisenberg, University of New Mexico, Albuquerque, New Mexico (377)

Anil P. Gore, University of Kentucky, Lexington, Kentucky (313)

Z. Govindarajulu, University of Kentucky, Lexington, Kentucky (313)

*Paper not published in this volume.

CONTENTS

CONTENTS

Numbers in parentheses refer to AMS (MOS) 1970 subject classifications.

ACADEMIC PRESS, INC.
111 Fifth Avenue, New York, New York 10003

United Kingdom Edition published by
ACADEMIC PRESS, INC. (LONDON) LTD.
Berkeley Square House, London W1X 6BA

LIBRARY OF CONGRESS CATALOG CARD NUMBER: 79-159624

AMS (MOS) 1970 Subject Classifications: 62-02,
62F07, 62C99, 62G99, 62C25

PRINTED IN THE UNITED STATES OF AMERICA

Statistical Decision Theory and Related Topics

Edited by

Shanti S. Gupta and James Yackel
Department of Statistics
Purdue University
Lafayette, Indiana

Proceedings of a Symposium Held at Purdue University
November 23–25, 1970

Academic Press New York and London 1971

ancestor (AB), and if both A and B depend on an element which is essentially the same, such as blood, then the evolution from (AB) to A in one direction and to B in another must have involved: (i) changes in some genes ("drastic" changes) determining the distinction between A and B, and (ii) lack of drastic changes in some other genes that determine the elements common to both A and B.

Broadly, the subject of evolutionary studies on the molecular level consists of the unraveling of chains of events in particular molecules and in genes, some drastic and some apparently inconsequential, and in constructing lineages linking the currently living species to their hypothetical common ancestors. An essential point in this general problem is the estimation of the time of separation between ancestors of, say, Carp on the one hand and Man on the other.

In the above connection I feel impressed by a several years' effort [4] to identify a molecule (a protein) which, in all living forms, is the expression of a homologous gene, thereby presumably bespeaking the common ancestry of life as seen on Earth. The particular molecule tried indicated possible common ancestry of Rabbit, Flounder, Yeast and a bacterium *E-Coli*. On the other hand, the authors raise doubts regarding two other microorganisms studied.

Of course, the occurrence of changes in genes, termed mutations, are common knowledge. At least some mutations are induced by radiation. It may be presumed that changes in molecules involved in important functions of particular organisms reflect gene mutations. The general scheme of these molecular changes is, approximately, as follows. The molecules in question, the macromolecules, may be thought of as long structures, involving a number N of "sites". The number N varies from one macromolecule to another, ranging from possibly 50 to perhaps over 1000. To each site of a macromolecule there corresponds a certain number s of possible occupants which I shall call submolecules. The presumed inconsequential change in a macromolecule consists of the substitution of the earlier occupant of a site by some other submolecule. How inconsequential such substitutions are is a subject of discussion and it seems probable that the situation may vary from one site to another and from one macromolecule to the next. However, the attempts at timing the separations of ancestors of particular known species all appear to be based on the assumption that the substitutions considered do not create pressures of selection and also that they occur at a more or less constant rate. The rate of occurrence of substitutions may depend on the site, some sites being "hot" and some others "cold", and also on the macromolecule.

In some cases it is quite apparent that, in the thinking of the molecular biologists, the submolecules that are potential occupants of a given site are arranged in a sequence, say $a_1, a_2, \ldots, a_s$ so that one of them, a_i, can follow the earlier one a_{i-1}, but not the one before a_{i-2}. Some authors are explicit on the possibility of backward mutations. The observable data underlying the molecular evolutionary studies are numbers of sites in a given macromolecule in which the occupant in a species A differs from that in a species B. Another datum frequently given is the minimum number of substitutions required to create the observed difference in occupants of a given site.

A SOURCE OF STATISTICAL PROBLEMS

In order to illustrate the type of evolutionary studies, I wish to report on the subject of the paper [1] by Wilson and Sarich which the two scholars were also kind enough to describe personally at two sessions of the seminar in the Statistical Laboratory. The principal problem of the two authors was the choice between two alternative hypotheses on the lineage of Man, the African Ape and the Old World Monkey. Figure 1, redrawn from the original paper [1] illustrates these hypotheses.

The two authors favor the hypothesis B, according to which the relationship between Man and Ape is much closer than those of these two species and Monkey. Their convincing arguments include the following Table 1, which I reproduce with a small change in headings.

Table 1. Comparison of sites of hemoglobins

Species compared	No. of sites with different occupants	Minimum no. of substitutions
Man vs Chimpanzee (Ape)	0	0
Man vs. Gorilla (Ape)	2	2
Monkey vs Man	12	15
Monkey vs Chimpanzee	12	15
Monkey vs Gorilla	14	17
Horse vs Man	43	52
Horse vs Chimpanzee	43	52
Horse vs Gorilla	45	54
Horse vs Monkey	43	52

The data in Table 1 illustrate clearly that the hemoglobins in Man and in the two Apes are very similar, that Man and the two Apes differ more strongly from the Monkey and that the differences between these species and the Horse are all of the same order of magnitude and about three times as numerous.

One of the subjects studied by Kimura [2] is illustrated in Table 2 which gives the comparison of hemoglobin α chains in Carp and in several mammals. The quantity K is Kimura's estimate of the rate of substitutions per site of the hemoglobin α chain and per unit of time equal to the number of years between the present and the moment of separation of the ancestor of Carp and that of the mammals compared. As rightly pointed out by Kimura, the estimates of rates of substitutions are remarkably similar.

Table 2. Comparison of hemoglobin α chains of Carp with those of several mammals.

Mammal	No. of sites with different occupants	Total no. of sites	K
Man	68	140	.665 ± .082
Mouse	68	140	.665 ± .082
Rabbit	73	140	.722 ± .087
Horse	67	140	.651 ± .081
Bovine	65	140	.642 ± .079
Average	68.2	140	

The point in Table 2 that will be referred to below is that, with one exception, the number of sites in Carp with occupant submolecules different from those in mammals is just a little less than 70, which is one-half of the total number of sites studied.

3. *Statistical problems and stochastic models.* Some of the ideas found in the literature combine, so to speak, substantive biological considerations with the purely statistical aspects of the study. Thus, for example, various biological findings lead Kimura to take it for granted that the separation of the ancestors of Lamprey and Man preceded that of Carp and Man. Also, anatomical considerations lead some

authors to regret that, judging from the first two entries in Table 1, Man appears to be closer to Chimpanzee than to Gorilla. As I see it, some of the biologists are right in insisting, that, once it is admitted (however tentatively) that some chance mechanisms were operating in the general process of evolution, it is desirable to build the models of these mechanisms purely from stochastic considerations. Later, when the probabilistic problem of the distribution of the observable random variables is satisfactorily solved, the solution of the problem of estimation would provide both the structure of the complicated lineages and the relative time scale of the successive separations of the various species studied. Again, prior to considering that a given stochastic model is really satisfactory, a number of tests against plausible alternatives might suggest modifications of the model.

To illustrate these ideas, consider first the case of some three species, say A (perhaps for Ape), C (for Carp) and M (for Man). The assumption of a common ancestor implies just one "structure" of the evolution. At some early time, T units ago, the common ancestor (ACM) must have split into two entities, say ϑ_1 and $(\vartheta_2\vartheta_3)$. Here the symbol ϑ_1 may have one of the three possible values, either A, C, or M. Next, some T_1 units of time ago, the common ancestor $(\vartheta_2\vartheta_3)$ of the other two species must have split into ϑ_2 and ϑ_3, yielding the phylogenetic tree as in Figure 2.

Here, then, the state of nature is characterized by a two dimensional parameter which I shall describe as basic. One component may be symbolized by ϑ_1 which is capable of assuming three values only: either A, C, or M. The other basic component may be symbolized by $\tau = T_1/T \in (0,1)$. In addition to these two parameters, the characterization of the state of nature may require some additional ones which I will describe as secondary. These may be exemplified by the rate of substitutions per site, per unit of time, as in Kimura [2], which may well vary from one macromolecule to the next. Another possible example is the number s of potential occupants of a given site which, while chemically different, are all consistent enough to allow the macromolecule to perform the same function and to maintain its identity. It is quite likely that s varies from site to site and that its average value for one macromolecule is different from that for another.

If the number of species is larger than three, the basic parameter characterizing the state of nature becomes substantially more complicated. In fact, already with four species the phylogenetic tree (see Figure 3) may have two different structures. The first split (T units of time ago) of the common ancestor (ACMW) of the three species A, C, and M as above plus the fourth W(perhaps Whale) may be either into the ancestor ϑ_1 of just one of them plus the ancestor of the three others $(\vartheta_2\vartheta_3\vartheta_4)$, or into the ancestors of two pairs $(\vartheta_1\vartheta_2)$ and $(\vartheta_3\vartheta_4)$. With either structure two new splits must have occurred T_1 and T_2 units of time ago, respectively, leading to four separate species living at the present epoch.

Because of the uncertainty of time T of the first split, combined with that of the rates of substitution, all that one may hope to estimate from the data on differences among particular macromolecules are the ratios $T_1/T = \tau_1$ and $T_2/T = \tau_2$. With the first structure we have $0 \leqq \tau_2 \leqq \tau_1 \leqq 1$. With the second structure it is known only that $0 \leqq \tau_1, \tau_2 \leqq 1$. Here, then, the basic possible states states of nature are characterized by a three-dimensional parameter. One of the components referring to (structure x ϑ identification) is capable of assuming 18 discrete values. The other two components are τ_1 and τ_2, varying continuously either within limits $0 \leqq \tau_2 \leqq \tau_1 \leqq 1$ or each between zero and unity, independently from the other. The following sections are limited to cases of two and of three species presumed to have a common ancestor.

As illustrated by Tables 1 and 2, the observable variables involved in the molecular studies of evolution are, customarily, the numbers of sites in which some two species have different occupants. Occasionally, as in Table 1, this information is supplemented by the minimum number of substitutions. In the following only the first of these data will be considered but it will be assumed that a little more information is available. Consider a particular site in a macromolecule carried by each of some three species A, C, and M. If the number s of potential occupants of the given site is at least three, then the comparison of the three species would lead to the following five mutually exclusive results:

1. Occupants of the given site in the three species are all different;

2, 3, 4. Some two species have the same submolecule in the site considered, but the third species does not;

5. All three species have the same occupant of the site.

These possibilities may be symbolized as follows.

$$
(1)\qquad
\begin{array}{l}
1.\ A \neq C \neq M \neq A \\
2.\ A \neq C = M \\
3.\ C \neq A = M \\
4.\ M \neq A = C \\
5.\ A = C = M
\end{array}
$$

It seems plausible that when three species are studied for differences in occupancies of N sites in a given macromolecule, then the numbers, say N_i, of sites characterized by the results of the comparison symbolized in the above formulas (1), with $i = 1,2,3,4,5$, must be known. Because the numbers N_i must add up to N, the total number of sites, only four of them need be considered. With the notation introduced, the number of sites in which A and C differ is, say

$$(2)\qquad \Delta(AC) = N_1 + N_2 + N_3,$$

and, similarly,

$$(3)\qquad \Delta(AM) = N_1 + N_2 + N_4$$

$$(4)\qquad \Delta(CM) = N_1 + N_3 + N_4$$

and it is seen that the four variables N_i determine the three differences Δ, but not conversely. In fact we have

$$(5)\qquad N_2 = \frac{1}{2}[\Delta(AM) + \Delta(AC) - \Delta(CM) - N_1] \quad ,$$

$$(6)\qquad N_3 = \frac{1}{2}[\Delta(CM) + \Delta(AC) - \Delta(AM) - N_1] \quad ,$$

$$(7)\qquad N_4 = \frac{1}{2}[\Delta(AM) + \Delta(CM) - \Delta(AC) - N_1] \quad .$$

In particular, the data in Table 1 referring to the three species Horse (say A), Chimpanzee (say C) and Monkey (say M), with

$$(8)\qquad \Delta(AC) = \Delta(AM) = 43 \quad \text{and} \quad \Delta(CM) = 12,$$

are consistent with seven different values of $N_1 = 0,2,4,6,8,10,12$ and the consequent systems of values of N_2, N_3 and N_4 obtainable from (5) to (7). The importance of the loss of information due to the use of the numbers of differences Δ alone will depend upon the details of the chance mechanism considered. In particular, it is possible that, with some mechanisms, the three variables Δ will form a sufficient statistic in which case the variables N_i will be irrelevant. However, *a priori*, it seems prudent to begin with the sample space, say $*$, composed of all possible combinations of four non-negative and integer valued variables N_1, N_2, N_3, and N_4, subject to the restriction that their total does not exceed the number N of sites in the macromolecule studied. Further refinements are likely to become necessary when empirical studies bring out distinctions among sites, perhaps with categories "hot" and "cold", etc..

With the above setup, a great variety of statistical problems is to be expected. From the substantive point of view of the actual evolutionary process, the most interesting question seems to be whether the studies of several different macromolecules, carried by the species compared, all lead to mutually consistent estimates of what I described as the basic parameters: the same structure of the lineage with the same identification [say ϑ_1 = Carp and $(\vartheta_2\vartheta_3)$ = (Ape Man)] and the absence of significant differences between the time parameters τ. The differences in secondary parameters would be quite acceptable.

From the purely statistical point of view, the problems of the above type are interesting because they are so different from those customarily considered. First, there is the peculiar basic parameter space Ω indexed by a vector parameter with at least two components, one with only a finite number of possible values and the other varying continuously within a range, possibly dependent on the value assumed by the first component. The second difference between the present and the customary statistical problems is in the distributions of the observable random variables as determined by particular parameter values. Whatever the details of the models that may come under consideration, it is safe to expect that changes in the parameter values will not be constrained to location, scale, etc., in the familiar densities. The third important novelty is that, in a sense, the "experiments" in evolutionary phenomena are not repeatable. The best that a statistician may hope to see is the study of lineage of the same group of species, say Ape, Carp and Man, based on several different macromolecules. The basic parameter space Ω is expected to be the same for all macromolecules, but the secondary parameters are likely to be different. Thus, the data stemming from studies of different molecules will be "consistent" with respect to Ω but "not consistent" with respect to secondary parameters. Some time ago I was connected with a study of this kind, distinguishing between "structural" and "incidental" parameters [5], but then drifted away from the subject. Another possibility of quasi-repetition of the experiment is illustrated by the work of Kimura [2]. Here the same macromolecule is studied for rate of substitution, by comparing a far away species, Carp, with several others, presumed to be more closely related. In the sense of the earlier terminology [5], here the data are "consistent" with respect to one "structural" parameter, namely the rate of substitution, but "not consistent" with respect to some others.

Depending upon personal attitudes, the above theoretical statistical novelties may appear attractive for their own sake, quite apart from interest in the substantive questions as to whether, for example, a convincing lineage can be traced, complete with approximate timings, linking to a common ancestor not only Man, Ape and Monkey, but also Carp, Whale, Yeast and some bacteria.

Incidentally, the statistical problems of evolution of species have a degree of similarity (also a considerable degree of dissimilarity) with one aspect of the problem of evolution of galaxies [6]. The principal question here is the direction of evolution: whether from elliptical types to spirals, to irregulars, or vice versa. The point of departure is (presumed) physical pairs of galaxies, with the two components supposed to have been formed at the same epoch and then having evolved independently of each other, with a degree of random variation.

4. *Two tentative stochastic models of inconsequential changes in macromolecules reflecting evolution of species.* The simplest chance mechanisms which may perhaps approximate the actual phenomena of supposedly inconsequential changes in macromolecules, which open the way to the reconstruction of lineages of now living species, are two familiar Markov processes. Both models that come to my mind involve the assumption of homogeneity and of mutual independence of sites in the macromolecule. This is that to each of the N sites there corresponds the same number s of potential occupant

submolecules, that substitutions occurring at one site are independent of those at all other sites and that the chance mechanism of these substitutions at any one site is identical with that at any other. In other words, we assume, basically, that all the N sites considered are independent copies of each other. Naturally, this aspect of homogeneity applies only to the chance mechanism of substitutions, but not to the identity and functions of potential occupants of particular sites. In consequence of the assumption of homogeneity adopted, further assumptions on the chance mechanism governing the substitutions need be formulated for one site only.

Another general assumption of homogeneity that we adopt is that the probabilities of substitutions in any interval of time, from t to $t + dt$, are the same for all t. Also we adopt the Markovian assumption that these probabilities may perhaps depend upon the submolecule occupying the given site at time t, but not upon the past history of the site. Further assumptions underlying the two models differ. Before discussing them, it will be convenient to mention a particular consequence of the hypotheses already adopted.

When the same macromolecule is studied in two species only, and if the only thing that the analysis can provide is whether in the two species the occupant submolecules are the same or different, then the only observable variable is, say X, the number of those sites, out of the N studied, in which the two species differ. In this case, the hypotheses of homogeneity and independence of sites imply that X is a binomial variable, with the probability $p(T)$ depending on the time interval T between the split of the two species and the present, and on the mechanism of substitutions.

When the number of species studied is three, the discussion in the last section indicates that, for each site, the comparison of one macromolecule in these species may lead to one of five exclusive outcomes. Becuase of the same hypotheses of homogeneity and independence, the observable variables, labeled N_i with $i = 1,2,3,4,5$, and $\Sigma N_i = N$ are multinomial variables, with probabilities $P_i(T,T_1)$ depending upon the times T and $T_1 = T\tau$ of the two splits, on the identification of the parameter ϑ_1 and, naturally, on the mechanism of substitutions.

One more property of the variables N_i must be mentioned. Given the identity of the species ϑ_1 that splits from ancestor $(\vartheta_2\vartheta_3)$ of the others, the probability that the variables $N_i(\vartheta_1)$ will assume some stated values n_i adding up to N is, say

$$P\{\cap N_i(\vartheta_1) = n_i\} = \frac{N!}{\Pi n_i!} \Pi P_i^{n_i}(T,T_1) \quad . \tag{9}$$

It will be noticed that, because of the symmetry of ϑ_2 and ϑ_3,

$$P_3(T,T_1) = P_4(T,T_1) \tag{10}$$

with the consequence that, whatever the details of the mechanism governing the substitutions, the sum $N_3(\vartheta_1) + N_4(\vartheta_1)$ forms a statistic which, jointly with $N_1(\vartheta_1)$ and $N_2(\vartheta_1)$, is sufficient for all parameters involved.

After these preliminaries, we may proceed to the details of the two alternative mechanisms supposed to be operating in each of the N sites. Both are Markov processes; see for example [7].

Model 1. The first mechanism considered is the continuous time process with s states $a_1, a_2, \ldots, a_s$ symbolizing the s submolecules, potential occupants of the given site. Given that at time t the site is occupied by a_i, the probability of there being no substitution up to $t + dt$ is assumed to be given by

$$1 - \lambda dt + o(dt) \tag{11}$$

where λ, described as rate of substitution, is a positive constant number. The probability of the substitution $a_i \to a_j$, with $j \neq i$, is assumed to be

$$\lambda r_{ij} dt + o(dt), \tag{12}$$

where r_{ij} stands for the conditional probability that the substitution is from a_i to a_j. As usual, the probability of more than one substitution in time dt is assumed to be $o(dt)$. In general, the numbers r_{ij} may depend upon both i and j and it is quite likely that future studies will lead to the consideration of such distinctions. However, at the present moment we will assume that, for all i and j, the probabilities r_{ij} have the same value $1/(s-1)$. Familiar calculations lead then to the following formulas for transition probabilities, say

$$P_{ii}(t_1, t_2) = (1 + (s-1)e^{-k(t_2 - t_1)})/s \tag{13}$$

and

$$P_{ij}(t_1, t_2) = (1 - e^{-k(t_2 - t_1)})/s \tag{14}$$

for any $i = 1, 2, \ldots, s$ and for any $j \neq i$, where, for simplicity, $k = s\lambda/(s-1)$.

As the first application of formulas (13) and (14) we shall now calculate the probability, say $P\{\vartheta_1(T) = \vartheta_2(T)\}$

that two species which, T units of time ago, split from the common ancestor, will have the given site of the macromolecule considered occupied by the same submolecule. Denoting by a_1 the submolecule that the two species carried at the time of split, we have

$$
\begin{aligned}
P\{\vartheta_1(T) = \vartheta_2(T)\} &= P^2_{11}(0,T) + \sum_{j=2}^{s} P^2_{1j}(0,T) \\
&= \frac{1}{s^2}\{1 + 2(s-1)e^{-kT} + (s-1)^2 e^{-2kT} \\
&\qquad + (s-1)[1 - 2e^{-kT} + e^{-2kT}]\} \qquad (15) \\
&= \frac{1}{s}\{1 + (s-1)e^{-2kT}\} \quad .
\end{aligned}
$$

Accordingly, the probability that the occupants of the site will differ is

$$
P\{\vartheta_1(T) \neq \vartheta_2(T)\} = \frac{s-1}{s}\left(1 - e^{-2kT}\right) \quad . \qquad (16)
$$

For large T, that is, for two species with a very distant common ancestor, this probability will be just less than $(s-1)/s$. It will be remembered that, as shown in Table 2, the total number of sites at which the hemoglobin α of Carp differs from those of the several mammals is a little less than one-half of the total. The comparison of this result with formula (16) suggests that, for the particular macromolecule $s = 2$. If, as is reported in some cases, about 75 percent of the sites of a macromolecule in two distant species are found carrying different submolecules, formula (16) suggests that the number of potential occupants per site is $s = 4$. It will be noticed that formula (16) does not depend upon the homogeneity assumptions adopted, but applies to each site separately from others. Therefore, if it is admitted that the number s varies from one site to the next, but that the other assumptions of Model 1 are approximately realistic, the interpretation of the proportion of sites in which the two distant species have the same submolecule is that its reciprocal is approximately equal to the harmonic mean of the numbers $s_1, s_2, \ldots, s_N$.

Turning to the case of three species, we shall now compute the conditional probabilities, given the identity of ϑ_1, of the five possible outcomes of intercomparisons at one one site, indicated in formulas (1). Putting $T = 1$ and $T_1/T = \tau$, these five probabilities will be denoted by $P_i(\tau)$, $i = 1,2,\ldots, 5$. Because of the special role of the submolecule carried in the given site at the moment of split between ϑ_1 and $(\vartheta_2\vartheta_3)$ and because of the assumed unrestricted interchangeability of all the s potential occupants, the initial occupant submolecule (at the time of the first split) will be denoted by a_1. In order to avoid complicated summation signs in the formulas, we will write them using appropriate multiples of probabilities relating to a_1, a_2, a_3 and a_4. In particular, with obvious symbolism, we have

$$\begin{aligned} P_1(\tau) &= P\{\vartheta_1, \vartheta_2, \vartheta_3, \text{ all different}\} \\ &= (s-1)(s-2)\ P\{\vartheta_1 = a_1\}P\{\vartheta_2 = a_2,\ \vartheta_3 = a_3\} \\ &\quad + 2(s-1)(s-2)P\{\vartheta_1 = a_2\}P\{\vartheta_2 = a_1, \vartheta_3 = a_3\} \\ &\quad + (s-1)(s-2)(s-3)P\{\vartheta_1 = a_2\}P\{\vartheta_2 = a_3,\ \vartheta_3 = a_4\} \end{aligned} \tag{17}$$

The probabilities relating to ϑ_1 are given by (13) and (14) with substitutions $t_1 = 0$ and $t_2 = 1$,

$$P\{\vartheta_1 = a_1\} = \left(1 + (s-1)e^{-k}\right)/s \tag{18}$$

(19) $$P\{\vartheta_1 = a_2\} = \left(1 - e^{-k}\right) /s$$

Probabilities relating to the pair ϑ_2, ϑ_3 m
lated taking into account that these two now se
cies split at time $1 - \tau$ after their common ar
rated from ϑ_1. At the time of the second spli
tor $(\vartheta_2\vartheta_3)$ could have had either a_1 or so
molecule in the given site. The probabilities
events are given by formulas (18) and (19) wit
tutions of $k(1-\tau)$ for k. After the split,
ϑ_2 and ϑ_3 evolved independently over the pe
τ, ending at the present epoch. Simple calcu
on these remarks yield the following four form
bolism of which must be obvious:

(20) $$\begin{aligned} \alpha &= P\{\vartheta_2 = \vartheta_3 = a_1\} \\ &= 1+(s-1)e^{-2k\tau}+2(s-1)e^{-k}+(s-1)(s-2)e^{-} \end{aligned}$$

(21) $$\begin{aligned} \beta &= P\{\vartheta_2 = \vartheta_3 = a_2\} \\ &= \{1+(s-1)e^{-2k\tau}-2e^{-k}-(s-2)e^{-k(1+\tau)}\}/s^2 \end{aligned}$$

(22) $$\begin{aligned} \gamma &= P\{\vartheta_2 = a_1,\ \vartheta_3 = a_2\} \\ &= 1-e^{-2k\tau}+(s-2)e^{-k}-(s-2)e^{-k(1+\tau)}\}/s^2 \end{aligned}$$

(23) $$\begin{aligned} \delta &= P\{\vartheta_2 = a_2,\ \vartheta_3 = a_3\} \\ &= \{1-e^{-2k}\ -2e^{-k}+2e^{-k(1+\ )}\}/s^2 \end{aligned}$$

As a check, it is easy to verify that

(24) $$\alpha + (s-1)\beta + (2(s-1)\gamma + (s-1)(s-2)\delta$$

Obvious combinations of (17) with formulas (
yield then

$$P_1(\tau) = (s-1)(s-2)\{1-e^{-2k\tau}-2e^{-2k}+2e^{-k(2+\tau)}\}/s^2$$

$$P_2(\tau) = (s-1)\{1+(s-1)e^{-2k\tau}-2e^{-2k}-(s-2)e^{-k(2+\tau)}\}/s^2$$

$$P_3(\tau) = P_4(\tau) = (s-1)\{1-e^{-2k\tau}+(s-2)e^{-2k} -(s-2)e^{-k(2+\tau)}\}/s^2$$

$$P_5(\tau) = \{1+(s-1)e^{-2k\tau}+2(s-1)e^{-2k} +(s-1)(s-2)e^{-k(2+\tau)}\}/s^2 .$$

'or any particular tentative identification of ϑ_1, for ıple $\vartheta_1 = C$, three of the above formulas are mutually ependent. The maximum likelihood estimates of the three ›abilities are given by the formulas

$$\hat{P}_1(\tau) = N_1/N$$

$$\hat{P}_2(\tau) = N_2/N \qquad \text{and}$$

$$\hat{P}_3(\tau) = \hat{P}_4(\tau) = (N_3 + N_4)/2N$$

ıce that N_1 and also N_5 are independent of the iden- ıcation of ϑ_1. This is not true for N_2, N_3 and N_4. ı any particular identification of ϑ_1, formulas (29) be used for estimating the three unknown parameters s, ınd τ. First, formulas (25) to (27) might be solved for e^{-k} and $e^{-k\tau}$. The correctness of identification of ϑ_1 ıt be tested by inquiring whether N_3 and N_4 differ ıificantly, etc.. The complete solution of the problem ıt be forthcoming from the deduction of the confidence ion for the parameter point determined by τ, s, λ and

The adequacy of the model to represent the evolution of three species, say A, C and M, might be judged from

the comparison of the estimates of ϑ_1 and of τ, derived from studying several different macromolecules.

Model 2. The perusal of the biological literature suggests the existence of at least two distinct categories. In one category the observable variables seem to be limited to numbers of sites of a macromolecule in which some two species carry identical (or different) submolecules. Model 1 described above came to my mind primarily under the influence of this particular section of the literature. The other section of the literature [3], [4] is much more complex. Here, the potential occupants of a given site, denoted above by $a_1, a_2, \ldots, a_s$, are dealt with individually, have known chemical composition and structure, and their functions in the organisms concerned are being investigated. Also it is in this section of the literature that one finds indications of ordering of substitutions. The effort to follow ideas of this kind indicated the applicability of another familiar chance mechanism, that of random walk with two reflecting barriers. This is what I describe as Model 2.

For a given site of a macromolecule we consider a number s of *ordered* potential occupants $a_1, a_2, \ldots, a_s$. At any time t, the site considered can be occupied by any of these submolecules, say a_i. The probability that this will happen is denoted by $p_i(t)$. We visualize the following possibilities for any period of time $[t, t+dt]$. If $a_i = a_1$, then the only passage possible is from a_1 to a_2, with the probability of this happening equal to $\lambda_1 dt + o(dt)$, where λ_1 is a constant rate of the indicated substitution. If $a_i = a_s$, then the only substitution possible in the period dt is the "backward" substitution $a_s \to a_{s-1}$. Its probability is supposed to be $\mu_s dt + o(dt)$ where μ_s is a constant positive number. For each i exceeding unity but less than s, we contemplate two possible substitutions, the "forward" substitution $a_i \to a_{i+1}$, with probability $\lambda_i dt + o(dt)$, and the "backward" substitution $a_i \to a_{i-1}$ with probability $\mu_i dt + o(dt)$. Here, rates λ_i and μ_i are assumed constant in time and, in order to give effect to the terms "backward" and "forward", satisfying the relations $0 < \mu_i \leqq \lambda_i$. As usual, probabilities of more than one substitution are assumed $o(dt)$.

With these assumptions, the probabilities $p_i(t)$ satisfy a system of $s-1$ linear differential equations with constant coefficients

$$p_1'(t) = -\lambda_1 p_1(t) + \mu_2 p_2(t) \tag{30}$$

and, for $i \leqq s-1$

$$p_i'(t) = \lambda_{i-1}p_{i-1}(t) - (\lambda_i+\mu_i)p_i(t) + \mu_{i+1}p_{i+1}(t) . \tag{31}$$

Here $p_s(t)$ is determined by the condition that the sum of all $p_i(t)$ must be equal to unity.

The above system of equations can be solved and the solutions are known to be combinations of exponentials. As t is increased, the probabilities $p_i(t)$ tend to limits [7] obtainable by putting to zero the left hand sides of (30) and (31), namely, say

$$p_i = \lim_{t\to\infty} p_i(t) = p_1\lambda_1 \frac{\lambda_2}{\mu_2}\frac{\lambda_3}{\mu_3} \cdots \frac{\lambda_{i-1}}{\mu_{i-1}}\frac{1}{\mu_i} \tag{32}$$

and it is seen that p_i is likely to be less than p_{i+1}. In particular, if the rates of substitution λ_i, μ_i do not depend on i and $\lambda_i > \mu_i$, the limiting probabilities p_i will increase in a geometric progression.

Here, then, we have a sharp distinction between models 1 and 2. According to model 1, formulas (13) and (14), the limiting probability that the given site will be occupied by any possible submolecule a_i is the same, 1/s. Contrary to this, the mechanism of random walk with reflecting barriers, and with "forward" rates exceeding "backward" rates, implies $p_1 < p_2 < \dots < p_s$. This circumstance may have some bearing on the interpretation of empirical results.

Another point should be mentioned at this time. This is that, while the possibility of backward mutation is admitted by some authors, this possibility is ignored in their calculations. It is easy to see that, if rates μ_i of backward mutations are put equal to zero, then, as time goes on, the probability $p_s(t)$ will tend to unity. The practical conclusion would be that the given site would be always occupied by the ultimate submolecule a_s and that there would be no differences among the species concerned. Thus, when the occupants of a particular site vary from one species to the next, possibilities of backward mutations cannot be ignored.

5. *Concluding remarks*. The statistical problems connected with the above two tentative models of substitutions in macromolecules, which I term "inconsequential" substitutions, particularly the problem of set estimation of the "basic" vector parameter, are certainly novel and intriguing. They are interesting irrespective of how realistic the two models are. The degree of realism of these models is another source of statistical problems, those of testing hypotheses. While I do not expect these models to be very

realistic, the identification of points requiring modification may be important from the substantive point of view and may serve as a stimulus for construction of better models. In addition, the development of evolutionary studies on the molecular level will require a conceptual effort to harmonize the findings with the results of classical population genetics, as symbolized by the names of R. A. Fisher, J.B.S. Haldane and Sewall Wright. In conclusion, the statistical community seems to have gained a broad novel field of interesting research.

6. *A postscript.* The above pages were discussed with Vincent M. Sarich and Allan C. Wilson, my colleagues in Berkeley and authors of the first paper [1] which attracted my attention to the present subject. As a result of this discussion, for which I am very grateful, I came to realize that the mechanism of random walk in one dimension, described as Model 2, is not realistic. On the other hand, there seems to be some hope for a specialization of Model 1, representing a multidimensional random walk. Essentially, this means that, for each subscript i, there is a set of values of j, for which the probabilities r_{ij} of formula (12) are are equal to zero.

Let Σ stand for the set of possible occupants of the given site. To each potential occupant a_i there corresponds a non-empty subset Σ_i of Σ, composed of those submolecules termed neighbors of a_i, that can replace a_i in a single substitution. If a_m belongs to Σ but not to Σ_i, then it can replace a_i only through a sequence of at least two substitutions of the type $a_i \to a_j \to \ldots \to a_k \to a_m$, where a_j must be a neighbor of a_i and a_k a neighbor of a_m. With this setup, the calculation of probabilities, such as P_i of formulas (25) through (28), would require a number of hypotheses regarding the "neighborhoods" Σ_i and also quite a bit of interesting work.

Acknowledgment. I am grateful to Rose Ray and to Robert Traxler for their assistance in correcting proofs and for their helpful suggestions tending to improve the intelligibility of the paper.

References

1. Wilson, A. C.and Sarich, V. M. (1969). "A molecular time scale of human evolution, "*Proc. Nat. Acad. Sci.* 63, pp. 1088-1093.

2. Kimura, Motoo, "The rate of molecular evolution considered from the standpoint of population genetics," *ibidem*, pp. 1181-1188.

3. Zuckerkandl, Emile and Pauling, Linus (1965). "Evolutionary divergence and convergence in proteins," *Evolving Genes and Proteins*, Vernon Bryson and Henry J. Vogel, editors, Academic Press, New York and London. pp.97-166.

4. Joshi, J. G., Hoshimoto, T., Hanabusa, K., Dougherty,H.W. and Handler, P., "Comparative aspects of the structure and function of Phosphoglucomutase," *ibidem*, pp.207-220.

5. Neyman, J. and Scott, E. L.,(1948}. "Consistent estimates based on partially consistent observations," *Econometrica* 16, pp. 1-32.

6. Neyman, J.,(1969), "An unsolved problem stemming from astronomy," *Proc. 37th Session, Intern. Stat. Inst.*43-2, pp. 217-219.

7. Cox, D. R. and Miller, H. D. (1965). *The Theory of Stochastic Processes*. John Wiley and Sons, New York.

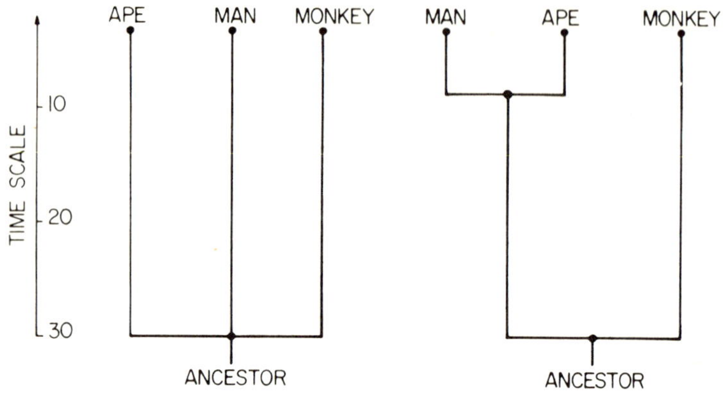

Figure 1

Alternative hypotheses as to the phylogenetic relationship of Man to the African Apes and the Old World Monkey (redrawn from ref. [1]).

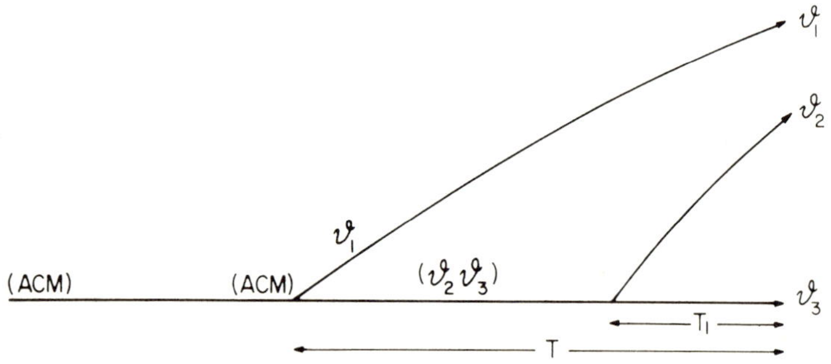

Figure 2

Lineage of three species A, C and M stemming from common ancestor (ACM): a single possible structure with three identifications determined by the identity of ϑ_1, either A, or C, or M.

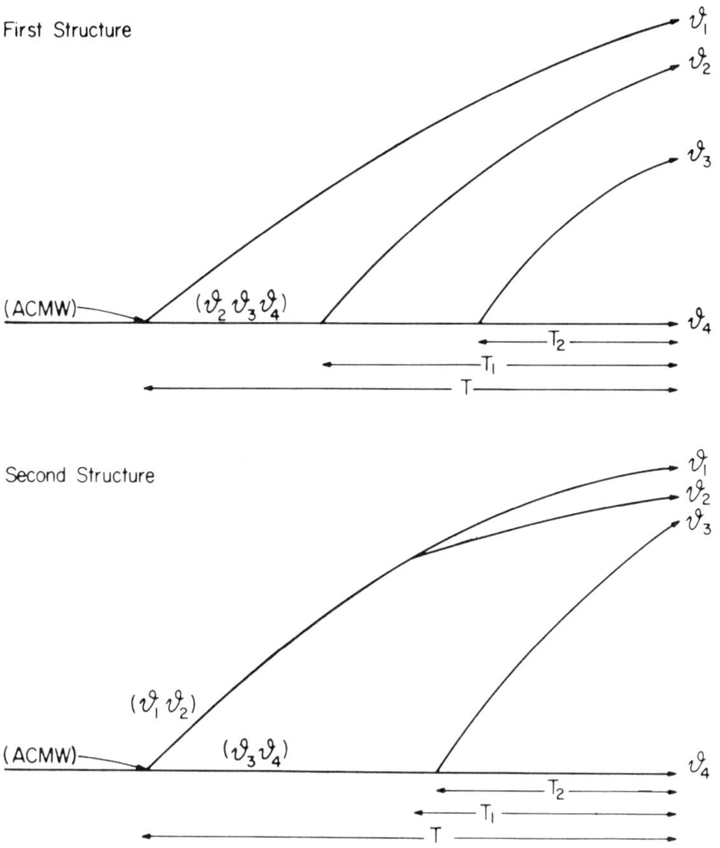

Figure 3

Lineage of four species, A, C, M and W stemming from the common ancestor (ACMW): two possible structures combined with 18 different identifications. The structure in the upper part of the figure allows for 12 different identifications, determined by the 12 ordered pairs of values of ϑ_1 and ϑ_2, either (A,C) or (C,A) or (A,M) or (M,A) etc.. or (W,M). The structure in the lower part of the figure allows for only six different identifications, determined by the unordered pairs of values of ϑ_1 and ϑ_2, either (A,C) or (A,M) or, etc... (M,W).

ASYMPTOTICALLY EFFICIENT ESTIMATION
OF NONPARAMETRIC REGRESSION COEFFICIENTS

By L. Weiss[1] and J. Wolfowitz[2]

Cornell University and University of Illinois

1. *Introduction.* In our paper [1] we constructed asymptotically efficient estimators of translation and scale parameters, separately and jointly, when the form of the density function is completely unknown to the statistician. Here "asymptotically efficient" is meant in the classical sense of minimal variance of the limiting normal distribution. (However, see also [3] and [4].) Asymptotic efficiency was proved by showing that the limiting distributions of our (normalized) estimators are the same as those of the asymptotically best estimators obtained when the form of the density function is known to the statistician.

In the present paper we obtain asymptotically efficient estimators of regression parameters when the density function is unknown. Our method involves a non-trivial use of the results of [1]. Formulas like those of (1.3), (1.4), (1.7), and (1.8) of [1] are not and cannot be available to us, the ordering of the observations being essentially changed by the parameters being estimated.

[1]Research supported by National Science Foundation Grant No. GP21184.

[2]Research supported by the U. S. Air Force under Grant AF-AFOSR-70-1947,monitored by the Office of Scientific Research.

It was pointed out in [1] (see also [5]) that, if one made use only of the "middle" $n(1-2p)$ observations, where $0 < p < 1/2$, weaker regularity conditions on the density function are needed. In the present paper we carry out the argument for such a p. If the regularity conditions are fulfilled for $p = 0$, the present results carry over with only trivial changes.

Without the requirement of symmetry of the density function (see Section 2 below) or an equivalent requirement, the parameter θ_1 (defined in Section 2) is not uniquely determined and hence cannot be estimated. The parameter θ_2 can be estimated without this requirement.

2. *Assumptions and notation.* For each n, let $X_1(n),\ldots, X_n(n)$ be independent random variables, $X_i(n)$ having density $f(x-\theta_1-\theta_2 t_i(n))$, where θ_1,θ_2 are the unknown parameters to be estimated, $t_i(n)$ is known and $-\infty < A \leqq t_i(n) \leqq B < \infty$ for all i and n. The density f is unknown but satisfies the following conditions:

(1) f is symmetric about zero.

(2) $\int_{-\infty}^{\infty} |y|\ f(y)dy < \infty$.

(3) $\int_{-\infty}^{\infty} [\frac{f'(y)}{f(y)}]^2\ f(y)dy = J$, say, where $0 < J < \infty$.

(4) $\int_{-\infty}^{\infty} [\frac{f(y-\Delta)}{f(y)}]^2\ f(y)dy = 1 + O(\Delta^2)$ for small Δ.

(5) Let $W_1',\ldots, W_m'$ be independently distributed, each with density f. Let $F(w)$ denote $\int_{-\infty}^{w} f(t)dt$. Let $W_1 \leq \ldots \leq W_m$ denote the ordered values of $W_1',\ldots, W_m'$. Define $U_i = F(W_i)$. We assume that $f(F^{-1}(r)) > D > 0$ for all r in $[p,1-p]$,

and that for all integers i,j,k,h in $[[np],[n(1-p)]]$ and all b_i, b_j, b_k, b_h (each equal to either 0 or 1),

$$E\left\{ (W_i - F^{-1}(\tfrac{i}{m+1}))^{b_i} (W_j - F^{-1}(\tfrac{j}{m+1}))^{b_j} (W_k - F^{-1}(\tfrac{k}{m+1}))^{b_k} \times \times (W_h - F^{-1}(\tfrac{h}{m+1}))^{b_h} \right\} =$$

$$\frac{E\{(U_i - \frac{i}{m+1})^{b_i}(U_j - \frac{j}{m+1})^{b_j}(U_k - \frac{k}{m+1})^{b_k}(U_h - \frac{h}{m+1})^{b_h}\}}{(f(F^{-1}(\frac{i}{m+1})))^{b_i}(f(F^{-1}(\frac{j}{m+1})))^{b_j}(f(F^{-1}(\frac{k}{m+1})))^{b_k}(f(F^{-1}(\frac{h}{m+1})))^{b_h}} \times \times [1 + 0(\tfrac{1}{m})] .$$

(This is a smoothness condition often imposed in the literature. It is implied by a suitable expansion

$$W_i = F^{-1}(U_i) = F^{-1}(\tfrac{i}{m+1}) + (U_i - \tfrac{i}{m+1})\frac{1}{f(F^{-1}(\frac{i}{m+1}))} + \ldots).$$

(6) The conditions satisfied by g of the paper [1] are to be satisfied by f.

3. *Reduction of the original problem to an asymptotically equivalent problem.* For each n, divide $[A,B]$ into subintervals of length Δ_n, such that $\sqrt{n}\ \Delta_n \to 0$ as $n \to \infty$. For each n, let $u_i(n)$ denote the center of the subinterval in which $t_i(n)$ lies. (If $t_i(n)$ lies on the boundary between two subintervals, let $u_i(n)$ be the smaller of the two possible values.) Thus $|u_i(n) - t_i(n)| \leq \frac{\Delta_n}{2}$ for all i. We will show that

$$\prod_{i=1}^{n} \frac{f(X_i - \theta_1 - \theta_2 u_i(n))}{f(X_i - \theta_1 - \theta_2 t_i(n))} = Q(n), \quad \text{say},$$

converges stochastically to one as n increases.

First, the expected value of $Q(n)$ is exactly one. Then

$$E\{Q^2(n)\} = \prod_{i=1}^{n} \{\int_{-\infty}^{\infty} [\frac{f(y-\theta_2(u_i(n)-t_i(n))}{f(y)}]^2 f(y)dy\}.$$ From assumption 4 of Section 2 it follows easily that this expression approaches one as n increases. It follows that $Q(n)$ converges stochastically to one as n increases. This implies that for our purposes, we can (and will) assume that $X_i(n)$ has density $f(x-\theta_1-\theta_2 u_i(n))$, rather than $f(x-\theta_1-\theta_2 t_i(n))$, at the point x.

Let $m_j(n)$ denote the midpoint of the jth subinterval of $[A,B]$, so that $A < m_1(n) < \ldots < m_{k(n)}(n) < B$, where $k(n)\Delta_n = B - A$. Let $N_j(n)$ denote the number of $t_i(n)$ in the jth subinterval. We assume that

$$\lim_{n\to\infty} \frac{1}{n} \sum_{j=1}^{k(n)} N_j(n)m_j(n)$$ exists and equals T, say, and that

$$\lim_{n\to\infty} \frac{1}{n} \sum_{j=1}^{k(n)} N_j(n)[m_j(n) - T]^2$$ exists and equals S, say,

with $S > 0$.

If $Q_1(n)$, $Q_2(n)$ denote the asymptotically efficient estimators of θ_1, θ_2 respectively, when f is known, then $\sqrt{n}(Q_1(n) - \theta_1), \sqrt{n}(Q_2(n) - \theta_2)$ have asymptotically a joint normal distribution with zero means and covariance matrix

$$\begin{pmatrix} \frac{1}{J} + \frac{T^2}{JS} & -\frac{T}{JS} \\ -\frac{T}{JS} & \frac{1}{JS} \end{pmatrix}.$$

Let $\overline{k}(n)$ denote the number of intervals (among the $k(n)$ intervals) for which $N_j(n) > 0$, and let $\overline{N}(n)$ denote the set of these indices j. Let $N(n)$ (respectively $N'(n)$) denote the minimum (respectively the maximum) of the $N_j(n)$ in $\overline{N}(n)$. We assume that $N(n) \to \infty$ and that one of the following cases (conditions) holds:

Case A: $\overline{k}(n) \leqq K < \infty$ for all n.

Case B: $k(n) \to \infty$, and

$$\frac{N'(n)}{N(n)} = O(1), \qquad \frac{N'(n)}{\sqrt{n}} = o(1) \quad .$$

Henceforth the indices j and j' are always assumed to be in the set $\overline{N}(n)$, whose elements we number $1,2,\ldots,\overline{k}(n)$.

4. *Estimation in Case* A. Choose a p in the open interval $(0, \frac{1}{2})$, as discussed in Section 1. For each j, let $V_1(j,n) < \ldots < V_{N_j(n)}(j,n)$ denote the ordered values of the $X_i(n)$ which have density $f(x-\theta_1-\theta_2 m_j(n))$ at the point x. Use $V_{[N_j(n)p]}(j,n),\ldots,V_{[N_j(n)(1-p)]}(j,n)$ to construct an estimator of $\theta_1 + \theta_2 m_j(n)$, as in Section 7 of [1]. Call the estimator $Y_j(n)$. The asymptotic distribution of $\sqrt{N_j(n)}\,(Y_j(n)-\theta_1-\theta_2 m_j(n))$ is normal, with zero mean and variance $\frac{1}{H(p)}$, where

$$H(p) = \frac{2f^2(F^{-1}(p))}{p} + \int_{F^{-1}(p)}^{F^{-1}(1-p)} \left(\frac{f'(y)}{f(y)}\right)^2 f(y)\,dy \quad .$$

$Y_j(n)$, $Y_{j'}(n)$ are independent if $j \neq j'$. Define

$$\overline{Q}_1(n) = \sum_{j=1}^{\overline{k}(n)} \frac{N_j(n)}{n} \left\{1 + \frac{T^2}{S} - \frac{Tm_j(n)}{S}\right\} Y_j(n)$$

$$\bar{Q}_2(n) = \sum_{j=1}^{\bar{k}(n)} \frac{N_j(n)}{n} \{-\frac{T}{S} + \frac{m_j(n)}{S}\} Y_j(n) .$$

Since $\bar{k}(n) \leqq K$, the asymptotic joint distribution of $\sqrt{n}(\bar{Q}_1(n) - \theta_1)$, $\sqrt{n}(\bar{Q}_2(n) - \theta_2)$ is normal, with zero means and covariance matrix

$$M = \begin{pmatrix} \frac{1}{H(p)} + \frac{T^2}{SH(p)} & -\frac{T}{SH(p)} \\ -\frac{T}{SH(p)} & \frac{1}{SH(p)} \end{pmatrix} .$$

Thus $\bar{Q}_1(n)$, $\bar{Q}_2(n)$, which do not require a knowledge of f, are asymptotically efficient, modulo the fact that only essentially $n(1-2p)$ observations have been used.

5. *Estimation in Case* B. In case B, we proceed differently. Let $N_{c(n)}(n) = N'(n)$. For each n, we use the observations whose density is $f(x-\theta_1-\theta_2 m_{c(n)}(n))$ at the point x to construct estimators of $f(F^{-1}(y))$, $f'(F^{-1}(y))$, and $f''(F^{-1}(y))$ for all y in $[p,\frac{1}{2}]$. This is done as described in Section 7 of [1]. Call the resulting estimators $g(G^{-1}(y))$, $g'(G^{-1}(y))$, $g''(G^{-1}(y))$, respectively. (Since f is symmetric about zero, $f(F^{-1}(1-y)) = f(F^{-1}(y))$, etc., and the same relationships hold for g, etc.). Define

$$\bar{A}_j^{(m)} = \left(\frac{g'(G^{-1}(\frac{j}{m}))}{g(G^{-1}(\frac{j}{m}))}\right)^2 - \frac{g''(G^{-1}(\frac{j}{m}))}{g(G^{-1}(\frac{j}{m}))}$$

$$\bar{A}'^{(m)}_{mp} = \bar{A}'^{(m)}_{m(1-p)} = -[g'(G^{-1}(p)) - \frac{1}{p} g^2(G^{-1}(p))]$$

(see (2.15) of [1]). We note that $\bar{A}_j^{(m)} = \bar{A}_{m-j}^{(m)}$.

For each $j \neq c(n)$ we define

$$Y_j(n) = \frac{\bar{A}'^{(N_j(n))}_{N_j(n)p}\left(V_{N_j(n)p}(j,n) + V_{N_j(n)(1-p)}(j,n)\right) + \frac{1}{N_j(n)}\sum_{i=N_j(n)p+1}^{N_j(n)(1-p)-1} \bar{A}_i^{(N_j(n))} V_i(j,n)}{2\,\bar{A}'^{(N_j(n))}_{N_j(n)p} + \frac{1}{N_j(n)}\sum_{i=N_j(n)p+1}^{N_j(n)(1-p)-1} \bar{A}_i^{(N_j(n))}}.$$

Then we define

$$\bar{Q}_1(n) = \sum_{\substack{j=1\\ j\neq c(n)}}^{\bar{k}(n)} \frac{N_j(n)}{n}\left\{1 + \frac{T^2}{S} - \frac{Tm_j(n)}{S}\right\} Y_j(n)$$

$$\bar{Q}_2(n) = \sum_{\substack{j=1\\ j\neq c(n)}}^{\bar{k}(n)} \frac{N_j(n)}{n}\left\{-\frac{T}{S} + \frac{m_j(n)}{S}\right\} Y_j(n) \quad .$$

We shall prove that $\bar{Q}_1(n)$ and $\bar{Q}_2(n)$ are asymptotically efficient estimators of θ_1 and θ_2, modulo the fact that only essentially $n(1-2p)$ observations have been used. For ease of exposition we divide the proof into two cases.

Case B1: For each large n, the coefficients $\bar{A}$ and $\bar{A}'$ in $Y_j(n)$ are known exactly and do not have to be estimated.

Case B2: The actual case, where the coefficients are estimated as described above.

Until the contrary is stated, we shall give the proof for the Case B1.

From the symmetry properties of g, g', g'' and hence of the $\bar{A}$'s, we have $E\{Y_j(n)\} = \theta_1+\theta_2 m_j(n)$, and it follows that $\sqrt{n}[E\{\bar{Q}_1(n)\} - \theta_1] \to 0$, $\sqrt{n}[E\{\bar{Q}_2(n)\} - \theta_2] \to 0$. From

assumption 5 of Section 2 it follows that
$N_j(n)E\{(Y_j(n)-\theta_1-\theta_2 m_j(n))^2\} \to \frac{1}{H(p)}$, and
$(N_j(n))^2 E\{(Y_j(n)-\theta_1-\theta_2 m_j(n))^4\} = 0(1)$, as $N_j(n) \to \infty$, uniformly in j, θ_1, and θ_2. It follows that
$(N_j(n))^{3/2} E\{|Y_j(n)-\theta_1-\theta_2 m_j(n)|^3\} = 0(1)$. Define, for
$j = 1,\ldots, \bar{k}(n)$, and $j \neq c(n)$,

$$\alpha_j(n) = \frac{N_j(n)}{n}\{1 + \frac{T^2}{S} - \frac{Tm_j(n)}{S}\}\ (Y_j(n) - E\{Y_j(n)\})$$

$$\beta_j(n) = \frac{N_j(n)}{n}\{-\frac{T}{S} + \frac{m_j(n)}{S}\}\ (Y_j(n) - E\{Y_j(n)\}) .$$

Making use of the other assumptions of Case B and the fact that the $Y_j(n)$ are independent, we obtain the following, where $\mathcal{D}(n) = \Omega(\frac{1}{n})$ means that

$$0 < \lim_n \inf\ n\mathcal{D}(n) \leq \lim_n \sup\ n\mathcal{D}(n) < \infty :$$

$$\sum_j E\{(\alpha_j(n))^2\} = \Omega(\tfrac{1}{n})$$

$$\sum_j E\{(\beta_j(n))^2\} = \Omega(\tfrac{1}{n})$$

$$\sum_j E\{\alpha_j^2(n)|\beta_j(n)|\} = 0(\frac{1}{n^{3/2}(\bar{k}(n))^{1/2}})$$

$$\sum_j E\{|\alpha_j(n)|\beta_j^2(n)\} = 0(\frac{1}{n^{3/2}(\bar{k}(n))^{1/2}})$$

$$\sum_j E\{|\alpha_j(n)|^3\} = 0(\frac{1}{n^{3/2}(\bar{k}(n))^{1/2}})$$

$$\sum_j E\{|\beta_j(n)|^3\} = 0(\frac{1}{n^{3/2}(\bar{k}(n))^{1/2}}) .$$

We now use these relationships, the fact that the $Y_j(n)$ are independent, and the fact that $\overline{k}(n) \to \infty$, to verify that the bivariate Liapounoff condition for the third absolute moment is satisfied by $\overline{Q}_1(n)$, $\overline{Q}_2(n)$. For the univariate condition see, e.g., [2], page 215. The bivariate condition is easily obtained from the proof on page 216 of [2]. Although the Liapounoff condition is usually stated for a sequence of chance variables, it follows easily from its proof (e.g., op. cit.) that it applies to a sequence of finite sequences (triangular array of chance variables). We conclude that the limiting joint distribution of the pair $\sqrt{n}(\overline{Q}_1(n)-\theta_1)$, $\sqrt{n}(\overline{Q}_2(n)-\theta_2)$ is normal, with means zero and covariance matrix M. This proves the asymptotic efficiency of our estimators in Case B1.

6. *Proof of efficiency in the Case* B2. We now drop the assumption that g, g', and g'' are known exactly. Let $\varepsilon > 0$ be arbitrary. It is proved in [1] that, for each large n, except for an event of probability less than ε, the errors in the estimators g, g', and g'' are uniformly less than $K(\varepsilon)[N_{c(n)}(n)]^{-d}$, where $K(\varepsilon)$ depends only on ε, and $d > 0$ is a constant which does not depend on ε. An easy computation shows that these errors can add to $N_j(n)E\{(Y_j(n) - \theta_1 - \theta_2 m_j(n))^2\}$ only a quantity $O[N_{c(n)}(n)]^{-d}$, and to $(N_j(n))^2E\{(Y_j(n)-\theta_1-\theta_2 m_j(n))^4\}$ only a quantity $O[N_{c(n)}(n)]^{-d}$. The remainder of the argument in Case B1 therefore follows exactly as before, and we conclude: The joint distribution of the pair $\sqrt{n}(\overline{Q}_1(n)-\theta_1), \sqrt{n}(\overline{Q}_2(n)-\theta_2)$, except for an event of probability ε, approaches the normal distribution with means zero and covariance matrix M. Since

$\varepsilon > 0$ was arbitrary, it follows that the limiting joint distribution is normal, with means zero and covariance matrix M. This proves the asymptotic efficiency of the estimators $(\bar{Q}_1(n), \bar{Q}_2(n))$ in the general case.

7. *Concluding remarks.* The solution of the problem of the present paper and that of [1] are truly "robust" in the full statistical meaning of this word, as used in the papers of Huber and others (see [6] for some most recent references). These papers judge the efficiency of a procedure by its asymptotic variance, just as is done here and in [1]. All assume that the parametric form of the density f is known up to a small "contaminating" component; no such assumption is made here or in [1].

In a paper ([7]) to appear elsewhere, we give sequential, asymptotically optimal, non-parametric confidence intervals for the translation parameter (median) of a symmetric density (which therefore is not known to belong to a given parametric class). In another paper we shall give sequential confidence intervals for the problem of the present paper.

References

1. Weiss, L., and Wolfowitz, J., (1970). "Asymptotically efficient non-parametric estimators of location and scale parameters," *Zeitschrift f. Wahrscheinlichkeitstheorie verw. Geb.*, 16, 134-150.

2. Cramer, H., (1961). *Mathematical methods of statistics*, Princeton University Press.

3. Weiss, L., and Wolfowitz, J.,(1967). "Maximum probability estimators", *Ann. Inst. Stat. Math.*, 19, 193-206.

4. Weiss, L., and Wolfowitz, J., (1969). "Maximum probability estimators with a general loss function," *Proc. McMaster University Symposium.* Berlin-Heidelberg-New York: Springer Lecture Notes in Mathematics, 89, 232-256.

5. Weiss, L., (1964). "On estimating location and scale parameters from truncated samples," *Naval Research Logistics Quarterly*, 11, 125-134.

6. Jaeckel, L.A., (1971). "Robust estimates of location; symmetry and asymmetric contamination", *Ann. Math. Stat.*, 42, No. 3.

7. Weiss, L., and Wolfowitz, J., "Optimal, bounded length, non-parametric, sequential confidence limits for a translation parameter," to appear.

OPTIMAL ALLOCATION OF OBSERVATIONS WHEN COMPARING SEVERAL TREATMENTS WITH A CONTROL (III): GLOBALLY BEST ONE-SIDED INTERVALS FOR UNEQUAL VARIANCES*

By Robert Bechhofer and Bruce Turnbull
Cornell University

1. *Introduction and Summary.* In this paper we continue our earlier studies [2],[3] of optimal allocation of observations when comparing several treatments with a control. In [2] and [3] we considered one-sided and two-sided comparisons, respectively, and described in detail a general allocation procedure which is globally optimal for the case in which the known variances of the "test" populations are equal, but possibly unequal to the known variance of the "control" population; this same procedure is suboptimal for the case in which the known variances of the "test" populations are *unequal* (although it is optimal for this latter case within a more restricted class of procedures, see Remark 1 in [2]). In the present paper we generalize the results in [2] to obtain the globally optimal procedure for one-sided comparisons for the case in which the known variances of the "test" populations are unequal. The earliest correct work on multiple comparisons with a control was carried out by Dunnett [4] who posed (but did not solve) the optimal allocation problem.

Let $\Pi_0, \Pi_1, \ldots, \Pi_p$ be $p+1$ normal populations with

*Prepared under Grants DA-31-124-ARO-D-474,U.S.Army Research Office-Durham and Nonr-401(53),Office of Naval Research.

unknown population means $\mu_0, \mu_1, \ldots, \mu_p$ and known population variances $\sigma_0^2, \sigma_1^2, \ldots, \sigma_p^2$. We shall refer to Π_0 as the "control" population, and Π_i $(1 \leqq i \leqq p)$ as the ith "test" population. Based on N_i independent observations X_{ij} $(j = 1,2,\ldots,N_i)$ from $\Pi_i (i = 0,1,\ldots,p)$, where $N = \sum_{i=0}^{p} N_i$ is specified prior to experimentation, it is desired to make an exact joint confidence statement concerning the p differences $\mu_i - \mu_0$ $(1 \leqq i \leqq p)$. In designing the experiment the $N_i (i = 0,1,\ldots,p)$ are to be chosen in such a way as to maximize the confidence coefficient, and at the same time guarantee a specified value for the one-sided or two-sided "widths" of the confidence intervals.

In [2] we considered one-sided comparisons in which the joint confidence statement took the form

$$\bar{x}_0 - \bar{x}_i - d < \mu_0 - \mu_i \quad (1 \leqq i \leqq p) \quad , \tag{1.1}$$

while in [3] we considered two-sided comparisons in which the joint confidence statement took the form

$$\bar{x}_0 - \bar{x}_i - d < \mu_0 - \mu_i < \bar{x}_0 - \bar{x}_i + rd \quad (1 \leqq i \leqq p). \tag{1.2}$$

In the above, $\bar{x}_i = \sum_{j=1}^{N_i} x_{ij}/N_i$ is the observed value of the sample mean from $\Pi_i (0 \leqq i \leqq p)$ while d and $(r+1)d$ are the specified values for the one-sided and two-sided widths, respectively; $d > 0$ is a "yardstick" in the units of x, and $r \geqq 0$ is a pure number, both d and r being *specified* prior to the start of experimentation.

In the present paper we shall show for one-sided*

*Analogous results for two-sided comparisons $(0 \leqq r \leqq \infty)$, particularly for $r \neq 1$, are also of interest, but we do not plan to undertake such studies.

comparisons that for *given* p and σ_i^2 $(0 \leq i \leq p)$ and *specified* N and d, the globally optimal proportion of observations $\hat{\gamma}_i$ to be taken from Π_i $(0 \leq i \leq p)$ depends only on $\theta_1, \theta_2, \ldots, \theta_p$ and λ where $\theta_i = \sigma_i^2/\sigma_0^2$ and $\lambda = d\sqrt{N}/\sigma_0$. A discussion of the behavior of the $\hat{\gamma}_i$ as functions of the arguments that determine them is given in Section 4.2. Our fundamental theorem concerning the $\hat{\gamma}_i$ is contained, along with some important corollaries, in Section 4.3. Special analytic results for $p = 2$ are given in Section 5 -- e.g., the interesting result that $\hat{\gamma}_1/\hat{\gamma}_2 \sim \sqrt{\theta_1/\theta_2}$ for λ sufficiently small, while $\hat{\gamma}_1/\hat{\gamma}_2 \sim \theta_1/\theta_2$ for λ arbitrarily large. Values of the $\hat{\gamma}_i$ and associated confidence coefficients for $p = 2$ and selected θ_i $(i = 1,2)$ are given as a function of λ in the tables of the Appendix. Use of the tables is described in Section 6. Savings obtained through optimal allocation are discussed in Section 7 with numerical results being given for $p = 2$ in Table I of Section 7.2.

2. *A discrete and continuous formulation of the optimal allocation problem.* In Section 2.1 we shall formulate the optimal allocation problem. The formulation is a discrete one, and it turns out that its solution involves the solution of an integer programming problem. In Section 2.2 we give the continuous version of the same problem. It is the latter problem that we solve in the present paper.

2.1. *An integer programming formulation of the problem.* For $1 \leq i \leq p$ we define

$$(2.1) \qquad Z_i = [(\bar{X}_0 - \bar{X}_i) - (\mu_0 - \mu_i)] \left(\frac{\sigma_0^2}{N_0} + \frac{\sigma_i^2}{N_i}\right)^{-1/2} ,$$

and for fixed $d'^{(i)}$ $(1 \leq i \leq p)$ we consider

(2.2) $$P\{Z_i < d'^{(i)} \quad (i = 1,2,\ldots,p)\} \quad .$$

We note that the Z_i have a p-variate normal distribution with $E\{Z_i\} = 0$, $\mathrm{Var}\{Z_i\} = 1$, and for $i \neq j$

(2.3) $$E\{Z_i Z_j\} = \rho_{ij} = [(1+\theta_i N_0/N_i)(1+\theta_j N_0/N_j)]^{-1/2} \quad .$$

Suppose now that for given N and $\theta_i (1 \leq i \leq p)$ and specified $\lambda > 0$ we limit consideration to those $d'^{(i)}$ for which

(2.4a) $$d'^{(i)}\left(\frac{\sigma_0^2}{N_0} + \frac{\sigma_i^2}{N_i}\right)^{1/2} = d \ ,$$

or equivalently

(2.4b) $$d'^{(i)}\left(\frac{N}{N_0} + \frac{N}{N_i}\theta_i\right)^{1/2} = \lambda$$

for $(1 \leq i \leq p)$. Our optimal allocation problem can then be posed as the following *integer programming* problem:

(2.5) $$\underset{N_0,N_1,\ldots,N_p}{\text{Maximize}} \ P\{Z_i < \lambda\left(\frac{N}{N_0} + \frac{N}{N_i}\theta_i\right)^{-1/2} (1 \leq i \leq p) | \underline{P}\}$$
$$\text{subject to} \quad \sum_{i=0}^{p} N_i = N \quad ,$$

the N_i $(0 \leq i \leq p)$ being *integers*. In (2.5) we have denoted the $p \times p$ matrix of the ρ_{ij} (2.3) by $\underline{P}$. The space of possible solutions in N_i/N $(1 \leq i \leq p)$ is the lattice of points which satisfy the inequalities $N_i/N \geq 0$ $(1 \leq i \leq p)$ and $\sum_{i=1}^{p} N_i/N \leq 1$ with the N_i integers. For $p = 2$ we have

Figure 1

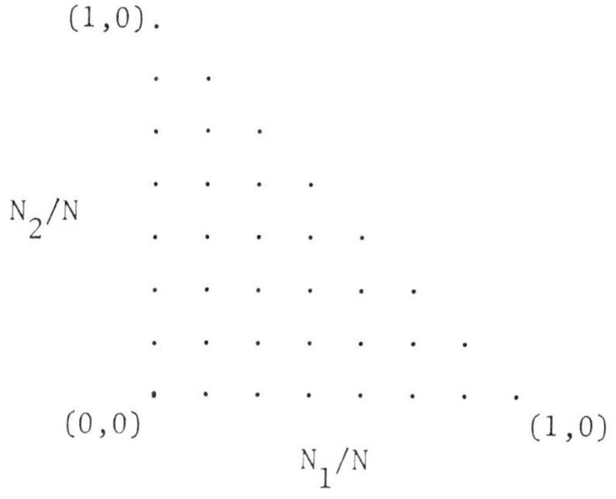

2.2. *A continuous approximation to the integer programming problem.* Ignoring the computational difficulties associated with the numerical evaluation of the probability in (2.5) for any particular

$$\lambda\left(\frac{N}{N_0} + \frac{N}{N_i}\ \theta_i\right)^{-1/2} \qquad (1 \leq i \leq p)$$

and $\underline{P}$, we remark that the problem (2.5) can be solved in principle by enumeration, but for large N the finding of a solution could be a long and computationally costly one (especially since one does not know in which region to concentrate the search). Hence we shall adopt the device used in [2] and [3] (see also the paper [6] on optimal design by Kiefer and Wolfowitz, and later related papers) and replace the discrete (in N_i/N) problem by its continuous (in γ_i) analogue. Then for *large* N the exact discrete problem can be solved to a high degree of approximation by the continuous theory, and for *small* N the exact discrete problem can be solved by enumeration (the initial search being conducted in the region suggested by the continuous theory).

In the continuous theory we consider the following problem:

$$\text{(2.6)}\quad \begin{aligned} &\underset{\gamma_0,\gamma_1,\ldots,\gamma_p}{\text{Maximize}}\ P\{Z_i < \lambda\left(\frac{1}{\gamma_0}+\frac{\theta_i}{\gamma_i}\right)^{-1/2} (1 \leqq i \leqq p) \,|\, \underline{P}_c\} \\ &\text{subject to}\ \sum_{i=0}^{p} \gamma_i = 1,\ \ \gamma_i \geqq 0 \ \ (0 \leqq i \leqq p), \end{aligned}$$

the γ_i $(0 \leqq i \leqq p)$ being continuous variables. In (2.6) we have denoted the $p \times p$ matrix of the

$$\text{(2.7)}\qquad \rho_{ij} = [(1 + \theta_i\gamma_0/\gamma_i)(1 + \theta_j\gamma_0/\gamma_j)]^{-1/2}$$

by $\underline{P}_c$. The space of possible solutions in γ_i $(1 \leqq i \leqq p)$ is the set of points which satisfy the inequalities

$$\gamma_i \geqq 0 \ (1 \leqq i \leqq p) \quad \text{and} \quad \sum_{i=1}^{p} \gamma_i \leqq 1.$$

In the remaining sections we shall consider only the continuous theory.

3. *An alternative expression for the probability.* It will be convenient to work with an alternative expression for the probability in (2.6). In terms of the quantities already defined, this probability can be rewritten as

$$\text{(3.1)}\qquad \begin{aligned} &g_p(\gamma_1,\gamma_2,\ldots,\gamma_p \,|\, \theta_1,\theta_2,\ldots,\theta_p;\ \lambda) \\ &= \int_{-\infty}^{\infty} \prod_{j=1}^{p} F\left[\sqrt{\frac{\gamma_j}{\theta_j}}\left(\frac{x}{\sqrt{\gamma_0}} + \lambda\right)\right] f(x)dx \end{aligned}$$

where $F(\cdot)$ is the standard normal distribution function, and $f(\cdot)$ is the corresponding density function; for simplicity of notation we shall denote (3.1) by g. (For details of the equivalence of the two expressions for g, see [2].)

We note from (2.6) (or (3.1)) that

$$\lim_{\gamma_0 \to 0} g = 1/2 , \qquad \lim_{\gamma_0 \to 1} g = (1/2)^p \tag{3.2}$$

since (see (2.7)) for all $i \neq j$ we have $\rho_{ij} = 1$ and 0, respectively, in these cases.

4. *The maximization problem.* We propose to maximize g with respect to the γ_i $(0 \leqq i \leqq p)$. To do so we replace γ_0 in g by $1 - \sum_{i=1}^{p} \gamma_i$, determine $\partial g/\partial \gamma_i$ $(1 \leqq i \leqq p)$, set the p resulting equations equal to zero, and solve them for the maximizing values $\hat{\gamma}_i$ $(1 \leqq i \leqq p)$. We henceforth refer to the vector $\hat{\gamma} = (\hat{\gamma}_0, \hat{\gamma}_1, \ldots, \hat{\gamma}_p)$, where $\hat{\gamma}_0 = 1 - \sum_{i=1}^{p} \hat{\gamma}_i$, as the *optimal allocation*. In doing so, we must, of course, be assured that a solution exists, that it is unique, and that it is in fact associated with the maximum. (We discuss this problem in Section 4.2.)

4.1. *Evaluation and simplification of the partial derivative,* $\partial g/\partial \gamma_t$. We shall evaluate $\partial g/\partial \gamma_t$ where g is given by (3.1). For $t = 1,2,\ldots,p$ we note that

$$\frac{\partial}{\partial \gamma_t} \prod_{j=1}^{p} F\left[\sqrt{\frac{\gamma_j}{\theta_j}} \left(\frac{x}{\sqrt{\gamma_0}} + \lambda\right)\right]$$

$$= \sum_{i=1}^{p} \prod_{\substack{j=1 \\ j \neq i}}^{p} F\left[\sqrt{\frac{\gamma_j}{\theta_j}} \left(\frac{x}{\sqrt{\gamma_0}} + \lambda\right)\right] \frac{\partial}{\partial \gamma_t} F\left[\sqrt{\frac{\gamma_i}{\theta_i}} \left(\frac{x}{\sqrt{\gamma_0}} + \lambda\right)\right], \tag{4.1}$$

(where we have written γ_0 for $1 - \sum_{i=1}^{p} \gamma_i$) and hence

$$\frac{\partial g}{\partial \gamma_t} = \int_{-\infty}^{\infty} \{ \sum_{i=1}^{p} \prod_{\substack{j=1 \\ j \neq i}}^{p} F[\sqrt{\frac{\gamma_j}{\theta_j}}(\frac{x}{\sqrt{\gamma_0}} + \lambda)] \cdot \frac{\partial}{\partial \gamma_t} F[\sqrt{\frac{\gamma_i}{\theta_i}}(\frac{x}{\sqrt{\gamma_0}} + \lambda)]\} f(x)dx \tag{4.2}$$

$$= K_1/2\gamma_0^{3/2} + K_{2t}/2\sqrt{\gamma_t\theta_t}$$

where

$$K_1 = \int_{-\infty}^{\infty} x \sum_{i=1}^{p} \sqrt{\frac{\gamma_i}{\theta_i}} f[\sqrt{\frac{\gamma_i}{\theta_i}}(\frac{x}{\sqrt{\gamma_0}} + \lambda)] \cdot \prod_{\substack{j=1 \\ j \neq i}}^{p} F[\sqrt{\frac{\gamma_j}{\theta_j}}(\frac{x}{\sqrt{\gamma_0}} + \lambda)] f(x)dx \tag{4.3}$$

and

$$K_{2t} = \int_{-\infty}^{\infty} (\frac{x}{\sqrt{\gamma_0}} + \lambda) f[\sqrt{\frac{\gamma_t}{\theta_t}}(\frac{x}{\sqrt{\gamma_0}} + \lambda)] \cdot \prod_{\substack{j=1 \\ j \neq t}}^{p} F[\sqrt{\frac{\gamma_j}{\theta_j}}(\frac{x}{\sqrt{\gamma_0}} + \lambda)] f(x)dx \quad . \tag{4.4}$$

Although the expression (4.2) - (4.4) could be used for numerical evaluation of $\hat{\gamma}$ for arbitrary $p \geqq 2$, it turns out that certain analytical studies of the solution, such as the limiting optimal allocations as $\lambda \to \infty$ and $\lambda \downarrow \lambda^*$ (where $\lambda^* > 0$ is defined by (4.34)),which are carried out in later sections depend on a further simplification of (4.2) - (4.4); in addition this simplification yields a particularly compact and usable result for $p = 2$. The derivation of the simplification is long and somewhat tedious. The final form of the result is given as (4.24) and also as (4.25).

Letting $y = \sqrt{\gamma_i/\theta_i}\,(\lambda + x/\sqrt{\gamma_0})$ in (4.3) we have

$$K_1 = \gamma_0 \sum_{i=1}^{p} \sqrt{\frac{\theta_i}{\gamma_i}}\, L_{1i} - \gamma_0 \lambda L_2 \tag{4.5}$$

where for $i = 1,2,\ldots,p$

$$L_{1i} = \int_{-\infty}^{\infty} y f(y) \prod_{\substack{j=1 \\ j\neq i}}^{p} F\left[\sqrt{\frac{\gamma_j \theta_i}{\theta_j \gamma_i}}\, y\right] f_i^*(y)\,dy \quad , \tag{4.6}$$

$$f_i^*(y) = f\left[\sqrt{\gamma_0}\left(\sqrt{\frac{\theta_i}{\gamma_i}}\, y - \lambda\right)\right] \quad , \tag{4.7}$$

and

$$L_2 = \sum_{i=1}^{p} \int_{-\infty}^{\infty} f(y) \prod_{\substack{j=1 \\ j\neq i}}^{p} F\left[\sqrt{\frac{\gamma_j \theta_i}{\theta_j \gamma_i}}\, y\right] f_i^*(y)\,dy \quad . \tag{4.8}$$

Then

$$\frac{\partial g}{\partial \gamma_t} = \frac{1}{2\sqrt{\gamma_0}} \sum_{i=1}^{p} \sqrt{\frac{\theta_i}{\gamma_i}}\, L_{1i} - \frac{\lambda}{2\sqrt{\gamma_0}} L_2 + \frac{1}{2\sqrt{\gamma_t \theta_t}} K_{2t} \quad . \tag{4.9}$$

We next consider L_{1i} (4.6) and integrate by parts letting

$$U = f_i^*(y) \prod_{\substack{j=1 \\ j\neq i}}^{p} F\left[\sqrt{\frac{\gamma_j \theta_i}{\theta_j \gamma_i}}\, y\right], \quad dV = y f(y)\,dy \quad ,$$

obtaining

$$(4.10)\qquad L_{1i} = -\gamma_0 \frac{\theta_i}{\gamma_i} L_{1i} + \gamma_0 \lambda \sqrt{\frac{\theta_i}{\gamma_i}}\, M_{1i} + M_{2i}$$

where

$$(4.11)\qquad M_{1i} = \int_{-\infty}^{\infty} f(y) \prod_{\substack{j=1\\ j\neq i}}^{p} F\left[\sqrt{\frac{\gamma_j\theta_i}{\theta_j\gamma_i}}\; y\right] f_i^*(y)\,dy$$

and

$$(4.12)\qquad M_{2i} = \int_{-\infty}^{\infty} f(y) f_i^*(y)\; d \prod_{\substack{j=1\\ j\neq i}}^{p} F\left[\sqrt{\frac{\gamma_j\theta_i}{\theta_j\gamma_i}}\; y\right] \quad .$$

Solving for L_{1i} we obtain

$$(4.13)\qquad L_{1i} = \frac{\gamma_0\lambda\sqrt{\theta_i\gamma_i}}{\gamma_i + \gamma_0\theta_i} M_{1i} + \frac{\gamma_i}{\gamma_i + \gamma_0\theta_i} M_{2i} \quad .$$

Combining (4.8) - (4.12) we see that

$$(4.14)\qquad \frac{\partial g}{\partial \gamma_t} = -\frac{\lambda}{2\sqrt{\gamma_0}} \sum_{i=1}^{p} \frac{\gamma_i}{\gamma_i + \gamma_0\theta_i} M_{1i}$$

$$+ \frac{1}{2\sqrt{\gamma_0}} \sum_{i=1}^{p} \frac{\sqrt{\theta_i\gamma_i}}{\gamma_i + \gamma_0\theta_i} M_{2i} + \frac{1}{2\sqrt{\gamma_t\theta_t}} K_{2t}$$

We now evaluate (4.11) obtaining

$$M_{1i} = f[\lambda \sqrt{\frac{\gamma_0\gamma_i}{\gamma_i + \gamma_0\theta_i}}\,] \cdot$$

$$(4.15)\quad \int_{-\infty}^{\infty} f[\sqrt{\frac{\gamma_i+\gamma_0\theta_i}{\gamma_i}}(y - \frac{\lambda\gamma_0\sqrt{\theta_i\gamma_i}}{\gamma_i+\gamma_0\theta_i})] \prod_{\substack{j=1\\ j\neq i}}^{p} F[\sqrt{\frac{\gamma_j\theta_i}{\theta_j\gamma_i}}$$

$$= f[\lambda\sqrt{\frac{\gamma_0\gamma_i}{\gamma_i+\gamma_0\theta_i}}] \sqrt{\frac{\gamma_i}{\gamma_i+\gamma_0\theta_i}}\; D_i$$

where

$$D_i = \int_{-\infty}^{\infty} f(z) \prod_{\substack{j=1\\ j\neq i}}^{p} F[\sqrt{\frac{\gamma_j\theta_i}{\theta_j(\gamma_i+\gamma_0\theta_i)}}\,z + \frac{\lambda\ \gamma_0}{\gamma_i}$$

$$(4.16)\quad = P\left\{\frac{Y_j - Y_0\sqrt{\frac{\gamma_j\theta_i}{\theta_j(\gamma_i+\gamma_0\theta_i)}}}{\sqrt{1+\frac{\gamma_j\theta_i}{\theta_j(\gamma_i+\gamma_0\theta_i)}}} < \frac{\lambda\ \gamma_0\theta}{\sqrt{(\gamma_i+\gamma_0\theta_i)(\gamma}} \quad (j \neq i;\ j\right.$$

$$= P\{Z_{ij} < d_{ij}\quad (j \neq i;\ j = 1,2,\ldots,p)\}$$

here the Y_j $(j = 0,1,\ldots,p)$ are normal with $E\{Y_j\} = 0$, $\mathrm{Var}\{Y_j\} = 1$, and hence $j = 1,2,\ldots,p)$ have a $(p-1)$-variate norm with $E\{Z_{ij}\} = 0$, $\mathrm{Var}\{Z_{ij}\} = 1$, and

$$E\{Z_{ij_1} Z_{ij_2}\} =$$

$$(4.17)\quad \theta_i \sqrt{\frac{\gamma_{j_1}\gamma_{j_2}}{[\gamma_i\theta_{j_1}+\gamma_{j_1}\theta_i+\gamma_0\theta_{j_1}\theta_i][\gamma_i\theta_{j_2}+\gamma_{j_2}\theta_i+\gamma_0\theta_{j_2}\theta_i]}}$$

$$(j_1 \neq j_2 \neq i;\ j_1, j_2 = 1,2,\ldots,p)\ .$$

We next evaluate (4.12). Since

$$d \prod_{\substack{j=1\\ j\neq i}}^{p} F\left[\sqrt{\frac{\gamma_j\theta_i}{\theta_j\gamma_i}}\, y\right]$$

$$(4.18)\quad = \sum_{\substack{h=1\\ h\neq i}}^{p} \prod_{\substack{j=1\\ j\neq h\neq i}}^{p} F\left[\sqrt{\frac{\gamma_j\theta_i}{\theta_j\gamma_i}}\, y\right] f\left[\sqrt{\frac{\gamma_h\theta_i}{\theta_h\gamma_i}}\, y\right] \sqrt{\frac{\gamma_h\theta_i}{\theta_h\gamma_i}}\, dy\ ,$$

obtain (following steps analogous to those used in deriv- the expression for M_{1i})

$$M_{2i} = \int_{-\infty}^{\infty} f(y) f_i^*(y) \sum_{\substack{h=1\\ h\neq i}}^{p} \prod_{\substack{j=1\\ j\neq h\neq i}}^{p} F\left[\sqrt{\frac{\gamma_j\theta_i}{\theta_j\gamma_i}}\, y\right] f\left[\sqrt{\frac{\gamma_h\theta_i}{\theta_h\gamma_i}}\, y\right] \cdot$$

$$(4.19)\quad \sqrt{\frac{\gamma_h\theta_i}{\theta_h\gamma_i}}\, dy$$

$$= \frac{1}{\sqrt{2\pi}} \sum_{\substack{h=1\\ h\neq i}}^{p} f\left[\lambda\sqrt{\frac{\gamma_0(\gamma_h\theta_i+\gamma_i\theta_h)}{\gamma_h\theta_i+\gamma_i\theta_h+\gamma_0\theta_i\theta_h}}\right] \sqrt{\frac{\gamma_h\theta_i}{\gamma_h\theta_i+\gamma_i\theta_h+\gamma_0\theta_i\theta_h}}\, E_{hi}$$

for $p = 2$ we have $E_{hi} \equiv 1$, and for $p > 2$

$$E_{hi} = P\{Z_{hij} < (\lambda\ \gamma_0\theta_i\theta_h\sqrt{\gamma_j}) \div$$

$$\sqrt{[\gamma_h\theta_i+\gamma_i\theta_h+\gamma_0\theta_i\theta_h][\theta_j(\gamma_h\theta_i+\gamma_i\theta_h+\gamma_0\gamma_i\theta_h)+\gamma_j\theta_i\theta_h)]} \tag{4.20}$$

$$(j \neq h \neq i;\ j = 1,2,\ldots,p)\};$$

here the Z_{hij} $(j \neq h \neq i;\ j = 1,2,\ldots,p)$ have a (p-2)-variate normal distribution with $E\{Z_{hij}\} = 0$, $Var\{Z_{hij}\} = 1$, and

$$E\{Z_{hij_1} Z_{hij_2}\} = \theta_h\theta_i\sqrt{\gamma_{j_1}\gamma_{j_2}} \div$$

$$\sqrt{[\theta_{j_1}(\gamma_i\theta_h+\gamma_h\theta_i+\gamma_0\theta_h\theta_i)+\gamma_{j_1}\theta_h\theta_i)]}\cdot \tag{4.21}$$

$$\sqrt{[\theta_{j_2}(\gamma_i\theta_h+\gamma_h\theta_i+\gamma_0\theta_h\theta_i)+\gamma_{j_2}\theta_h\theta_i]}$$

$$(j_1 \neq j_2 \neq h \neq i;\ j_1,j_2= 1,2,\ldots,p).$$

Finally we evaluate (4.4). After letting

$$y = \sqrt{\gamma_t/\theta_t}\ (\lambda + x/\sqrt{\gamma_0})$$

in (4.4) we obtain

$$K_{2t} = \sqrt{\gamma_0}\ \frac{\theta_t}{\gamma_t}\ L_{1t} \tag{4.22}$$

where L_{1t} is defined by (4.6). From (4.13), (4.15), (4.19) we see that

$$K_{2t} = \frac{\lambda(\gamma_0\theta_t)^{3/2}/\sqrt{\gamma_t}}{\gamma_t+\gamma_0\theta_t} M_{1t} + \frac{\sqrt{\gamma_0}\theta_t}{\gamma_t+\gamma_0\theta_t} M_{2t}$$

$$= \lambda\left(\frac{\gamma_0\theta_t}{\gamma_t+\gamma_0\theta_t}\right)^{3/2} f\left[\lambda\sqrt{\frac{\gamma_0\gamma_t}{\gamma_t+\gamma_0\theta_t}}\right] D_t$$

$$(4.23)\qquad + \frac{1}{\sqrt{2\pi}} \sum_{\substack{h=1\\h\neq t}}^{p} f\left[\lambda\sqrt{\frac{\gamma_0(\gamma_h\theta_t+\gamma_t\theta_h)}{\gamma_h\theta_t+\gamma_t\theta_h+\gamma_0\theta_t\theta_h}}\right]$$

$$\cdot \frac{\theta_t^{3/2}}{\gamma_t+\gamma_0\theta_t} \sqrt{\frac{\gamma_0\gamma_h}{\gamma_h\theta_t+\gamma_t\theta_h+\gamma_0\theta_t\theta_h}} E_{ht} \quad .$$

Combining (4.14), (4.15), (4.19), (4.23) we obtain our final result, namely that for $t = 1,2,\ldots,p$ we have

$$\frac{\partial g}{\partial\gamma_t} = -\frac{1}{2\sqrt{\gamma_0}}\{\lambda[\sum_{i=1}^{p}\left(\frac{\gamma_i}{\gamma_i+\gamma_0\theta_i}\right)^{3/2} f\left[\lambda\sqrt{\frac{\gamma_0\gamma_i}{\gamma_i+\gamma_0\theta_i}}\right] D_i$$

$$- \frac{\gamma_0^2\theta_t}{\sqrt{\gamma_t}(\gamma_t+\gamma_0\theta_t)^{3/2}} f\left[\lambda\sqrt{\frac{\gamma_0\gamma_t}{\gamma_t+\gamma_0\theta_t}}\right] D_t]$$

$$(4.24)\qquad - \frac{1}{\sqrt{2\pi}}[\sum_{i=1}^{p}\sum_{\substack{h=1\\h\neq i}}^{p} \frac{\theta_i}{\gamma_i+\gamma_0\theta_i}\sqrt{\frac{\gamma_i\gamma_h}{\gamma_h\theta_i+\gamma_i\theta_h+\gamma_0\theta_i\theta_h}} \cdot$$

$$f\left[\lambda\sqrt{\frac{\gamma_0(\gamma_h\theta_i+\gamma_i\theta_h)}{\gamma_h\theta_i+\gamma_i\theta_h+\gamma_0\theta_i\theta_h}}\right] E_{hi}$$

$$+ \sum_{\substack{h=1\\h\neq t}}^{p} \frac{\gamma_0\theta_t}{\sqrt{\gamma_t}(\gamma_t+\gamma_0\theta_t)} \sqrt{\frac{\gamma_h}{\gamma_h\theta_t+\gamma_t\theta_h+\gamma_0\theta_t\theta_h}} \cdot f[\lambda \sqrt{\frac{\gamma_0(\gamma_h\theta_t+\gamma_t\theta_h)}{\gamma_h\theta_t+\gamma_t\theta_h+\gamma_0\theta_t\theta_h}}]E_{ht}]\}$$

where $D_i (i = 1,2,\ldots,p)$ and $E_{hi} (h \neq i; h,i = 1,2,\ldots,p)$ are given by (4.16) and (4.20), respectively.

An alternative form of (4.24) is given by

$$\frac{\partial g}{\partial \gamma_t} = -\frac{1}{2\sqrt{\gamma_0}} \{\lambda [\sum_{\substack{i=1\\i\neq t}}^{p} (\frac{\gamma_i}{\gamma_i+\gamma_0\theta_i})^{3/2} f[\lambda \sqrt{\frac{\gamma_0\gamma_i}{\gamma_i+\gamma_0\theta_i}}] D_i$$

$$+ \frac{\gamma_t^2 - \gamma_0^2 \theta_t}{\sqrt{\gamma_t} (\gamma_t+\gamma_0\theta_t)^{3/2}} f[\lambda \sqrt{\frac{\gamma_0\gamma_t}{\gamma_t+\gamma_0\theta_t}}] D_t]$$

$$(4.25) \quad - \frac{1}{\sqrt{2\pi}} [\sum_{\substack{i=1\\i\neq t}}^{p} \sum_{\substack{h=1\\h\neq i}}^{p} \frac{\theta_i}{\gamma_i+\gamma_0\theta_i} \sqrt{\frac{\gamma_i\gamma_h}{\gamma_h\theta_i+\gamma_i\theta_h+\gamma_0\theta_i\theta_h}} \cdot f[\lambda \sqrt{\frac{\gamma_0(\gamma_h\theta_i+\gamma_i\theta_h)}{\gamma_h\theta_i+\gamma_i\theta_h+\gamma_0\theta_i\theta_h}}] E_{hi}$$

$$+ \sum_{\substack{h=1\\h\neq t}}^{p} \frac{(\gamma_t+\gamma_0)\theta_t}{\sqrt{\gamma_t}(\gamma_t+\gamma_0\theta_t)} \sqrt{\frac{\gamma_h}{\gamma_h\theta_t+\gamma_t\theta_h+\gamma_0\theta_t\theta_h}} f[\lambda \sqrt{\frac{\gamma_0(\gamma_h\theta_t+\gamma_t\theta_h)}{\gamma_h\theta_t+\gamma_t\theta_h+\gamma_0\theta_t\theta_h}}] E_{ht}]\} .$$

4.2. *Dependence of the solution of the maximization problem on the value of* λ.

4.2.1. *Description of the probability surface.* It will be helpful to regard the probability g (3.1) as a response surface in $(p+1)$-space with the γ_i $(1 \leqq i \leqq p)$ as independent variables, and the θ_i $(1 \leqq i \leqq p)$ as known fixed constants; $\lambda = d\sqrt{N}/\sigma_0$ $(0 < \lambda < \infty)$ is specified, and then held fixed.

All of our calculations and studies lead us to conclude that when $\lambda^* < \lambda < \infty$ (where $\lambda^* > 0$ is given by (4.34)), the response surface g, regarded as a function of the γ_i $(1 \leqq i \leqq p)$, has a *unique* maximum at $\hat{\gamma} = (\hat{\gamma}_0, \hat{\gamma}_1, \ldots, \hat{\gamma}_p)$ in the interior of the region given by $\gamma_i \geqq 0$ $(1 \leqq i \leqq p)$, $\sum_{i=1}^{p} \gamma_i \leqq 1$. We have also noted that as $\lambda \downarrow \lambda^*$ we have

$\sum_{i=1}^{p} \hat{\gamma}_i = 1 - \hat{\gamma}_0 \rightarrow 1$, i.e., $\hat{\gamma}_0 \rightarrow 0$; as $\lambda \downarrow \lambda^*$ the response surface becomes ridge-like, and in the limit $(\lambda = \lambda^*)$ it has a constant maximum value of $1/2$ along the hyperplane

$\sum_{i=1}^{p} \gamma_i = 1$. For *all* $\lambda (0 \leqq \lambda < \lambda^*)$ the response surface also is ridge-like, and has a constant maximum value of $1/2$ along the hyperplane $\sum_{i=1}^{p} \gamma_i = 1$. (These remarks are consistent with those given in Section 5 of [2]; however, the analysis in [2] was less complicated than that required here.)

As indicated above, we have not yet *proved* analytically the existence of a *unique* maximum for g when $\lambda^* < \lambda < \infty$ (nor did we actually *prove* the corresponding result in [2]), although all of our numerical calculations and certain analytical considerations all point to this conclusion.

4.2.2. *Definition of* λ^* *and limiting results as* $\hat{\gamma}_0 \to 0$. Throughout this section we assume that $\theta = (\theta_1, \theta_2, \ldots, \theta_p)$ is fixed. We shall first find for arbitrary $\lambda > 0$, the optimal allocation, $\hat{\gamma}(\gamma_0) = (\gamma_0, \hat{\gamma}_1(\gamma_0), \ldots, \hat{\gamma}_p(\gamma_0))$, conditioned on γ_0 being some fixed number in $(0,1)$. We shall then find the limiting conditional optimal allocation $\hat{\gamma}^* = \lim \hat{\gamma}(\gamma_0)$ as $\hat{\gamma}_0 \to 0$. Finally, we shall show that there is a unique value of λ, which we denote by λ^*, such that when $\lambda = \lambda^*$ the p+1 equations $\partial g/\partial \gamma_t = 0$ $(1 \leqq t \leqq p)$, $\sum_{i=0}^{p} \gamma_i = 1$ are satisfied when γ_0 is arbitrarily close to zero. Hence $\hat{\gamma}^*$ is the globally optimal allocation as $\lambda \to \lambda^*$.

First we consider the problem of maximizing g (3.1) with respect to the γ_i $(1 \leqq i \leqq p)$ subject to the condition that $\sum_{i=1}^{p} \gamma_i = 1 - \gamma_0$ with $\gamma_0 > 0$ and $\lambda > 0$ fixed but arbitrary. Denoting $g(\gamma_1, \gamma_2, \ldots, \gamma_p | \theta_1, \theta_2, \ldots, \theta_p; \lambda) + \mu(\sum_{i=1}^{p} \gamma_i - 1 + \gamma_0)$ by $h(\gamma_1, \gamma_2, \ldots, \gamma_p; \mu | \theta_1, \theta_2, \ldots, \theta_p; \lambda)$ or h (say), where μ is a Lagrange multiplier, we see that the maximizing value of $\gamma = (\gamma_0, \gamma_1, \ldots, \gamma_p)$, call it $\hat{\gamma}(\gamma_0)$, is found by solving simultaneously the p + 1 equations

$$\frac{\partial h}{\partial \mu} = 0, \quad \frac{\partial h}{\partial \gamma_t} = 0 \quad (1 \leqq t \leqq p). \tag{4.26}$$

This is equivalent to solving the p equations

$$\sum_{i=1}^{p} \gamma_i = 1 - \gamma_0, \quad \frac{\partial g}{\partial \gamma_1} = \frac{\partial g}{\partial \gamma_s} \quad (2 \leqq s \leqq p). \tag{4.27}$$

From (4.24) we see that (4.27) implies that

$$\gamma_0^{3/2}\,\lambda\left[\frac{\theta_1 f[\lambda\sqrt{\frac{\gamma_0\theta_1}{\gamma_1+\gamma_0\theta_1}}]\,D_1}{\sqrt{\gamma_1}\,(\gamma_1+\gamma_0\theta_1)^{3/2}}-\frac{\theta_s f[\lambda\sqrt{\frac{\gamma_0\theta_s}{\gamma_s+\gamma_0\theta_s}}]\,D_s}{\sqrt{\gamma_s}\,(\gamma_s+\gamma_0\theta_s)^{3/2}}\right]$$

$$= \frac{\gamma_0^{1/2}}{\sqrt{2\pi}}\Bigg(\sum_{h=2}^{p}\frac{\theta_1}{\sqrt{\gamma_1}\,(\gamma_1+\gamma_0\theta_1)}\sqrt{\frac{\gamma_h}{\gamma_h\theta_1+\gamma_1\theta_h+\gamma_0\theta_1\theta_h}}\cdot f[\lambda\sqrt{\frac{\gamma_0(\gamma_h\theta_1+\gamma_1\theta_h)}{\gamma_h\theta_1+\gamma_1\theta_h+\gamma_0\theta_1\theta_h}}]\,E_{h1}$$

(4.28)

$$-\sum_{\substack{h=1\\h\neq s}}^{p}\frac{\theta_s}{\sqrt{\gamma_s}\,(\gamma_s+\gamma_0\theta_s)}\sqrt{\frac{\gamma_h}{\gamma_h\theta_s+\gamma_s\theta_h+\gamma_0\theta_s\theta_h}}\cdot f[\lambda\sqrt{\frac{\gamma_0(\gamma_h\theta_s+\gamma_s\theta_h)}{\gamma_h\theta_s+\gamma_s\theta_h+\gamma_0\theta_s\theta_h}}]\,E_{hs}\Bigg)$$

$$(s = 2,3,\ldots,p), \quad \sum_{i=1}^{p}\gamma_i = 1-\gamma_0 ,$$

where for convenience of notation we have written $\hat{\gamma}(\gamma_0)$ as γ. We now study the behavior of $\hat{\gamma}(\gamma_0)$ as $\gamma_0 \to 0$. For $\gamma_0 \to 0$ the dominating term in each of the first p-1 equations of (4.28) is the one with coefficient $\gamma_0^{1/2}$. Thus, in the limit as $\gamma_0 \to 0$ we must have

$$\sum_{h=2}^{p} \frac{\theta_1 E_{h1}^0}{(\gamma_1^*)^{3/2}} \sqrt{\frac{\gamma_h^*}{\gamma_h^*\theta_1+\gamma_1^*\theta_h}}$$

$$(4.29) \qquad = \sum_{\substack{h=1\\ h\neq s}}^{p} \frac{\theta_s E_{hs}^0}{(\gamma_s^*)^{3/2}} \sqrt{\frac{\gamma_h^*}{\gamma_h^*\theta_s+\gamma_s^*\theta_h}}$$

$$(s = 2,3,\ldots,p), \quad \sum_{i=1}^{p} \gamma_i^* = 1 ,$$

where E_{hi}^0 $(i = 1,2,\ldots,p)$ is defined by setting $\gamma_0 = 0$ in (4.20). In the foregoing we have let $\hat{\gamma}^* = (0,\hat{\gamma}_1^*,\ldots,\hat{\gamma}_p^*) = \lim \hat{\gamma}(\gamma_0)$ as $\gamma_0 \to 0$ denote the solution to the equations (4.29). Note that the equations (4.29) are independent of λ, and therefore so is the solution $\hat{\gamma}^*$. For example, for $p = 2$ we note that $E_{12}^0 = E_{21}^0 = 1$, and hence the solution to (4.29) is

$$(4.30) \qquad \hat{\gamma}^* = (0,\sqrt{\theta_1}/(\sqrt{\theta_1}+\sqrt{\theta_2}),\ \sqrt{\theta_2}/(\sqrt{\theta_1}+\sqrt{\theta_2})) .$$

As noted above, for all p we have $\hat{\gamma}^*$ independent of λ. Thus, if we can find a value of λ, say λ^*, such that as $\lambda \to \lambda^*$ we have $\gamma_0 \to 0$ satisfies the equations $\partial g/\partial\gamma_t = 0$ $(1 \leq t \leq p)$, $\sum_{i=0}^{p} \gamma_i = 1$, then $\hat{\gamma}^*$ is the *unconditional* optimal allocation in the limit $(\lambda = \lambda^*)$.

In order to find λ^* we write $\partial g/\partial\gamma_t$ $(1 \leq t \leq p)$ as

$$(4.31) \qquad \frac{\partial g}{\partial \gamma_t} = -\frac{1}{2\sqrt{\gamma_0}} Q_t(\gamma_0,\gamma_1,\ldots,\gamma_p|\theta_1,\theta_2,\ldots,\theta_p;\lambda)$$

where Q_t is given by the outer { } in (4.24). We note that $Q_t = Q$ (say) is independent of t $(1 \leq t \leq p)$ when $\gamma_0 = 0$. In order for $\gamma_0 = 0$ to be associated with a global optimal allocation, we must have

$$\lambda = \bar{\lambda}_p\ (0,\gamma_1,\ldots,\gamma_p;\ \theta_1,\theta_2,\ldots,\theta_p) = \bar{\lambda}$$

(say) where $\bar{\lambda}$ satisfies the equation

$$Q(0,\gamma_1,\ldots,\gamma_p|\theta_1,\theta_2,\ldots,\theta_p;\ \bar{\lambda}) = 0\ , \tag{4.32}$$

i.e.,

$$\bar{\lambda} = \frac{1}{\sqrt{2\pi}}\ \frac{\sum_{i=1}^{p}\sum_{\substack{h=1\\h\neq i}}^{p}\theta_i\sqrt{\frac{\gamma_h}{\gamma_i(\gamma_h\theta_i+\gamma_i\theta_h)}}\ E_{hi}^0}{\sum_{i=1}^{p} D_i^0} \tag{4.33}$$

where D_i^0 $(1 \leqq i \leqq p)$ and E_{hi}^0 $(h \neq i;\ h,i = 1,2,\ldots,p)$ are obtained by substituting $\gamma_0 = 0$ in (4.16) and (4.20), respectively.

Combining (4.33) with the fact that $\hat{\gamma}^*$ is optimal as $\gamma_0 \to 0$ independently of λ, we see that

$$\lambda^* = \bar{\lambda}_p(0,\gamma_1^*,\ldots,\gamma_p^*;\ \theta_1,\theta_2,\ldots,\theta_p)\ , \tag{4.34}$$

and λ^* is unique. In summary, as $\lambda \to \lambda^*$ we have $\hat{\gamma} \to \hat{\gamma}^*$ with $\hat{\gamma}_0 \to 0$.

Thus, for example, when $\theta_1 = \theta_2 = \ldots = \theta_p = \theta$ (say), in which case we have $\hat{\gamma}^* = (0,1/p,\ldots,1/p)$ (because of symmetry), we see that

$$\lambda_p^*(\theta) = \frac{(p-1)}{2}\sqrt{\frac{p\theta}{\pi}}\ \frac{F_{p-2}(0|1/3)}{F_{p-1}(0|1/2)} \tag{4.35}$$

where $F_n(z|\rho)$ is the equicoordinate n-variate standard normal distribution function with $E\{Z_iZ_j\} = \rho_{ij} = \rho(i \neq j;\ i,j=1,2,\ldots,n)$. Since $F_{p-1}\ (0|1/2) = 1/p$, we note that (4.35) reduces to (see also, (28) in [2])

(4.36) $$\lambda_p^*(\theta) = \frac{p(p-1)}{2}\sqrt{\frac{p\theta}{\pi}}\ F_{p-2}(0|1/3) .$$

It is known (see, e.g., Gupta [5], Section 6) that $F_0(0|1/3) = 1$, $F_1(0|1/3) = 1/2$, $F_2(0|1/3) = (1/4) + (1/2\pi)\arcsin(1/3)$, and $F_3(0|1/3) = (1/8) + (3/4\pi)\arcsin(1/3)$; $F_n(0|1/3)$ has been computed to 5 decimals for $n = 1(1)12$ by Gupta ([5], Table II, p. 817).

Also, for $p = 2$ with arbitrary θ_1, θ_2 we have, since $\hat{\gamma}^*$ is given by (4.30), that

(4.37) $$\lambda_2^*(\theta_1,\theta_2) = \frac{\sqrt{\theta_1}+\sqrt{\theta_2}}{\sqrt{2\pi}} .$$

Remark 1: If we consider (2.6) for $p = 2$, and seek to maximize the probability as $\gamma_0 \to 0$, we see that this is equivalent to maximizing

(4.38) $$P\{Z_i < 0 \quad (i = 1,2)\} = \frac{1}{4} + \frac{1}{2\pi}\arcsin \rho_{12}$$

as $\gamma_0 \to 0$ where ρ_{12} is given by (2.7). For fixed $\gamma_0 > 0$, maximizing (4.38) is accomplished by maximizing ρ_{12}, and it is straightforward to show that this occurs when

(4.39) $$\hat{\gamma}_1(\gamma_0) = \frac{B(A-B)}{\theta_2-\theta_1},\quad \hat{\gamma}_2(\gamma_0) = \frac{A(A-B)}{\theta_2-\theta_1} ,$$

where $A = \sqrt{\theta_2(1-\gamma_0+\gamma_0\theta_1)}$, $B = \sqrt{\theta_1(1-\gamma_0+\gamma_0\theta_2)}$. For $\gamma_0 = 0$, (4.39) reduces to $\hat{\gamma}_i^*$ $(i = 1,2)$ of (4.30). This method of obtaining the optimal allocation as $\gamma_0 \to 0$, i.e., by maximizing (4.38), suggests an approach that might be useful for $p > 2$.

4.2.3. *The case* $0 \leq \lambda \leq \lambda^*$. Referring to (3.1) we note that g is a strictly increasing function of λ for fixed θ_i $(1 \leq i \leq p)$ and γ_i $(0 \leq i \leq p)$. Also, as $\lambda \to \lambda^*$ we have $\gamma_0 \to 0$ and $\hat{\gamma}(\gamma_0) \to \hat{\gamma}^*$. Finally (see (3.2)), $\lim g = 1/2$ as $\gamma_0 \to 0$ for all λ and θ_i. Hence, for all $0 \leqq \lambda \leqq \lambda^*$ we must have

$$\begin{aligned} & g_p(\gamma_0,\gamma_1,\ldots,\gamma_p|\theta_1,\theta_2,\ldots,\theta_p;\lambda) \\ (4.40) \qquad & \leqq g_p(\gamma_0,\gamma_1,\ldots,\gamma_p|\theta_1,\theta_2,\ldots,\theta_p;\lambda^*) \\ & \leqq g_p(0,\hat{\gamma}_1^*,\ldots,\hat{\gamma}_p^*|\theta_1,\theta_2,\ldots,\theta_p;\lambda^*) = 1/2 \quad . \end{aligned}$$

Thus, for all $\lambda(0 \leqq \lambda \leqq \lambda^*)$, g is bounded above by 1/2, and this bound is attained when $\hat{\gamma}_0 = 0$ and $\hat{\gamma}_i = \hat{\gamma}_i^*$ $(1 \leqq i \leqq p)$ which is thus the optimal allocation. [Actually, when $0 \leqq \lambda \leqq \lambda^*$ we have $\partial g/\partial\gamma_t > 0$ $(1 \leqq t \leqq p)$ for all $\gamma = (\gamma_0,\gamma_1,\ldots,\gamma_p)$, and hence the $p+1$ equations $\partial g/\partial\gamma_t = 0$ $(1 \leqq t \leqq p)$, $\sum_{i=0}^{p} \gamma_i = 1$ do *not* have a solution; the supremum of g is taken on at the boundary, $\gamma_0 = 0$.]

4.2.4. *Limiting results as* $\lambda \to \infty$. Using (4.24) we shall study the behavior of the solution $\hat{\gamma}$ of the $p+1$ equations $\partial g/\partial\gamma_t = 0$ $(1 \leqq t \leqq p)$, $\sum_{i=0}^{p} \gamma_i = 1$ as $\lambda \to \infty$. In order that these equations have a solution as $\lambda \to \infty$, the coefficient of λ in (4.24) must approach 0 as $\lambda \to \infty$. Thus as $\lambda \to \infty$ we must have

$$\sum_{i=1}^{p} \left(\frac{\hat{\gamma}_i}{\hat{\gamma}_i+\hat{\gamma}_0\theta_i}\right)^{3/2} f\left[\lambda\hat{\gamma}_0 \sqrt{\frac{\hat{\gamma}_i\theta_t-\hat{\gamma}_t\theta_i}{(\hat{\gamma}_i+\hat{\gamma}_0\theta_i)(\hat{\gamma}_t+\hat{\gamma}_0\theta_t)}}\right]$$

$$(4.41) \qquad - \frac{1}{\sqrt{2\pi}} \frac{\hat{\gamma}_0^2\theta_t}{\sqrt{\hat{\gamma}_t}(\hat{\gamma}_t-\hat{\gamma}_0\theta_t)^{3/2}} \to 0 \quad (1 \leqq t \leqq p) ,$$

$$\sum_{i=0}^{p} \hat{\gamma}_i = 1.$$

But this is possible only if

$$(4.42) \qquad \lambda^2 \hat{\gamma}_0^2 \frac{\hat{\gamma}_i \theta_t - \hat{\gamma}_t \theta_i}{(\hat{\gamma}_i + \hat{\gamma}_0 \theta_i)(\hat{\gamma}_t + \hat{\gamma}_0 \theta_t)} \to \Delta_{it} \quad \text{(say)}$$

where Δ_{it} is a *finite* limit. Since $\hat{\gamma}_0 = 0$ is clearly not a solution of (4.41), this implies that as $\lambda \to \infty$ we must have

$$(4.43) \qquad \hat{\gamma}_i \theta_t - \hat{\gamma}_t \theta_i \to 0 \quad (i,t = 1,2,\ldots,p) \quad .$$

But the case $\gamma_1/\theta_1 = \gamma_j/\theta_j$ $(2 \leqq j \leqq p)$ is the one studied in [2] (see (10) of [2]), and by Corollary 1 (p. 470 of [2]) we have that for this case the optimal allocation in the limit (as $\lambda \to \infty$) is

$$(4.44) \qquad \hat{\gamma}_0 = 1/(1 + \sqrt{\beta}), \; \hat{\gamma}_i = \theta_i/\sqrt{\beta}(1 + \sqrt{\beta}) \quad (1 \leqq i \leqq p)$$

where $\beta = \sum_{i=1}^{p} \theta_i$. Thus (4.44) is the desired limiting result for our present problem. (Note: This implies that in (4.42) we must have $\Delta_{it} = \log_e(\theta_i/\theta_t)$.)

4.3. *Fundamental theorem and summary of results.* Our basic results concerning optimal allocation are summarized in the following theorem and corollaries:

Theorem 1. *Let* λ^* *be defined as in* (4.34)

a) *For fixed* $\lambda (0 < \lambda \leqq \lambda^*)$, *the optimal allocation is* $\hat{\gamma}^* = (0, \hat{\gamma}_1^*, \ldots, \hat{\gamma}_p^*)$ *where* $\hat{\gamma}^*$ *is defined as the solution to the* p *equations* (4.29).

b) *For fixed* $\lambda (\lambda^* < \lambda < \infty)$, *the optimal allocation is* $\hat{\gamma} = (\hat{\gamma}_0, \hat{\gamma}_1, \ldots, \hat{\gamma}_p)$ *where* $\hat{\gamma}$ *is the unique* [1] *root of the* p+1 *equations* $\partial g/\partial \gamma_t = 0$ $(1 \leq t \leq p)$, $\sum_{i=0}^{p} \gamma_i = 1$ *where* $\partial g/\partial \gamma_t$ *is given*

---

[1] See the comment at the end of Section 4.2.1.

by (4.24). *Here* $\hat{\gamma}^*$ *and* $\hat{\gamma}$ *are functions of* $p \geqq 1$, $\theta_i = \sigma_i^2/\sigma_0^2$ $(1 \leqq i \leqq p)$ *and* $\lambda = d\sqrt{N}/\sigma_0$ *which are assumed to be fixed.*

Corollary 1: *For the setup of* Theorem 1, *we have in the limit* $(\lambda \downarrow \lambda^*)$ *that* $\hat{\gamma}_0 = 0$, $\hat{\gamma}_i = \hat{\gamma}_i^*$ $(1 \leqq i \leqq p)$.

Corollary 2: *For the setup of* Theorem 1, *we have in the limit* $(\lambda \to \infty)$ *that* $\hat{\gamma}_0 = (1 + \sqrt{\beta})^{-1}$, $\hat{\gamma}_i = \theta_i/\sqrt{\beta}(1 + \sqrt{\beta})$ $(1 \leqq i \leqq p)$ *where* $\beta = \sum_{i=1}^{p} \theta_i$.

Remark 2: If $\theta_1 = \theta_2 = \ldots = \theta_p$, then (by symmetry) $\hat{\gamma}_1 = \hat{\gamma}_2 = \ldots = \hat{\gamma}_p$ and the results of [2] apply and are globally optimal.

Remark 3: The result of Corollary 2 can be obtained directly in a very simple way if one notes that for $\lambda \to \infty$ the probability in (2.6) does not depend, to the first order, on the ρ_{ij} (2.7). Thus we could consider maximizing the probability in (2.6) when $\rho_{ij} = 0$ (all $i \neq j$). By symmetry, this occurs when the θ_i/γ_i $(1 \leqq i \leqq p)$ are equal, and then the results of Corollary 2 of [2] apply.

5. *Computation of the optimal allocation for* p=2. For p=2 we have already noted (see (4.37) and (4.30)) that $\lambda_2^*(\theta_1, \theta_2) = (\sqrt{\theta_1} + \sqrt{\theta_2})/\sqrt{2\pi}$ and $\hat{\gamma}^* = (0, \sqrt{\theta_1}/(\sqrt{\theta_1} + \sqrt{\theta_2}), \sqrt{\theta_2}/(\sqrt{\theta_1} + \sqrt{\theta_2}))$ which is the optimal allocation for $0 < \lambda \leqq \lambda^*$. Also, as $\lambda \to \infty$ $\lim \hat{\gamma} = (1 + \sqrt{\theta_1 + \theta_2})^{-1}(1, \theta_1/\sqrt{\theta_1 + \theta_2}, \theta_2/\sqrt{\theta_1 + \theta_2})$. Thus, for $\lambda \downarrow \lambda^*$ and $\lambda \to \infty$ we have $\hat{\gamma}_1/\hat{\gamma}_2 \to \sqrt{\theta_1/\theta_2}$ and θ_1/θ_2, respectively.

For p = 2 the equation (4.24) simplifies somewhat, and the optimal allocation $\hat{\gamma}$ for $\lambda_2^* < \lambda < \infty$ is the solution to the three equations

$$- \frac{\lambda}{\sqrt{\gamma_0}} \{ [\frac{\gamma_j}{\gamma_j + \theta_j \gamma_0}]^{3/2} f_j F_{ij} + \frac{\gamma_i^2 - \theta_i \gamma_0^2}{\sqrt{\gamma_i}(\gamma_i + \theta_i \gamma_0)^{3/2}} f_i F_{ji} \}$$

$$+ \frac{f_3}{\sqrt{2\pi}} \frac{\sqrt{\gamma_j / \gamma_i}}{\sqrt{\gamma_0 (\gamma_1 \theta_2 + \gamma_2 \theta_1 + \gamma_0 \theta_1 \theta_2}} [\frac{\theta_j \gamma_i}{\gamma_j + \theta_j \gamma_0} + \frac{\theta_i (1 - \gamma_j)}{\gamma_i + \theta_i \gamma_0}] = 0 \tag{5.1}$$

$$(i = 1, j = 2), \ (i = 2, \ j = 1) \ ,$$

$$\sum_{i=0}^{2} \gamma_i = 1 \quad ,$$

where

$$f_j = f[\lambda \sqrt{\frac{\gamma_0 \gamma_j}{\gamma_j + \theta_j \gamma_0}}] \qquad (j = 1,2)$$

$$f_3 = f[\lambda \sqrt{\frac{\gamma_0 (\gamma_1 \theta_2 + \gamma_2 \theta_1)}{\gamma_1 \theta_2 + \gamma_2 \theta_1 + \gamma_0 \theta_1 \theta_2}}] \tag{5.2}$$

$$F_{ij} = F[\frac{\lambda \theta_i \gamma_0 \sqrt{\gamma_j}}{\sqrt{[\gamma_i + \theta_i \gamma_0][\gamma_1 \theta_2 + \gamma_2 \theta_1 + \gamma_0 \theta_1 \theta_2]}}] \qquad \begin{matrix} (i=1, j=2) \\ (i=2, j=1) \end{matrix}$$

which involve the standard normal density function $f(\cdot)$ and cdf $F(\cdot)$.

We have computed the solution to (5.1) for selected values of (θ_1, θ_2) and λ obtaining the optimal allocation $\hat{\gamma}$; we then used $\hat{\gamma}$ in g (3.1) to obtain the associated maximum probabilities $\hat{P}$. These numerical results are given in Tables A1 - A15; the entries are correct to 5 significant figures.

The path of the optimal allocation $\hat{\gamma}$ as λ increases from λ_2^* to ∞ is plotted for the cases $\theta_1 = \theta_2$, $\theta_1 < \theta_2$ and $\theta_1 > \theta_2$ in Figure 2.

Figure 2.

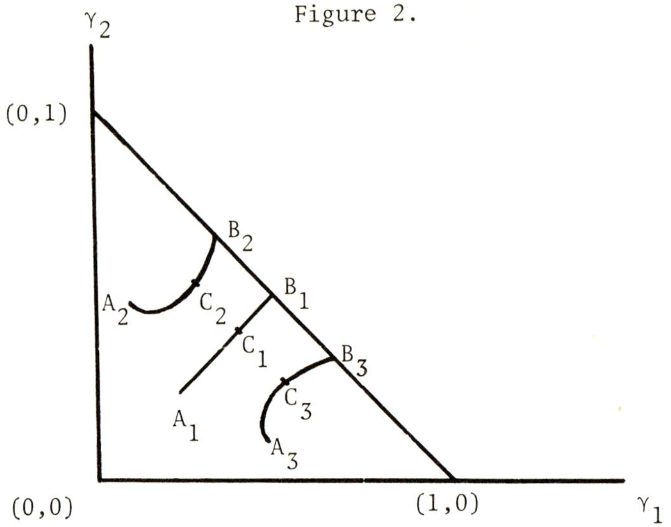

The segment $A_1C_1B_1$ represents the path of $\hat{\gamma}$ for $\theta_1 = \theta_2$, the segment $A_2C_2B_2$ the path for $\theta_1 < \theta_2$, and the segment $A_3C_3B_3$ the path for $\theta_1 > \theta_2$. As λ increases from 0 to λ_2^*, the optimal allocation remains stationary at B_i with coordinates $\gamma_1 = \sqrt{\theta_1}/(\sqrt{\theta_1}+\sqrt{\theta_2})$, $\gamma_2 = \sqrt{\theta_2}/(\sqrt{\theta_1}+\sqrt{\theta_2})$. As λ increases from λ_2^* to ∞, the optimal allocation moves away from the point B_i, through C_i, and approaches a limiting point A_i with $\gamma_1 = \theta_1/[\theta_1+\theta_2+\sqrt{\theta_1+\theta_2}]$, $\gamma_2 = \theta_2/[\theta_1+\theta_2+\sqrt{\theta_1+\theta_2}]$.

6. *Use of the tables.* Tables of $(\hat{\gamma}_0, \hat{\gamma}_1, \ldots, \hat{\gamma}_p)$ and the associated $\hat{P}$ as a function of λ for fixed p and $(\theta_1, \theta_2, \ldots, \theta_p)$ would be used as follows by a practitioner when he is designing his experiment: p and the σ_i^2 $(0 \leq i \leq p)$ are given as data of the problem; the latter determine the θ_i $(1 \leq i \leq p)$. The experimenter *specifies* d (his "yard-stick") and N, the total number of observations available

for experimentation, which together determine $\lambda = d\sqrt{N}/\sigma_0$. Then p, the θ_i $(1 \leq i \leq p)$ and λ determine the $\hat{\gamma}_i$ $(0 \leq i \leq p)$ and the associated $\hat{P}$. If $\hat{P}$ is too low (high) for the experimenter's requirements, he can increase (decrease) d and/or N.

Remark 4: In practice, one would never choose $\hat{\gamma}_0 = 0$ (the optimal allocation of Theorem 1 for $0 \leq \lambda \leq \lambda_p^*$), but rather one would approximate this allocation by (say) $\hat{\gamma}_0 = 1/N$. Since the N_i $(0 \leq i \leq p)$ are integers, the $\hat{\gamma}_i$ $(0 \leq i \leq p)$ must also be approximated unless $\hat{\gamma}_i N$ is an integer $(0 \leq i \leq p)$. For large N these approximations should be quite close.

7. *Savings obtained through optimal allocation.* In this section we discuss savings in total sample size achieved through optimal allocation.

7.1. *Relative efficiency considerations.* Suppose that we have a specified confidence coefficient $P^* > 1/2$ which the experimenter wishes to guarantee. For given p and σ_i^2 $(0 \leq i \leq p)$ and specified d, one might be interested in knowing the total sample size N which would be required using different allocation rules. In this section we compare the total sample size $\hat{N}$ required under the globally optimal allocation rule $\hat{R}$, with the total sample sizes $N^{(j)}$ required under three alternative allocation rules R_j $(j=1,2,3)$; these latter rules are

$$R_1: \quad \gamma_i = 1/(p+1) \quad (0 \leq i \leq p)$$

$$R_2: \quad \gamma_i = \gamma_j \sigma_i^2/\sigma_j^2 \quad (i,j = 0,1,\ldots,p) \tag{7.1}$$

$$R_3: \quad \gamma_i = \gamma_j \sigma_i^2/\sigma_j^2 \quad (i,j = 1,2,\ldots,p)$$ with γ_0 being chosen optimally subject to this restriction.

We point out that in general R_1 and R_2 are not optimal for any σ_i^2 $(0 \leqq i \leqq p)$. R_3 (which is the rule proposed in [2]) is equivalent to $\hat{R}$ (and therefore optimal) if $\sigma_1^2 = \sigma_2^2 = \ldots = \sigma_p^2$ and $\lambda < \infty$; it is also equivalent to $\hat{R}$ for arbitrary σ_i^2 $(1 \leqq i \leqq p)$ as $\lambda \to \infty$.

We define the efficiency of R_j $(j = 1,2,3)$ relative to $\hat{R}$ for given p, θ_i $(1 \leqq i \leqq p)$ and specified P^* as

$$(7.2) \qquad e_j = \frac{\hat{N}}{N^{(j)}} = \left(\frac{\hat{\lambda}}{\lambda_j}\right)^2 \qquad (1 \leqq j \leqq 3) ,$$

where $\hat{\lambda} = d\sqrt{\hat{N}}/\sigma_0$ and $\lambda_j = d\sqrt{N^{(j)}}/\sigma_0$ are the λ-values associated with P^* for the given p and θ_i $(1 \leqq i \leqq p)$ when $\hat{R}$ and R_j, respectively, are used with the same d. Clearly $0 < e_j \leqq 1$ $(1 \leqq j \leqq 3)$.

7.2. *Relative efficiency calculations for* $p = 2$. We consider the special case $p = 2$ (which is the smallest p-value which will illustrate the results), and compute the $\hat{\lambda}$, λ_j and e_j $(j = 1,2,3)$ for $\theta_1, \theta_2 = 0.1, 1, 10$ and $P^* = 0.60.0.90,0.99$. These are given in Table I, below. The values of $\hat{\lambda}$ were obtained by interpolation (actually by forming a finer λ-grid) in the appropriate tables of the Appendix; the values of λ_1 were computed especially for the present purpose using (3.1); the values of λ_2 and λ_3 were obtained from [1] (using the method described in Section 3, (ii)) and by solving numerically equation (34) of [2], respectively. The values of $\hat{\lambda}$, λ_1, and λ_3 are correct to the number of figures recorded; λ_2 is correct to 4 significant figures.

Table I

P^*	$\hat{\lambda}$	λ_1	λ_2	λ_3	e_1	e_2	e_3
	$\theta_1 = 0.1$			$\theta_2 = 0.1$			
0.60	0.7366	0.7619	0.9696	0.7366	0.9347	0.5772	1
0.90	2.2075	2.6035	2.4430	2.2075	0.7189	0.8165	1
0.99	3.6654	4.4765	3.9630	3.6654	0.6704	0.8555	1
	$\theta_1 = 0.1$			$\theta_2 = 1.0$			
0.60	1.1195	1.1816	1.2820	1.2324	0.8977	0.7625	0.8252
0.90	3.0371	3.3469	3.2310	3.2297	0.8233	0.8836	0.8844
0.99	5.0441	5.7368	5.2420	5.2418	0.7730	0.9258	0.9260
	$\theta_1 = 0.1$			$\theta_2 = 10$			
0.60	2.0311	2.2224	2.9480	2.8822	0.8352	0.4747	0.4966
0.90	5.6423	7.3624	7.4290	6.7391	0.5874	0.5769	0.7009
0.99	9.8465	13.3640	12.0500	10.7424	0.5429	0.6677	0.8402
	$\theta_1 = 1$			$\theta_2 = 1$			
0.60	1.5216	1.5332	1.5332	1.5216	0.9849	0.9849	1
0.90	3.8375	3.8628	3.8628	3.8375	0.9868	0.9868	1
0.99	6.1893	6.2654	6.2654	6.1893	0.9760	0.9760	1
	$\theta_1 = 1$			$\theta_2 = 10$			
0.60	2.5501	2.6410	3.0660	2.9880	0.9324	0.6918	0.7283
0.90	6.3674	7.3923	7.7250	6.9662	0.7420	0.6795	0.8354
0.99	10.5794	13.3640	12.5300	11.0996	0.6267	0.7128	0.9084
	$\theta_1 = 10$			$\theta_2 = 10$			
0.60	3.8676	4.2255	4.0560	3.8676	0.8377	0.9093	1
0.90	8.8576	9.3434	10.2200	8.8576	0.8987	0.7512	1
0.99	14.0773	14.7870	16.5800	14.0773	0.9063	0.7210	1

The e-values demonstrate that substantial savings can be made by optimal allocation when θ_1, θ_2 differ markedly from unity; these savings then depend critically on P^*. As wou' be expected, $e_3 \geqq e_2$.

8. *Directions of future research.* It would be interesting to generalize the results of the present paper to the

case of two-sided comparisons; however, we do not plan to undertake such studies. It would be useful to extend the tables of the Appendix to the case $p > 2$, and also to study the relative efficiencies of Section 7 for large p.

9. *Acknowledgement.* We are happy to acknowledge the assistance of Professor John E. Dennis, Jr. of Cornell's Department of Computer Science who gave us valuable advice on certain problems in numerical analysis arising in our computations.

References

1. Bechhofer, R.E. (1954). "A single-sample multiple decision procedure for ranking means of normal populations with known variances," *Annals of Mathematical Statistics*, Vol. 25, pp. 16-39.

2. Bechhofer, R.E. (1969). "Optimal allocation of observations when comparing several treatments with a control," *Multivariate Analysis*, II, Academic Press, Inc., New York., pp. 463-473.

3. Bechhofer, R.E. and Nocturne, D.J.M. (1970). "Optimal allocation of observations when comparing several treatments with a control, II: 2-sided comparisons," Technical Report No. 110, Department of Operations Research, Cornell University.

4. Dunnett, C.W. (1955). "A multiple comparison procedure for comparing several treatments with a control," *Journal of the American Statistical Association*, Vol. 50, pp. 1096-1121.

5. Gupta, S.S. (1963), "Probability integrals of multivariate normal and multivariate t," *Annals of Mathematical Statistics*, Vol. 34, pp. 792-828.

6. Kiefer, J. and Wolfowitz, J. (1959), "Optimum designs in regression problems," *Annals of Mathematical Statistics*, Vol. 30, pp. 271-294.

Optimal Allocation $(\hat{\gamma}_0, \hat{\gamma}_1, \hat{\gamma}_2)$, and Associated Maximum Probability (P) for Selected λ, θ_1, θ_2 when $p = 2$

Table A1. $\theta_1 = 1/10$, $\theta_2 = 1/10$

λ	$\hat{\gamma}_0$	$\hat{\gamma}_1$	$\hat{\gamma}_2$	$\hat{P}$
λ^*	0.00000	0.50000	0.50000	0.50000
0.3	0.10877	0.44562	0.44562	0.50432
0.4	0.25852	0.37074	0.37074	0.52128
0.5	0.35163	0.32418	0.32418	0.54269
0.6	0.41493	0.29253	0.29253	0.56622
0.7	0.46061	0.26969	0.26969	0.59084
0.8	0.49503	0.25249	0.25249	0.61596
0.9	0.52181	0.23909	0.23909	0.64118
1.0	0.54321	0.22840	0.22840	0.66621
1.2	0.57513	0.21243	0.21243	0.71480
1.4	0.59769	0.20116	0.20116	0.76036
1.6	0.61439	0.19281	0.19281	0.80197
1.8	0.62718	0.18641	0.18641	0.83909
2.0	0.63724	0.18138	0.18138	0.87145
2.2	0.64533	0.17734	0.17734	0.89906
2.4	0.65194	0.17403	0.17403	0.92210
2.6	0.65741	0.17130	0.17130	0.94093
2.8	0.66199	0.16900	0.16900	0.95600
3.0	0.66587	0.16706	0.16706	0.96780
3.2	0.66917	0.16541	0.16541	0.97686
3.4	0.67201	0.16400	0.16400	0.98367
3.6	0.67445	0.16278	0.16278	0.98868
3.8	0.67656	0.16172	0.16172	0.99230
4.0	0.67840	0.16080	0.16080	0.99486
5.0	0.68462	0.15769	0.15769	0.99948
$\lim_{\lambda\to\infty}$	0.69098	0.15451	0.15451	1.00000

$\lambda^* = (\sqrt{1/10} + \sqrt{1/10})/\sqrt{2\pi} = 0.25231$

Table A2. $\theta_1 = 1/10$, $\theta_2 = 8/10$

λ	$\hat{\gamma}_0$	$\hat{\gamma}_1$	$\hat{\gamma}_2$	$\hat{P}$
λ^*	0.00000	0.26120	0.73880	0.50000
0.7	0.22270	0.21696	0.56034	0.52826
0.8	0.27972	0.20498	0.51530	0.54672
0.9	0.32217	0.19566	0.48217	0.56640
1.0	0.35473	0.18812	0.45715	0.58673
1.2	0.40080	0.17640	0.42280	0.62807
1.4	0.43121	0.16739	0.40140	0.66896
1.6	0.45228	0.15997	0.38775	0.70837
1.8	0.46739	0.15355	0.37906	0.74562
2.0	0.47851	0.14784	0.37365	0.78026
2.2	0.48685	0.14263	0.37052	0.81199
2.4	0.49319	0.13783	0.36897	0.84068
2.6	0.49808	0.13336	0.36856	0.86627
2.8	0.50187	0.12918	0.36895	0.88882
3.0	0.50483	0.12525	0.36991	0.90845
3.2	0.50716	0.12156	0.37129	0.92533
3.4	0.50899	0.11807	0.37294	0.93968
3.6	0.51044	0.11478	0.37478	0.95174
3.8	0.51158	0.11167	0.37675	0.96176
4.0	0.51248	0.10874	0.37878	0.96999
4.2	0.51319	0.10597	0.38083	0.97667
4.4	0.51375	0.10336	0.38289	0.98205
4.6	0.51418	0.10090	0.38492	0.98632
4.8	0.51452	0.09857	0.38691	0.98967
5.0	0.51477	0.09638	0.38885	0.99228
$\lim_{\lambda\to\infty}$	0.51317	0.05409	0.43274	1.00000

$\lambda^* = (\sqrt{1/10} + \sqrt{8/10})/\sqrt{2\pi} = 0.48298$

Table A3. $\theta_1 = 1/10$, $\theta_2 = 1$

λ	$\hat{\gamma}_0$	$\hat{\gamma}_1$	$\hat{\gamma}_2$	$\hat{P}$
λ^*	0.00000	0.24025	0.75975	0.50000
0.7	0.18565	0.20989	0.60446	0.52062
0.8	0.24878	0.19884	0.55238	0.53783
0.9	0.29509	0.19025	0.51467	0.55656
1.0	0.33020	0.18328	0.48652	0.57611
1.1	0.35751	0.17742	0.46507	0.59607
1.2	0.37918	0.17235	0.44847	0.61618
1.3	0.39666	0.16787	0.43547	0.63623
1.4	0.41095	0.16381	0.42523	0.65609
1.5	0.42276	0.16010	0.41714	0.67564
1.6	0.43261	0.15665	0.41074	0.69478
1.7	0.44089	0.15341	0.40569	0.71345
1.8	0.44790	0.15035	0.40175	0.73157
1.9	0.45386	0.14744	0.39870	0.74910
2.0	0.45895	0.14465	0.39639	0.76600
2.1	0.46333	0.14198	0.39469	0.78223
2.2	0.46709	0.13940	0.39350	0.79778
2.3	0.47035	0.13692	0.39274	0.81262
2.4	0.47316	0.13451	0.39233	0.82674
2.5	0.47560	0.13218	0.39222	0.84015
2.6	0.47773	0.12992	0.39235	0.85283
2.7	0.47957	0.12772	0.39270	0.86479
2.8	0.48118	0.12559	0.39322	0.87605
2.9	0.48259	0.12352	0.39389	0.88661
3.0	0.48381	0.12150	0.39468	0.89650
4.0	0.48999	0.10415	0.40586	0.96306
5.0	0.49127	0.09105	0.41768	0.98938
6.0	0.49114	0.08127	0.42759	0.99755
7.0	0.49064	0.07400	0.43536	0.99955
8.0	0.49010	0.06857	0.44133	0.99993
$\lim_{\lambda\to\infty}$	0.48809	0.04654	0.46537	1.00000

$\lambda^* = (\sqrt{1/10} + \sqrt{1})/\sqrt{2\pi} = 0.52510$

Table A4. $\theta_1 = 1/10$, $\theta_2 = 10/8$

λ	$\hat{\gamma}_0$	$\hat{\gamma}_1$	$\hat{\gamma}_2$	$\hat{P}$
λ^*	0.00000	0.22048	0.77952	0.50000
0.7	0.14342	0.20225	0.65433	0.51310
0.8	0.21505	0.19233	0.59262	0.52887
0.9	0.26651	0.18461	0.54889	0.54655
1.0	0.30489	0.17831	0.51680	0.56525
1.1	0.33435	0.17297	0.49268	0.58448
1.2	0.35757	0.16830	0.47423	0.60394
1.3	0.37592	0.16412	0.45996	0.62343
1.4	0.39086	0.16030	0.44884	0.64279
1.5	0.40308	0.15677	0.44015	0.66190
1.6	0.41319	0.15345	0.43337	0.68066
1.7	0.42160	0.15030	0.42810	0.69901
1.8	0.42865	0.14730	0.42405	0.71687
1.9	0.43459	0.14442	0.42099	0.73420
2.0	0.43961	0.14165	0.41874	0.75097
2.1	0.44387	0.13897	0.41716	0.76713
2.2	0.44750	0.13638	0.41613	0.78266
2.3	0.45059	0.13386	0.41555	0.79755
2.4	0.45323	0.13141	0.41536	0.81178
2.5	0.45549	0.12903	0.41548	0.82534
2.6	0.45742	0.12672	0.41586	0.83823
2.7	0.45908	0.12446	0.41646	0.85046
2.8	0.46050	0.12226	0.41724	0.86202
2.9	0.46170	0.12012	0.41818	0.87294
3.0	0.46274	0.11803	0.41923	0.88320
4.0	0.46725	0.09992	0.43283	0.95470
5.0	0.46742	0.08617	0.44641	0.98549
6.0	0.46662	0.07590	0.45749	0.99617
7.0	0.46573	0.06826	0.46601	0.99917
8.0	0.46496	0.06258	0.47246	0.99985
$\lim_{\lambda\to\infty}$	0.46256	0.03981	0.49763	1.00000

$\lambda^* = (\sqrt{1/10} + \sqrt{10/8})/\sqrt{2\pi} = 0.57219$

Table A5. $\theta_1 = 1/10$, $\theta_2 = 10$

λ	$\hat{\gamma}$	$\hat{\gamma}$	$\hat{\gamma}$	$\hat{P}$
λ^*	0.00000	0.09091	0.90909	0.50000
1.6	0.31866	0.13838	0.54296	0.54209
1.8	0.32946	0.13402	0.53652	0.56952
2.0	0.33236	0.12885	0.53879	0.59598
2.2	0.33114	0.12337	0.54549	0.62135
2.4	0.32769	0.11782	0.55449	0.64561
2.6	0.32304	0.11235	0.56461	0.66874
2.8	0.31783	0.10702	0.57515	0.69077
3.0	0.31241	0.10189	0.58570	0.71170
3.2	0.30701	0.09698	0.59601	0.73156
3.4	0.30177	0.09229	0.60594	0.75039
3.6	0.29677	0.08783	0.61540	0.76821
3.8	0.29205	0.08360	0.62435	0.78506
4.0	0.28763	0.07960	0.63277	0.80096
4.5	0.27795	0.07049	0.65156	0.83680
5.0	0.27008	0.06259	0.66733	0.86745
5.5	0.26379	0.05575	0.68046	0.89340
6.0	0.25880	0.04985	0.69135	0.91516
6.5	0.25487	0.04477	0.70036	0.93319
7.0	0.25179	0.04040	0.70780	0.94798
7.5	0.24938	0.03665	0.71397	0.95995
8.0	0.24749	0.03342	0.71910	0.96953
8.5	0.24599	0.03064	0.72337	0.97709
9.0	0.24481	0.02824	0.72696	0.98298
9.5	0.24388	0.02617	0.72996	0.98751
10.0	0.24312	0.02437	0.73251	0.99095
10.5	0.24252	0.02280	0.73469	0.99353
11.0	0.24202	0.02143	0.73655	0.99543
11.5	0.24162	0.02022	0.73815	0.99681
12.0	0.24129	0.01917	0.73955	0.99781
12.5	0.24101	0.01823	0.74076	0.99851
13.0	0.24078	0.01740	0.74182	0.99900
$\lim_{\lambda\to\infty}$	0.23935	0.00753	0.75312	1.00000

$\lambda^* = (\sqrt{1/10} + \sqrt{10})/\sqrt{2} = 1.38772$

Table A6. $\theta_1 = 8/10$, $\theta_2 = 8/10$

λ	$\hat{\gamma}$	$\hat{\gamma}$	$\hat{\gamma}$	$\hat{P}$
λ^*	0.00000	0.50000	0.50000	0.50000
0.8	0.07400	0.46300	0.46300	0.50628
0.9	0.13611	0.43195	0.43195	0.51848
1.0	0.18220	0.40890	0.40890	0.53296
1.1	0.21773	0.39114	0.39114	0.54870
1.2	0.24591	0.37705	0.37705	0.56519
1.3	0.26879	0.36560	0.36560	0.58213
1.4	0.28772	0.35614	0.35614	0.59931
1.5	0.30362	0.34819	0.34819	0.61659
1.6	0.31715	0.34143	0.34143	0.63385
1.7	0.32879	0.33560	0.33560	0.65101
1.8	0.33891	0.33054	0.33054	0.66799
1.9	0.34777	0.32611	0.32611	0.68472
2.0	0.35560	0.32220	0.32220	0.70116
2.2	0.36874	0.31563	0.31563	0.73297
2.4	0.37933	0.31033	0.31033	0.76310
2.6	0.38801	0.30599	0.30599	0.79135
2.8	0.39522	0.30239	0.30239	0.81756
3.0	0.40129	0.29936	0.29936	0.84162
3.5	0.41280	0.29360	0.29360	0.89231
4.0	0.42077	0.28962	0.28962	0.93007
4.5	0.42644	0.28678	0.28678	0.95666
5.0	0.43056	0.28472	0.28472	0.97436
5.5	0.43357	0.28322	0.28322	0.98553
6.0	0.43578	0.28211	0.28211	0.99221
6.5	0.43741	0.28129	0.28129	0.99600
7.0	0.43861	0.28070	0.28070	0.99804
7.5	0.43947	0.28026	0.28026	0.99908
8.0	0.44010	0.27995	0.27995	0.99959
$\lim_{\lambda\to\infty}$	0.44152	0.27924	0.27924	1.00000

$\lambda^* = (\sqrt{8/10} + \sqrt{8/10})/\sqrt{2} = 0.71365$

Table A7. $\theta_1 = 8/10$, $\theta_2 = 1$

λ	$\hat{\gamma}_0$	$\hat{\gamma}_1$	$\hat{\gamma}_2$	$\hat{P}$
λ^*	0.00000	0.47214	0.52786	0.50000
0.9	0.10733	0.42395	0.46871	0.51264
1.0	0.15709	0.40145	0.44145	0.52597
1.1	0.19499	0.38422	0.42079	0.54084
1.2	0.22481	0.37057	0.40462	0.55660
1.3	0.24887	0.35948	0.39165	0.57291
1.4	0.26867	0.35027	0.38105	0.58953
1.5	0.28525	0.34250	0.37225	0.60631
1.6	0.29931	0.33585	0.36484	0.62313
1.7	0.31138	0.33008	0.35854	0.63989
1.8	0.32184	0.32502	0.35313	0.65652
1.9	0.33099	0.32055	0.34846	0.67295
2.0	0.33905	0.31656	0.34439	0.68914
2.2	0.35257	0.30975	0.33768	0.72058
2.4	0.36344	0.30412	0.33244	0.75054
2.6	0.37233	0.29938	0.32829	0.77880
2.8	0.37971	0.29533	0.32496	0.80517
3.0	0.38590	0.29183	0.32227	0.82956
3.5	0.39765	0.28481	0.31753	0.88160
4.0	0.40578	0.27955	0.31467	0.92122
4.5	0.41157	0.27548	0.31295	0.94981
5.0	0.41577	0.27226	0.31198	0.96939
5.5	0.41885	0.26967	0.31148	0.98214
6.0	0.42112	0.26758	0.31131	0.99002
6.5	0.42279	0.26586	0.31135	0.99467
7.0	0.42402	0.26445	0.31153	0.99727
7.5	0.42492	0.26329	0.31179	0.99867
8.0	0.42557	0.26232	0.31211	0.99937
$\lim_{\lambda\to\infty}$	0.42705	0.25464	0.31831	1.00000

$\lambda^* = (\sqrt{8/10} + \sqrt{1})/\sqrt{2\pi} = 0.75577$

Table A8. $\theta_1 = 8/10$, $\theta_2 = 10/8$

λ	$\hat{\gamma}_0$	$\hat{\gamma}_1$	$\hat{\gamma}_2$	$\hat{P}$
λ^*	0.00000	0.44444	0.55556	0.50000
0.9	0.07490	0.41510	0.51000	0.50710
1.0	0.12980	0.39327	0.47692	0.51897
1.1	0.17087	0.37670	0.45243	0.53283
1.2	0.20278	0.36363	0.43359	0.54791
1.3	0.22830	0.35300	0.41870	0.56340
1.4	0.24915	0.34416	0.40669	0.57942
1.5	0.26651	0.33665	0.39683	0.59565
1.6	0.28118	0.33018	0.38864	0.61198
1.7	0.29371	0.32453	0.38176	0.62830
1.8	0.30454	0.31953	0.37593	0.64454
1.9	0.31398	0.31506	0.37095	0.66063
2.0	0.32228	0.31104	0.36668	0.67652
2.2	0.33615	0.30404	0.35980	0.70750
2.4	0.34726	0.29813	0.35461	0.73718
2.6	0.35631	0.29303	0.35066	0.76533
2.8	0.36380	0.28857	0.34763	0.79178
3.0	0.37007	0.28461	0.34532	0.81641
3.5	0.38192	0.27638	0.34170	0.86964
4.0	0.39007	0.26986	0.34007	0.91105
4.5	0.39586	0.26454	0.33960	0.94170
5.0	0.40005	0.26014	0.33981	0.96330
5.5	0.40312	0.25646	0.34042	0.97781
6.0	0.40538	0.25335	0.34127	0.98712
6.5	0.40705	0.25070	0.34225	0.99283
7.0	0.40827	0.24845	0.34327	0.99616
7.5	0.40917	0.24652	0.34431	0.99803
8.0	0.40982	0.24486	0.34532	0.99903
$\lim_{\lambda\to\infty}$	0.41122	0.22977	0.35901	1.00000

$\lambda^* = (\sqrt{8/10} + \sqrt{10/8})/\sqrt{2\pi} = 0.80286$

Table A9. $\theta_1 = 8/10$, $\theta_2 = 10$

λ	$\hat{\gamma}_0$	$\hat{\gamma}_1$	$\hat{\gamma}_2$	$\hat{P}$
λ^*	0.00000	0.22048	0.77952	0.50000
1.8	0.16690	0.27225	0.56085	0.52215
2.0	0.19676	0.27152	0.53172	0.54527
2.2	0.21450	0.26771	0.51780	0.56851
2.4	0.22601	0.26255	0.51144	0.59151
2.6	0.23378	0.25670	0.50952	0.61407
2.8	0.23912	0.25049	0.51039	0.63610
3.0	0.24278	0.24412	0.51309	0.65750
3.2	0.24527	0.23771	0.51701	0.67822
3.4	0.24692	0.23134	0.52174	0.69823
3.6	0.24795	0.22507	0.52698	0.71748
3.8	0.24853	0.21892	0.53255	0.73597
4.0	0.24879	0.21292	0.53829	0.75368
4.2	0.24879	0.20711	0.54410	0.77059
4.4	0.24862	0.20147	0.54990	0.78672
4.6	0.24833	0.19603	0.55564	0.80206
4.8	0.24794	0.19078	0.56128	0.81661
5.0	0.24749	0.18573	0.56678	0.83039
5.2	0.24699	0.18087	0.57213	0.84341
5.4	0.24648	0.17621	0.57732	0.85569
5.6	0.24595	0.17173	0.58232	0.86724
5.8	0.24541	0.16744	0.58715	0.87808
6.0	0.24488	0.16332	0.59179	0.88824
7.0	0.24244	0.14522	0.61235	0.92960
8.0	0.24044	0.13068	0.62888	0.95765
9.0	0.23889	0.11901	0.64210	0.97570
10.0	0.23769	0.10961	0.65270	0.98671
11.0	0.23677	0.10200	0.66123	0.99308
12.0	0.23605	0.09579	0.66816	0.99657
13.0	0.23550	0.09070	0.67381	0.99838
14.0	0.23506	0.08648	0.67846	0.99927
$\lim_{\lambda\to\infty}$	0.23330	0.05679	0.70991	1.00000

$\lambda^* = (\sqrt{8/10} + \sqrt{10})/\sqrt{2\pi} = 1.61839$

Table A10. $\theta_1 = 1$, $\theta_2 = 1$

λ	$\hat{\gamma}_0$	$\hat{\gamma}_1$	$\hat{\gamma}_2$	$\hat{P}$
λ^*	0.00000	0.50000	0.50000	0.50000
1.0	0.13150	0.43425	0.43425	0.51958
1.2	0.20358	0.39821	0.39821	0.54851
1.4	0.24963	0.37518	0.37518	0.58021
1.6	0.28156	0.35922	0.35922	0.61284
1.8	0.30495	0.34753	0.34753	0.64546
2.0	0.32276	0.33862	0.33862	0.67750
2.2	0.33673	0.33163	0.33163	0.70854
2.4	0.34795	0.32602	0.32602	0.73828
2.6	0.35713	0.32144	0.32144	0.76648
2.8	0.36474	0.31763	0.31763	0.79296
3.0	0.37114	0.31443	0.31443	0.81762
3.2	0.37657	0.31171	0.31171	0.84036
3.4	0.38122	0.30939	0.30939	0.86117
3.6	0.38522	0.30739	0.30739	0.88004
3.8	0.38869	0.30566	0.30566	0.89702
4.0	0.39171	0.30414	0.30414	0.91217
4.2	0.39435	0.30282	0.30282	0.92558
4.4	0.39667	0.30166	0.30166	0.93736
4.6	0.39872	0.30064	0.30064	0.94761
4.8	0.40052	0.29974	0.29974	0.95648
5.0	0.40211	0.29894	0.29894	0.96408
5.2	0.40352	0.29824	0.29824	0.97055
5.4	0.40477	0.29761	0.29761	0.97602
5.6	0.40588	0.29706	0.29706	0.98060
5.8	0.40687	0.29657	0.29657	0.98440
6.0	0.40774	0.29613	0.29613	0.98755
7.0	0.41084	0.29458	0.29458	0.99634
8.0	0.41252	0.29374	0.29374	0.99909
$\lim_{\lambda\to\infty}$	0.41421	0.29289	0.29289	1.00000

$\lambda^* = (\sqrt{1} + \sqrt{1})/\sqrt{2\pi} = 0.79788$

Table A11. $\theta_1 = 1$, $\theta_2 = 10/8$

λ	$\hat{\gamma}_0$	$\hat{\gamma}_1$	$\hat{\gamma}_2$	$\hat{P}$
λ^*	0.00000	0.47214	0.52786	0.50000
1.0	0.10340	0.42627	0.47032	0.51328
1.2	0.18130	0.39127	0.42743	0.54022
1.4	0.23005	0.36901	0.40095	0.57058
1.6	0.26347	0.35346	0.38307	0.60215
1.8	0.28777	0.34191	0.37032	0.63392
2.0	0.30620	0.33294	0.36086	0.66528
2.2	0.32060	0.32575	0.35365	0.69583
2.4	0.33214	0.31982	0.34804	0.72524
2.6	0.34155	0.31484	0.34361	0.75329
2.8	0.34935	0.31058	0.34007	0.77979
3.0	0.35589	0.30690	0.33721	0.80462
3.2	0.36144	0.30367	0.33489	0.82768
3.4	0.36618	0.30082	0.33300	0.84893
3.6	0.37027	0.29828	0.33145	0.86835
3.8	0.37381	0.29600	0.33019	0.88597
4.0	0.37689	0.29396	0.32915	0.90183
4.2	0.37959	0.29210	0.32831	0.91600
4.4	0.38196	0.29042	0.32763	0.92856
4.6	0.38404	0.28888	0.32708	0.93961
4.8	0.38588	0.28747	0.32664	0.94926
5.0	0.38751	0.28619	0.32630	0.95764
5.4	0.39023	0.28392	0.32585	0.97101
5.8	0.39238	0.28199	0.32563	0.98064
6.2	0.39407	0.28034	0.32558	0.98739
6.6	0.39541	0.27893	0.32566	0.99198
7.0	0.39647	0.27771	0.32582	0.99503
8.0	0.39822	0.27534	0.32644	0.99865
9.0	0.39915	0.27366	0.32719	0.99968
$\lim_{\lambda\to\infty}$	0.40000	0.26667	0.33333	1.00000

$\lambda^* = (\sqrt{1} + \sqrt{10/8})/\sqrt{2\pi} = 0.84497$

Table A12. $\theta_1 = 1$, $\theta_2 = 10$

λ	$\hat{\gamma}_0$	$\hat{\gamma}_1$	$\hat{\gamma}_2$	$\hat{P}$
λ^*	0.00000	0.24025	0.75975	0.50000
1.8	0.14060	0.28758	0.57182	0.51588
2.0	0.17592	0.28873	0.53535	0.53811
2.2	0.19649	0.28575	0.51776	0.56073
2.4	0.20999	0.28110	0.50891	0.58328
2.6	0.21933	0.27562	0.50505	0.60551
2.8	0.22597	0.26970	0.50432	0.62731
3.0	0.23077	0.26356	0.50567	0.64857
3.2	0.23425	0.25733	0.50842	0.66923
3.4	0.23679	0.25110	0.51212	0.68924
3.6	0.23861	0.24492	0.51647	0.70856
3.8	0.23990	0.23885	0.52124	0.72716
4.0	0.24080	0.23291	0.52629	0.74502
4.2	0.24138	0.22712	0.53150	0.76214
4.4	0.24174	0.22149	0.53677	0.77849
4.6	0.24192	0.21604	0.54204	0.79409
4.8	0.24196	0.21077	0.54727	0.80892
5.0	0.24190	0.20568	0.55242	0.82300
5.4	0.24157	0.19605	0.56239	0.84892
5.8	0.24106	0.18713	0.57181	0.87197
6.2	0.24048	0.17890	0.58063	0.89227
6.6	0.23986	0.17131	0.58883	0.91002
7.0	0.23925	0.16433	0.59642	0.92538
8.0	0.23783	0.14926	0.61292	0.95477
9.0	0.23664	0.13704	0.62632	0.97384
10.0	0.23567	0.12713	0.63720	0.98557
11.0	0.23489	0.11904	0.64606	0.99242
12.0	0.23427	0.11242	0.65331	0.99620
13.0	0.23377	0.10695	0.65928	0.99819
14.0	0.23337	0.10241	0.66422	0.99918
$\lim_{\lambda\to\infty}$	0.23166	0.06985	0.69849	1.00000

$\lambda^* = (\sqrt{1} + \sqrt{10})/\sqrt{2\pi} = 1.66051$

Table A13. $\theta_1 = 10/8$, $\theta_2 = 10/8$

λ	$\hat{\gamma}_0$	$\hat{\gamma}_1$	$\hat{\gamma}_2$	$\hat{P}$
λ^*	0.00000	0.50000	0.50000	0.50000
1.0	0.07405	0.46298	0.46298	0.50781
1.2	0.15862	0.42069	0.42069	0.53251
1.4	0.21032	0.39484	0.39484	0.56146
1.6	0.24536	0.37732	0.37732	0.59194
1.8	0.27068	0.36466	0.36466	0.62283
2.0	0.28980	0.35510	0.35510	0.65349
2.2	0.30472	0.34764	0.34764	0.68351
2.4	0.31665	0.34168	0.34168	0.71256
2.6	0.32638	0.33681	0.33681	0.74041
2.8	0.33444	0.33278	0.33278	0.76688
3.0	0.34120	0.32940	0.32940	0.79181
3.2	0.34693	0.32653	0.32653	0.81512
3.4	0.35184	0.32408	0.32408	0.83674
3.6	0.35607	0.32196	0.32196	0.85665
3.8	0.35974	0.32013	0.32013	0.87484
4.0	0.36294	0.31853	0.31853	0.89134
4.2	0.36574	0.31713	0.31713	0.90621
4.4	0.36821	0.31590	0.31590	0.91950
4.6	0.37038	0.31481	0.31481	0.93131
4.8	0.37230	0.31385	0.31385	0.94172
5.0	0.37401	0.31300	0.31300	0.95084
5.4	0.37686	0.31157	0.31157	0.96562
5.8	0.37912	0.31044	0.31044	0.97650
6.2	0.38092	0.30954	0.30954	0.98431
6.6	0.38235	0.30883	0.30883	0.98976
7.0	0.38348	0.30826	0.30826	0.99347
7.5	0.38457	0.30772	0.30772	0.99640
8.0	0.38537	0.30731	0.30731	0.99809
8.5	0.38597	0.30702	0.30702	0.99902
9.0	0.38640	0.30680	0.30680	0.99951
$\lim_{\lambda\to\infty}$	0.38743	0.30629	0.30629	1.00000

$\lambda^* = (\sqrt{10/8} + \sqrt{10/8})/\sqrt{2\pi} = 0.89206$

Table A14. $\theta_1 = 10/8$, $\theta_2 = 10$

λ	$\hat{\gamma}_0$	$\hat{\gamma}_1$	$\hat{\gamma}_2$	$\hat{P}$
λ^*	0.00000	0.26120	0.73880	0.50000
1.8	0.11102	0.30191	0.58707	0.50967
2.0	0.15378	0.30580	0.54042	0.53078
2.2	0.17752	0.30382	0.51866	0.55266
2.4	0.19310	0.29978	0.50713	0.57465
2.6	0.20403	0.29474	0.50123	0.59647
2.8	0.21199	0.28917	0.49884	0.61796
3.0	0.21791	0.28332	0.49877	0.63901
3.2	0.22238	0.27734	0.50027	0.65954
3.4	0.22579	0.27133	0.50288	0.67949
3.6	0.22841	0.26534	0.50625	0.69883
3.8	0.23041	0.25943	0.51016	0.71750
4.0	0.23195	0.25362	0.51443	0.73549
4.2	0.23312	0.24794	0.51894	0.75277
4.4	0.23401	0.24240	0.52359	0.76933
4.6	0.23467	0.23702	0.52831	0.78517
4.8	0.23515	0.23180	0.53305	0.80027
5.0	0.23550	0.22674	0.53776	0.81464
5.4	0.23587	0.21714	0.54699	0.84121
5.8	0.23595	0.20820	0.55585	0.86494
6.2	0.23586	0.19991	0.56423	0/88594
6.6	0.23566	0.19224	0.57210	0.90438
7.0	0.23539	0.18515	0.57946	0.92041
8.0	0.23461	0.16973	0.59565	0.95130
9.0	0.23384	0.15713	0.60902	0.97156
10.0	0.23315	0.14683	0.62002	0.98415
11.0	0.23255	0.13837	0.62908	0.99158
12.0	0.23205	0.13139	0.63656	0.99574
13.0	0.23163	0.12561	0.64277	0.99794
14.0	0.23128	0.12078	0.64794	0.99906
$\lim_{\lambda\to\infty}$	0.22967	0.08559	0.68474	1.00000

$\lambda^* = (\sqrt{10/8} + \sqrt{10})/\sqrt{2\pi} = 1.70760$

Table A15. $\theta_1 = 10$, $\theta_2 = 10$

λ	$\hat{\gamma}_0$	$\hat{\gamma}_1$	$\hat{\gamma}_2$	$\hat{P}$
λ^*	0.00000	0.50000	0.50000	0.50000
3.0	0.07929	0.46035	0.46035	0.53187
3.2	0.09282	0.45359	0.45359	0.54729
3.4	0.10344	0.44828	0.44828	0.56299
3.6	0.11212	0.44394	0.44394	0.57881
3.8	0.11936	0.44032	0.44032	0.59465
4.0	0.12553	0.43723	0.43723	0.61044
4.2	0.13085	0.43457	0.43457	0.62611
4.4	0.13549	0.43225	0.43225	0.64163
4.6	0.13957	0.43021	0.43021	0.65694
4.8	0.14319	0.42840	0.42840	0.67203
5.0	0.14642	0.42679	0.42679	0.68685
5.4	0.15192	0.42404	0.42404	0.71561
5.8	0.15642	0.42179	0.42179	0.74303
6.2	0.16016	0.41992	0.41992	0.76899
6.6	0.16329	0.41835	0.41835	0.79338
7.0	0.16594	0.41703	0.41703	0.81614
8.0	0.17102	0.41449	0.41449	0.86570
9.0	0.17452	0.41274	0.41274	0.90500
10.0	0.17699	0.41150	0.41150	0.93492
11.0	0.17874	0.41063	0.41063	0.95682
12.0	0.17998	0.41001	0.41001	0.97225
13.0	0.18086	0.40957	0.40957	0.98273
14.0	0.18148	0.40926	0.40926	0.98959
15.0	0.18190	0.40905	0.40905	0.99392
16.0	0.18220	0.40890	0.40890	0.99656
17.0	0.18239	0.40880	0.40880	0.99811
18.0	0.18252	0.40874	0.40874	0.99900
19.0	0.18261	0.40870	0.40870	0.99948
20.0	0.18266	0.40867	0.40867	0.99974
$\lim_{\lambda\to\infty}$	0.18274	0.40863	0.40863	1.00000

$\lambda^* = (\sqrt{10} + \sqrt{10})/\sqrt{2\pi} = 2.52313$

ON SOME CONTRIBUTIONS TO MULTIPLE DECISION THEORY*

By Shanti S. Gupta and Klaus Nagel
Purdue University

Summary. In this paper we discuss the multiple decision (*selection and ranking*) rules in a general decision theoretic framework. More specifically, we discuss the subset selection problem. The earlier part of the paper describes the general framework and gives some known results for sake of completeness; in the latter part of the paper we give some new results dealing with the subset selection problem for a class of discrete distributions (Section 2). Some relevant tables for these procedures are included. The derivation of rules with some desirable property is made in Section 3 using the likelihood ratio criterion.

1. *Preliminary Definitions and General Formulation*. We are given k populations $\Pi_1, \Pi_2, \ldots, \Pi_k$ where the population Π_i is described by the probability space $(\mathcal{X}, \mathcal{B}, P_i)$, where P_i belongs to some family $\mathcal{P}$. We assume that there is a partial order relation ($\succ$) defined in $\mathcal{P}$. $P_i \succ P_j$ is equivalent to saying that P_i is better than or equal to P_j; or, in other words P_i is preferred over P_j. For example,

---

*This research was supported in part by the Office of Naval Research Contract N00014-67-A-0226-00014 and the Aerospace Research Laboratories Contract AF33(615)67C1244 at Purdue University. Reproduction in whole or in part is permitted for any purposes of the United States Government.

if $\mathcal{P}$ is a one-parameter family, $P_i(x) = P(\theta_i, x)$, we may define: $P_i \succ P_j$ iff $\theta_i \geq \theta_j$. In many problems $\succ$ denotes stochastic ordering. Other partial orderings that have been considered are: star-shaped ordering, convex ordering, tail ordering.

In the above set-up, we assume that there exists a population Π_j such that $\Pi_j \succ \Pi_i$ for all i. This population Π_j will be referred to as the 'best' population. In case of more than one population satisfying the condition we will consider one of them to be tagged as the best.

From each population we observe a random element X_i. The space of observations is: $\mathcal{X}^k = \{x=(x_1,x_2,\ldots,x_k),\ x_i \in \mathcal{X},\ i = 1,2,\ldots,k\}$. In most applications $\mathcal{X}^k$ will be a real vector space.

The decision space $\mathcal{D}$ consists of the 2^k subsets d of the set $\{1,2,\ldots,k\}$: to put it formally,

$$\mathcal{D} = \{d \mid d \subseteq \{1,2,\ldots,k\}\} \quad . \tag{1.1}$$

In other words, a decision d corresponds to the selection of a subset of k populations.

A decision $d \in \mathcal{D}$ is called a correct selection (CS) if $j \in d$ which means that the best population Π_j is included in the selected subset d. It should be pointed out that in many subset selection procedures investigated earlier, the null set ϕ is excluded from $\mathcal{D}$ to guarantee the selection of a non empty subset.

Def. 1. *A measurable function* δ *defined on* $\mathcal{X}^k \times \mathcal{D}$ *is called a selection procedure provided that for each* $x \in \mathcal{X}^k$, *we have,*

$$\delta(x,d) \geq 0 \qquad \textit{and}$$

(1.2)

$$\sum_{d \in \mathfrak{D}} \delta(x,d) = 1 \quad ,$$

where $\delta(x,d)$ *denotes the probability that the subset* d *is selected when* x *is observed. The individual selection probability* $p_i(x)$ *for the population* Π_i *is then given by*

(1.3) $$p_i(x) = \sum_{d \ni i} \delta(x,d) \quad ,$$

where the summation is over all d *containing* i. *If the selection probabilities* $p_1(x), p_2(x), \ldots, p_k(x)$ *take on only the values* 0 *and* 1, *then the selection procedure* $\delta(x,d)$ *is completely specified.*

In general, we can assume that the selection of a subset $d \in \mathfrak{D}$ results in a loss. Let us consider the situation where $P_i = P(\theta_i, x)$ and assume the loss $L(\theta,d) = L((\theta_1,\theta_2,\ldots,\theta_k),d) = \sum_{i \in d} L_i(\theta)$ where $L_i(\theta)$ is the loss if the ith population is selected. We may assume an additional loss L if a correct selection is not made. The overall risk for the nonrandomized rule δ is:

(1.4) $$R(\theta,\delta) = \sum_{i=1}^{k} L_i(\theta)\, E_\theta p_i(x) + L[1-P_\theta(CS|\delta)].$$

In many problems it has been assumed that $L_i(\theta) = 1$ and $L = 0$, in which case, $R(\theta,\delta)$ gives the expected size of the selected subset. In general, our aim is to minimize the risk $R(\theta,\delta)$ which will be done under the usual symmetry condition.

The subset selection problems investigated earlier have been concerned with obtaining selection rules δ which select non empty subsets and guarantee a correct selection with probability at least equal to P^* i.e.

(1.5) $$\inf_{\Omega} P_{\omega}(CS|\delta) \geq P^*$$

where Ω is the space of joint probability measures. The points of Ω are denoted by $\omega = (P_1,P_2,\ldots,P_k)$, $P_i \in \mathcal{P}$. The condition in (1.5) has been called the basic probability requirement.

In general, we wish rules with large probability of a correct selection and a small value of the expected size. The ratio $\eta_{\omega}(\delta) = k\, P_{\omega}(CS|\delta)/E_{\omega}(S|\delta)$ can, among others, be considered as a measure of the efficiency of the procedure δ at ω. It should be pointed out that both $P_{\omega}(CS|\delta)$ and $E_{\omega}(S|\delta)$ depend on δ only through the individual selection probabilities and hence if we restrict our attention to these quantities, we can define two rules δ and δ' as equivalent if they have the same individual selection probabilities $p(x)$ and $p'(x)$ for all x. Hence, we can use the following simplified definition, replacing δ by R.

Def. 2. *A subset selection rule* R *is a measurable mapping from* $\mathcal{X}^k$ *into* E^k (k dimensional Euclidean space), *namely,*

$$R: x \to (p_1(x),p_2(2),\ldots,p_k(x)),\ 0 \leq p_i(x) \leq 1,\quad i = 1,2,\ldots,k\ .$$

If p_i's *are* 0 *or* 1, *the rule is nonrandomized; in this case,* δ *can also be defined by the sets* $A_i = \{x \in \mathcal{X}^k | p_i(x) = 1\}$, $i = 1,2,\ldots,k$. A_i *is the set of observations for which* Π_i *is selected.*

Def. 3. R *is unbiased iff*

$$\Pi_j \succ \Pi_i,\ i=1,2,\ldots,k \Rightarrow P_{\omega,j} \geq P_{\omega,i} \quad \textit{for all} \quad \omega \in \Omega$$

where $P_{\omega,i} = E_{\omega}p_i(x)$ = *probability that* Π_i *is selected.*

Def. 4. R *is monotone iff*

$$\Pi_j > \Pi_i \Rightarrow P_{\omega,j} \geq P_{\omega,i} \text{ for all } i,j \text{ and all } \omega \in \Omega .$$

We shall restrict ourselves to selection rules which are invariant under permutation.

Def. 5. *A rule* R *is invariant under permutation* (or R is symmetric) *iff*

$$(p_1(gx),\ldots,p_k(gx)) = g(p_1(x),\ldots,p_k(x)) \text{ for all } x\varepsilon\mathcal{X}^k, g\varepsilon G$$

where G *denotes the group of permutations* g *of the integers* 1,2,...,k. The minimization of the risk under the symmetry condition imposed by G is also discussed in [6].

In addition to the several desirable properties and criteria for selection rules given above, one important concept is that of "just" selection rules investigated in [5]. This concept is examined in some detail in the present paper.

Let $(\mathcal{X},\mathcal{B},P)$ be a probability space where a partial order $>$ is defined on $\mathcal{X}$ [$y > x$ or, equivalently, $x < y$ means that y is better than x].

Def. 6. *A selection rule* R, *defined by its individual selection probabilities* $p_i(x_1,\ldots,x_k)$, $i = 1,2,\ldots,k$ *is said to be just iff*

$$\left.\begin{array}{l} x_i < y_i \\ x_j > y_j, j \neq i \end{array}\right\} \Rightarrow p_i(y_1,\ldots,y_k) \geq p_i(x_1,\ldots,x_k) \quad .$$

For nonrandomized rules determined by acceptance regions $A_1,A_2,\ldots,A_k$, we can give an equivalent definition of a just rule in terms of increasing sets and general stochastic ordering. A subset $A \subset \mathcal{X}^k$ is said to be *increasing* iff $x \varepsilon A$ and $y > x \Rightarrow y \varepsilon A$. P is stochastically better than $Q(P \underset{St}{>} Q)$ iff $P(A) \geq Q(A)$ for all increasing sets $A \varepsilon \mathcal{B}$.

We note that if $\mathcal{X}$ is the real line and $\succ$ stands for $>$(or $\geq$) then the increasing sets are the intervals $[a,\infty)$ and (a,∞) which induce the usual stochastic ordering on the distribution functions.

Def. 7. R *is just iff*

$$\left.\begin{array}{l} x \in A_i \\ x_i \prec y_i \\ x_j \succ y_j,\ j \neq i \end{array}\right\} \text{ implies } y \in A_i \ .$$

As mentioned earlier, frequently we require a selection rule to satisfy the basic probability requirement (1.5). Hence, a central problem in the subset selection theory is to determine $\inf_{\omega\in\Omega} P_\omega(CS|R)$. For many rules investigated in the literature, this infimum is attained in Ω_0 where $\Omega_0 \subseteq \Omega$ is the set of ω where P_i are identical. This could reasonably be expected of a good rule, because in Ω_0, no stati tical information can be employed to find the arbitrarily tagged population. It has been proved in [5] that this property holds for a just selection rule i.e.

(1.6) $$\inf_{\omega\in\Omega} P(CS|R) = \inf_{\omega\in\Omega_0} P_\omega(CS|R), \text{ if } R \text{ is just.}$$

The above result enables us to restrict our attention to Ω_0 for determining the infimum of the probability of a correct selection. Thus, in the case of a one-parameter family of distributions the problem is reduced to finding the infimum of a univariate function. This problem is even more simplified in some cases; for example the rule studied in [3] for selecting a subset of normal populations with means $\sigma_1,\sigma_2,\ldots,\sigma_k$ and a common known variance σ^2 is: Select Π_i iff $\bar{x}_i \geq \bar{x}_{max} - D\sigma/\sqrt{n}$ where $D = D(k,P^*)$ is determined to satisfy the P^* condition. It can easily be seen that this rule is just and that it is invariant under shift in location. Since Ω_0 also is invariant under shift in location, this implies that $P_\omega(CS|R)$ is constant for $\omega \in \Omega_0$. Hence $P_{\omega_0}(CS|R) \geq P^*$ for some $\omega_0 \in \Omega_0$ implies the P^*-condition. It is also a reasonable requirement that $P_\omega(CS|R)$ be constant over Ω_0 because in stating the P^*-condition, we express that we are content if $P_\omega(CS|R)$ is at least P^* and we are not interested in exceeding P^*, at least not in Ω_0 where it can be achieved only by increasing the expected number of populations in the selected subset.

Now we state a lemma which can be applied to construct just subset selection rules with constant probability of a correct selection in Ω_0.

Lemma 1.1. *Let* $X_1, X_2, \ldots, X_k$ *be independent and identically distributed random variables with joint distribution* P_θ. *Let* $T(X_1, X_2, \ldots, X_k)$ *be a sufficient statistic for* θ.

(i) *If* $E(\delta(X_1, \ldots, X_k)|T) = P^*$ *for all* T *then* $E_\theta\delta = P^*$ *for all* θ.

(ii) *If* T *is complete w.r.t.* $\{P_\theta(x)\}$, *then* $E_\theta(\delta(X_1, \ldots, X_k)|T) = P^*$ *is also necessary for* $E_\theta\delta = P^*$ *for all* θ.

The proof is simple and is omitted. This lemma plays a role in some selection procedures discussed in the next section.

2. *Some Selection Rules for Discrete Distributions.* In this section we discuss some new selection rules in the cases of binomial, Poisson, and negative binomial distributions. Very little work has been done under subset selection

formulation in the cases of Poisson and negative binomial distriburions. For the binomial distributions, a subset selection rule was proposed and studied in [4].

Binomial Case: Let $\Pi_1,\Pi_2,\ldots,\Pi_k$ be k binomial populations $B(\theta_i,n)$, $i = 1,\ldots,k$. Since θ_i's are the unknown parameters, $\Omega = \{\omega\colon \omega = (\theta_1,\theta_2,\ldots,\theta_k)$ and $\Omega_0 = \{\omega\colon \omega = (\theta,\theta,\ldots,\theta)\}$. We will construct a just selection rule R for selecting the population with the largest θ_i, which is also stochastically the largest, such that $P_{\omega_0}(CS|R) = P^*$ holds for all $\omega \in \Omega_0$. It is clear that this goal cannot be achieved with a nonrandomized rule, because when $\omega = (0,0,\ldots,0)$ or $\omega = (1,1,\ldots,1)$ the observations will be $x = (0,0,\ldots,0)$ or $x = (n,n,\ldots,n)$ with probability one, requiring the use of individual selection probabilities $p_i = P^*$, $i = 1,2,\ldots,k$, in these cases.

The joint density for $\omega \in \Omega_0$ is

$$(2.1)\quad f_\omega(x_1,x_2,\ldots,x_k) = (1-\theta)^{nk}\exp\Big[\Big(\sum_1^k x_i\Big)\log\frac{\theta}{1-\theta}\Big]\prod_1^k \binom{n}{x_i} .$$

We see that $T = \sum_{i=1}^k X_i$ is a sufficient statistic for θ.

Since we are interested in symmetric rules R it is sufficient to know one of the individual selection probabilities, say, p_k. From the lemma of the previous section it follows

$$(2.2)\qquad E(p_k(X)|T) = P^* \quad \text{for } T = 0,1,\ldots,kn.$$

The requirement that R be just leads to

$$(2.3)\quad \left.\begin{array}{l} y_i \le x_i,\, i=1,2,\ldots,k-1 \\ \\ y_k \ge x_k \end{array}\right\} \Rightarrow p_k(x_1,x_2,\ldots,x_k) \le p_k(y_1,y_2,\ldots,y_k).$$

Figure 1 shows the partial ordering induced by (2.3) among

the observation vectors for the case $k = 3$, $n = 2$. The individual selection probability $p_3(x_1, x_2, x_3)$ defines a just rule if its values are nondecreasing in the direction of the arrows. Because of symmetry only one of the two permutations (x_1, x_2, x_3) and (x_2, x_1, x_3) is plotted. The numbers underneath the observation vectors denote the corresponding T values.

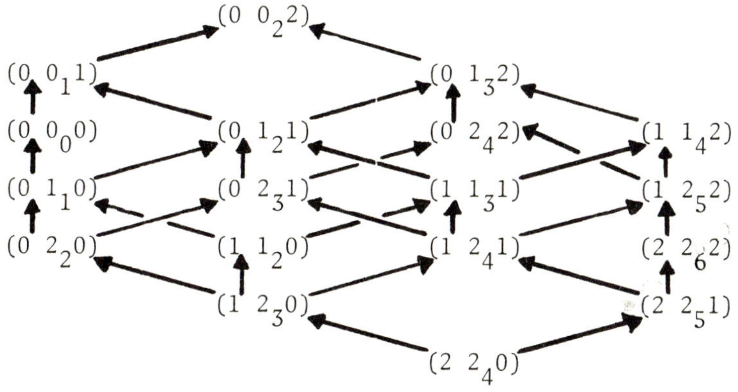

Figure 1. Partial Ordering for Binomial Observations $k = 3$, $n = 2$.

The conditions (2.2) and (2.3) do not determine a rule uniquely. We propose the following rule R_0:

$$(2.4) \qquad p_k(x) = \begin{cases} 1 & \text{if} \quad x_k > c_T \\ \rho & \text{if} \quad x_k = c_T \\ 0 & \text{if} \quad x_k < c_T \end{cases}$$

where $\rho = \rho(T, P^*, k)$ and $c_T = c_T(P^*, k)$ are determined to satisfy

$$(2.5) \qquad E(p_k(X) \mid T) = P\{X_k > c_T \mid T\} + \rho P\{X_k = c_T \mid T\} = P^* .$$

The conditional distribution of X_k given T is hypergeometric.

$$P\{X_k = i|T\} = \frac{\binom{n}{i}\binom{(k-1)n}{T-i}}{\binom{kn}{T}} \quad . \tag{2.6}$$

Let Z_T have the same distribution as X_k given T. Then (2.5) becomes

$$P\{Z_T > c_T\} + \rho P\{Z_T = c_T\} = P^* \tag{2.7}$$

and the constant c_T is the smallest integer determined from the inequalities

$$P\{Z_T > c_T\} \leq P^* \tag{2.8}$$

and

$$P\{Z_T \geq c_T\} > P^* \quad . \tag{2.9}$$

From (2.7), we have

$$\rho = \frac{P^* - P\{Z_T > c_T\}}{P\{Z_T = c_T\}} \quad . \tag{2.10}$$

Now, we show that R_0 is just.

Theorem 2.1. R_0 *is just.*

Proof: *Let* $x = (x_1, x_2, \ldots, x_k)$, $y = (y_1, y_2, \ldots, y_k)$ *and denote the preference relation induced* (2.3) *by* $y \underset{k}{\succ} x$. Let $T_x = \Sigma x_i$.

Case 1. $T_x = T_y$. In this case $y \underset{k}{\succ} x$ implies $y_k \geq x_k$ and the assertion follows from (2.4).

Case 2. $T_x \neq T_y$. It suffices to show that $p_k(y) \geq p_k(x)$ for those pairs (x,y) where y ranks immediately above x i.e. $y \underset{k}{\succ} x$ and there is no y' such that $y \underset{k}{\succ} y' \underset{k}{\succ} x$ holds. There are two types of such y's for each x:

Type 1: $y_k = x_k + 1$, $y_i = x_i$, $i \neq k$; Type 2; $y_k = y_k, y_j = x_j - 1$, for some $j \neq k$ and $y_j = x_j$ for all other j.

Type 1. Here $T_y = T_x + 1$. If $p_k(x) = 1$, then by (2.8) $P\{Z_T > x_k\} \leq p^*$ holds, therefore,

(2.11) $$P\{Z_{T_y} > y_k\} = P\{Z_{T_x+1} > x_k + 1\} \leq P\{Z_{T_x} > x_k\} \leq P^*,$$

hence $p_k(y) = 1 \geq p_k(x)$.

If $p_k(x) = \rho > 0$ then by (2.8), (2.9)

(2.12) $$P\{Z_{T_x} > x_k\} \leq P^* \quad \text{and} \quad P\{Z_{T_x} \geq x_k\} = P^*, \quad \text{holds.}$$

From (2.11), we get

(2.13) $$P\{Z_{T_y} > y_k\} \leq P^* \quad .$$

If also

(2.14) $$P\{Z_{T_y} \geq y_k\} \leq P^*$$

holds, then

$$p_k(y) = 1 \geq p_k(x) \quad .$$

If (2.13) holds but (2.14) does not, we have

(2.15) $$\begin{aligned} p_k(y) &= \frac{P^* - P\{Z_{T_y} > y_k\}}{P\{Z_{T_y} > y_k - 1\} - P\{Z_{T_y} > y_k\}} \\ &\geq \frac{P^* - P\{Z_{T_x} > x_k\}}{P\{Z_{T_x} > x_k - 1\} - P\{Z_{T_k} > x_k\}} = p_k(x) \end{aligned}$$

where the inequality is of the kind $\frac{P^*-a}{b-a} \geq \frac{P^*-A}{B-A}$ with $0 < a \leq A \leq P^* < b \leq B$ and is seen to be true as follows: $\frac{P^*-a}{b-a} \geq \frac{P^*-a}{B-a} \geq \frac{P^*-A}{B-A}$ where the second inequality holds because the expression in the middle is a decreasing function in a.

The third possibility $p_k(x) = 0$ is trivially true.

Type 2. Here $T_y = T_x - 1$. The proof is analogous to that for type 1 with (2.11) replaced by

(2.16) $$P\{Z_{T_y} > y_k\} = P\{Z_{T_x - 1} > x_k\} < P\{Z_{T_x} > x_k\} \quad .$$

This concludes the proof of Theorem 2.1.

Table 1 gives the values of c_T and ρ for several selected values of P^*, k and n. Since T takes on the values $0, 1, \ldots, kn$ these tables become very extensive for large values of k and n. Therefore it is desirable to find approximations for c_T and ρ. The normal approximation for the hypergeometric distribution gives good results when n is large and T is not extreme (close to 0 or kn). The expectation and variance of Z_T are $\mu = \frac{T}{k}$ and $\sigma^2 = \frac{T(kn-T)(k-1)}{(kn-1)k^2}$ respectively. Using the fact that asymptotically Z_T is $N(\mu, \sigma^2)$, we obtain approximate value $\tilde{c}_T$ given by

$$\tilde{c}_T = [\tfrac{1}{2} + \mu - \sigma\,\Phi^{-1}(P^*)]$$

where Φ^{-1} is the inverse of the standard normal cdf and $[x]$ is the integral part of x. For ρ we get the approximate value $\tilde{\rho} = \tilde{c}_T + 0.5 - (\mu - \sigma\Phi^{-1}(P^*))$. The exact and approximate values of c_T and ρ were compared for $k = 2,3,5,10$; $n = 5,10,20$; and some selected values of T and P^*. The results showed no change in the values of c_T and $\tilde{c}_T$ and small derivations in the values of ρ and $\tilde{\rho}$.

The nonrandomized version R_0' of R_0,

R_0': Select Π_i iff $x_i \geq c_T$, is conservative in the sense of meeting the basic probability requirement. However, R_0' may not be just and it selects large subsets if the θ_i's are close to zero or one.

The performance of a rule R,

$$R: \text{ Select } \Pi_i \text{ iff } x_i \geq \max_{1 \leq j \leq k} x_j - D \quad ,$$

was studied in [4] and a table was given for the expected proportion under various slippage configurations $(\theta,\theta,\ldots,\theta,\theta+\delta)$. A comparison of R_0 and R is difficult because $\inf_\Omega P_\omega(CS|R)$ is not known. Since it takes place near $\theta = \frac{1}{2}$, the P*-value for R_0 was chosen to satisfy $P_\omega(CS|R) = P^*$ with $\omega = (\frac{1}{2},\frac{1}{2},\ldots,\frac{1}{2})$ which makes the comparison slightly more favorable for R. The numerical computations showed that R_0 yields better results for small values of δ, while R is better for large δ. Hence R_0 should be applied if small differences in the success probabilities are expected. This disadvantage of R_0 becomes more evident in the case of equally spaced configurations, where almost surely more than half of the populations will be retained in the selected subset if the number of observations is increased indefinitely, whereas R will eventually select only the best one. In Section 3 a rule will be proposed, which combines the advantages of both R and R_0.

Poisson Case:

A selection rule similar to the rule R_0 for the binomial case has been constructed for the Poisson case. The conditional probability in this case is

$$(2.17) \qquad P\{X_k = x|T\} = \binom{T}{x}\frac{(k-1)^{T-x}}{k^T} \quad .$$

The rule is of the same type as R_0 defined in (2.4) and the constant c_T and ρ are determined as before except that the conditional distribution is now given by (2.17). Table 2 gives the values of c_T and ρ for various k, T and P^*.

Negative Binomial Case:

A selection rule for large θ for the negative binomial distribution with probability function $\binom{x-1}{r-1}\theta_i^r(1-\theta_i)^{x-r}$ is similar to R_0 except that $p_i(x) = 1$ or 0 according as $x_i < c_T$ or $> c_T$. The evaluation of the constants c_T and ρ is accomplished as before. Table 3 gives values of these for selected values of k, P^* and r.

Similar selection rules have also been computed for Fisher's logarithmic distribution [5].

Remark 2.1. It should be pointed out that the rules discussed in this section overcame the difficulty in the evaluation of the infimum of the probability of a correct selection encountered in rules of the type R for the binomial case that was studied in [4]. The conditional rules of the type R_0 lead to $P(CS|R_0)$ which is constant in Ω_0 which is not the case for rules of type R.

3. *Some Rules with Constant* $P(CS|R)$ *in* Ω_0 *derived from the Likelihood Ratio Criterion.* From a likelihood ratio test under slippage hypotheses a derivation was given in [1] for the following rule for selecting a subset containing the one with highest mean from several normal populations. This derivation can be generalized for Koopman-Darmois families and more general hypotheses.

Let X_i, $i = 1,2,\ldots,k$, have the probability densities

$$f(\theta_i,X_i) = c(\theta_i)e^{Q(\theta_i)T(x_i)}h(x_i) \quad . \tag{3.1}$$

If we make the usual assumption that $Q(\theta_i)$ is strictly monotone, say increasing, so that we can consider $Q(\theta_i)$ as the parameter and rename it θ_i, simplifying (3.1) to

$$f(\theta_i,X_i) = c(\theta_i)e^{\theta_i T(x_i)}h(x_i) \quad . \tag{3.2}$$

Let us assume we know that the θ_i take on the values $\theta'_1 \leq \theta'_2 \leq \dots \leq \theta'_k$, but that the correct pairing is not known. Consider the set of hypotheses

$$(3.3) \qquad H_i: \quad \theta_i = \theta'_k; \quad i = 1,\dots,k,$$

i.e. H_i is the hypothesis that θ_i corresponds to θ'_k without specifying the parameters of the remaining $(k-1)$ populations. If Ω_i, $i = 1,2,\dots,k$, denotes the subset of Ω where H_i is true, then the likelihood ratio test of H_k against the alternatives $H_1,\dots,H_{k-1}$ yields the region of acceptance:

$$(3.4) \qquad \lambda = \frac{\max\limits_{\omega\varepsilon\Omega_k} \prod\limits_{i=1}^{k} f(\theta'_i, x_i)}{\max\limits_{\omega\varepsilon\Omega_k} \prod\limits_{i=1}^{k} f(\theta'_i, x_i)} = e^{\Sigma\theta'_i[T'_{[i]} - T_{[i]}]} \geq c$$

where the $T_{[i]}$ are the ordered values of $T_i = T(x_i)$, $i = 1,2,\dots,k$, and $T'_{[i]}$ are the ordered values of T_i, $i = 1,2,\dots,k-1$, $T'_{[k]} = T_k$. Let r be the rank of T_k among the T_i's, i.e. $T_{[r]} = T_k$. Then (3.4) becomes

$$(3.5) \qquad \sum_{i=1}^{k} \theta_i (T'_{[i]} - T_{[i]}) = \sum_{j=r+1}^{k} (\theta_{j-1} - \theta_j) T_{[j]} + (\theta_k - \theta_r) T_k \geq c_1 .$$

Under slippage configuration $\omega_k = (\theta'_1,\dots,\theta'_k) = (\theta,\dots,\theta,\theta+\delta)$, (3.5) simplifies to

$$(3.6) \qquad -\delta T_{[k]} + \delta T_k \geq c_1$$

or

$$(3.7) \qquad T_k \geq T_{[k]} - c_2 .$$

If θ and δ are known this gives rise to the selection rule

(3.8) $\quad R$: Select Π_i if $T_i \geq T_{[k]} - c_2$

where $c_2 = c_2(k,P^*,\theta,\delta)$ is determined from the P^*-condition

(3.9) $$P_{\omega_k}\{T_k \geq T_{[k]} - c_2\} = P^* .$$

The rule given in (3.8) was introduced by Gupta [1,3]. It can easily be seen that this rule is just, hence if we keep θ fixed the minimum of $P(CS)$ takes place of when $\delta = 0$, in which case (3.9) becomes

(3.10) $$\int_{-\infty}^{\infty} F_\theta^{k-1}(t+c_2)dF_\theta(t) = P^* ,$$

where F_θ is the cumulative distribution function of T. For normal distributions with θ as location parameter, c_2 in (3.10) does not depend on θ. For this case the constants c_2 are tabulated in [2]. In general c_2 depends on θ and if θ is not known an estimator for θ may be used in (3.9). Since ΣT_i is a sufficient statistic for θ, this leads to a selection rule of the form

(3.11) $\quad$ Select Π_i, if $T_i \geq T_{[k]} - c(\Sigma T_i,P^*)$.

By Lemma 1.1 this rule has constant $P(CS)$ in Ω_0, if $c(\Sigma T_i,P^*)$ is determined to satisfy:

(3.12) $$P_{\omega_0}\{T_i \geq T_{[k]} - c(\Sigma T_i,P^*)|\Sigma T_j\} = P^* \quad \text{for all } \Sigma T_i,\ \omega_0 \varepsilon\ \Omega_0 .$$

However it is not known whether (4.11) is a just rule.

Acknowledgment. The authors wish to thank Professor S. Panchapakesan of Southern Illinois University for assistance and discussion during the writing of this paper.

References

1. Gupta, S. S. (1956). On a decision-rule for a problem in ranking means. Ph.D. Thesis, University of North Carolina, Chapel Hill, N. C.

2. Gupta, S. S. (1963). Probability integrals of the multivariate normal and multivariate t. *Ann. Math. Statist.*, 34, 792-828.

3. Gupta, S. S. (1965). On some multiple decision (selection and ranking) rules. *Technometrics*, 7, 225-245.

4. Gupta, S. S. and Sobel, M. (1960). Selecting a subset containing the best of several binomial populations. *Contributions to Probability and Statistics*. (I. Olkin, ed), 224-248, Stanford University Press, Stanford, California.

5. Nagel, K. (1970). On Subset Selection Rules with Certain Optimality Properties. Mimeo Series 222, Department of Statistics, Purdue University, Lafayette, Indiana.

6. Studden, W. J. (1967). On selecting a subset of k populations containing the best. *Ann. Math. Statist.* 38, 1072-78.

Table 1. c_T and ρ_T for Binomial Distributions

K = 2 N = 5

	P=.75		P=.90		P=.95		P=.99	
T	c_T	ρ_T	c_T	ρ_T	c_T	ρ_T	c_T	ρ_T
0	0	.75	0	.90	0	.95	0	.99
1	0	.50	0	.80	0	.90	0	.98
2	1	.95	0	.55	0	.78	0	.96
3	1	.60	1	.96	0	.40	0	.88
4	1	.05	1	.68	1	.89	0	.58
5	2	.63	1	.03	1	.54	1	.94
6	2	.05	2	.68	2	.89	1	.58
7	3	.60	3	.96	2	.40	2	.88
8	4	.95	3	.55	3	.78	3	.96
9	4	.50	4	.80	4	.90	4	.98
10	5	.75	5	.90	5	.95	5	.99

K = 3 N = 5

T	c_T	ρ_T	c_T	ρ_T	c_T	ρ_T	c_T	ρ_T
0	0	.75	0	.90	0	.95	0	.99
1	0	.63	0	.85	0	.93	0	.98
2	0	.42	0	.77	0	.88	0	.98
3	0	:05	0	.62	0	.81	0	.96
4	1	.78	0	.35	0	.68	0	.94
5	1	.53	1	.95	0	.40	0	.88
6	1	.17	1	.77	1	.97	0	.76
7	2	.83	1	.50	1	.81	0	.46
8	2	.54	1	.00	1	.54	1	.97
9	2	.15	2	.78	2	.99	1	.82
10	3	.79	2	.45	2	.78	1	.42
11	3	.48	3	.93	2	.37	2	.91
12	4	.98	3	.65	3	.87	2	.55
13	4	.68	4	.99	3	.48	3	.90
14	4	.25	4	.70	4	.85	4	.97
15	5	.75	5	.90	5	.95	5	.99

K = 5 N = 5

T	c_T	ρ_T	c_T	ρ_T	c_T	ρ_T	c_T	ρ_T
0	0	.75	0	.90	0	.95	0	.99
1	0	.69	0	.87	0	.94	0	.99
2	0	.61	0	.84	0	.92	0	.98
3	0	.50	0	.80	0	.90	0	.98
4	0	.35	0	.74	0	.87	0	.97
5	0	.14	0	.66	0	.83	0	.97
6	1	.93	0	.54	0	.77	0	.95
7	1	.78	0	.38	0	.69	0	.94
8	1	.63	0	.14	0	.57	0	.91
9	1	.46	1	.94	0	.39	0	.88
10	1	.25	1	.83	0	.12	0	.82
11	2	.99	1	.70	1	.94	0	.73
12	2	.82	1	.53	1	.84	0	.59

K = 5 N = 5 (Cont'd.)

	P=.75		P=.90		P=.95		P=.99	
T	c_T	ρ_T	c_T	ρ_T	c_T	ρ_T	c_T	ρ_T
13	2	.65	1	.30	1	.71	0	.33
14	2	.45	2	.98	1	.53	1	.99
15	2	.22	2	.85	1	.24	1	.91
16	3	.95	2	.69	2	.95	1	.80
17	3	.77	2	.47	2	.81	1	.60
18	3	.58	2	.13	2	.63	1	.19
19	3	.34	3	.89	2	.31	2	.93
20	3	.01	3	.71	3	.94	2	.77
21	4	.81	3	.44	3	.78	2	.39
22	4	.62	4	.98	3	.48	3	.94
23	4	.35	4	.80	4	.95	3	.70
24	5	.94	4	.50	4	.75	4	.95
25	5	.75	5	.90	5	.95	5	.99

K = 2 N = 10

T	c_T	ρ_T	c_T	ρ_T	c_T	ρ_T	c_T	ρ_T
0	0	.75	0	.90	0	.95	0	.99
1	0	.50	0	.80	0	.90	0	.98
2	1	.98	0	.58	0	.79	0	.96
3	1	.63	0	.05	0	.53	0	.91
4	1	.17	1	.77	1	.97	0	.77
5	2	.72	1	.38	1	.75	0	.38
6	2	.26	2	.88	1	.31	1	.93
7	3	.77	2	.51	2	.85	1	.69
8	3	.31	3	.94	2	.47	2	1.00
9	4	.79	3	.57	3	.90	2	.77
10	4	.33	4	.96	3	.51	2	.14
11	5	.79	4	.57	4	.90	3	.77
12	5	.31	5	.94	4	.47	4	1.00
13	6	.77	5	.51	5	.85	4	.69
14	6	.26	6	.88	5	.31	5	.93
15	7	.72	6	.38	6	.75	5	.38
16	7	.17	7	.77	7	.97	6	.77
17	8	.63	7	.05	7	.53	7	.91
18	9	.98	8	.58	8	.79	8	.96
19	9	.50	9	.80	9	.90	9	.98
20	10	.75	10	.90	10	.95	10	.99

K = 3 N = 10

T	c_T	ρ_T	c_T	ρ_T	c_T	ρ_T	c_T	ρ_T
0	0	.75	0	.90	0	.95	0	.99
1	0	.63	0	.85	0	.93	0	.98
2	0	.43	0	.77	0	.89	0	.98
3	0	.11	0	.64	0	.82	0	.96
4	1	.82	0	.43	0	.72	0	.94
5	1	.58	0	.08	0	.54	0	.91

Table 1 (Continued)

K = 3 N = 10 (Cont'd.)								
	P=.75		P=.90		P=.95		P=.99	
T	c_T	ρ_T	c_T	ρ_T	c_T	ρ_T	c_T	ρ_T
6	1	.29	1	.87	0	.23	0	.85
7	2	.94	1	.67	1	.94	0	.74
8	2	.68	1	.41	1	.78	0	.54
9	2	.38	2	1.00	1	.57	0	.15
10	2	.00	2	.80	1	.22	1	.93
11	3	.73	2	.54	2	.91	1	.80
12	3	.43	2	.18	2	.70	1	.56
13	3	.05	3	.86	2	.38	1	.11
14	4	.75	3	.60	3	.96	2	.89
15	4	.44	3	.23	3	.74	2	.67
16	4	.05	4	.87	3	.42	2	.26
17	5	.74	4	.60	4	.96	3	.90
18	5	.42	4	.19	4	.73	3	.66
19	5	.00	5	.84	4	.36	3	.15
20	6	.70	5	.53	5	.91	4	.85
21	6	.36	5	.04	5	.63	4	.50
22	7	.94	6	.75	5	.13	5	.94
23	7	.63	6	.37	6	.79	5	.67
24	7	.24	7	.90	6	.39	6	.98
25	8	.84	7	.57	7	.88	6	.72
26	8	.50	8	.98	7	.52	7	.97
27	8	.01	8	.68	8	.91	7	.66
28	9	.68	8	.03	8	.52	8	.90
29	9	.25	9	.70	9	.85	9	.97
30	10	.75	10	.90	10	.95	10	.99
K = 5 N = 10								
0	0	.75	0	.90	0	.95	0	.99
1	0	.69	0	.88	0	.94	0	.99
2	0	.61	0	.84	0	.92	0	.98
3	0	.50	0	.80	0	.90	0	.98
4	0	.37	0	.75	0	.87	0	.97
5	0	.20	0	.68	0	.84	0	.97
6	1	.98	0	.59	0	.79	0	.96
7	1	.84	0	.46	0	.73	0	.95
8	1	.69	0	.30	0	.65	0	.93
9	1	.54	0	.08	0	.54	0	.91
10	1	.37	1	.93	0	.39	0	.88
11	1	.17	1	.83	0	.19	0	.84

K = 5 N = 10 (Cont'd.)								
	P=.75		P=.90		P=.95		P=.99	
T	c_T	ρ_T	c_T	ρ_T	c_T	ρ_T	c_T	ρ_T
12	2	.96	1	.72	1	.98	0	.78
13	2	.80	1	.58	1	.90	0	.71
14	2	.64	1	.41	1	.80	0	.60
15	2	.46	1	.20	1	.69	0	.44
16	2	.27	2	.97	1	.54	0	.22
17	2	.04	2	.85	1	.36	1	.98
18	3	.86	2	.72	1	.11	1	.92
19	3	.69	2	.56	2	.94	1	.85
20	3	.51	2	.36	2	.82	1	.75
21	3	.31	2	.12	2	.69	1	.61
22	3	.08	3	.92	2	.51	1	.41
23	4	.88	3	.78	2	.29	1	.13
24	4	.70	3	.61	3	1.00	2	.95
25	4	.52	3	.41	3	.88	2	.85
26	4	.31	3	.16	3	.73	2	.72
27	4	.07	4	.94	3	.56	2	.54
28	5	.87	4	.78	3	.32	2	.27
29	5	.68	4	.60	3	.01	3	.97
30	5	.49	4	.39	4	.87	3	.86
31	5	.27	4	.11	4	.71	3	.71
32	5	.00	5	.90	4	.50	3	.50
33	6	.82	5	.73	4	.22	3	.16
34	6	.63	5	.52	5	.95	4	.93
35	6	.42	5	.26	5	.79	4	.78
36	6	.17	6	.96	5	.59	4	.57
37	7	.93	6	.80	5	.31	4	.22
38	7	.74	6	.59	6	.97	5	.93
39	7	.53	6	.33	6	.81	5	.77
40	7	.30	7	.98	6	.59	5	.50
41	8	1.00	7	.81	6	.28	5	.01
42	8	.81	7	.60	7	.94	6	.86
43	8	.60	7	.30	7	.75	6	.62
44	8	.36	8	.94	7	.48	6	.09
45	8	.04	8	.75	8	.99	7	.87
46	9	.82	8	.49	8	.81	7	.56
47	9	.62	9	.99	8	.52	8	.96
48	9	.35	9	.81	9	.96	8	.73
49	10	.94	9	.50	9	.75	9	.95
50	10	.75	10	.90	10	.95	10	.99

Table 2. c_T and ρ_T for Poisson Distributions

K = 2								
	P=.75		P=.90		P=.95		P=.99	
T	c_T	ρ_T	c_T	ρ_T	c_T	ρ_T	c_T	ρ_T
0	0	.75	0	.90	0	.95	0	.99
1	0	.50	0	.80	0	.90	0	.98
2	0	0.00	0	.60	0	.80	0	.96
3	1	.67	0	.20	0	.60	0	.92
4	1	.25	1	.85	0	.20	0	.84
5	2	.80	1	.56	1	.88	0	.68
6	2	.40	1	.10	1	.63	0	.36
7	3	.91	2	.77	1	.23	1	.96
8	3	.52	2	.41	2	.86	1	.81
9	3	.02	3	.94	2	.57	1	.54
10	4	.62	3	.61	2	.11	1	.08
11	4	.15	3	.16	3	.79	2	.85
12	5	.71	4	.78	3	.43	2	.58
13	5	.26	4	.38	4	.96	2	.13
14	6	.79	5	.92	4	.65	3	.84
15	6	.35	5	.56	4	.22	3	.55
16	7	.87	5	.08	5	.83	3	.07
17	7	.43	6	.70	5	.46	4	.80
18	8	.94	6	.27	6	.97	4	.47
19	8	.51	7	.83	6	.65	5	.98
20	8	.01	7	.43	6	.21	5	.72
21	9	.58	8	.94	7	.80	5	.34
22	9	.10	8	.57	7	.42	6	.91
23	10	.65	8	.09	8	.94	6	.61
24	10	.18	9	.69	8	.59	6	.17
25	11	.72	9	.24	8	.12	7	.81
26	11	.25	10	.80	9	.74	7	.46
27	12	.78	10	.38	9	.32	8	.97
28	12	.32	11	.91	10	.87	8	.68
29	13	.83	11	.50	10	.48	8	.26
30	13	.38	11	.00	11	.99	9	.85
31	14	.89	12	.62	11	.63	9	.50
32	14	.44	12	.15	11	.17	9	.00
33	15	.95	13	.72	12	.76	10	.70
34	15	.50	13	.27	12	.34	10	.28
35	16	1.00	14	.82	13	.88	11	.86
36	16	.55	14	.39	13	.48	11	.50
37	16	.06	15	.91	14	.99	11	.01
38	17	.61	15	.50	14	.62	12	.69
39	17	.12	16	1.00	14	.15	12	.26
40	18	.66	16	.60	15	.74	13	.84

K = 2 (Cont'd.)								
	P=.75		P=.90		P=.95		P=.99	
T	c_T	ρ_T	c_T	ρ_T	c_T	ρ_T	c_T	ρ_T
41	18	.18	16	.12	15	.30	13	.47
42	19	.71	17	.69	16	.85	14	.98
43	19	.23	17	.23	16	.44	14	.63
44	20	.76	18	.78	17	.95	14	.20
45	20	.29	18	.34	17	.56	15	.80
46	21	.80	19	.86	17	.08	15	.41
47	21	.34	19	.43	18	.68	16	.94
48	22	.85	20	.94	18	.22	16	.58
49	22	.39	20	.53	19	.78	16	.11
50	23	.90	20	.03	19	.35	17	.73

K = 3								
0	0	.75	0	.90	0	.95	0	.99
1	0	.63	0	.85	0	.93	0	.98
2	0	.44	0	.77	0	.89	0	.98
3	0	.16	0	.66	0	.83	0	.97
4	1	.87	0	.49	0	.75	0	.95
5	1	.64	0	.24	0	.62	0	.92
6	1	.38	1	.95	0	.43	0	.89
7	1	.07	1	.80	0	.15	0	.83
8	2	.80	1	.61	1	.93	0	.74
9	2	.54	1	.37	1	.80	0	.62
10	2	.25	1	.05	1	.62	0	.42
11	3	.93	2	.84	1	.40	0	.14
12	3	.68	2	.64	1	.09	1	.95
13	3	.39	2	.39	2	.89	1	.85
14	3	.07	2	.07	2	.71	1	.73
15	4	.79	3	.84	2	.49	1	.55
16	4	.51	3	.62	2	.21	1	.30
17	4	.21	3	.35	3	.93	2	.99
18	5	.90	3	.02	3	.75	2	.88
19	5	.62	4	.80	3	.52	2	.73
20	5	.32	4	.57	3	.24	2	.53
21	6	.99	4	.28	4	.95	2	.27
22	6	.72	5	.97	4	.76	3	.97
23	6	.43	5	.74	4	.52	3	.84
24	6	.11	5	.48	4	.24	3	.66
25	7	.81	5	.18	5	.94	3	.43
26	7	.52	6	.90	5	.74	3	.13
27	7	.21	6	.66	5	.49	4	.91
28	8	.89	6	.38	5	.20	4	.74

Table 2 (Continued)

K = 3 (Cont'd.)								
	P=.75		P=.90		P=.95		P=.99	
T	c_T	ρ_T	c_T	ρ_T	c_T	ρ_T	c_T	ρ_T
29	8	.61	6	.05	6	.92	4	.53
30	8	.30	7	.81	6	.70	4	.25
31	9	.97	7	.55	6	.44	5	.96
32	9	.69	7	.25	6	.13	5	.79
33	9	.39	8	.94	7	.87	5	.58
34	9	.06	8	.70	7	.64	5	.32
35	10	.77	8	.42	7	.37	6	.99
36	10	.47	8	.10	7	.05	6	.83
37	10	.15	9	.83	8	.81	6	.62
38	11	.84	9	.57	8	.57	6	.36
39	11	.55	9	.27	8	.28	6	.03
40	11	.23	10	.95	9	.96	7	.84
41	12	.91	10	.70	9	.74	7	.63
42	12	.62	10	.42	9	.48	7	.38
43	12	.31	10	.10	9	.17	7	.05
44	13	.98	11	.83	10	.89	8	.85
45	13	.69	11	.56	10	.65	8	.63
46	13	.38	11	.26	10	.37	8	.37
47	13	.05	12	.94	10	.04	8	.05
48	14	.75	12	.69	11	.80	9	.84
49	14	.45	12	.40	11	.54	9	.62
50	14	.13	12	.08	11	.25	9	.35
K = 5								
0	0	.75	0	.90	0	.95	0	.99
1	0	.69	0	.87	0	.94	0	.99
2	0	.61	0	.84	0	.92	0	.98
3	0	.51	0	.80	0	.90	0	.98
4	0	.39	0	.76	0	.88	0	.98
5	0	.24	0	.69	0	.85	0	.97
6	0	.05	0	.62	0	.81	0	.96
7	1	.89	0	.52	0	.76	0	.95
8	1	.75	0	.40	0	.70	0	.94
9	1	.62	0	.25	0	.63	0	.93
10	1	.47	0	.07	0	.53	0	.91
11	1	.31	1	.94	0	.42	0	.88
12	1	.12	1	.85	0	.27	0	.85
13	2	.94	1	.75	0	.09	0	.82

K = 5 (Cont'd.)								
	P=.75		P=.90		P=.95		P=.99	
T	c_T	ρ_T	c_T	ρ_T	c_T	ρ_T	c_T	ρ_T
14	2	.79	1	.64	1	.96	0	.77
15	2	.64	1	.51	1	.89	0	.72
16	2	.48	1	.36	1	.81	0	.64
17	2	.31	1	.19	1	.71	0	.56
18	2	.12	2	.99	1	.61	0	.44
19	3	.94	2	.89	1	.48	0	.31
20	3	.79	2	.77	1	.33	0	.13
21	3	.63	2	.65	1	.16	1	.98
22	3	.46	2	.51	2	.98	1	.94
23	3	.28	2	.36	2	.89	1	.88
24	3	.09	2	.18	2	.79	1	.81
25	4	.91	3	.99	2	.68	1	.74
26	4	.76	3	.87	2	.55	1	.64
27	4	.59	3	.74	2	.41	1	.54
28	4	.42	3	.61	2	.24	1	.40
29	4	.24	3	.46	2	.05	1	.25
30	4	.04	3	.29	3	.93	1	.06
31	5	.87	3	.10	3	.82	2	.95
32	5	.71	4	.94	3	.70	2	.88
33	5	.54	4	.81	3	.57	2	.80
34	5	.36	4	.67	3	.42	2	.71
35	5	.17	4	.52	3	.25	2	.60
36	6	.98	4	.36	3	.06	2	.47
37	6	.81	4	.18	4	.93	2	.32
38	6	.65	5	.99	4	.81	2	.14
39	6	.47	5	.86	4	.69	3	.98
40	6	.29	5	.72	4	.55	3	.90
41	6	.09	5	.57	4	.39	3	.81
42	7	.91	5	.41	4	.22	3	.71
43	7	.74	5	.23	4	.02	3	.59
44	7	.57	5	.03	5	.90	3	.46
45	7	.39	6	.89	5	.77	3	.30
46	7	.20	6	.75	5	.64	3	.12
47	7	.01	6	.60	5	.49	4	.96
48	8	.84	6	.43	5	.33	4	.88
49	8	.67	6	.26	5	.14	4	.78
50	8	.49	6	.06	6	.96	4	.66

Table 3. c_T and ρ_T for Negative Binomial Distributions

K = 2, r = 5

	P=.75		P=.90		P=.95		P=.99	
T	c_T	ρ_T	c_T	ρ_T	c_T	ρ_T	c_T	ρ_T
10	5	.75	5	.90	5	.95	5	.99
11	6	.50	6	.80	6	.90	6	.98
12	7	.08	7	.63	7	.82	7	.96
13	7	.73	8	.37	8	.69	8	.94
14	8	.38	8	.99	9	.49	9	.90
15	8	.95	9	.79	10	.21	10	.84
16	9	.61	10	.54	10	.94	11	.76
17	10	.22	11	.22	11	.77	12	.65
18	10	.82	11	.91	12	.56	13	.51
19	11	.45	12	.66	13	.31	14	.32
20	12	.04	13	.37	13	.99	15	.08
21	12	.67	14	.03	14	.81	15	.94
22	13	.28	14	.77	15	.60	16	.84
23	13	.88	15	.49	16	.35	17	.71
24	14	.51	16	.17	17	.05	18	.57
25	15	.11	16	.87	17	.84	19	.40
26	15	.72	17	.60	18	.62	20	.20
27	16	.34	18	.30	19	.37	20	.98
28	16	.93	18	.97	20	.08	21	.87
29	17	.56	19	.70	20	.85	22	.74
30	18	.16	20	.41	21	.63	23	.59
31	18	.77	21	.09	22	.38	24	.42
32	19	.39	21	.80	23	.10	25	.23
33	19	.98	22	.52	23	.86	26	.01
34	20	.60	23	.20	24	.63	26	.88
35	21	.21	23	.90	25	.38	27	.74
36	21	.82	24	.62	26	.11	28	.59
37	22	.43	25	.31	26	.87	29	.42
38	23	.03	25	.99	27	.64	30	.23
39	23	.65	26	.71	28	.39	31	.02
40	24	.26	27	.42	29	.12	31	.88
41	24	.86	28	.10	29	.87	32	.74
42	25	.48	28	.81	30	.64	33	.58
43	26	.08	29	.52	31	.39	34	.41
44	26	.69	30	.21	32	.12	35	.22
45	27	.30	30	.91	32	.87	36	.02
46	27	.90	31	.62	33	.64	36	.88
47	28	.52	32	.32	34	.39	37	.73
48	29	.12	32	1.00	35	.12	38	.57
49	29	.73	33	.72	35	.87	39	.40
50	30	.34	34	.42	36	.64	40	.21
51	30	.94	35	.11	37	.39	41	.01
52	31	.56	35	.81	38	.12	41	.87
53	32	.16	36	.52	38	.87	42	.71
54	32	.77	37	.21	39	.64	43	.55
55	33	.39	37	.91	40	.39	44	.38
56	33	.99	38	.62	41	.12	45	.20
57	34	.60	39	.32	41	.87	45	1.00
58	35	.21	40	.00	42	.64	46	.85
59	35	.82	40	.71	43	.38	47	.70
60	36	.43	41	.42	44	.12	48	.53

K = 3, r = 5

	P=.75		P=.90		P=.95		P=.99	
T	c_T	ρ_T	c_T	ρ_T	c_T	ρ_T	c_T	ρ_T
15	5	.75	5	.90	5	.95	5	.99
16	6	.25	6	.70	6	.85	6	.97
17	6	.70	7	.20	7	.60	7	.92
18	7	.10	7	.78	8	.03	8	.81
19	7	.58	8	.33	8	.76	9	.56
20	7	.95	8	.83	9	.35	10	.08
21	8	.43	9	.38	9	.88	10	.86
22	8	.83	9	.85	10	.51	11	.60
23	9	.26	10	.40	10	.98	12	.18
24	9	.68	10	.87	11	.63	12	.86
25	10	.08	11	.41	12	.14	13	.58
26	10	.53	11	.88	12	.73	14	.16
27	10	.92	12	.42	13	.28	14	.83
28	11	.36	12	.89	13	.82	15	.52
29	11	.76	13	.42	14	.40	16	.09
30	12	.18	13	.89	14	.91	16	.79
31	12	.60	14	.42	15	.50	17	.45
32	12	.99	14	.89	15	.99	17	1.00
33	13	.43	15	.41	16	.60	18	.72
34	13	.84	15	.89	17	.10	19	.36
35	14	.26	16	.41	17	.68	19	.94
36	14	.67	16	.88	18	.22	20	.64
37	15	.07	17	.40	18	.77	21	.25
38	15	.50	17	.87	19	.32	21	.87
39	15	.90	18	.39	19	.85	22	.55
40	16	.33	18	.87	20	.41	23	.14
41	16	.74	19	.38	20	.93	23	.80
42	17	.15	19	.86	21	.50	24	.45
43	17	.57	20	.37	22	.00	25	.02
44	17	.96	20	.85	22	.59	25	.71
45	18	.39	21	.36	23	.11	26	.34
46	18	.80	21	.84	23	.67	26	.94
47	19	.21	22	.35	24	.20	27	.61
48	19	.63	22	.83	24	.75	28	.22
49	20	.03	23	.33	25	.30	28	.85
50	20	.46	23	.82	25	.83	29	.51
51	20	.86	24	.32	26	.39	30	.10
52	21	.28	24	.81	26	.91	30	.76
53	21	.69	25	.31	27	.47	31	.40
54	22	.10	25	.80	27	.99	31	.98
55	22	.52	26	.29	28	.56	32	.66
56	22	.92	26	.78	29	.08	33	.28
57	23	.34	27	.28	29	.64	33	.89
58	23	.75	27	.77	30	.17	34	.55
59	24	.16	28	.27	30	.72	35	.16
60	24	.58	28	.76	31	.26	35	.80
61	24	.98	29	.25	31	.80	36	.44
62	25	.41	29	.75	32	.35	37	.04
63	25	.81	30	.24	32	.88	37	.70
64	26	.23	30	.73	33	.43	38	.32
65	26	.64	31	.22	33	.95	38	.93

Table 3 (Continued)

K = 5 r = 5	P=.75		P=.90		P=.95		P=.99	
T	c_T	ρ_T	c_T	ρ_T	c_T	ρ_T	c_T	ρ_T
25	5	.75	5	.90	5	.95	5	.99
26	5	.94	6	.50	6	.75	6	.95
27	6	.34	6	.83	6	.99	7	.78
28	6	.62	7	.14	7	.63	8	.16
29	6	.84	7	.59	7	.92	8	.81
30	7	.10	7	.87	8	.40	9	.24
31	7	.42	8	.22	8	.77	9	.78
32	7	.67	8	.60	9	.07	10	.18
33	7	.90	8	.87	9	.55	10	.72
34	8	.17	9	.21	9	.86	11	.05
35	8	.46	9	.57	10	.24	11	.63
36	8	.70	9	.86	10	.64	11	.96
37	8	.93	10	.18	10	.93	12	.52
38	9	.20	10	.53	11	.35	12	.89
39	9	.48	10	.82	11	.71	13	.37
40	9	.72	11	.12	11	.99	13	.79
41	9	.95	11	.48	12	.42	14	.21
42	10	.22	11	.78	12	.76	14	.68
43	10	.49	12	.06	13	.08	15	.02
44	10	.73	12	.42	13	.48	15	.54
45	10	.96	12	.73	13	.81	15	.91
46	11	.24	12	.99	14	.15	16	.38
47	11	.50	13	.36	14	.54	16	.79
48	11	.74	13	.67	14	.86	17	.20
49	11	.97	13	.94	15	.21	17	.66
50	12	.25	14	.28	15	.58	18	.01
51	12	.51	14	.60	15	.90	18	.51
52	12	.75	14	.89	16	.26	18	.89
53	12	.98	15	.21	16	.62	19	.34
54	13	.25	15	.54	16	.93	19	.75
55	13	.51	15	.83	17	.31	20	.15
56	13	.75	16	.13	17	.66	20	.61
57	13	.99	16	.46	17	.97	20	.97
58	14	.26	16	.76	18	.35	21	.44
59	14	.51	17	.05	18	.70	21	.84
60	14	.76	17	.39	19	.01	22	.26
61	14	.99	17	.70	19	.40	22	.69
62	15	.26	17	.98	19	.74	23	.07
63	15	.51	18	.31	20	.05	23	.53
64	15	.76	18	.62	20	.43	23	.91
65	15	.99	18	.91	20	.77	24	.36
66	16	.26	19	.23	21	.10	24	.77
67	16	.51	19	.55	21	.47	25	.18
68	16	.76	19	.84	21	.80	25	.62
69	16	.99	20	.15	22	.14	25	.99
70	17	.26	20	.47	22	.50	26	.45
71	17	.52	20	.77	22	.83	26	.84
72	17	.76	21	.07	23	.18	27	.27
73	17	1.00	21	.40	23	.54	27	.69
74	18	.26	21	.70	23	.86	28	.08
75	18	.51	21	.99	24	.21	28	.53

K = 2 r = 10	P=.75		P=.90		P=.95		P=.99	
T	c_T	ρ_T	c_T	ρ_T	c_T	ρ_T	c_T	ρ_T
20	10	.75	10	.90	10	.95	10	.99
21	11	.50	11	.80	11	.90	11	.98
22	12	.05	12	.62	12	.81	12	.96
23	12	.70	13	.30	13	.65	13	.93
24	13	.32	13	.92	14	.38	14	.88
25	13	.88	14	.69	14	.98	15	.79
26	14	.51	15	.37	15	.81	16	.65
27	15	.06	15	.96	16	.57	17	.42
28	15	.68	16	.70	17	.24	18	.09
29	16	.27	17	.37	17	.91	18	.92
30	16	.84	17	.97	18	.68	19	.78
31	17	.44	18	.68	19	.39	20	.59
32	17	.99	19	.34	19	1.00	21	.33
33	18	.61	19	.95	20	.77	21	1.00
34	19	.18	20	.65	21	.49	22	.85
35	19	.76	21	.30	22	.13	23	.67
36	20	.35	21	.92	22	.84	24	.43
37	20	.92	22	.61	23	.57	25	.13
38	21	.52	23	.25	24	.23	25	.90
39	22	.08	23	.88	24	.90	26	.72
40	22	.67	24	.56	25	.63	27	.49
41	23	.25	25	.19	26	.31	28	.21
42	23	.82	25	.84	26	.96	28	.94
43	24	.41	26	.51	27	.69	29	.75
44	24	.97	27	.13	28	.38	30	.52
45	25	.57	27	.79	29	.02	31	.25
46	26	.14	28	.45	29	.75	31	.96
47	26	.72	29	.07	30	.45	32	.77
48	27	.30	29	.73	31	.10	33	.54
49	27	.87	30	.39	31	.80	34	.28
50	28	.46	30	1.00	32	.50	34	.98
51	29	.02	31	.68	33	.17	35	.78
52	29	.61	32	.32	33	.85	36	.56
53	30	.19	32	.95	34	.56	37	.29
54	30	.77	33	.62	35	.23	37	1.00
55	31	.35	34	.25	35	.90	38	.79
56	31	.92	34	.89	36	.61	39	.57
57	32	.50	35	.55	37	.28	40	.31
58	33	.07	36	.18	37	.94	41	.01
59	33	.66	36	.83	38	.65	41	.80
60	34	.23	37	.49	39	.34	42	.57
61	34	.81	38	.11	39	.99	43	.31
62	35	.39	38	.77	40	.70	44	.02
63	35	.96	39	.42	41	.39	44	.80
64	36	.54	40	.04	42	.04	45	.57
65	37	.11	40	.70	42	.75	46	.31
66	37	.70	41	.35	43	.44	47	.02
67	38	.27	41	.97	44	.10	47	.80
68	38	.84	42	.64	44	.79	48	.57
69	39	.43	43	.28	45	.48	49	.31
70	39	.99	43	.91	46	.15	50	.03

Table 3 (Continued)

K = 3 r = 10								
	P=.75		P=.90		P=.95		P=.99	
T	c_T	ρ_T	c_T	ρ_T	c_T	ρ_T	c_T	ρ_T
30	10	.75	10	.90	10	.95	10	.99
31	11	.25	11	.70	11	.85	11	.97
32	11	.69	12	.15	12	.58	12	.92
33	12	.07	12	.75	12	.97	13	.77
34	12	.56	13	.23	13	.70	14	.43
35	12	.92	13	.75	14	.17	14	.95
36	13	.38	14	.22	14	.76	15	.72
37	13	.77	14	.72	15	.27	16	.28
38	14	.17	15	.17	15	.80	16	.87
39	14	.59	15	.68	16	.32	17	.54
40	14	.95	16	.10	16	.82	17	.99
41	15	.40	16	.62	17	.35	18	.71
42	15	.78	17	.02	17	.83	19	.25
43	16	.18	17	.55	18	.36	19	.83
44	16	.59	17	.96	18	.84	20	.45
45	16	.96	18	.48	19	.36	20	.94
46	17	.38	18	.90	19	.84	21	.59
47	17	.77	19	.39	20	.35	22	.08
48	18	.16	19	.83	20	.83	22	.72
49	18	.57	20	.30	21	.34	23	.26
50	18	.94	20	.75	21	.82	23	.82
51	19	.36	21	.20	22	.33	24	.41
52	19	.75	21	.67	22	.81	24	.92
53	20	.13	22	.09	23	.31	25	.53
54	20	.54	22	.58	23	.79	26	.01
55	20	.92	22	.99	24	.28	26	.65
56	21	.33	23	.48	24	.77	27	.16
57	21	.72	23	.91	25	.26	27	.75
58	22	.10	24	.38	25	.75	28	.30
59	22	.51	24	.82	26	.23	28	.84
60	22	.89	25	.28	26	.72	29	.42
61	23	.29	25	.73	27	.20	29	.93
62	23	.68	26	.17	27	.70	30	.53
63	24	.06	26	.64	28	.17	31	.02
64	24	.47	27	.06	28	.67	31	.63
65	24	.85	27	.54	29	.14	32	.15
66	25	.25	27	.96	29	.64	32	.73
67	25	.64	28	.44	30	.10	33	.27
68	26	.02	28	.87	30	.61	33	.82
69	26	.43	29	.34	31	.07	34	.38
70	26	.81	29	.78	31	.58	34	.90
71	27	.20	30	.23	32	.03	35	.49
72	27	.60	30	.68	32	.55	35	.98
73	27	.98	31	.12	32	1.00	36	.58
74	28	.38	31	.58	33	.52	37	.09
75	28	.77	32	.00	33	.97	37	.68
76	29	.16	32	.48	34	.49	38	.21
77	29	.56	32	.91	34	.94	38	.76
78	29	.94	33	.37	35	.45	39	.32
79	30	.34	33	.81	35	.91	39	.85
80	30	.73	34	.27	36	.41	40	.42

K = 5 r = 10								
	P=.75		P=.90		P=.95		P=.99	
T	c_T	ρ_T	c_T	ρ_T	c_T	ρ_T	c_T	ρ_T
50	10	.75	10	.90	10	.95	10	.99
51	10	.94	11	.50	11	.75	11	.95
52	11	.34	11	.82	11	.98	12	.77
53	11	.62	12	.10	12	.60	12	1.00
54	11	.84	12	.56	12	.89	13	.75
55	12	.08	12	.83	13	.29	13	.99
56	12	.40	13	.12	13	.69	14	.65
57	12	.65	13	.52	13	.94	14	.94
58	12	.87	13	.79	14	.38	15	.48
59	13	.12	14	.03	14	.72	15	.84
60	13	.41	14	.43	14	.97	16	.23
61	13	.65	14	.72	15	.39	16	.69
62	13	.87	14	.95	15	.72	16	.97
63	14	.12	15	.31	15	.97	17	.47
64	14	.40	15	.62	16	.37	17	.82
65	14	.64	15	.87	16	.70	18	.17
66	14	.86	16	.16	16	.95	18	.62
67	15	.10	16	.49	17	.33	18	.92
68	15	.37	16	.76	17	.66	19	.36
69	15	.62	17	.00	17	.92	19	.73
70	15	.84	17	.35	18	.28	20	.02
71	16	.07	17	.64	18	.61	20	.49
72	16	.34	17	.89	18	.88	20	.82
73	16	.58	18	.19	19	.21	21	.18
74	16	.81	18	.50	19	.55	21	.59
75	17	.04	18	.77	19	.84	21	.90
76	17	.30	19	.02	20	.13	22	.30
77	17	.55	19	.35	20	.49	22	.68
78	17	.78	19	.63	20	.78	22	.97
79	17	1.00	19	.89	21	.05	23	.41
80	18	.26	20	.18	21	.41	23	.76
81	18	.51	20	.48	21	.71	24	.07
82	18	.74	20	.76	21	.98	24	.49
83	18	.96	20	1.00	22	.33	24	.83
84	19	.22	21	.32	22	.64	25	.18
85	19	.47	21	.61	22	.92	25	.57
86	19	.70	21	.87	23	.24	25	.89
87	19	.92	22	.15	23	.57	26	.27
88	20	.17	22	.45	23	.85	26	.64
89	20	.42	22	.72	24	.15	26	.95
90	20	.66	22	.97	24	.49	27	.35
91	20	.88	23	.28	24	.78	27	.71
92	21	.12	23	.57	25	.06	28	.01
93	21	.37	23	.83	25	.40	28	.42
94	21	.61	24	.10	25	.70	28	.77
95	21	.84	24	.41	25	.97	29	.09
96	22	.07	24	.68	26	.31	29	.49
97	22	.32	24	.94	26	.62	29	.82
98	22	.57	25	.23	26	.90	30	.17
99	22	.80	25	.52	27	.21	30	.55
100	23	.08	25	.79	27	.53	30	.88

A DECISION-THEORETIC APPROACH TO THE PROBLEM OF TESTING A NULL HYPOTHESIS*

By Herman Rubin
Purdue University

1. *Summary.* We consider the testing of the "*null hypothesis*" $\theta = 0$ against the one-dimensional alternative $\theta \neq 0$. In most problems, the investigator knows that $\theta = 0$ is unreasonable, and would prefer to "*accept*" $\theta = 0$ if $|\theta|$ is sufficiently small. We make the assumption that the problem is sufficiently regular, that is, that the likelihood function is sufficiently close to that of a sample from a normal distribution with mean θ and variance 1, after normalization if necessary. We give a mathematical formulation of this problem and investigate the solution. It is shown that a crude procedure based on a "*small sample*" treatment and a "*very large sample*" treatment can be very bad in the transition region; also, there is not enough information in those treatments to get robust results. Further work is contemplated to see if a small amount of additional information will suffice to obtain robust procedures using only information which the user can reasonably supply.

---

*Research was supported in part by the Office of Naval Research Contract N00014-67-A-0226-0008. Project Number NR042-216 at Purdue University. Reproduction in whole or in part is permitted for any purpose of the United States Government.

2. *Mathematical treatment.* Let X be the mean of a sample of size n from $N(\theta,1)$. Let the weight density for accepting $\theta = 0$ be $c\theta^2$, and let the weight measure for rejecting $\theta = 0$ be μ. Then the risk of accepting if $|X| < \xi$ is

$$\text{(1)} \qquad \int_{-\infty}^{\infty} \int_{-\xi}^{\xi} c\theta^2 \sqrt{\frac{n}{2\pi}}\, e^{-n(x-\theta)^2/2}\, dx\, d\theta + \int \int_{|x|>\xi} \sqrt{\frac{n}{2\pi}}\, e^{-(x-\theta)^2/2}\, d\mu(\theta) \quad .$$

Now the first integral in (1) can readily be evaluated as

$$\text{(2)} \qquad 2c\left(\frac{\xi}{n} + \frac{\xi^3}{3}\right) \quad .$$

Suppose $\theta = \alpha\phi$, $x = \alpha y$, $\xi = \alpha\eta$, $n = \alpha^{-2}m$. Then (1) becomes

$$\text{(3)} \qquad 2c\alpha^3\left(\frac{\eta}{m} + \frac{\eta^3}{3}\right) + \int \int_{|y|>\eta} \sqrt{\frac{m}{2\pi}}\, e^{-m(y-\phi)^2/2}\, d\mu(\alpha\phi) \quad .$$

Suppose $|\mu| < \infty$. Then if α is chosen so that

$$\text{(4)} \qquad c\alpha^3 = \frac{1}{\sqrt{2\pi}}\, |\mu| \quad ,$$

and $d\nu(\phi) = d\mu(\alpha\phi)/|\mu|$, the risk is

$$\text{(5)} \qquad |\mu|\left[\frac{2}{\sqrt{2\pi}}\left(\frac{\eta}{m} + \frac{\eta^3}{3}\right) + \nu * N(0,\tfrac{1}{m})(\{y : |y| > \eta\})\right] \quad .$$

We will take this as our standard form. Suppose ν is symmetric. Then it is easily seen by differentiating that

$$\text{(6)} \qquad \frac{1}{\sqrt{2\pi}}\left(\frac{1}{m} + \eta^2\right) = \frac{d\, \nu * N(0,\frac{1}{m})\,(\eta)}{d\eta} \quad .$$

Unfortunately, the solution of this equation for the optimal $\hat{\eta}$ depends heavily on ν. Let us first see what happens in two special cases.

The case in which ν is concentrated at 0 corresponds to the situation in which there is positive prior probability that $\theta = 0$, and for any deviation from $\theta = 0$ rejection would be preferred. In this case, (6) becomes

$$\frac{1}{\sqrt{2\pi}}\left(\frac{1}{m} + \eta^2\right) = \frac{\sqrt{m}}{\sqrt{2\pi}}\, e^{-\frac{1}{2} m \eta^2}, \tag{7}$$

so that if $m \geq 1$ acceptance is possible. (This is the reason for choosing the particular normalization.) Let us call the solution for this case η_N.

Another case is that in which the sample size is so large that (6) is approximately

$$\frac{1}{\sqrt{2\pi}}\,\eta^2 = \frac{d\nu(\eta)}{d\eta}. \tag{8}$$

This is the case in which sampling error is unimportant and the question is merely whether θ is small enough that $\theta = 0$ should be accepted. Let the optimal η for this be η_D.

The first simple procedure which comes to mind is to consider $\eta^* = \max(\eta_N, \eta_D)$. That this can be very bad is easily seen computationally in the case ν normal.

From a theoretical analysis of the problem with 0-th power loss for ν normal, a procedure $\tilde{\eta}$ suggested itself. Let P_N be the probability of type I error under the null hypothesis of rejection beyond η_N and let P_D be the probability of rejection beyond η_D. Then the probability of rejection beyond $\tilde{\eta}$ is $P_N P_D$. This does not give as good results far away from the critical values of n as η^*, but rarely is much worse if ν is normal.

The optimal procedure $\hat{\eta}$ and the risks of $\hat{\eta}$, η^*, and $\tilde{\eta}$ were computed for ν $N(0,\sigma^2)$, $\sigma^2 = 10^{-k}$, $k = 1(1)20$, and $m = 10^j$, $j = .1(.1)20$. The most striking results were at the extreme for $\sigma^2 = 10^{-20}$ (see table). Note that a sample of "size" 10^{20} is 25,000 times as bad as one of half the size for the crude procedure η^*. One might argue that 10^{20} is too large a sample size; however, there is a scale factor involved, and 10^{20} might correspond to a much smaller sample. However, the bad behavior of the crude procedure holds for $\sigma^2 < 10^{-3}$, and a table is included for $\sigma^2 = 10^{-8}$.

While the central limit theorem gives us reason to make a normal approximation for the statistic, there does not seem to be a compelling reason for the weight measure ν to be normal. Computations with ν double-exponential turned out to be feasible, and this was done for scale factors 10^{-k}, $k = .5(.5)10$ and m as before. As is seen in the enclosed tables for scale factors 10^{-10} and $10^{-4.5}$, the crude procedure η^* shows the same type of behavior as before, but not as extreme; the procedure $\tilde{\eta}$ is not too good, giving risks 45% too high and regrets (excesses of risk over that of knowledge of the parameter) of 80% too high. It is possible to develop an analog of $\tilde{\eta}$ for the double-exponential, but then the double-exponential was chosen only for computational convenience, and no clear brief can be made for it.

In the case of ν the Cauchy distribution, the only case we have done is for $m = 10^{20}$, $\eta_N = \eta_D$. Here η^* gives a risk of 1.56×10^{-27}, $\hat{\eta}$, 1.55×10^{-27}, and $\tilde{\eta}$, 1.95×10^{-27}. This indicates that the tail nature of ν near η_D is very important and further investigation is being made of this problem.

Acknowledgment. The author wishes to acknowledge the invaluable help of Arthur Rubin in the construction and especially the debugging of the programs for the numerical results.

References

1. Rubin, H. "Occam's Razor needs new blades", Purdue Mimeo Series No. 216, to appear in the Proceedings of the Symposium on the Foundations of Statistical Inference held at Waterloo, 1970.

2. Rubin, H. and Sethuraman, J. (1965). "Bayes risk efficiency". *Sankyā*, A, Vol. 27 pp. 347-356.

Table 1

ν double exponential, scale factor 10^{-10}			
m	10^{26} risk $(\hat{\eta})$	10^{26} risk (η^*)	10^{26} risk $(\tilde{\eta})$
$10^{17.3}$	365.80	366.10	402.71
$10^{17.7}$	96.52	97.87	119.92
10^{18}	37.01	45.64	52.80
$10^{18.3}$	17.53	4,424.52	26.21
$10^{18.5}$	12.54	2,049,000	17.89
$10^{18.7}$	9.94	6,409.12	13.15
10^{19}	8.02	50.29	9.45
$10^{19.3}$	7.16	9.73	7.75
$10^{19.7}$	6.70	6.88	6.82
∞	6.36	6.36	6.36

ν double exponential, scale factor $10^{-4.5}$			
m	10^{10} risk $(\hat{\eta})$	10^{10} risk (η^*)	10^{10} risk $(\tilde{\eta})$
10^{7}	26.05	26.27	31.03
$10^{7.3}$	10.39	11.09	13.88
$10^{7.7}$	3.84	19.97	5.56
$10^{7.9}$	2.78	85.98	3.85
10^{8}	2.46	24.54	3.29
$10^{8.3}$	1.92	3.24	2.28
$10^{8.7}$	1.63	1.73	1.73
∞	1.45	1.45	1.45

ν normal $(0,10^{-20})$			
m	10^{27} risk $(\hat{\eta})$	10^{27} risk (η^*)	10^{27} risk $(\tilde{\eta})$
10^{18}	349.35	351.01	351.48
$10^{18.7}$	34.93	45.60	35.53
10^{19}	13.58	85.00	13.91
$10^{19.3}$	5.60	3,194.46	5.77
$10^{19.7}$	2.01	44,893,000	2.08
10^{20}	1.11	1.112×10^{12}	1.14
∞	.40	.40	.40

ν normal $(0,10^{-8})$			
m	10^{10} risk $(\hat{\eta})$	10^{10} risk (η^*)	10^{10} risk $(\tilde{\eta})$
10^{6}	636.50	637.17	642.63
10^{7}	28.66	34.44	29.97
$10^{7.3}$	12.21	31.57	12.96
$10^{7.7}$	4.53	369.49	4.86
10^{8}	2.54	10,860	2.71
$10^{8.3}$	1.68	183.85	1.76
$10^{8.7}$	1.21	3.95	1.24
10^{9}	1.06	1.37	1.08
∞	.93	.93	.93

THE ROLE OF SYMMETRY AND APPROXIMATION
IN EXACT DESIGN OPTIMALITY

By J. Kiefer*
Cornell University

1. *Introduction.* For brevity, we treat the simplest framework: Let $f = (f_1,\ldots,f_k)$ where the f_i are known real continuous functions on a compact space $\mathcal{X}$. The coefficient parameter space R^k is coordinatized by $\theta=(\theta_1,\ldots,\theta_k)$. In the *exact theory* the statistician must choose an element (= "exact design") $x^* = (x_1,\ldots,x_N)$ in a specified subset $\mathcal{X}^*$ of $\mathcal{X}^N$. He then observes an N-vector $Y(x^*)$ of uncorrelated rv's $Y_1,\ldots,Y_N$ with common (known or unknown) variance σ^2, and with Y_i having expectation

$$(f(x_i),\theta) = \sum_{j=1}^{k}\theta_j f_j(x_i) \quad .$$

We shall also restrict attention to problems of *point estimation* of a collection of linear forms $\{(c,\theta),\ c \in C\}$, where C is specified, and will consider only nonrandomized linear estimators

$$(Y(x^*),h_c) = \sum_1^N h_{ci}Y_i$$

of the (c,θ). Moreover, we shall be concerned only with functionals of the expected squared errors; and, although the results pertain also to certain settings where biased estimators are called for (Box and Draper, Hader et al, etc.), we treat here only unbiased estimators. Thus, $(Y(x^*),h_c)$

*Research performed under an NSF Grant.

may be assumed to be the Gauss-Markov estimator of (c,θ) if the latter is estimable under x^*, and it has variance

$$\sigma^2 v(c,x^*) = \sigma^2 (c, c\, A_{x^*}^{-1})$$

where

$$A_{x^*} = \sum_1^N f(x_i)'\, f(x_i) \quad .$$

(All expressions involving inverses have obvious meanings in singular cases.)

In block design settings there are usually restrictions which make $\mathcal{X}^* \neq \mathcal{X}^N$. When, as in common regression experiments with unlimited exactly repeatable observation expectations, there are no such restrictions, we can define the discrete probability measure ξ_{x^*} on $\mathcal{X}$ by $N\xi_{x^*}(x) =$ [number of i such that $x_i = x$], and we then see that $N^{-1}A_{x^*}$ equals

$$M(\xi) = \int_{\mathcal{X}} f(x)'\, f(x)\xi(dx)$$

with $\xi = \xi_{x^*}$. We are restricted here, in the exact theory, to the class Ξ_N of those ξ's whose range consists of integer multiples of $1/N$. If we omit this last restriction and consider the class Ξ of *all* probability measures on $\mathcal{X}$ relative to some σ-field which includes all one-point sets, we have the *approximate theory*, and any element of Ξ is called an *approximate design*.

We omit discussion of admissibility and complete classes to concentrate on specific optimality criteria. If Φ is a real functional on the space of variance functions $v(\cdot;x^*)$ on C, we say that $\bar{x}^*$ is *Φ-optimum for C* if it minimizes $\Phi(v(\cdot;x^*))$ over $\mathcal{X}^*$. The corresponding definition of an *approximate Φ-optimum design* $\bar{\xi}$ in the approximate theory is obvious. Among the most commonly employed optimality criteria are, expressed as functionals on the class M_k of $k \times k$ nonnegative definite matrices $M = A_{x^*}$ above,

$$\Phi_1(M) = \operatorname{tr} BM^{-1}, \quad \Phi_2(M) = \det BM^{-1},$$

$$\Phi_3(M) = \max_C (Hc', M^{-1}Hc'),$$

where B (in M_k) and H are specified. We hereafter assume Φ lower semi-continuous to avoid worrying about attainment of optimality.

2. *Symmetry*. A discussion of symmetry has been given in several papers. In the approximate theory, if a compact group G operates appropriately on $(\mathcal{X}, f, C, \Phi)$, which includes convexity in ξ of some increasing function of $\Phi(M(\xi))$, then there is an approximate Φ-optimum $\bar{\xi}$ which is G-invariant ($\bar{\xi}(gA) = \bar{\xi}(A)$ for all g in G and measurable A). Common applications of the Φ_i's listed above fall into this framework, and we have used this to treat regression problems on spheres, cubes, and simplices.

The corresponding result applies less often in the exact theory; we can still represent x^* as a probability measure ξ' on $\mathcal{X}^*$ (not on $\mathcal{X}$), but the "symmetrical" (G-invariant) design ξ'_G defined formally by $\xi'_G(x) = \int_G \xi'(gx)\mu(dg)$ (where μ is Haar probability measure), and which will improve on ξ' if Φ is invariant and convex, need not correspond to an element of $\mathcal{X}^*$. However, sometimes a particular $\bar{x}^*$ can be shown to be better than all competitors in $\mathcal{X}^*$, as follows: Suppose there are u linear parametric functions of interest, which we can take to be $\theta_1, \ldots, \theta_u$. Partition A_{x^*} as $\binom{BC'}{CD}$ with B $u \times u$, and write $\tilde{A}_{x^*} = B - C'D^{-1}C$. The f_i need not be linearly independent, especially in block design settings, and hence not all linear functions of $\theta_1,\ldots,\theta_u$ need be estimable. If $\theta_1,\ldots,\theta_u$ are all estimable for some design, we write $s = u$ and $A^* = \tilde{A}$. If only contrasts of $\theta_1,\ldots,\theta_u$ are estimable, all contrasts being estimable for some design, we write $s = u-1$ and $A^* = L\tilde{A}L'$ where L is $s \times u$ and has orthonormal rows, each summing to zero. (Other cases of $s-u$, such as arise when estimating all main-order contrasts in r-way analysis of variance, have a similar treatment.) Then $A^*_{x^*}$ is proportional to the inverse of the covariance matrix of the s parametric functions being estimated, and we suppose $\Phi(A_{x^*}) = \Phi^*(A^*_{x^*})$ for some Φ^*. We also suppose a compact group $G = \{g\}$ operates on the problem in such a way that $\xi' \in \mathfrak{X}^*$ implies $\xi' g \in \mathfrak{X}^*$ and that $\int_G A^*_{\xi' g}\mu(dg)$ is a multiple of the identity; this last is automatic if G is homomorphic to the orthogonal group $\tilde{G} = \{\tilde{g}\}$ operating on M_s as $A^*_{\xi' g} = \tilde{g}A^*_{\xi'}\tilde{g}'$, or in the case $s = u-1$ if G is the permutation group on the u coordinates in $\mathfrak{X}$ and if (often the case) all rows of $\tilde{A}_{x^*}$ sum to zero for each x^*. Our simple result is then:

In the above setting, suppose $\Phi^*(bA^*) \leq \Phi^*(A^*)$ *for all* $b > 1$, *that* Φ^* *is convex, and that* $\Phi^*(A^*_{\xi'}) = \Phi^*(A^*_{\xi' g})$ *for* $\xi' \in \mathfrak{X}^*$ *and* $g \in G$. *If* $\bar{x}^*$ *maximizes* $\operatorname{tr} A^*_{x^*}$ *over* $\mathfrak{X}^*$, *and if* $A^*_{\bar{x}^*}$ *is a multiple of the identity, then* $\bar{x}^*$ *is* Φ*-optimum.*

This tool yielded our 1958 results on A-, D-, and E-optimality (Φ_1-, Φ_2-, Φ_3-optimality for appropriate B,C,H) of balanced block designs (BBD), and also of generalized Youden squares (GYS) under certain conditions. For estimating all treatment contrasts, all conditions for using this tool are satisfied if $\bar{x}^*$ is the usual "symmetric" design (a BBD or GYS if one exists), except for the condition on $\text{tr}\, A^*_{\bar{x}^*}$ in the case of a GYS. In these settings $\tilde{A}$ has all row sums zero; and $\tilde{A}_{\bar{x}^*}$ has equal diagonal entries and equal off-diagonal entries, so it suffices to show that $\text{tr}\tilde{A}_{x^*}$ is maximized by $\bar{x}^*$, which is a great simplification over looking directly at $\Phi(A_{x^*})$. In the usual setting of 2-way heterogeneity on a $k_1 \times k_2$ array of plots, with the common model of row-plus-column-plus-treatment-effects for expectations, it was shown in 1958 only that a GYS (if one exists) is optimum (where k_1 and k_2 might be $> u$, unlike the usual YS setting) if k_1 or k_2 is divisible by u.

3. *Counterexamples to "symmetry implies optimality".* Having proved E-optimality (minimization of the maximum eigenvalue of A^{*-1}) for the GYS without divisibility some dozen years ago, we were motivated to search for a D-optimality proof. We discovered recently that *the* GYS *is sometimes not* D-*optimum in the absence of the above divisibility property*. The exact determination of which cases yield an optimum GYS and which do not, seems difficult; there are some cases of optimality without divisibility; but there are infinitely many cases of nonoptimality in the absence of divisibility.

These are the first cases we know of where an "exotic design" with full symmetry has been proved nonoptimum for a symmetric estimation problem. (Nonoptimality results in my 1958 paper were concerned with hypothesis testing.)

The simplest case is that of a 6×6 array with 4 treatments, the setting that was used for the example on p. 690

of my 1958 paper, where the GYS d* had rows (134324), (412233), (241342), (124123), (313412), (321441), $a_{ii} = 25/4$ $a_{ij} = -25/12(i \neq j)$. This example illustrated that the proof of Section 2 above did not work in this setting, i.e., that the GYS d* had tr $\tilde{A}_{d*} <$ tr $\tilde{A}_{d'}$ for some competitor d'. However, the d' considered there yielded det $A^*_{d'} <$ det A^*_{d*}, so no counterexample to D-optimality was obtained. If, instead, we consider the design d" with rows (122334), (213344), (231442), (334122), (344213), (442231), we obtain for the entries of $\tilde{A}_{d''}$ the values $a_{11} = 5$, $a_{22} = a_{33} = a_{44} = 61/9$, $a_{12} = a_{13} = a_{14} = -5/3$, $a_{23} = a_{34} = a_{24} = -23/9$. The eigenvalues of $A^*_{d''}$ are seen to be 28/3, 28/3, 20/3, and det $A^*_{d''} = 15680/27 > 15625/27 =$ det A^*_{d*}; thus, d* is not D-optimum.

The simplest other examples are obtained in a sequence of settings which use the same idea and exhibit the same phenomenon: with four treatments on a square array of side 6t, t odd, one treatment is "short-changed" by 3 replications while each of the other 3 treatments receives one extra replication over the average number of replications $9t^2$. A suitable design (as symmetric as possible) with these parameters yields smaller generalized variance than the fully symmetric GYS.

The degree of departure of d* from D-optimality in the above example is not great, but of course that is not the point. We do not yet know how bad fully symmetric designs can be in other settings.

4. *What to do when no exact theory symmetric design exists.*

A. *Block design problems.* For certain values of the

number of treatments u, of the block size, and of number of blocks, there do not exist BBD's; and, in the setting of two-way heterogeneity of the previous section there similarly do not always exist GYS's. These are two familiar examples of a common phenomenon. Very little has been done in such cases.

Let us fix attention on the setting where we know BBD's, if they exist, are optimum, since the discussion of the previous section shows in the setting of two-way heterogeneity that a phenomenon additional to nonexistence of fully symmetric designs may complicate matters and even lead to a choice of fairly asymmetric designs for some Φ. Since $\mathrm{tr}\,\tilde{A}_{x*}$ is the same value $(u-1)J$ (say) for all $x*$ in the BBD setting, it is tempting when no BBD exists to try to obtain a Φ-optimum design by finding a design which minimizes some simple measure Ψ of the departure of A^*_{x*} from JI_{u-1}.

It appears difficult to make this approach precise in general settings where a fully symmetric design does not exist. Among other difficulties, one can give examples where the Φ-optimum design depends on Φ. An obvious choice of Ψ, suggested by expanding a symmetric Φ about its ideal (unattainable) minimum, is $\Psi = \sum_1^{u-1}(\lambda_{x*i} - J)^2 = \mathrm{tr}(\tilde{A}_{x*})^2 - (u-1)J^2$ where the λ_{x*i} are the eigenvalues of A^*_{x*}. This was discussed by K.R. Shah (1960), but no applications were made. In a few examples we can show that Ψ is so small for some near-symmetric design $x*$, that $x*$ is A-, D-, or E-optimum, but results here are very fragmentary.

The only proof of optimality through direct comparison of the values $\Phi(A_{x*})$ is due to Takeuchi (1961), who proved A-

and E-optimality for certain PBIBD's in some of the settings where no BIBD exists.

B. *Relation of approximate to exact theory when* $\mathcal{X}^* = \mathcal{X}^N$. The practical importance of the continuous theory is that, when N is large, an approximate Φ-optimum design ξ^* can be implemented in terms of an exact design ξ_N (in Ξ_N), close to ξ^*, and consequently close to being exactly Φ-optimum if Φ is smooth. To make this precise with brevity, consider ξ^* to be Φ-optimum with finite support S; such a ξ^* always exists, although a prescription like that which follows can also be given for other ξ^*. If $\Phi(M(\xi))$ for ξ with support S, considered as a function of the values $\xi(x)$ for x in S, is twice continuously differentiable in a neighborhood of ξ^*, then

$$\Phi(M(\xi)) = \Phi(M(\xi^*)) + O(\max_{x \in S} |\xi(x)-\xi^*(x)|^2) \quad .$$

Consequently, if ξ_N is chosen in Ξ_N to minimize $\max_{x \in S} |\xi(x)-\xi^*(x)|$, we have $\Phi(M(\xi_N))/\Phi(M(\xi^*)) = 1 + O(N^{-2})$. This is the situation for A- or D-optimality; for E-optimality or G-optimality ($\Phi(M(\xi)) = \max_{x \in \mathcal{X}} (f(x), f(x)M^{-1}(\xi))$), we obtain $1 + O(N^{-1})$ in the worst cases.

There remains a possibility that the ξ_N constructed as above, while typically *not an approximate* Φ*-optimum design* if $\xi_N \neq \xi^*$, *is nevertheless* Φ*-optimum in the exact theory.* This result is too much to hope for in general, and in fact one of the motivations for considering the approximate theory is the common occurrence of problems where there is a fine structure that makes the support of the exactly Φ-optimum ξ_N' from Ξ_N depend on N. A remarkable result of

Salaevskii is that, for the criterion of D-optimality in estimating all parameters in univariate polynomial regression of degree $k-1$ on an interval, where ξ^* is the well known Guest-Hoel design, *the* ξ_N *of the previous paragraph is exactly* D-*optimum for* N *sufficiently large!* Some special results for small N have been obtained by Granovskii.

Note that, in this last example, $\xi_N \neq \xi^*$ and $\det M(\xi_N) < \det M(\xi^*)$ unless k divides N. Thus, for cubic regression $(k = 4)$ on $[-1,1]$ with $N = 5$, the measure ξ^* assigns measure 1/4 to each of the points ± 1, $\pm 1/2$, while $5\xi_5$ puts two observations at any one of these points (it doesn't matter which one) and one observation at each of the other three. Thus, ξ_5 lacks symmetry in its weights. This brings us back to the role of symmetry: since the development of the first paragraph of Section 2 implied that there was a symmetric D-optimum *approximate* ξ^* in this setting, it is surely tempting to seek an exactly D-optimum design among the symmetric designs $5\xi_5''$ which assign one observation to each of 5 points $0, \pm b_1, \pm b_2$. (It is a common error to suppose designs on more than 4 points can be eliminated by invoking the moment-space result which applies to the approximate theory.) But there is nothing in the development of Section 5 to imply that this will succeed, and indeed the best symmetric design is inferior to ξ_5.

The determination of general conditions on χ, f, Φ which imply exact Φ-optimality for some symmetric design, or which which imply it for ξ_N, is an outstanding problem in exact design theory.

References

1. Box, G.E.P. and Draper, N.R., (1959). "A basis for the selection of a response surface design". *JASA*, 54, 622-654.

2. Hader, R.J., Karson, M.J., and Manson, A.R. (1969). "Minimum bias estimation and experimental design for response surfaces", *Technometrics*, 11, 461-475.

3. Kiefer, J. (1958). "On the nonrandomized optimality and randomized nonoptimality of symmetrical designs" *Ann. Math. Statist.* 29, 675-699.

4. Kiefer, J. (1959). "Optimum experimental designs, *JRSS* (B), 21, 272-319.

5. Kiefer, J., (1960). "Optimum experimental designs V, with applications to systematic and rotatable designs, *Proc. Fourth Berk. Symp.* , Vol. 1, 381-405.

6. Salaevskii, O.V., (1965). "The problem of the distribution of observations in polynomial regression", *Proc. Steklov Inst.* 79, *Amer. Math. Soc. Transl.*, (1966).

7. Shah, K.R., (1960). "Optimality criteria for incomplete block designs", *Ann. Math. Statist.* 31, 791-794.

8. Takeuchi, K., (1961). "On the optimality of certain type of PBIB designs", *Rep. Stat. Appl. Res. JUSE* 8, 140-145.

SYMMETRIC BINOMIAL GROUP-TESTING WITH THREE OUTCOMES

By M. Sobel[1], S. Kumar, and S. Blumenthal[2]
University of Minnesota, University of Wisconsin-Milwaukee,
and New York University

1. *Introduction*. Consider a problem of classifying N units into one of two disjoint categories; each unit is either good or defective. A test on an individual unit classifies it as good or defective. A test on x units, for $x \geq 2$, has one of the following three outcomes: (i) all the x units are good, (ii) all the x units are defective, or (iii) there are at least one good and at least one defective unit among the x units. Each unit is assumed to represent an independent observation from a binomial population with a common known a priori probability q of being good and $p = 1-q$ of being defective. The problem is to define an efficient procedure for separating all the defective units from the good units. The objective is to minimize the expected total number of tests and the extent to which this minimum is attained is the criterion of efficiency. The related problem of maximizing the number of units classified in a fixed number of tests is considered in [4]. A classification procedure R_S for $N < \infty$ is proposed in Section 3, and a procedure R_S^{∞} for N (countably) infinite is proposed

[1]Research supported by NSF Grant GP-11021.

[2]Research supported by NSF Grant GP-23171.

in Section 9. In Section 4 we illustrate the procedure R_S by a simple numerical example. Some of the properties of R_S are investigated in Section 5. The optimal procedure R^o is investigated in Section 6, and a comparison of R^o with R_S is made in Section 7. Section 8 discusses upper bounds for the expected number of tests under the optimal procedure. Lower bounds for any procedure are also obtained using information theory and coding theory. In Section 10 we define 2 modifications R_S' and R_S'' of procedure R_S, which allow the mixing of units from different sets. They result in an increase in efficiency. Tables II and IV give the test group sizes (x-values) to be used under procedures R_S and R_S^{∞}. Table III gives the expected number of tests and the x-values for $q = .9$ and $N \leq 5$ under procedure R_S. Table V gives some comparisons for procedures R_S, R_S' and R_S'' for $q = .9$.

One application of this formulation is to testing electrical devices such as conductors (not light bulbs that give a visual result). These conductors are connected both in parallel and in series and the results for these two arrangements are obtained separately by throwing a switch. If we get current for the series configuration then all are good. If we get no current for the parallel configuration then all are defective. In the one remaining case (no current for the series configuration and current for the parallel configuration), we have at least one good unit and at least 1 defective unit. Hence for our purposes, this compound test to determine which of these three situations holds is to be regarded as a single test and we wish to minimize the expected number of such tests.

Another possible application is in the chemical analysis of several specimens where it is known a priori that each specimen contains either A or B but not both, which are two specific substances of interest. Suppose a mixture of several specimens is formed and then we split the result into 2 aliquot parts. By using reagent α, which precipitates A and does not react with B, we can detect "no A" by no precipitate in one of the 2 aliquots. Similarly, by using reagent β, which precipitates B and does not react with A, we can detect "no B" by no precipitate in the other of the 2 aliquots. "Some A and some B" is indicated if both reagents cause precipitation. Regarding this compound test as a single test, we want to classify the specimens as containing A or containing B in the smallest expected number of tests.

2. *Preliminaries*. A set of units S_B will be called a binomial set or B-type set if, given the past history of testing, the units in this set can be represented by independent binomial random variables with probability q and $p = 1-q$ of being good and defective, respectively. The initial set with N units is a B-type set denoted by $S_B(N)$.

A set of units of size $m \geq 2$ will be called of DG-type and denoted by $S_{DG}(m)$ if it is known to contain at least one defective unit and at least one good unit. Then, for a set S of size $m \geq 2$, the conditional probability that there are i good units in S given $S = S_{DG}(m)$ is

$$(2.1) \qquad P\{i \mid S_{DG}(m)\} = \frac{\binom{m}{i} q^i p^{m-i}}{1 - p^m - q^m}, \quad i = 1, 2, \ldots, m-1 \quad .$$

We use x for the size of the sampled subset and let $X(Y)$

denote the random number of good (defective) units in the subset of size x. Then the probability that a randomly chosen proper subset of fixed size $x(1 \leq x < m)$, taken from $S_{DG}(m)$ with $m \geq 2$, has only good units is given by

$$\text{(2.2)} \qquad P\{X = x | S_{DG}(m), x\} = \sum_{i=x}^{m-1} \frac{\binom{i}{x}}{\binom{m}{x}} \frac{\binom{m}{i} q^i p^{m-i}}{1 - p^m - q^m} = \frac{q^x(1-q^{m-x})}{1 - p^m - q^m}.$$

Similarly, the probability that a randomly chosen proper subset of fixed size $x(1 \leq x < m)$, taken from $S_{DG}(m)$ with $m \geq 2$, has only defective units is given by

$$\text{(2.3)} \qquad P\{Y = x | S_{DG}(m), x\} = \frac{p^x(1-p^{m-x})}{1 - p^m - q^m} .$$

Hence the probability that a randomly chosen proper subset of size $x(1 \leq x < m)$, taken from $S_{DG}(m)$ with $m \geq 2$, is also of DG-type (i.e., that $X \geq 1$ and $Y \geq 1$) is easily shown to be

$$\text{(2.4)} \qquad P\{X \geq 1, Y \geq 1 | S_{DG}(m), x\} = \frac{1 - p^x - q^x}{1 - p^m - q^m} .$$

A set of units $S = S_D$ will be called of D-type (resp., of G-type and written $S = S_G$) if it is known to contain at least one defective unit (resp., at least one good unit). Then for a set S of size $m \geq 2$ the conditional probability that there are i good units, given that $S = S_D(m)$, is

$$\text{(2.5)} \qquad P\{i | S_D(m)\} = \frac{\binom{m}{i} q^i p^{m-i}}{1 - q^m}, \quad i = 0,1,\ldots, m-1 .$$

The probability that a randomly chosen subset of fixed size $x(1 \leq x \leq m)$, taken from $S_D(m)$ with $m \geq 2$, contains only good units is

(2.6) $$P\{X = x|S_D(m),x\} = \sum_{i=x}^{m-1} \frac{\binom{i}{x}}{\binom{m}{x}} \frac{\binom{m}{i}q^i p^{m-i}}{1 - q^m} = \frac{q^x(1-q^{m-x})}{1 - q^m}.$$

The probability that a randomly chosen subset of fixed size $x(1 \leq x \leq m)$, taken from $S_D(m)$ with $m \geq 2$ contains only defective units is

(2.7) $$P\{Y = x|S_D(m),x\} = \sum_{i=0}^{m-x} \frac{\binom{m-i}{x}}{\binom{m}{x}} \frac{\binom{m}{i}q^i p^{m-i}}{1 - q^m} = \frac{p^x}{1 - q^m}.$$

Hence the probability that a randomly chosen proper subset of size $x(1 \leq x \leq m)$, taken from $S_D(m)$ with $m \geq 2$, is a set of DG-type is easily shown to be

(2.8) $$P\{X \geq 1,\ Y \geq 1|S_D(m),x\} = \frac{1 - p^x - p^x}{1 - q^m}.$$

Similarly, the probability that a randomly chosen subset of fixed size $x(1 \leq x \leq m)$, taken from $S_G(m)$ with $m \geq 2$, contains only good units, only defective units, and at least one of each, respectively, is

(2.9) $$P\{X = x|S_G(m),x\} = \frac{q^x}{1 - p^m},$$

(2.10) $$P\{Y = x|S_G(m),x\} = \frac{p^x(1-p^{m-x})}{1 - p^m},$$

(2.11) $$P\{X \geq 1,\ Y \geq 1|S_G(m),x\} = \frac{1 - p^x - q^x}{1 - p^m}.$$

We will need the following

Lemma 1. *Given a set* S *equal to one of the three types* $S_D(m)$ *or* $S_G(m)$ *or* $S_{DG}(m)$ *of size* $m \geq 2$ *and given that a randomly chosen subset of size* $x(2 \leq x \leq m)$ *is of* DG-type, *then the posterior distribution associated with the remaining* m-x *units is binomial, i.e., each unit is an independent Bernoulli chance variable with probability* p *(respectively,* q*) of being defective (respectively, good).*

The proof of lemma 1 is straightforward and is omitted. It appears in an early version [5] of this paper.

We state another lemma and omit its proof because of its similarity to the proof of lemma 1 in [6] and the lemma in [2].

Lemma 2. *Given a set* $S_D(m)$ *(respectively,* $S_G(m)$*) of size* $m \geq 2$ *and given that a randomly chosen subset of size* x *contains only defective units (respectively, only good units), then the posterior distribution associated with the remaining* m-x *units is binomial, i.e., each unit is an independent Bernoulli chance variable with probability* p *(respectively,* q*) of being defective (respectively, good).*

3. The Classification Procedure R_S.

A. *Notation.*

Under procedure R_s we always have at most 2 types of sets present and (if there are two) one of these is an S_B set. If there are two sets present say, $S_B(n-m)$ and $S_j(m)$ for j = D, G or DG, then the next test group is always taken from the set $S_j(m)$ without mixing. Let DG(m,n) denote the expected number of additional group-tests required to classify n units if the procedure R_S is used starting with a DG-situation with one set $S_{DG}(m)$ of size m and the other set $S_B(n-m)$ of size n-m. Similarly, D(m,n) (respectively, G(m,n)) will be used to denote the expected number of additional group-tests required, if the procedure R_S is used, starting with a D (respectively, G) situation with one set $S_D(m)$ (respectively, $S_G(m)$) of size m and the other set $S_B(n-m)$ of size n-m.

For the special case when $m = 0$ we shall use the notation $B(n)$ instead of $DG(0,n)$, $D(0,n)$ and $G(0,n)$. The situation for the unclassified units is referred to as a DG-situation or a D-situation or a G-situation, if $m \geq 2$, according as we have a DG-set or a D-set or a G-set, respectively, and as a B-situation if $m = 0$. The case when $m = 1$ is excluded, since the D or G-situation can be immediately changed into a B-situation by classifying that unit without further testing; this property forms one of our boundary conditions below.

B. *Recursion Formulas Defining Procedure* R_S.

If $n = 1$ and we have a B-situation, the testing procedure is trivial, i.e., we test this unit individually; hence we need only give the recursion formulas for $n \geq 2$.

For any B-situation and any set $S_B(n)$ with $n \geq 2$, we take a sample of size $x(1 \leq x \leq n)$ for testing from this set and obtain

$$(3.1) \qquad B(n) = 1 + \min_{1 \leq x \leq n} \{(p^x+q^x)B(n-x) + (1-p^x-q^x)DG(x,n)\}.$$

The expression $DG(1,n)$ never arises since for $x = 1$ the coefficient is zero. Moreover, it is shown below that the value $x = 1$ is used only if we have a B-situation with one unit left to be classified.

For any DG-situation with $3 \leq m \leq n$, we take a sample of size $x(1 \leq x \leq m-1)$ from $S_{DG}(m)$ for testing and obtain (using lemma 1)

$$(3.2)\quad DG(m,n) = 1 + \min_{1\le x<m} \left\{ \frac{q^x(1-q^{m-x})}{1-p^m-q^m} D(m-x,n-x) + \frac{p^x(1-p^{m-x})}{1-p^m-q^m} G(m-x,n-x) + \left(\frac{1-p^x-q^x}{1-p^m-q^m}\right) DG(x,n) \right\} .$$

For any D-situation with $2 \le m \le n$, we take a sample of size $x(1 \le x \le m)$ from $S_D(m)$ for testing and obtain (using lemmas 1 and 2)

$$(3.3)\quad D(m,n) = 1 + \min_{1\le x\le m} \left\{ \left(\frac{q^x(1-q^{m-x})}{1-q^m}\right) D(m-x,n-x) + \left(\frac{p^x}{1-q^m}\right) B(n-x) + \left(\frac{1-p^x-q^x}{1-q^m}\right) DG(x,n) \right\} .$$

Similarly, for any G-situation with $2 \le m \le n$, we take a sample of size $x(1 \le x \le m)$ from $S_G(m)$ for testing and obtain (using lemmas 1 and 2)

$$(3.4)\quad G(m,n) = 1 + \min_{1\le x\le m} \left\{ \frac{p^x(1-p^{m-x})}{1-p^m} G(m-x,n-x) + \left(\frac{q^x}{1-p^m}\right) B(n-x) + \left(\frac{1-p^x-q^x}{1-p^m}\right) DG(x,n) \right\} .$$

The boundary conditions (that hold for all q) are:

$$(3.5)\quad B(0) = 0 ,$$

$$(3.6)\quad B(1) = 1 ,$$

$$(3.7)\quad DG(2,n) = 1 + B(n-2) \quad \text{for all } n \ge 2,$$

$$(3.8)\quad D(1,n) = G(1,n) = B(n-1) \quad \text{for all } n \ge 1 .$$

It is surmised that for $m \ge 3$ the minimum is never

attained at $x = 1$ in (3.2), but this has not been proved. (The proof for $m = 3$ is not difficult and we wish to thank the referee for furnishing an additional proof for $m = 3$; the general case is still not proved.) Note that $x = m$ is allowed in (3.3) and (3.4) but not in (3.2), where it provides no new information.

4. *Illustration of the procedure* R_S. In the following figure the test result that all x units are good (respectively, defective) is denoted by G(respectively, D) and the outcome of DG-type is denoted by DG. The symbol E_j $(j = 1,2,\ldots,2^N)$ denotes an endpoint of the entire experiment.

We illustrate the use of R_S with $N = 4$ and $q = .9$. From Table II we observe that the first test group is of size $x = 4$. If the test on these four units shows that all units are good or all units are defective, the experiment is over; if this group of 4 units turns out to be of DG-type, the next test group is of size $x = 2$ (cf. Table II). If the test on these two units shows that both of these are good (respectively, defective), we have a D-type (respectively, G-type) set of size 2 and the next test group will come from this group. If the test on these two units shows that the pair is of DG-type, then we test one of these two in the next test. The complete tree with all 16 end points is shown in Figure 1.

The expected number of tests is $B(4) = 1.9828$. Without affecting the properties of the procedure R_S, it is assumed that the order of the units is randomized only once at the outset; units tested are then taken in that order. The experiment terminates after one test if all the units are

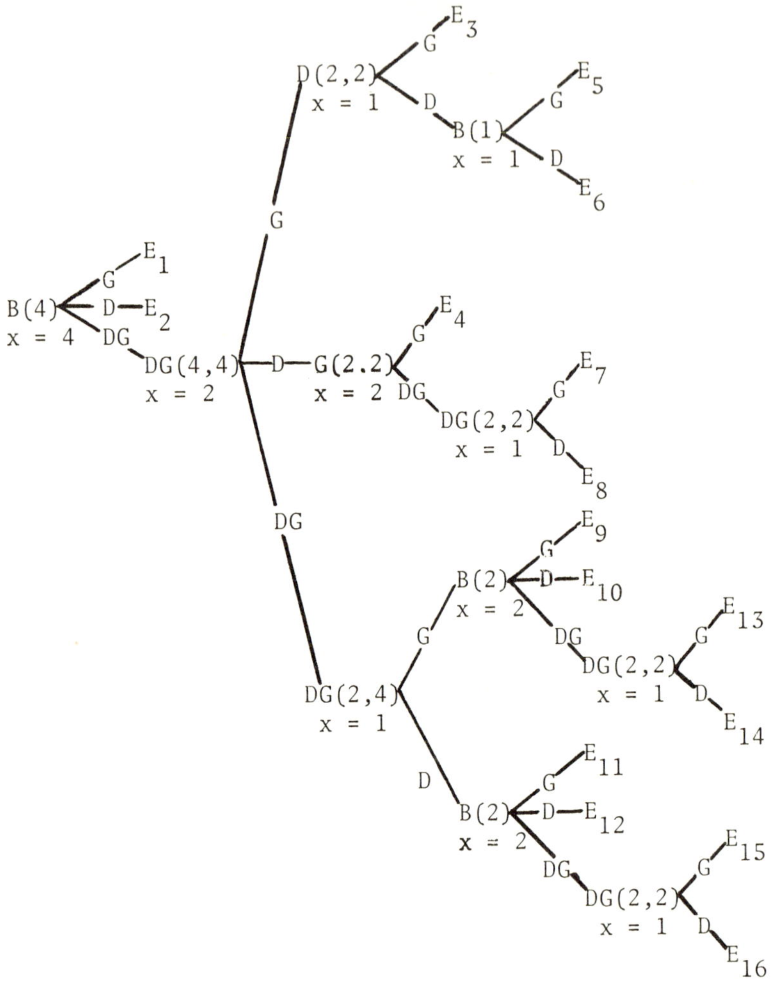

Figure 1: *The group test under procedure* R_S *for* $N = 4$ *and* $q = .9$.

good or all the units are defective; the probability of this event is $p^4 + q^4 = .6562$. The number of tests required is 5 if and only if the first two units and the last two units are both of DG-type; the probability of this event is easily seen to be $4p^2q^2 = .0324$. The probability function for the number of tests T required under R_S when $q = .5(.1)1.0$ and $N = 4$ is given below:

Table 1: Probability Function of T under Procedure R_S for $q = .5(.1)1.0$.

q \ T→	1	2	3	4	5	$E\{T\|R_S\}$	$\sigma\{T\|R_S\}$
.5	0	.2500	.5000	.2500	0	3.0000	.7071
.6	0	.2704	.4992	.2304	0	2.9600	.7065
.7	0	.3364	.4872	.1764	0	2.8400	.6979
.8	0	.4624	.4352	.1024	0	2.6400	.6596
.9	.6562	0	.0810	.2304	.0324	1.9828	1.3965
1.0	1	0	0	0	0	1	0

For $q = .9$ we find that $E\{T\} = 1.9828$ and $\sigma(T) = 1.3965$. If we test units one-at-a-time (call this R_0), it is easily seen that $E\{T|R_0\} = 4$. Thus in our example we have reduced $E\{T\}$ to about 50% of the value under R_0.

5. *Properties of the procedure* R_S. Let $B(n;q)$ denote the $B(n)$-value under q.

Property 1.

$$B(n;q) = B(n; 1-q).$$

The proof depends on symmetry and is omitted (cf [5]).

Property 2.

The integer x that achieves the minimization in the right side of (3.3) for any q also achieves the minimization in the right side of (3.4) if we replace q by $1 - q$. Furthermore, the value of $D(m,n)$ for any q is identical with $G(m,n)$, if q is replaced by $1 - q$.

Property 3.

It is conjectured that $B(n;q)$ has its maximum at $q=1/2$ for all n. (Heuristically, it is clear that $p = q = 1/2$ is the most difficult case for classifying units in our symmetric group-testing problem, but this has not been proved.)

Property 4.

In the $D(2,n)$-situation with $q \geq 1/2$ and any n, the minimization in (3.3) is achieved by taking $x = 1$.

Proof:

We rewrite (3.3) as

$$D(2,n) = 1 + \operatorname*{Min}_{1 \leq x \leq 2} \left\{ \left(\frac{q^x(1-q^{2-x})}{1 - q^2}\right) D(2-x,n-x) + \left(\frac{p^x}{1-q^2}\right) B(n-x) + \left(\frac{1 - p^x - q^x}{1 - q^2}\right) DG(x,n) \right\}. \tag{5.1}$$

Corresponding to $x = 1$, the right side of (5.1) is equal to

$$1 + \left(\frac{pq}{1-q^2}\right) D(1,n-1) + \frac{p}{1-q^2} B(n-1) \leq 1 + B(n-2) + \frac{p}{1-q^2} \tag{5.2}$$

by using (3.8) and the fact that $B(n-1) \leq 1 + B(n-2)$. Corresponding to $x = 2$, the right side of (5.1) is equal to

$$1 + B(n-2) + \frac{1-p^2-q^2}{1-q^2} = 1 + B(n-2) + \frac{2pq}{1-q^2} \tag{5.3}$$

by using (3.7). Clearly the right side of (5.2) $\leq$ (5.3) for $q \geq 1/2$. Hence the left side of (5.2) $\leq$ (5.3) for $q \geq 1/2$. Hence $x = 1$ is preferable to $x = 2$ in the $D(2,n)$-situation for $q \geq 1/2$.

6. *Properties of the optimal non-mixing procedure* R_S *and the optimal procedure* R^o. A procedure R^o is called optimal among all procedures if for every positive starting

integer N the expected number of tests for the classification of N units using R^o is less than or equal to the expected number of tests under any other procedure. The procedure R_S is optimal among non-mixing procedures. We discuss some properties of R_S and R^o.

Theorem 1. *Under procedure* R_S *and* R^o, *a subset of size* $x = 1$ *is never used for a* B(n)*-situation with* $n \geq 2$.

Proof: The stragegy $x = 1$ reduces the B(n)-situation with $n \geq 2$ immediately to a B(n-1)-situation with $n-1 \geq 1$. If we take $x = 1$ twice, then we note by direct computation that $x = 2$ for B(n) gives the better result $1 + 2pq < 2$ for all q. If we take $x = 1$ for B(n) and the optimal $x = x_0 \geq 2$ for B(n-1) then we can find a better procedure by putting aside one unit of the original n and using at the outset the procedure for B(n-1), which starts with $x = x_0$. If we reach a B(1)-situation, then we bring out the unit put aside and change to a B(2)-situation. If we do not reach a B(1)-situation, then the unit put aside is tested separately at the end. This procedure is better since we reduce the expected number of tests if we reach B(1) and do not increase it in any case.

Corollary. *For* $n \geq 2$ *we can write* $2 \leq x \leq n$ *in the right side of* (3.1).

The next theorem is similar to one proved by Ungar [10]. Let $\hat{R}$ denote any non-mixing procedure, i.e., one for which any group tested is a subset of a B(binomial) set or a G(good) set or a D(defective) set or a proper subset of a DG (mixed) set. Let $B(n|\hat{R})$ denote the expected number of group tests required for the B(n)-situation under any non-mixing procedure $\hat{R}$. We prove that for any such procedure there is an interval, symmetric about 1/2, where we never test more than 2 units. We conjecture that the same result holds for any "reasonable" procedure (see Ungar [10]), but this has not been shown.

Theorem 2. *Under procedure* $\hat{R}$ *(with* n *units at the outset) there is a symmetric interval about* $q = 1/2$ *for which we can pair off the* n *units in groups of size* 2 *(with possibly one group of size one) and treat each group separately, i.e., for* $(1/2)(1 - \frac{1}{\sqrt{5}}) < q < (1/2)(1 + \frac{1}{\sqrt{5}})$,

$$(6.1) \qquad B(n|\hat{R}) = \begin{cases} m(1+2pq) & \textit{if } n = 2m \textit{ is even} \\ 1+m(1+2pq) & \textit{if } n = 2m+1 \textit{ is odd.} \end{cases}$$

Proof: We show that for q in the range $(\frac{1}{2} - \frac{\sqrt{5}}{10}, \frac{1}{2} + \frac{\sqrt{5}}{10})$ the testing procedure cannot be optimal with $x > 2$ at any stage of testing.

We can represent a group-testing procedure by a tree in the following manner. The set S_0 on the top represents the set to be tested first. Sets S_1, S_2, S_3 represent the set to be tested next if S_0 turns out to be all good units, all defective units, or a set of DG-type, respectively. This gives a representation of the procedure (cf. Figure 2).

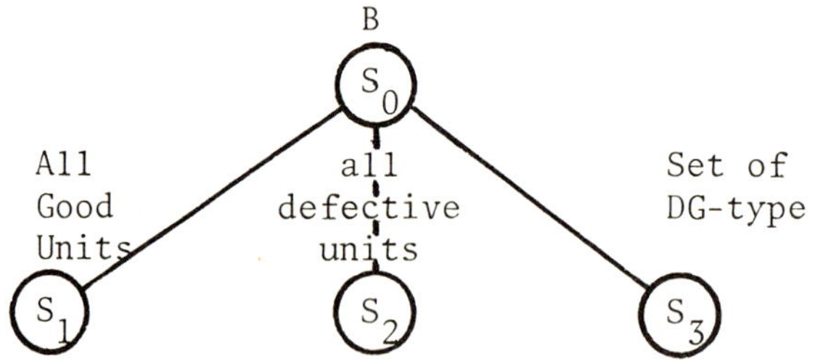

Figure 2.

Two sets are said to "occur on the same branch of the tree" if one of them can be reached from the other by moving only downwards along one of the connecting paths.

A group testing procedure is called "reasonable" if no test is used to obtain information that is already available. No reasonable procedure adds elements which have already been identified to a group which is to be tested. Any procedure which is not reasonable can be made reasonable by removing elements and skipping unnecessary tests. These changes do not increase the number of tests needed for the classification of any sample.

The theorem is proved by considering an arbitrary given (or old) procedure (that does not work with at most pairs of units) and modifying it so that the expected number of tests under the new modified procedure is less than that under the given (or old) procedure, whenever

$$.276\ldots = 1/2 - \frac{\sqrt{5}}{10} < q < 1/2 + \frac{\sqrt{5}}{10} = .724\ \ldots.$$

We start with an arbitrary given procedure that tests a set S of size $x \geq 3$ units at some branch point B(*not necessarily a binomial situation*) and all the testing points below B(if there are any below B) require the units to be tested in groups of size at most two. Now we introduce a new plan -- a modification of the given procedure. Denote by T the two-element set occurring immediately below S on the DG branch. (By an argument like that of Theorem 1, it is clear that this first test should not be on a single element.) Under the modified procedure, we test T first (instead of S) and then S - T. There are several possibilities:

(i) For $x \geq 4$ suppose T is DG and S - T is DG. We proceed as we would have under the old procedure after observing that S is DG and T is DG. We are ignoring some additional information available under the new plan and there is no increase in the number of tests used.

(ii) T is DG and S - T is all good (or all defective). The new plan uses 3 tests (one element of T is tested), while the old plan tests S(DG), T(DG) and then needs at least $[\frac{x - 1}{2}]$ tests on the (x - 2) elements of (S - T) and one test on an element of T. The net saving is at least $[\frac{x - 1}{2}]$ tests; i.e., the integer part of $\frac{x-1}{2}$.

(iii) For $x \geq 4$ suppose T is all good (or all defective) and S - T is DG. Proceed as the old plan would after finding that S is DG and T is good (or defective), ignoring the additional information available under the new plan. No increase occurs in the number of tests.

(iv) For $x \geq 4$ suppose T is all good (or all defective) and S - T is all defective (or all good). The new plan uses two tests, while the old plan uses two plus at least $[\frac{x - 1}{2}]$ tests on the remaining (x - 2) elements of S - T. For x = 3 there is no change in the number of tests.

(v) T is all good (or all defective) and S - T is all good (or all defective). In this case, the new plan uses one more test than the old would have.

We assume that the test set S satisfies the following conditions:

(a) If all elements of S *can* be good (respectively, defective), it is also possible for all elements of S - T to be good (respectively, defective) while one or both elements of T are defective (respectively, good) without affecting prior test results or the choice of strategy beyond this branch point.

(b) If all elements of S can be good (respectively, defective), it is also possible for all elements of S - T to be defective (respectively, good) while one or both elements of T are good (respectively, defective) without affecting prior test results or the choice of strategy beyond this branch point.

Below, we shall study the case where both all good and all defective sets are possible for S. The case where all good (defective) but not all defective (good) can occur, while (a) and (b) are satisfied, follows in a similar manner.

Let Q be the probability of a sample where S is all good. A sample with one chosen element of T changed has probability $(\frac{p}{q})Q$, and with both elements changed, $(\frac{p}{q})^2Q$. An all bad sample has probability $(\frac{p}{q})^xQ$, and S - T bad, with only the first element of T good: $(\frac{p}{q})^{x-1}Q$, and with S - T bad, both elements of T good: $(\frac{p}{q})^{x-2}Q$. Factoring out $(\frac{Q}{q^x})$, we note that each of the above probabilities then resembles a binomial probability and in the sequel we shall ignore this common, positive factor $(\frac{Q}{q^x})$. Consider first the case x = 3. Here, case (iv) results in no savings, but case (ii) gives a saving of one test while case (v) gives a loss of one test for the new plan, and the expected saving is:

$$(6.2) \qquad 2(pq^2 + p^2q) - (p^3 + q^3) = 2pq - (1 - 3pq^2 - 3p^2q)$$
$$= 5pq - 1$$

which is positive for q in the given range.

Next, consider x = 4. Considering case (iv) also, we have expected savings of

(6.3) $$2pq(p^2 + q^2) + 2p^2q^2 - (p^4 + q^4)$$

which reduces to

(6.4) $$6(pq) - 4(pq)^2 - 1 \ .$$

This is positive for $(pq) > (1/2)[1 - (\sqrt{5}/3)]$ which in turn gives a wider interval for q than stated above.

Finally consider $x > 4$. We ignore the saving possible in case (iv). Hence we have an expected saving of at least

(6.5) $$2[\frac{x - 1}{2}]pq(p^{x-2} + q^{x-2}) - (p^x + q^x) \quad .$$

Using $p^x + q^x = p^{x-1} + q^{x-1} - pq(p^{x-2} + q^{x-2})$ we obtain

(6.6) $$(2[\frac{x - 1}{2}] + 1)pq(p^{x-2} + q^{x-2}) - (p^{x-1} + q^{x-1}).$$

Since $(p^{x-2} + q^{x-2}) > (p^{x-1} + q^{x-1})$, the expected saving is positive if

(6.7) $$(2[\frac{x - 1}{2}] + 1)pq - 1 > 0 \quad \text{or} \quad pq > 1/(2[\frac{x - 1}{2}] + 1).$$

Since $(2[\frac{x - 1}{2}] + 1) \geq 5$ for $x \geq 5$, the saving is positive in an interval which at least contains the desired interval.

For a non-mixing procedure the group S appearing at the branch point B can be one of several types: Binomial, Good, Defective, or a subset of one of these or a subset of a DG group. By the definition of these groups it is clear that conditions a) and b) above are satisfied. Formula (6.1) is easily obtained by noticing that the number of pairs is m, and the expected number of tests per pair is $1 + 2pq$. This completes the proof of Theorem 2.

Remark 1: As already noted, the above does not prove that Theorem 2 holds for all procedures although we conjecture that the result is true in general. One example of a mixing procedure for $N = 6$ that is not covered by the above proof is the following: Label the units a,b,c,d,e,f. Test the pairs (a,b), (c,d) and (e,f). If exactly one pair is DG, test one of its elements. If exactly two pairs are DG, test a pair consisting of one element from each; then, if necessary, test one of this pair. If all three pairs are DG, test the triplet (a,c,e) followed, if necessary, by the tests (a,c), (c,e), (e). In the q-range indicated in Theorem 2, this can be improved upon by skipping the triplet test and going directly to (a,c). Here the result of Theorem 2 holds but the proof does not, since any change in the nature of a or c or e changes prior test results, so that the branch point B (the triplet test in this case) is no longer reached.

Remark 2: For procedures that allow mixing the proof of Theorem 2 shows that, for any branch point B satisfying a) and b) above, all subsequent tests will be done with at most 2 units per test; the optimal procedures for $N = 3$ and 4 in the Appendix shows that the units will not necessarily be paired off with pairs treated independently of one another.

7. *Comparison of* R_S *and* $\hat{R}$. For given q, the two procedures R and R' are said to be equivalent if $B(n|R) = B(n|R')$ for every n. We prove the

Theorem. *For* q *such that* $\frac{1}{2} - \frac{\sqrt{5}}{10} < q < \frac{1}{2} + \frac{\sqrt{5}}{10}$, R_s *and* $\hat{R}$ *are equivalent.*

Proof: Let $n = 2m$. Under R_S, from (3.1), we have by using $x = 2$

$$
\begin{aligned}
B(n|R_S) &= 1 + \operatorname*{Min}_{2 \le x \le n} \{(p^x+q^x)B(n-x)+(1-p^x-q^x)DG(x,n)\} \\
&\le 1+(p^2+q^2)B(n-2)+(1-p^2-q^2)DG(2,n) \qquad (7.1)\\
&= 1 + 2pq + B(n-2) \\
&\le m(1 + 2pq) \; .
\end{aligned}
$$

We have already shown that for $\frac{1}{2} - \frac{\sqrt{5}}{10} < q < \frac{1}{2} + \frac{\sqrt{5}}{10}$

$$B(n|\hat{R}) = m(1 + 2pq) \; . \tag{7.2}$$

Combining (7.1) and (7.2), we get

$$B(n|R_S) \le B(n|\hat{R}) \quad . \tag{7.3}$$

But the reverse inequality in (7.3) is always true. Hence R_S and $\hat{R}$ are equivalent if $n = 2m$ and $\frac{1}{2} - \frac{\sqrt{5}}{10} < q < \frac{1}{2} + \frac{\sqrt{5}}{10}$. The case of odd n is treated similarly.

8. *Bounds for group-testing procedures.* In this section we find an upper bound for the expected number of tests under the optimal group-testing procedure R^o. Also using information theory and coding theory we obtain lower bounds for the expected number of tests under any procedure R.

8a. *Upper bound for the optimal group-testing procedure* R^o. If we have two units, the optimal procedure is to test two units as a group first and, if necessary, then test a single unit. Thus

$$B(2|R^o) = 2 - p^2 - q^2 = 1 + 2pq. \tag{8.1}$$

If $n = 2m$, divide these units into subgroups of size 2 and use the optimal procedure for each subgroup. If $n = 2m+1$, divide these units into m subgroups of size 2 and one subgroup of size one. Let $H(n)$ be the expected number of tests under this scheme. Then

$$(8.2) \quad B(n|R^o) \le H(n) = \begin{cases} \frac{n}{2}(1 + 2pq) & \text{if } n \text{ is even} \\ 1+(\frac{n-1}{2})(1+2pq) & \text{if } n \text{ is odd.} \end{cases}$$

Remark. Since $pq \le \frac{1}{4}$, we observe that

$$(8.3) \qquad B(n|R^o) \le \begin{cases} 3n/4 & \text{if } n \text{ is even} \\ (3n+1)/4 & \text{if } n \text{ is odd.} \end{cases}$$

8b. *Lower bound for any procedure from information theory.* Let $B(n|R)$ denote the expected number of group-tests needed to classify n units under any procedure R for our problem. Then we have the following

Theorem.

$$B(n|R) \ge - n(p \log_3 p + q \log_3 q).$$

We omit its proof because it is similar to the proof of similar theorems in [2] and [7].

8c. *Lower bound for any procedure from coding theory.* Every group-testing procedure can be written as a 3-ary code; we arbitrarily associate 0(respectively, 1) with the test result that all units in test-group are good (respectively, defective) and 2 with the result that the test group is of DG-type. Representation of group-testing procedures by codes is discussed in [3], [7], [8] and [9]. Huffman [1] has given a procedure for the construction of a 3-ary code with the smallest expected word length. We use the Huffman algorithm for obtaining a lower bound on the expected number of tests under any procedure. The procedure can be illustrated with $N = 3$ and $q = .7$.

There are $2^N = 2^3 = 8$ states of nature (or possible subsets of good units). First we order the probabilities for various states of nature in decreasing order. Add the two lowest, reorder the resulting set. At subsequent steps we add the *three* smallest probabilities and reorder again, etc. Original probabilities are written in column 1. The totals obtained from columns j and to the left of j are written in column j + 1. The sum of the totals showing in columns 2, 3,... gives the cost of the Huffman code. For this illustration the Huffman cost is 1.747. The exact expected number of tests under the optimal procedure for this example is 2.09. (Cf. A(2) in the appendix).

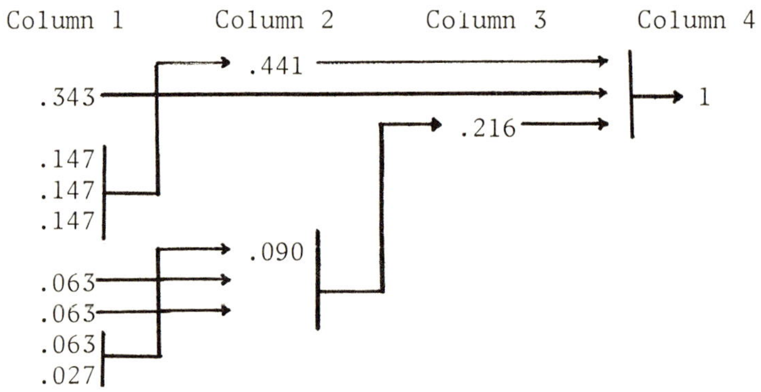

Figure 3: Scheme for obtaining the Huffman cost for procedure R_S ($N = 3$, $q = .7$).

For a group-test the number of rows in the first column of the Huffman algorithm is 2^N. This indicates that not all 3-ary codes can be interpreted as group-test codes. A 3-ary code has to satisfy several conditions to be a group-test code. A detailed discussion for the relation between group-test codes for binomial group-testing problem and binary code is given in [8] and [9]. We can improve on the lower bound obtained by the Huffman algorithm. Actually, we use a modified Huffman procedure to construct a code in which 3 items from column 1 are never combined. This modification is justified by the fact that the experiment does not terminate if the test-group shows to be DG-type. We shall illustrate this procedure with N = 3 and q = .7. First we order in column 1 the probabilities for various states of nature in decreasing order. Add the two lowest, reorder the resulting set subject to the condition that the lowest three uncombined numbers contain the result obtained in the 1st step. At the subsequent steps we add the lowest three of the uncombined numbers and reorder subject to the condition mentioned earlier. The sum of the totals showing in columns 2, 3,... (cf. Figure 4) gives the cost of the modified code. It is necessary for the group-testing code to have the structure of the modified code but not vice-versa. For this illustration the cost of the modified code is 1.816. It is obtained by adding the totals obtained after each step. These totals are shown in the various columns below.

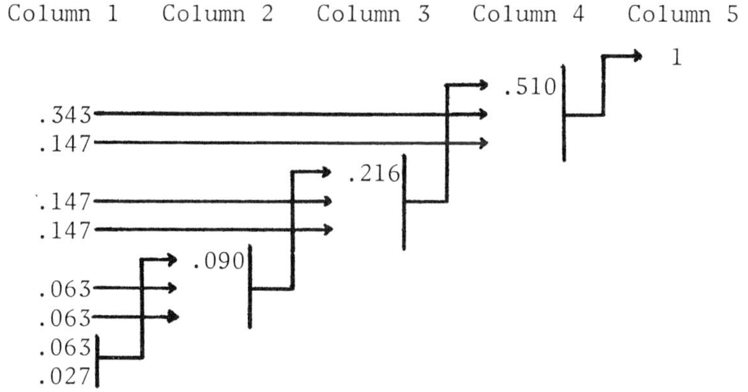

Figure 4: Huffman cost without combining 3 items from Column 1 (N = 3, q = .7).

This modification yields a higher value that is also a lower bound for any group-testing procedure. For this illustration the lower bound is increased by 1.816 - 1.747 = .069.

9. *Procedure* R_S^{∞} *for the infinite population* ($N = \infty$) *problem*. For convenience, we assume that the units are ordered at the outset and the units tested are then taken in that order. Thus no unit is classified before any predecessor so that the procedure R_S^{∞} has the "first come-first served" property. For the case $N = \infty$ we define the procedure R_S^{∞} so that it minimizes the expected number of tests per unit classified. Let $F_j(x)$ denote the expected number of tests required to get from a j-situation (j = B, D, G or DG) to the next binomial situation, if we start with a test group of size x. If we are in a B-situation, we take a sample of size x for testing. The size x is determined by the fact that the procedure minimizes the expected number of tests per expected unit classified. (Note that we use the ratio of expectations in (9.11) below and not the expected value of the ratio.) For $j = B$ we have

$$F_B(x) = 1 + (1-p^x - q^x)F_{DG}(x) = 1 + pqF^*_{DG}(x) \tag{9.1}$$

where, by definition, for (9.1) and below we use

$$F^*_{DG}(x) = \left(\frac{1-p^x-q^x}{pq}\right)F_{DG}(x), \quad F^*_D(m) = \left(\frac{1-q^m}{1-q}\right)F_D(m) \quad \text{and} \tag{9.2}$$

$$F^*_G(m) = \left(\frac{1-p^m}{1-p}\right)F_G(m) \quad .$$

For any DG-situation with $m \geq 3$, we take a sample of size x ($1 \leq x \leq m-1$) from $S_{DG}(m)$ for testing and obtain

$$F_{DG}(m) = 1 + \underset{1\le x<m}{\text{Min}} \left\{\frac{q^x(1-q^{m-x})}{1-p^m-q^m} F_D(m-x) + \frac{p^x(1-p^{m-x})}{1-p^m-q^m} F_G(m-x) + \left(\frac{1-p^x-q^x}{1-p^m-q^m}\right) F_{DG}(x)\right\} \tag{9.3}$$

or, equivalently,

$$F^*_{DG}(m) = \frac{1-p^m-q^m}{pq} + \underset{1\le x<m}{\text{Min}} \{q^{x-1}F^*_D(m-x) + p^{x-1}F^*_G(m-x) + F^*_{DG}(x)\} . \tag{9.4}$$

For any D-situation with $m \geq 2$, we take a sample of size x $(1 \leq x \leq m)$ from $S_D(m)$ for testing and obtain

$$F_D(m) = 1 + \underset{1\le x\le m}{\text{Min}} \left\{\frac{q^x(1-q^{m-x})}{1-q^m} F_D(m-x) + \left(\frac{1-p^x-q^x}{1-q^m}\right) F_{DG}(x)\right\} \tag{9.5}$$

or, equivalently,

$$F^*_D(m) = \frac{1-q^m}{p} + \underset{1\le x\le m}{\text{Min}} \{q^x F^*_D(m-x) + qF^*_{DG}(x)\} . \tag{9.6}$$

Similarly, for any G-situation with $m \geq 2$, we take a sample of size x $(1 \leq x \leq m)$ from $S_G(m)$ for testing and obtain

$$F_G(m) = 1 + \underset{1\le x\le m}{\text{Min}} \left\{\frac{p^x(1-p^{m-x})}{1-p^m} F_G(m-x) + \frac{1-p^x-q^x}{1-p^m} F_{DG}(x)\right\} \tag{9.7}$$

or, equivalently,

$$F^*_G(m) = \frac{1-p^m}{q} + \underset{1\le x\le m}{\text{Min}} \{p^x F^*_G(m-x) + pF^*_{DG}(x)\} . \tag{9.8}$$

The boundary conditions for all q are

(9.9) $$F^*_D(1) = F^*_G(1) = F_D(1) = F_G(1) = 0 ,$$

(9.10) $$F^*_{DG}(2) = 2; \quad F_{DG}(2) = 1 .$$

With (9.1), (9.4) and (9.6) we also need $F^*_D(0) = F^*_G(0) = F^*_{DG}(1) = 0$. Clearly $F_B(1) = 1$ and $F_B(2) = 1 + 2pq$. Let $EU(x)$ denote the expected number of units classified in a cycle, i.e., between the occurrences of two successive binomial situations. If we continue to take the same x for every binomial situation, then

(9.11) $$R(x) = \frac{F_B(x)}{EU(x)}$$

is the ratio of the expected number of tests per cycle to the expected number of units classified per cycle. $F_B(x)$ can be calculated from (9.1) by using the relations (9.2)-(9.10). Under the procedure R_S^∞, we take $x = x(q)$ in the binomial situation to be the sample size that minimizes $R(x)$.

We now develop the details of procedure R_S^∞ and illustrate its use. By direct calculation we find

(9.12) $$R(1) = \frac{F_B(1)}{EU(1)} = 1 ,$$

(9.13) $$R(2) = \frac{F_B(2)}{EU(2)} = \frac{1 + 2pq}{2} .$$

Note that $R(2) < R(1)$ when $1 + 2pq < 2$, which holds for all q. Hence we always prefer $x = 2$ to $x = 1$ for any B-situation.

By direct calculation in (9.4) we find that $F^*_{DG}(3) = 5$ and hence, by (9.1), we have $F_B(3) = 1 + 5pq$. Also it is easy to show that $EU(3) = 3 - 2pq$. Then, from (9.11)

(9.14) $$R(3) = (1 + 5pq)/(3 - 2pq) .$$

Thus $x = 3$ is preferable to $x = 2$ if $R(3) < R(2)$ or when

$$(9.15) \qquad (1 + 5pq)/(3 - 2pq) < (1 + 2pq)/2 \qquad \text{or}$$

$$4(pq)^2 + 6pq - 1 < 0.$$

This inequality holds (and we prefer $x = 3$ to $x = 2$) when

$$(9.16) \qquad pq < (-3 + \sqrt{13})/4 = .1514 \ldots .$$

Thus we take $x = 2$ if $pq > (-3 + \sqrt{13})/4$, i.e., $.1860 < q < .8140$; at either endpoint we can take $x = 2$ or $x = 3$ or randomize between them.

We also find that $x = 4$ is preferable to $x = 3$ if $R(4) < R(3)$ or

$$(9.17) \qquad \frac{1 + 8pq - 4(pq)^2}{4 - 5pq} < \frac{1 + 5pq}{3 - 2pq} \qquad \text{or}$$

$$1 - 7y + 3y^2 - 8y^3 > 0 \quad ,$$

where $y = pq$. Thus $x = 3$ is preferable when $.1486 < pq < .1514$ and hence we prefer $x = 3$ in the two intervals, symmetric about 1/2,

$$(9.18) \qquad .1816 < q < .1860 \qquad \text{and} \qquad .8140 < q < .8184 \, .$$

At the endpoints the appropriate randomizations can be made.

Similarly we find that $x = 5$ is preferable to $x = 4$ if $R(5) < R(4)$ or

$$(9.19) \qquad \frac{1 + 12y - 15y^2}{5 - 9y + 2y^2} < \frac{1 + 8y - 4y}{4 - 5y} \qquad \text{or}$$

$$1 - 12y + 30y^2 - 23y^3 - 8y^4 > 0 \, .$$

Thus $x = 4$ is preferable when $.1118 < pq < .1486$ and hence we prefer $x = 4$ in the two intervals, symmetric about 1/2,

$$(9.20) \qquad .1282 < q < .1816 \qquad \text{and} \quad .8184 < q < .8718.$$

At the endpoints the appropriate randomizations can be made. Proceeding in this manner we can determine the procedure R_S^∞ for any fixed value of $q(0 < q < 1)$.

If we apply the above procedure R_S^∞ to the problem in Figure 1 and stop when the 4 units are classified, then the only change is that for $G(2,2)$ in the center of Figure 1 we take $x = 1$ instead of $x = 2$ and the continuation after this is straightforward. This increases the expected number of tests from 1.9828 to 1.9900.

10. *Two modifications of procedure* R_S. In this section two modifications R_S' and R_S'' of R_S are considered. To see the need for these, we assume that $q = .9$ and that $G(2,3)$ (or $G(2,4)$, or $G(3,4)$) can arise starting from a B(N)-situation. Then we can throw away some information by mixing all the units and, for example, replace $G(2,3)$ by $G(3,3)$. Since $G(3,3) = 1.63063 < G(2,3) = 2.16364$, it follows that we have reduced the expected number of tests required without taking any observations. Such anomalies do arise when q is close to 0 or 1 (e.g., for $q = .9$ and $N = 10$) and the above two modifications are introduced to improve the efficiency of the procedure by using the anomaly (in the case of R_S') and by avoiding the anomaly (in the case of R_S'').

For R_S' we use equations (3.1), (3.2) and (3.5)-(3.8) as before with primes on all functions. In (3.4) we write $G_1'(m,n)$ on the left and primes on the right. We then define

$$G'(m,n) = \text{Min}\{G_1'(m,n),\ G_2'(m,n)\} \tag{10.1}$$

where $G_2'(m,n)$ is defined for $m < n$ by

$$G_2'(m,n) = 1 + \underset{m<x\leq n}{\text{Min}} \left\{ \left(\frac{q^x}{1-p^m}\right) B'(n-x) + \left(\frac{1-p^m-q^x}{1-p^m}\right) DG'(x,n) \right\} . \tag{10.2}$$

In (10.2) we allow the mixing of the good and binomial sets subject to the condition that for $x > m$, the entire good set of size m is included in the test group of size x. This modification can be carried out by keeping at most 2 groups of unclassified units at all times, without assuming that units within either group are identified (e.g., by being numbered). In writing $DG'(x,n)$ in (10.2) we have 'thrown away some information', namely, we say there is a good unit in the first $x > m$, rather than among the first m. A similar definition is made for $D'(m,n)$ in terms of $D_1'(m,n)$ and $D_2'(m,n)$ where the former is given by (3.3) with primes on the right.

By virtue of (10.1) this new procedure R_S' contains all the strategies possible under R_S plus new strategies for $m < n$. Hence the mixing procedure R_S' is uniformly as good or better than the non-mixing procedure R_S.

Illustration: Starting with the $B'(10)$-situation and $q=.9$, we take $x = 6$ and with positive probability can reach $DG'(6,10)$. Then we take $x = 2$ and with positive probability can reach $G'(4,8)$. Using (10.2) we obtain

$$\begin{aligned} G_2'(4,8) &= 1 + \left(\frac{1-(.1)^4-(.9)^8}{1-(.1)^4}\right) DG'(8,8) \\ &= 3.76084 < G_1'(4,8), \end{aligned} \tag{10.3}$$

since $G_1'(4,8) = 3.85494$. We also note that $G_2'(4,8) < G_1'(8,8) = 3.76105$, so that we can no longer 'throw away information' and improve our results.

The second modification R_S'' requires the identification of units and the introduction of a more general class of situations (say, GDG and DDG) with 3 sets of unclassified units (or 3 arguments) as follows. For $m < k \leq n$ we denote the expected number of tests by $GDG(m,k,n)$ if we start with the first m containing at least one good unit, the first k containing at least one of each type and the remaining $n - k$ being a binomial set.

We will need the additional

Lemma 3. *Start with an ordered set* $S_{DG}(k)$ *of size* $k \geq 2$. *Given that the first* $m(< k)$ *form a set* $S_G(m)$, *and that a randomly chosen subset of* $S_G(m)$ *of size* $x(1 \leq x \leq m)$ *contains all defective units, then the posterior distribution associated with the last* $k - m$ *units is binomial with the same probability* p *of a unit being defective.*

The proof is straightforward and is omitted (cf. [5]).

To see how the GDG-situation arises, we rewrite (10.2) without throwing away any information. Then, using double primes everywhere for procedure R_S'', we have

$$G_2''(m,n) = 1 + \min_{m<x\leq n} \left\{ \left(\frac{q^x}{1 - p^m}\right) B''(n-x) + \left(\frac{1 - p^m - q^x}{1 - p^m}\right) GDG''(m,x,n) \right\} . \tag{10.4}$$

For $GDG(m,k,n)$ we take $x(1 \leq x \leq m)$ randomly from the first m and use the recursion

$$GDG''(m,k,n) = 1 + \min_{1 \le x \le m} \left\{ \frac{q^x(1-q^{k-x})}{1-p^m-q^k} D''(k-x,n-x) \right.$$

$$(10.5) \qquad + \frac{p^x(1-p^{m-x})}{1-p^m-q^k} G''(m-x,n-x)$$

$$\left. + \left(\frac{1-p^x-q^x}{1-p^m-q^k}\right) DG''(x,n) \right\} .$$

The coefficient of $D''(k-x,n-x)$ in (10.5) is straightforward and is based on observing that the test group has only good units. In the term involving $G''(m-x,n-x)$ we utilize lemma 3. Since the $k - m$ units are binomial by lemma 3 and the $n - k$ units are independently binomial, the entire set of size $n - m$ is binomial with the same p; hence the second term in (10.5). The third term in (10.5) utilizes lemma 1 and is self-explanatory. Similar equations are written for $D_2''(m,n)$ and $DDG''(m,k,n)$.

There are some good reasons for the restriction $1 \le x \le m$ in (10.5). Firstly, allowing x to be greater than m, introduces serious complications in the new types of situations that can arise. Secondly, if we mixed the good and binomial units, it would destroy the "first come-first served' property. Thirdly, empirical calculations show that in a DG(m,n)-situation the optimal value of x is usually quite small compared to m; similarly, the optimal value of x in the GDG(m,k,n) situation is usually quite small compared to m.

Empirical calculations show that the results for R_S'' are very close to the results for R_S'. For example, for $q = .9$ we obtain for the last members of (10.2) and (10.4) with $m = 4$, $n = 8$ and $x = 8$

(10.6) $DG'(8,8) = 4.84793 > GDG''(4,8,8) = 4.84791.$

It follows that

(10.7) $G'(4,8) = G_2'(4,8) = 3.760845 > G''(4,8) =$
$= G_2''(4,8) = 3.760836.$

The improvement is negligible, especially in view of the deeper analysis that was required.

Table V shows that the B, B' and B''-values are all close together for $q = .9$ and $N \leq 50$. Thus, in addition to the fact that R_S is non-mixing and hence simpler, its existence is further justified by the fact that it gives results that are close to those of the more involved procedures R_S' and R_S''. Table V also shows that $B'(N)$ is smaller for some values of N and $B''(N)$ is smaller for others, when $q = .9$. It would be possible to combine these two to form a single procedure that allows the strategies of both, but this has not been done because the results are so close together. (See also Remark 3 in the Appendix.)

Appendix. *Optimal Procedures for Small* N. The development of procedure R_S and R_S' (but not R_S'') allows us to assume that the items within any set or test group need not be identified or distinguishable. If we assume that each item is individually labelled and that the history of its past tests and test results is kept, then further savings are possible in the expected number of tests. We illustrate this by developing below the optimal mixing tests for $N = 3$ and $N = 4$.

Consider $N = 3$ and label the units a,b,c. For $N = 3$ and $q \geq 1/2$ we consider 2 procedures, one for q near 1 and one for q near 1/2; for $q \leq 1/2$ the procedure is defined by symmetry. For q near 1 start by testing (a,b,c). If DG, test (a,b); otherwise we are done. If DG, test (a,c); otherwise we are done. If DG, test (a). Thus we have at most 4 tests. We used the labelling to select (a) for the last test. For this strategy it is easy to show that the expected number of tests is given by

$$\text{(A1)} \quad B(3) = (p^3 + q^3) + (p^2q + q^2p)(2 + 3 + 4) = 1 + 6pq.$$

For q near 1/2 we start by testing (a,b). If G or D, test (c); if DG, test (a,c). If G or D, we are through; if DG, test c. For this strategy we obtain

$$\text{(A2)} \quad B(3) = 2(p^2 + q^2) + 5(p^2q + q^2p) = 2 + pq.$$

Checking to see when (A2) is preferred, we find that (A2) is preferred whenever $5pq > 1$ or when

$$1/2 - \sqrt{5}/10 < q < 1/2 + \sqrt{5}/10$$

and (A1) is preferred otherwise. Comparing with Table II we find that this procedure is uniformly (i.e., for all p) better than its non-mixing, memoryless counterpart R_S. By exhausting all possibilities we found that the above was optimal.

Now we consider $N = 4$, labelling the units (a,b,c,d). Here we consider 3 different strategies, one near $q = 1$, one is intermediate and the third is near 1/2. For q near 1/2 we start with the test group size $x = 2$. In the other two strategies we start with $x = 4$; we never start with $x = 3$. For the 1st strategy we test all 4 units at the outset. If DG, test (a,b,c). If DG, test (a,b,d). If DG, test (a,c,d). If DG, test (b,c,d). If DG, test (a,b). If DG, test (a,c). If DG, test (a). In any order possibility, we stop and infer the results from tests already taken. This gives the result

(A3) $$B(4) = 1 + 10pq + 16(pq)^2 \quad .$$

In the second strategy we again start by testing $N = 4$. We describe it for $q > 1/2$ only. If DG, test (a,b). If G, test (c) and this leads to the use of inference if (c) is G and one more test if (c) is D. If (a,b) is D, test (c,d); the 2 possible results are G (requiring no more tests) and DG(requiring 1 more test). If (a,b) is DG, test (c,d); if G or D, then test (a). If DG, test (a,c). If D or G, then we are through; if DG, test (a) and get the others by inference. This algorithm gives the result

(A4) $$B(4) = 1 + pq(11 - 3pq + p^2) \quad .$$

The dividing point between A(4) and A(3) is the root (near $q = 1$) of $20x^2 - 21x + 2 = 0$, which is

(A5) $$\frac{21 + \sqrt{281}}{40} \sim .944 \ldots$$

and, of course, .056 is used in the symmetric strategy.

For the remaining strategy (near $q = 1/2$) we start with $x = 2$ and test (a,b). In any case, we then test (c,d). If (a,b) is DG and the other is not, or vice versa, we test one unit from the DG group. If both are DG, test (a,c). If (a,c) is DG, test (a). This gives the result

(A6) $$B(4) = 2 + 4pq - 2(pq)^2 \; .$$

The dividing point between (A6) and (A4) is the root $> 1/2$ in x of $2x^4 - 5x^3 + 11x^2 - 8x + 1 = 0$, which is .823 ... to 3 decimal places. Hence, in summary,

$$(A7)\qquad B(4) = \begin{cases} 2 + 4pq - 2(pq)^2 & \text{for } .177 < q < .823 \\ 1 + 11pq - 3(pq)^2 + p^3q & \text{for } .823 < q < .944 \\ 1 + 10pq + 16(pq)^2 & \text{for } .944 < q < 1 \end{cases} .$$

For $q < 1/2$ we interchange p and q in (A7). Here again, this is claimed to be optimal as a result of empirical investigation of many different possible strategies. We note from Table II that there is a saving of at least $2(pq)^2$ for all p, if we use the mixing procedure above corresponding to (A7).

Remark 3: The anomaly that arose for $G(2,3)$ at the beginning of Section 10 can also be handled by introducing the following mixing subroutine. (This idea has not been generalized nor have the numerical results of using it been computed.) Let $(a,b;c)$ denote the 3 units and (a,b) denote the "good" set. Test (a,c). Stop if D, test (b) if G, and test (b,c) if DG. For this plan $E\{T\}$ is proportional to $2(q^3 + 3pq^2) + 3p^2q = 2q + pq + pq^2$. Alternatively, for q close to one, we test (a,b,c) at the outset. If G, stop. If DG, test (a,c). Then, if (a,c) is G or D stop and if (a,c) is DG, test (b,c). For this plan $E\{T\}$ is proportional to $q^3 + 6pq^2 + 2pq^2 + 2p^2q + 3p^2q = q + 4pq + 2pq^2$. Here we prefer the latter plan for $q > \sqrt{3}-1 = .732\ldots$ and the former one otherwise. These mixing subroutines use the information available in an efficient manner and remove the anomaly.

Remark 4: It was noted that the expected saving obtained in the binomial case of Theorem 2 is a lower bound for all the cases considered and it is conjectured that this will remain true in all cases.

Table II. Expected Number of Tests and Sample Size under R_S for $N = 2,3,4,5$
(x denotes the test group size to be taken for the given situation)

$B(2) = 1 + 2pq$ for all q, $x = 2$.

$$B(3) = \begin{cases} 2 + 2pq & \text{for } p_1 = (5 - \sqrt{5})/10 \le q \le (5 + \sqrt{5})/10 = q_1,\ x = 2. \\ 1 + 7pq & \text{for } q < p_1 = .276\ldots \text{ or } q > q_1 = .724\ldots,\ x = 3. \\ \text{Here } q_1 & \text{is the root of } 5x^2 - 5x + 1 = 0 . \end{cases}$$

$$B(4) = \begin{cases} 1 + pq(11 - q + 2q^2) & \text{for } q \le p_2,\ x = 4. \\ 2(1 + 2pq) & \text{for } p_2 \le q \le q_2,\ x = 2. \\ 1 + pq(12 - 3q + 2q^2) & \text{for } q \ge q_2,\ x = 4. \\ \text{Here } q_2 = .823\ldots & \text{is the root of } 2x^4 - 5x^3 + 11x^2 - 8x + 1 = 0 . \end{cases}$$

$$B(5) = \begin{cases} 1 + pq(15 + p + 4q^2 - 2pq) & \text{for } q \le p_3,\ x = 5. \\ 2 + 7pq + 10p^2q^2 & \text{for } p_3 \le q \le p_1,\ x = 3. \\ 3 + 4pq & \text{for } p_1 \le q \le q_1,\ x = 2. \\ 2 + 7pq + 10p^2q^2 & \text{for } q_1 \le q \le q_3,\ x = 3. \\ 1 + pq(15 + q + 4p^2 - 2pq) & \text{for } q_3 \le q \le 1,\ x = 5. \\ \text{Here } q_3 = .836\ldots & \text{is the root of } 16x^4 - 35x^3 + 49x^2 - 48x + 19 = 0. \end{cases}$$

$DG(2,2) = 1$ for all q, $x = 1$.

$DG(2,3) = 2$ for all q, $x = 1$.

$DG(2,4) = 2 + 2pq$ for all q, $x = 1$.

$DG(2,5) = 1 + B(3)$ for all q, $x = 1$.

$DG(3,3) = 7/3$ for all q, $x = 2$.

Table II (Cont'd.)

$DG(3,4) = (8 + 4pq)/3$ for all q, $x = 2$.

$DG(3,5) = \{5 + 2B(3) + B(2)\}/3$ for all q, $x = 2$.

$$DG(4,4) = \begin{cases} (11-q+2q^2)/(4-2pq) \text{ for } q \le \frac{1}{2}, & x = 2. \\ (12-3q+2q^2)/(4-2pq) \text{ for } q \ge \frac{1}{2}, & x = 2. \end{cases}$$

$DG(4,5) = \{9-6pq+B(2) + 2B(3)\}/(4-2pq)$ for all q, $x = 2$.

$$DG(5,5) = \begin{cases} \{13-16pq+p+4q^2+2B(3)\}/5(1-pq) \text{ for } q \le \frac{1}{4}, & x = 2. \\ \{14-16pq+2B(3)\}/5(1-pq) \text{ for } \frac{1}{4} \le q \le \frac{3}{4}, & x = 2. \\ \{13+q+4p^2-16pq+2B(3)\}/(5(1-pq)) \text{ for } \frac{3}{4} \le q, & x = 2. \end{cases}$$

$$D(2,2) = \begin{cases} (1+3q)/(1+q) \text{ for } q \le \frac{1}{2}, & x = 2. \\ (2+q)/(1+q) \text{ for } q \ge \frac{1}{2}, & x = 1. \end{cases}$$

$D(2,3) = (2 + 4q - 2q^2)/(1 + q)$ for all q, $x = 1$.

$$D(2,4) = \begin{cases} 1 + B(2) + 2q/(1 + q) \text{ for } q \le \frac{1}{2}, & x = 2. \\ 1 + \{B(3) + qB(2)\}/(1 + q) \text{ for } q \ge \frac{1}{2}, & x = 1. \end{cases}$$

$$D(3,3) = \begin{cases} (1 + 8q + q^2)/(1 + q + q^2) \text{ for } q \le \frac{1}{4}, & x = 3. \\ (2 + 4q + q^2)/(1 + q + q^2) \text{ for } q \ge \frac{1}{4}, & x = 2. \end{cases}$$

$D(3,4) = 1 + \{2q+q^2+qB(2)+B(2)\ /(1+q+q^2)$ for all q, $x = 2$.

$$D(4,4) = \begin{cases} (1+12q+3q^3)/(1+q+q^2+q^3) \text{ for } q \le p_4, & x = 4. \\ (2+6q+2q^2+2q^3)/(1+q+q^2+q^3) \text{ for } p_4 \le q \le \frac{1}{2}, & x = 2. \\ (2+6q+3q^2)/(1+q+q^2+q^3) \text{ for } \frac{1}{2} \le q, & x = 2. \\ \text{where } p_4 = .175\ldots \text{is the root of } x^3-2x^2+6x-1 = 0. \end{cases}$$

The values for $G(2,2)$, $G(2,3)$, $G(2,4)$, $G(3,3)$, $G(3,4)$, $G(4,4)$ can be obtained from the respective D-functions, as pointed out in Property 2 in Section 5.

Table III

Numerical Results for Procedure R_S for $q = .9$ and $N \leq 5$

B(1) = 1	(take x=1)	DG(2,4) = 2.18000	(take x=1)
DG(2,2) = 1	(take x=1)	DG(3,4) = 2.78667	(take x=2)[§]
B(2) = 1.18000	(take x=2)	DG(4,4) = 2.85839	(take x=2)
D(2,2) = 1.52632	(take x=1)	B(4) = 1.98280	(take x=4)
G(2,2) = 1.18182	(take x=2)	D(2,4) = 2.41684	(take x=1)[§]
DG(2,3) = 2	(take x=1)	D(3,4) = 2.79041	(take x=2)[§]
DG(3,3) = 2.33333	(take x=2)	D(4,4) = 2.85844	(take x=2)[§]
B(3) = 1.63000	(take x=3)	G(2,4) = 2.36182	(take x=2)[§]
D(2,3) = 2.09474	(take x=1)[§]	G(3,4) = 2.35856	(take x=2)[§]
D(3,3) = 2.36531	(take x=2)	G(4,4) = 1.98290	(take x=4)[§]
G(2,3) = 2.16364	(take x=1)[§]	DG(2,5)= 2.63000	(take x=1)
G(3,3) = 1.63063	(take x=3)	DG(3,5) = 3.14667	(take x=2)[§]
		DG(4,5) = 3.37696	(take x=2)[§]
		DG(5,5) = 3.46374	(take x=2)
		B(5) = 2.41840	(take x=5)

[§]These items are not used for $q = .9$ and $N \leq 5$ to compute B(N). If G(2,3) or G(2,4) or G(3,4) were used then we immediately come up with the anomaly that we can 'throw away information' and reduce the expected number of tests by putting one or more units from the binomial set into the good set and 'forgetting' which units were added. For $q = .9$ and $N \geq 10$ such anomalies can actually arise (see discussion in Section 10).

Table IV

Intermediate Results for Procedure R_S^∞ for $q < .8718$

$$\left.\begin{aligned} F_B^*(2) &= 1 + 2pq \\ EU(2) &= 2 \end{aligned}\right\} \quad R(2) = \frac{1 + 2pq}{2} < R(1) = 1 \text{ for all } q$$

$F_D^*(2) = 1 + q$ (take $x = 1$)

$F_G^*(2) = 1 + p$ (take $x = 1$)

$F_{DG}^*(3) = 5$ (take $x = 2$)

$$\left.\begin{aligned} F_B(3) &= 1 + 5pq \\ EU(3) &= 3 - 2pq \end{aligned}\right\} \quad R(3) = \frac{1 + 5pq}{3 - 2pq}$$

For the dividing point q_{23} between $x = 2$ and $x = 3$, solve for the root y_0 of $1 - 6y - 4y^2 = 0$ and then solve $pq = y_0$, obtaining $y_0 = .1514$ and $q = .1860, .8140$.

$F_D^*(3) = 1 + 2q + 2q^2$ (take $x = 1$)

$F_G^*(3) = 1 + 2p + 2p^2$ (take $x = 1$)

$F_{DG}^*(4) = 4(2-pq)$ (take $x = 2$)

$$\left.\begin{aligned} F_B(4) &= 1 + 8pq - 4(pq)^2 \\ EU(4) &= 4 - 5pq \end{aligned}\right\} \quad R(4) = \frac{1 + 8pq - 4(pq)^2}{4 - 5pq}$$

For the dividing point q_{34} between $x = 3$ and $x = 4$, solve for the root y_0 of $1 - 7y + 3y^2 - 8y^3 = 0$ and then solve $pq = y_0$, obtaining $y_0 = .1486$ and $q = .1816, .8184$.

$$F_D^*(4) = \begin{cases} 1+2q+3q^2+3q^3 & \text{for } q < (\sqrt{5} - 1)/2 \quad (\text{take } x = 1) \\ 1+3q+2q^2+2q^3 & \text{for } q > (\sqrt{5} - 1)/2 \quad (\text{take } x = 2) \end{cases}$$

$$F_G^*(4) = \begin{cases} 1+2p+3p^2+3p^3 & \text{for } p < (\sqrt{5} - 1)/2 \quad (\text{take } x = 1) \\ 1+3p+2p^2+2p^3 & \text{for } p > (\sqrt{5} - 1)/2 \quad (\text{take } x = 2) \end{cases}$$

$F_{DG}^*(5) = 12 - 15\,pq$ (take $x = 2$)

$$\left.\begin{aligned} F_B(5) &= 1 + 12pq - 15(pq)^2 \\ EU(5) &= 5 - 9pq + 2(pq)^2 \end{aligned}\right\} \quad R(5) = \frac{1 + 12pq - 15(pq)^2}{5 - 9pq + 2(pq)^2}$$

Table IV (Cont'd.)

For the dividing point q_{45} between $x = 4$ and $x = 5$, solve for the root y_0 of $1 - 12y + 30y^2 - 23y^3 - 8y^4 = 0$ and then solve $pq = y_0$, obtaining $y_0 = .1118$ and $q = .1282, .8718$.

The resulting form for R_S^∞ is given in the text. The partial tree needed to compute $F_B(5)$ and $EU(5)$ is given below. The notation $B(j + \infty)$ below means that j units out of the 5 taken at the left were not classified before getting to the next B-situation.

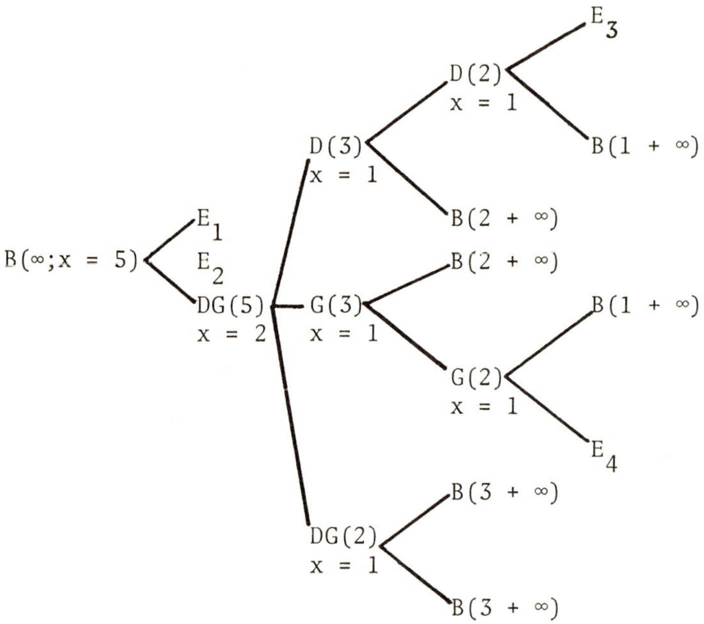

Figure 5: Partial Tree for R_S^∞ for $.1282 < q < .1816$ and $.8184 < q < .8718$.

Table V

Expected Number of Tests for Procedures R_S, R_S' and R_S'' (for N = 6(1)12(2)20(5)50 and q = .9)

N	B(N)	B'(N)	B''(N)
1 to 5	(B(N)=B'(N)=B''(N) for N = 1(1)9; see Table II)		
6	2.82152	2.82151900	2.82151900
7	3.30406	3.30405670	3.30405670
8	3.76105	3.76105339	3.76105339
9	4.24196	4.24195675	4.24195675
10	4.67688	4.67589885	4.67589871
11[§]	5.12163	5.12044002	5.12045473
12	5.54829	5.54767707	5.54767684
14	6.47176	6.47043097	6.47043066
16[§]	7.37964	7.37776527	7.37776581
18	8.26701	8.26545391	8.26545378
20	9.18141	9.17904766	9.17904745
25[§]	11.44045	11.43792902	11.43793258
30[§]	13.69487	13.69118824	13.69118833
35[§]	15.95895	15.95460632	15.95460999
40[§]	18.21529	18.20976098	18.20976126
45[§]	20.47660	20.47048715	20.47048946
50	22.73278	22.72559754	22.72559750

[§]For these values of N the procedure R_S' is better; for the remaining values of $N \geq 10$ the procedure R_S'' is better. However it should be noted that the results for these two procedures agree to 5 decimal places for all the values of N computed, except for N = 11 where the difference is 10^{-5}; this explains the 8 decimals.

References

1. Huffman, D. A. (1952). A method for the construction of minimum redundancy codes. *Proc. I.R.E.* 40, 1098.

2. Kumar, S. (1970). Multinomial group-testing. *SIAM Jour. Appl. Math.* 19, 340-350.

3. Kumar, S. (1971). Group-testing to classify all units in a trinomial sample. To appear in *Studia Sci. Math. Hungar.*

4. Kumar, S. and Sobel, M. (1970). Group-testing with at most c tests for finite c and $c \to \infty$. *Technical Report No.* 146. Dept. of Statistics, Univ. of Minnesota.

5. Sobel, M., Kumar, S. and Blumenthal, S. (1970). Symmetric binomial group-testing with 3 Outcomes. *Technical Report No.* 149 (or 149A). Dept. of Statistics, Univ. of Minnesota.

6. Sobel, M. and Groll, P. A. (1959). Group-testing to eliminate efficiently all defectives in a binomial sample. *Bell System Tech. Journal* 38, 1179-1252.

7. Sobel, M. (1960). Group-testing to classify all defectives in a binomial sample. *Information and Decision Processes*, ed. R. E. Machol. McGraw-Hill, 127-161.

8. Sobel, M. (1967). Optimal group-testing. *Proceedings of the Colloquium on Information Theory Organized by the Bolyai Mathematical Society*, Debrecen, (Hungary), 411-488.

9. Sobel, M. (1970). A characterization of binary codes that correspond to a class of group-testing procedures. *Technical Report No.* 148, Dept. of Statistics, Univ. of Minnesota.

10. Ungar, P. (1960). The cut-off point for group-testing. *Comm. Pure Appl. Math.* 13, 49-54.

DETECTION OF OUTLIERS*

By A. P. Dempster and Bernard Rosner
Harvard University

Summary. Outlier detection can be regarded as a decision process within several of the theoretical frameworks of statistical inference. A semi-Bayesian approach is described which uses as inputs to the decision process separate Bayesian analyses for each contemplated number k of outliers. Significance tests can be used for assessing k but should be supplemented by Bayesian analysis for judging which observations are outliers. In §3, an asymptotic theorem is given to clarify the difference between the Bayesian and significance testing messages. Solutions to computational problems are outlined in §4.

1. *Outlier detection and decision theory.* An outlier is an observation judged to be discrepant in the sense of not following a law which is accepted as explaining the values of some main body of observations. It is natural to regard such a judgment of discrepancy as a decision. What kind of statistical theory can or should be applied to these decisions?

---

*This work was facilitated by Grants GP-8774 and GP-19182 from the National Science Foundation.

Computer time was provided by IBM Cambridge Scientific Center under a joint study agreement.

A 2 x 2 classification of statistical decision theories can be created with cells labelled (F,U), (NF,U), (F,NU), (NF,NU) where the first coordinate refers to whether a frequency interpretation is required (F) or not required (NF) of the probability concept used in the theory, and the second coordinate refers to whether an explicit utility function appears (U) or does not appear (NU) in the theory.

Decision theory as formulated abstractly by Wald [10] falls in category (F,U). An application of Wald's theory to outlier detection was given by Anscombe [1] who took utility to be a measure of improvement in the estimator of some population characteristic when the contamination from the outlier is removed. Of course, if a detected outlier is a false positive, then the improvement is generally negative. Anscombe interpreted this loss as the premium to be paid for protection against true positives. The Neyman-Pearson theory of testing belongs in category (F,NU), but is really a special case of (F,U) where the utilities are simply probabilities of correct judgments. Detection of outliers is often considered as a problem of hypothesis testing, and applications of the Neyman-Pearson theory abound. Examples and references may be found in the review Chapter 8 of David [5].

The label NF refers to probabilities interpreted as degrees of certainty for specific events. Whereas frequency theory speaks to long run frequencies or averages, and can be used to compare the long run behavior of procedures, the degree of certainty theory provides judgments of uncertainty and expected utilities to guide individual actions. Against the advantage of specificity, one must weigh the disadvantage that the required probability assessments cannot always be made sufficiently objective. The methods proposed here attempt to make the NF approach work.

Personalistic Bayesian decision theory as expounded by Savage [9] belongs to category (NF,U). In this paper, however, we rely on simpler theory of the (NF,NU) type. For decisions leading to real world actions, utility theory is natural and almost inescapable, but outlier detection can be conceived as primarily an inductive operation, and the utilities or losses appearing in inductive decision theories are usually chosen because they are mathematically nice, not because they are practically compelling. Suppressing utility in the theory leads one to formulate a simple direct question: what is the posterior probability that a given observation is an outlier?

Box and Tiao [2] have described outlier detection procedures based on (NF,NU) theory. We differ mainly in advocating a more restricted application of Bayes. In particular, we put no prior distribution on the number of outliers but instead assign prior probabilities to events within the sample space of a specific number of outliers (k). We decide on k by significance testing techniques. We feel our method makes fewer assumptions and is computationally more feasible since we need only consider computations of at most $\binom{n}{k}$ weights $<< 2^n$ weights where n is the total sample size, especially in that k is typically small compared with n.

2. *A semi-Bayesian approach.* The practical art of outlier detection necessarily uses theory in a rough and ready way, and therefore appears and may always appear primitive relative to the sophisticated models of decision-making

which have been analyzed by mathematical statisticians. In practice, outliers are most often declared on the basis of visual inspection of plots, or if there is some doubt about the reality of an apparent outlier then a significance testing argument based on an extreme-value distribution may be introduced as evidence. We propose to supplement visual and significance testing evidence by means of a Bayesian argument which gives an indication of how probable it is *a posteriori* that various subsets of k observations are outliers, given that some plausible $k(= 1,2,3,...)$ has been selected. Our approach is introduced and described below in terms of a specific example. An earlier discussion of a similar idea placed in a broader context of many parameter problems may be found in [6].

Suppose that $X_1, X_2, ..., X_n$ denote a batch of observable quantities which may plausibly be regarded as independently drawn from identical $N(0,\sigma^2)$ populations with unknown variance σ^2. Suppose that a hypothesis of k outliers implies that an unknown subset I consisting of k of the n populations have suffered location shifts of unknown magnitudes. It will be convenient to denote the absolute values $|X_1|, |X_2|, ..., |X_n|$ by $Z_1, Z_2, ..., Z_n$ and to assume that the Z_i have been arranged in nondecreasing order.

Table 1 shows a batch of $n = 31$ values used by Daniel [3] to illustrate the application of outlier detection methods to the problem of judging which contrasts are meaningful in a 2^5 factorial experiment. For present purposes it will be assumed that the identification of the contrasts with specific main effects and interaction effects are excluded from the data.

.0000	.0281	-.0561	-.0842	-.0982	.1263	.1684
.1964	.2245	-.2526	.2947	-.3087	.3929	.4069
.4209	.4350	.4630	-.4771	.5472	.6595	.7437
-.7437	-.7577	-.8138	-.8138	-.8980	1.080	-1.305
2.147	-2.666	-3.143				

Table 1

A set of $n = 31$ data points taken from a set of contrasts quoted in Table 1 of Daniel [3]. These values are ordered by absolute value and scaled to have sum of squares 31.

Daniel [3] proposed an approach of the following kind. For each contemplated number k of outliers $(k=0,1,2,\ldots)$, plot $Z_1,\ldots,Z_{n-k}$ on half normal probability paper and calculate an estimated standard deviation

$$\hat{\sigma}_k = Z_i \tag{2.1}$$

where i is an integer satisfying

$$\left|\frac{i - .5}{n - k} - .683\right| \leq \left|\frac{j - .5}{n - k} - .683\right| \tag{2.2}$$

for all $j \neq i$, $i \leq j \leq n-k$. In words, $\hat{\sigma}_k$ is the order statistic Z_i closest to .683 of the way along the sequence $Z_1,Z_2,\ldots,Z_{n-k}$. Thence, plot straight lines on the half-normal plots to depict the estimates $\hat{\sigma}_k$. Select the smallest k which give "good" fit. Goodness-of-fit may be judged both visually and from quantitative guardrails indicating significant deviations for the largest observation. Figures 1-4 show the Daniel-type picture for the data of Table 1. The message is clear: the 3 largest observations are too far out, while no suspicions are raised about the remaining observations.

While accepting the value of procedures like the foregoing, we propose in addition to compute rough posterior probabilities that specific subsets of the observations are contaminated. This is done separately for each contemplated k, so that the posterior probabilities $p(I)$ sum to unity as I runs over all subsets of k out of the n original data points. The possibility of a plausible Bayesian argument here is due to the availability of a plausible prior distribution: assuming no knowledge distinguishing *a priori* among the observations, each of the $\binom{n}{k}$ subsets I can be taken as an equally probable candidate for the set of outliers. The prior distribution can then be completed by assigning relatively innocuous flat priors to $\log \sigma$ and the unknown location parameter. It follows that the posterior probability $p(I)$, given k and the data, is proportional to

$$\text{(2.3)} \qquad wt(I) = \Big(\sum_{i \notin I} Z_i^2 \Big)^{-\frac{n}{2}} ,$$

so that

$$\text{(2.4)} \qquad p(I) = wt(I) \Big/ \sum_{I^* \in \mathcal{J}} wt(I^*)$$

where $\mathcal{J}$ denotes the class of subsets of k out of n points.

These weights suggest a natural way to estimate σ^2 for each k, namely

$$\text{(2.5)} \qquad \hat{\sigma}_k^2 = \sum_{I \in \mathcal{J}} p(I)\, S^2(I)$$

where

$$\text{(2.6)} \qquad S^2(I) = \frac{1}{n-k} \sum_{i \notin I} X_i^2 .$$

Likewise they suggest computing a posterior probability that X_i is an outlier, namely

$$P_i = \sum_{I \supset \{i\}} p(I) \tag{2.7}$$

and a vector of estimated population means

$$(\hat{\mu}_1, \hat{\mu}_2, \ldots, \hat{\mu}_n) = \sum_{I \varepsilon \mathcal{I}} p(I)(\hat{\mu}_1(I), \hat{\mu}_2(I), \ldots, \hat{\mu}_n(I)) \tag{2.8}$$

where

$$\hat{\mu}_i(I) = \begin{cases} X_i & \text{if } i \varepsilon I \\ 0 & \text{otherwise} \end{cases} \quad . \tag{2.9}$$

Table 2 shows summaries of the Bayesian analyses for $k = 1,2,3,4,5$ applied to the data of Table 1. Figures 2-4 show $\hat{\hat{\sigma}}_k$, $k = 1,2,3$ as compared with $\hat{\sigma}_k$, $k = 1,2,3$ from the Daniel analysis.

How to choose k is a key question. By suggesting separate Bayesian analyses for each k, we implied above that the choice should not be attempted through a fully Bayesian analysis which would assign posterior probabilities to $k = 0,1,2,\ldots$. The central problem with a unitary Bayesian approach is not simply the requirement of a prior distribution for k, nor even the somewhat deeper problem that flat priors for the remaining parameters are essentially incommensurable for different k. The basic trouble lies with the conception of what is an outlier. We regard a value as an outlier, or alternatively declare the presence of an outlier without specifically pointing a finger, if the hypothesis accommodating the outlier fits the data sufficiently better

Table 2. Summary statistics from the separate Bayesian analyses for k = 1,2,3,4.5 as applied to the data of Table 1 (with signs omitted).

	k = 1		k = 2		k = 3		k = 4		k = 5	
X_i	μ_i	P_i	μ_i	P_i	μ_i	P_i	μ_i	P_i	μ_i	P_i
0.0000	0.0000	0.0019	0.0000	0.0015	0.0000	0.0016	0.0000	0.0127	0.0000	0.0160
0.0281	0.0001	0.0019	0.0000	0.0015	0.0000	0.0016	0.0004	0.0127	0.0004	0.0160
0.0561	0.0001	0.0019	0.0001	0.0015	0.0001	0.0016	0.0007	0.0128	0.0009	0.0161
0.0842	0.0002	0.0019	0.0001	0.0015	0.0001	0.0016	0.0011	0.0129	0.0014	0.0162
0.0982	0.0002	0.0019	0.0001	0.0015	0.0002	0.0016	0.0013	0.0129	0.0016	0.0163
0.1263	0.0002	0.0019	0.0002	0.0015	0.0002	0.0016	0.0016	0.0131	0.0021	0.0165
0.1684	0.0003	0.0019	0.0002	0.0015	0.0003	0.0016	0.0022	0.0133	0.0029	0.0169
0.1964	0.0004	0.0019	0.0003	0.0015	0.0003	0.0017	0.0027	0.0136	0.0034	0.0173
0.2245	0.0004	0.0019	0.0003	0.0015	0.0004	0.0017	0.0031	0.0139	0.0040	0.0177
0.2526	0.0005	0.0019	0.0004	0.0015	0.0004	0.0017	0.0036	0.0142	0.0046	0.0183
0.2947	0.0006	0.0020	0.0005	0.0015	0.0005	0.0018	0.0044	0.0148	0.0057	0.0192
0.3087	0.0006	0.0020	0.0005	0.0016	0.0005	0.0018	0.0046	0.0150	0.0060	0.0195
0.3929	0.0008	0.0020	0.0006	0.0016	0.0007	0.0019	0.0065	0.0166	0.0087	0.0222
0.4069	0.0008	0.0020	0.0007	0.0016	0.0008	0.0019	0.0069	0.0170	0.0092	0.0227
0.4209	0.0009	0.0020	0.0007	0.0017	0.0008	0.0019	0.0073	0.0173	0.0098	0.0233
0.4350	0.0009	0.0021	0.0007	0.0017	0.0009	0.0020	0.0077	0.0177	0.0104	0.0239
0.4630	0.0010	0.0021	0.0008	0.0017	0.0009	0.0020	0.0086	0.0185	0.0117	0.0252
0.4771	0.0010	0.0021	0.0008	0.0017	0.0010	0.0021	0.0090	0.0189	0.0124	0.0260
0.5472	0.0012	0.0022	0.0010	0.0018	0.0012	0.0022	0.0118	0.0215	0.0166	0.0304
0.6595	0.0015	0.0023	0.0013	0.0020	0.0017	0.0026	0.0181	0.0275	0.0270	0.0410
0.7437	0.0018	0.0025	0.0016	0.0022	0.0022	0.0030	0.0253	0.0341	0.0398	0.0535
0.7437	0.0018	0.0025	0.0016	0.0022	0.0022	0.0030	0.0253	0.0341	0.0398	0.0535
0.7577	0.0019	0.0025	0.0017	0.0022	0.0023	0.0031	0.0268	0.0354	0.0425	0.0561
0.8138	0.0021	0.0026	0.0019	0.0024	0.0028	0.0034	0.0340	0.0417	0.0559	0.0687
0.8138	0.0021	0.0026	0.0019	0.0024	0.0028	0.0034	0.0340	0.0417	0.0559	0.0687
0.8980	0.0025	0.0028	0.0024	0.0027	0.0037	0.0041	0.0492	0.0547	0.0865	0.0963
1.0804	0.0037	0.0034	0.0038	0.0035	0.0068	0.0063	0.1193	0.1104	0.4076	0.3773
1.3049	0.0059	0.0046	0.0071	0.0054	0.0163	0.0125	0.4414	0.3382	1.0523	0.8064
2.1468	0.0507	0.0236	0.1482	0.0690	1.9957	0.9296	2.1321	0.9932	2.1443	0.9989
2.6659	0.3029	0.1136	2.3677	0.8882	2.6537	0.9954	2.6650	0.9997	2.6658	1.0000
3.1430	2.5128	0.7995	3.1055	0.9881	3.1419	0.9996	3.1429	1.0000	3.1430	1.0000
$\hat{\hat{\sigma}}_k$	.8650		.7102		.5856		.5572		.5221	
max p(I)	.7995		.8762		.9247		.3311		.1825	

than the hypothesis of no outlier. Admittedly, the meaning of "sufficiently better" is difficult to tie down. We suggest below two approaches, one Bayesian and one non-Bayesian. What we are unable to understand or to find is a prior distribution for a complete Bayesian analysis which captures in the resulting posterior distribution of k the notion that good fit to the data is equivalent to high posterior probability.

The first suggested approach is to contemplate the sequence of maximum posterior probabilities for $k=1,2,3,\ldots$. In our example, these are defined by $p(I)$ for the subset I corresponding to the most extreme observations, and are shown at the bottom of Table 2. Note that $\max P(I)$ increases to a maximum of .925 at $k = 3$, and starts to drop off rapidly for larger k. The inference is that under the assumption $k = 3$, one can be reasonably sure that the 3 outliers are in fact the 3 largest observations. On the other hand, if one assumes $k = 5$, then it is no longer clear which 5 observations are contaminated. In general, if the objective is to declare a specific set of data points outliers, it would appear that a wise rule would be to take the largest k such that $\max p(I)$ is large enough to provide reasonable assurance that the k most discrepant data points are outliers. The data may then be said to concur or fit with the hypothesis of k specified outliers, but not with any $k + 1$ specified outliers.

Heuristically, it might be expected that a significance testing argument would declare that there are more outliers than are identified by the procedure of the preceding paragraph. The point is that rejection of a null hypothesis does not in itself speak directly to which among many alternatives might hold. For example, one might feel comfortable with the hypothesis that more than k observations were contaminated, for a specific k, while only k of these observations could be identified with reasonable certainty. The result of §3 suggests that such an outcome will commonly hold and will become pronounced as n increases.

Significance testing is a difficult art. Most tests in the literature are directed at distinguishing between $k = 0$ and $k = 1$. Practical work will often require looking at a sequence of tests of k against $k + 1$ for $k=0,1,2,\ldots$. Null distributions for $k = 1,2,\ldots$ will generally depend on nuisance parameters, namely the disturbances associated with k outliers, where these disturbances are not well determined by the data. A simple expedient is to use a $k = 0$ test, and if this rejects use the same test on the reduced sample eliminating the most discrepant observation, and so on until the test ceases to reject the next most extreme observation. In effect, the theory here assumes that detected discrepancies are very large, not always a reasonable assumption.

The Bayesian procedures of this paper suggest plausible test criteria for consideration alongside the familiar maximum deviation criteria. For example, the largest posterior probability for $k = 1$ may be used. Or the reduction in likelihood from $k = 0$ to $k = 1$ may be used, where likelihood for $k = 1$ is averaged over the posterior distribution of the n subhypotheses. The sampling distributions of such criteria are difficult to get at. In general, a combination of asymptotic theory for large n and experimental sampling for specified n will be required. We have barely begun to study these distributions, and have not applied a series of tests to the data of Table 1. Figure 4 suggests that $k = 3$ would be the choices of reasonable significance testing procedures.

Finally, as regards testing, how should one interpret the data if a believable sequence of tests should point, say to $k = 5$ while the Bayesian procedures show that only 3 outliers can be identified with confidence? First, one could say that the data indicate that $5/n$ is a plausible estimate of the fraction contaminated in the sample. Second, one could continue the Bayesian analysis to $k = 5$ in order to display degrees of uncertainty about the actual 5 outliers.

3. *A limit law related to Bayes vs. non-Bayes*. Consider a Bayesian analysis as suggested above with selected $k = 1$ and suppose for simplicity that the possibility of $k > 1$ need not be considered. To be "sure" that the most discrepant observation is an outlier, one might require that the corresponding largest posterior probability is at least .95. To be "sure" that some observation is an outlier, one might require that the largest posterior probability should exceed the .95 quantile of its sampling distribution under the null hypothesis of no outlier. If these judgments were to coincide, not just for $p = .95$ but for all p, the null sampling distributtion of the largest posterior probability would need to be uniform on $(0,1)$. The purpose of this section is to show, in a simple case, that the sampling distribution is not uniform, and in fact collapses on 0 at the rate $(\log n)^{-1}$. Consequently, if $n - 1$ data points fit the null distribution accurately while the extreme point is

somewhat off, a just significant value of the largest posterior probability does not generally imply a large posterior probability, and indeed for large n will generally imply a very small posterior probability, indicating that the presence of an outlier is generally detectable much more easily than the corresponding discrepant observation.

In the example of §2 we supposed normal data with unknown σ^2. Here we simplify further to the case of known σ, which may therefore be taken to be unity. Thus $k = 0$ will mean that $X_1, X_2, \ldots, X_n$ are independent $N(0,1)$ observations, while $k = 1$ will mean that one of the X_i is shifted by an unknown amount. The analog of (2.3) becomes

$$\text{wt}(I) = e^{-\frac{1}{2}\sum_{j \notin I} X_j^2} \quad . \tag{3.1}$$

Since the wt(I) are only determined up to a constant multiplier, we can multiply through by $\exp(\frac{1}{2}\sum X_i^2)$, and since we are considering only $k = 1$ we can identify subsets I with indices i and replace (3.1) by

$$Y_i = e^{\frac{1}{2}X_i^2} \quad . \tag{3.2}$$

It is convenient to denote the null density of the Y_i by

$$\phi(y) = \pi^{-\frac{1}{2}} y^{-2} (\log y)^{-\frac{1}{2}} \text{ for } 1 < y < \infty \tag{3.3}$$

and the upper tail cumulative of the Y_i by

$$f(y) = \int_y^\infty \phi(y)\, dy \ . \tag{3.4}$$

In the Bayesian analysis based on weights (3.1) or (3.2) the largest posterior probability may be denoted Y_n^*/S_n where

(3.5) $$Y_n^* = \max_{1 \le i \le n} Y_i$$

and

(3.6) $$S_n = \sum_{i=1}^{n} Y_i .$$

Our concern here is with the distribution of the ratio Y_n^*/S_n. It is important to notice first that $\phi(y)$ is a regularly varying function with exponent -2, i.e., that

(3.7) $$\lim_{y\to\infty} \frac{\phi(\lambda y)}{\phi(y)} = \lambda^{-2} .$$

Darling [4] has derived asymptotic distributions for the ratio Y_n^*/S_n in the cases where $\phi(y)$ is slowly varying with exponent γ where $-3 \le \gamma < -2$ or where $-2 < \gamma \le -1$, but our case $\gamma = -2$ has apparently not been resolved in general. We now derive the required distribution for the special case of $\phi(y)$ given by (3.3).

Theorem. *Suppose that* $Y_1, Y_2, \ldots, Y_n$ *are independently and identically distributed according to the density* (3.3). *Then the ratio* R_n *defined by* (3.5), (3.6) *and*

(3.8) $$R_n = \frac{S_n - Y_n^*}{Y_n^* \log n}$$

has a limiting distribution as $n \to \infty$ *with density* $\frac{1}{2}\exp(-\frac{1}{2}r)$ *on* $0 < r < \infty$.

Actually, we prove a stronger result. Standard extreme value theory gives a limiting distribution for Y_n^*, and we find in the following lemma a limiting conditional distribution, actually a single point distribution, for R_n given Y_n^*. Thus we have in effect a limiting joint distribution for R_n and Y_n^* from which the theorem follows easily.

Lemma. *Suppose that* Z_n *is the* p *quantile of* Y_n^*, *i.e.*,

(3.9) $$\Pr(Y_n^* \leq Z_n) = p,$$

for $n = 1,2,\ldots$. *Then the sequence of conditional distributions of* R_n *given that* $Y_n^* = Z_n$ *converges to a distribution concentrated at the single point* $-2 \log p$.

To deduce the theorem from the lemma, note that

$$\lim_{n\to\infty} \Pr(R_n > r) = \lim_{n\to\infty} \int_0^1 \Pr(R_n > r \mid Y_n^* = Z_n)dp$$

$$= \int_0^1 \lim_{n\to\infty} \Pr(R_n > r \mid Y_n^* = Z_n)dp = e^{-\frac{1}{2}r}$$

because

$$\lim_{n\to\infty} \Pr(R_n > r \mid Y_n^* = Z_n) = 1 \quad \text{if} \quad r < -2 \log p$$
$$= 0 \quad \text{otherwise} .$$

To prove the lemma, we study the mean E_n and variance V_n of the conditional distribution of R_n given $Y_n^* = Z_n$, and show that $E_n \to -2 \log p$ while $V_n \to 0$. The distribution of $S_n - Y_n^*$ given $Y_n^* = Z_n$ is the $(n-1)$ fold convolution of the distribution (3.3) restricted to the range $(1,Z_n)$. Consequently

(3.10) $$E_n = \frac{n-1}{Z_n \log n} \cdot \frac{2 (\log Z_n)^{\frac{1}{2}}}{\sqrt{\pi}\ (1-f(Z_n))} .$$

Since $Z_n \to\infty$, to show that $E_n \to -2 \log p$, it is equivalent to show that

(3.11) $$\frac{2}{\sqrt{\pi}} \cdot \frac{n}{\log n} \cdot \frac{(\log Z_n)^{\frac{1}{2}}}{Z_n} \underset{n\to\infty}{\to} -2 \log p.$$

Next we use the known limiting distribution of Y_n^*. From a result of Fisher and Gnedenko (c.f. Feller [7]),

$$\lim_{n\to\infty} \Pr\left(\frac{Y_n^*}{B_n} \leq \lambda\right) = e^{-1/\lambda} \tag{3.12}$$

where the sequence B_n is defined by

$$f(B_n) = \frac{1}{n} \quad . \tag{3.13}$$

It follows that, for the sequence Z_n defined above for a given p,

$$\lim_{n\to\infty} \frac{Z_n}{B_n} = \lambda \tag{3.14}$$

where

$$\lambda = -1/\log p. \tag{3.15}$$

Substituting from (3.13) into the second term of the left side of (3.11) and from (3.14) into the third term, and replacing Z_n by x, we see that (3.11) is equivalent to the relation

$$\frac{1}{\sqrt{\pi}} \cdot \frac{-1}{f(x)\log f(x)} \cdot \frac{(\log x)^{\frac{1}{2}}}{x} \underset{x\to\infty}{\to} 1 \quad . \tag{3.16}$$

Relation (3.16) follows directly from

$$\frac{f(x)}{x\phi(x)} \underset{x\to\infty}{\to} 1 \tag{3.17}$$

together with the specific form (3.3) of $\phi(x)$, while relation (3.17) follows from checking that

$$\frac{\frac{d}{dx} f(x)}{\frac{d}{dx}(x\phi(x))} \underset{x\to\infty}{\to} 1 \quad . \tag{3.18}$$

To see that $V_n \to 0$ we note that

$$V_n \le \frac{(n-1)}{(\log n)^2 Z_n^2} E(Y^2 \mid Y \le Z_n) \tag{3.19}$$

and we note Theorem I (VIII.9) in Feller [7] stating that

$$\lim_{n\to\infty} \frac{Z_n^3 \phi(Z_n)}{E(Y^2 \mid Y \le Z_n)} = 1 \quad . \tag{3.20}$$

Thus, we have from the (3.13), (3.17), (3.19) and (3.20) that

$$\begin{aligned} \lim_{n\to\infty} V_n &\le \lim_{n\to\infty} \frac{n Z_n \phi(Z_n)}{(\log n)^2} = \lim_{n\to\infty} \frac{n f(Z_n)}{(\log n)^2} \\ &= \lim_{n\to\infty} \frac{1}{\lambda(\log n)^2} = 0 \end{aligned} \tag{3.21}$$

and consequently $V_n \to 0$.

Comment. If (3.3) is generalized to

$$\phi(y) = \frac{1}{\Gamma(1-\alpha)} y^{-2} (\log y)^{-\alpha} \quad , \tag{3.22}$$

the above theorem and proof generalize directly to show that the density of the limiting distribution of R_n in (3.8) is $(1-\alpha) \exp((1-\alpha)r)$. Other special cases, such as a Pareto distribution in place of (3.3), can be easily handled. We have not yet obtained general theory for densities which are regularly varying with exponent -2.

4. *Computing algorithms.* The Bayesian analyses of §2 require that the weights wt(I) be computed for all $\binom{n}{k}$ subsets I. Clearly this may be computationally infeasible for commonly occurring choices of k and n. Fortunately, there are two mitigating circumstances. First, it is possible to define a sequence of subsets I such that consecutive

blocks within the sequence have decreasing weights wt(I) within each block and such that all weights above a certain threshold are found with reasonable efficiency by following the sequence. Second, it appears to be generally true that the number of weights making a numerically significant contribution to the total is relatively small and can be handled by a computer. For example, in the analysis shown in Table 2 it was found adequate to use a single substitution algorithm. That is, only $(n-k) \times k$ subsets I had to be passed through, where these subsets were found by substituting each of the $n-k$ least extreme observations into the k positions of the initial choice of I, which maximizes wt(I) by choosing the k most extreme observations. Further details of algorithms and why they are practicable will be reported in [8].

References

1. Anscombe, F. J. (1960). "Rejection of Outliers", *Technometrics*, 2, 123-148.

2. Box, G.E.P. and G.C. Tiao, (1968). "A Bayesian Approach to some Outlier problems", *Biometrika*, 55.

3. Daniel, Cuthbert, (1959). "Use of half-normal plots in interpreting factorial two-level experiments", *Technometrics*, 1, 311-41.

4. Darling, D. A. (1952). "The Influence of the Maximum Term in the Addition of Independent Random Variables", *Trans Amer. Math. Soc.*, 73, 95-107.

5. David, H. A. (1970). *Order Statistics*, John Wiley & Sons, Inc.

6. Dempster, A. P. (1970). "Model searching and estimation in the logic of inference", To appear in the *Proceedings of the International Symposium on Statistical Inference*, University of Waterloo.

7. Feller, W. (1966). *An Introduction to Probability Theory and its Applications*, Vol. II, John Wiley & Sons.

8. Rosner, Bernard. *Detection of Outliers*, Ph.D. Thesis, Harvard University, Department of Statistics, (in preparation).

9. Savage, L. J. (1954). *Foundation of Statistics*, John Wiley & Sons, Inc.

10. Wald, Abraham, (1950). *Statistical Decision Functions*, John Wiley & Sons, Inc.

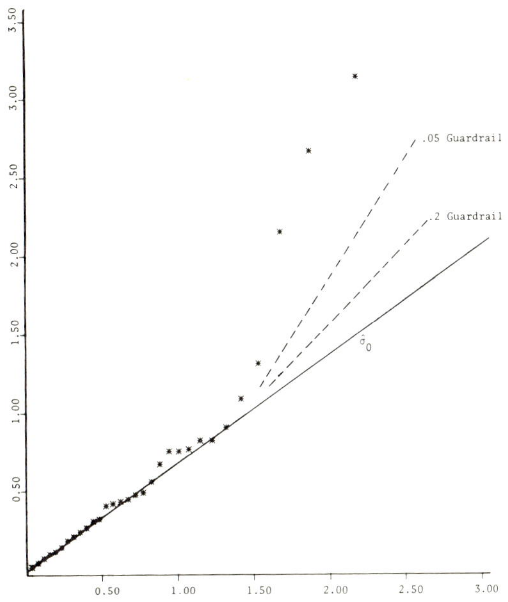

Figure 1. A half-normal probability plot of the data in Table 1 for the case $k = 0$. $\hat{\sigma}_0$ is the standard deviation estimated by Daniel.

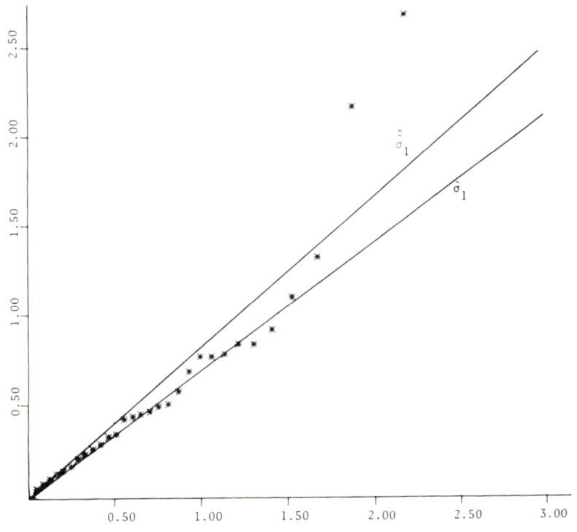

Figure 2. A half normal probability plot of the data in Table 1 for the case $k = 1$. $\hat{\sigma}_1$ is the standard deviation estimated by Daniel, $\hat{\hat{\sigma}}_1$, is our estimated standard deviation.

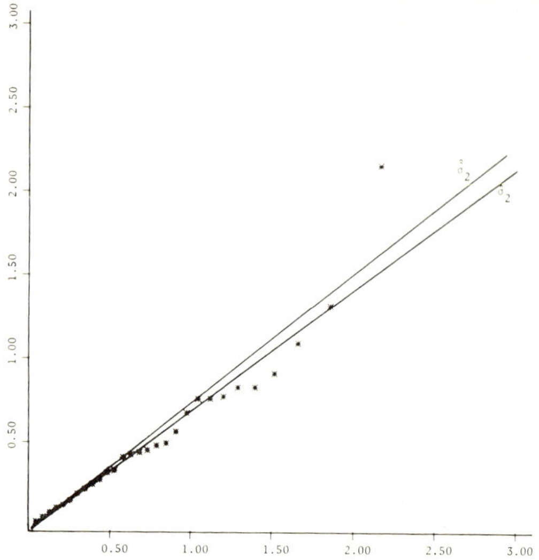

Figure 3. A half normal probability plot of the data in Table 1 for the case k = 2. $\hat{\sigma}_2$ is the standard deviation estimated by Daniel $\hat{\hat{\sigma}}_2$ is our estimated standard deviation.

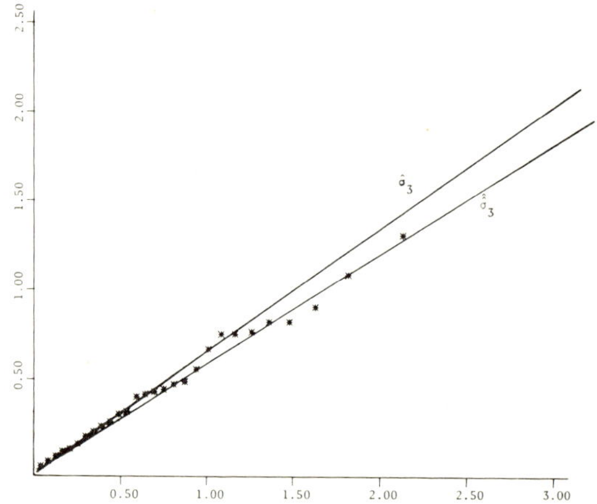

Figure 4. A half normal probability plot of the data in Table 1 for the case k = 3. $\hat{\sigma}_3$ is the standard deviation estimated by Daniel, $\hat{\hat{\sigma}}_3$, is our estimated standard deviation.

EMPIRICAL BAYES SLIPPAGE TESTS*

By J. Van Ryzin
University of Wisconsin

1. *Introduction and summary.* The empirical Bayes approach to statistical decision theory is applicable when one is confronted repeatedly and independently with the same decision problem. In such instances it is reasonable to formulate the component problems in the sequence as Bayes decision problems with respect to a completely *unknown* prior distribution on the parameter space and then use the accumulated observations to improve the decision rule at each stage. This approach is due to H. Robbins [4] and is best presented in his paper [5]. We assume familiarity with [5].

Many empirical Bayes procedures have been shown to be asymptotically optimal in the sense that the risk for the nth decision problem converges to the optimal Bayes risk. This risk is obtained if the prior distribution were *known* and the Bayes rule with respect to this prior distribution were used.

This paper studies slippage tests from an empirical Bayes point of view. In so doing we apply certain earlier results of the author [6] concerning general empirical Bayes multiple decision problems. For a discussion of multiple

*This research was supported by the National Science Foundation Grant NSF Contract No. GP-9324 at the University of Wisconsin.

decision problems and in particular the slippage problem see Chapter 6 of Ferguson [2]. References for the slippage problem are contained therein. Additional references on empirical Bayes theory may be found in the papers [3] - [6].

Section 2 discusses empirical Bayes slippage tests in the general framework of empirical Bayes multiple decision problems. Section 3 contains theorems on asymptotic optimality and convergence rate properties of empirical Bayes procedures for slippage problems in which the distributions are known. In Section 4, we study empirical Bayes procedures for slippage problems on an unknown location parameter. Asymptotically optimal procedures with rate results are obtained for tests based on the maximal invariant. Finally, the case of empirical Bayes slippage tests for normal distribution families is treated in Section 5.

2. *Empirical Bayes slippage tests.* Consider the following slippage problem, referred to hereafter as the component problem. Let $\underset{\sim}{X} = (X_1,\ldots,X_k)$ be an observable random variable with values in $\mathcal{X}^k$, a k-dimensional space. Let P_0 and P_1 be two probability measures on $(\mathcal{X},\mathcal{B})$ ($\mathcal{B}$ a σ-field) which are dominated by a σ-finite measure μ^*. Let $f_i(x) = (dP_i/d\mu^*)(x)$ be the μ^*-density of X under P_i, $i = 0,1$.

In the slippage problem, the statistician is interested in a multiple hypothesis testing problem between hypotheses $H_0,\ldots,H_k$. Under H_0, $\underset{\sim}{X}$ is distributed with joint density $f_0(\underset{\sim}{x}) = \Pi_{j=1}^k f_0(x_j)$, while under H_i, $\underset{\sim}{X}$ is distributed with joint density $f_i(\underset{\sim}{x}) = \{\Pi_{j\neq i} f_0(x_j)\} f_1(x_i)$. Under H_i, $i = 1,\ldots,k$ we say X_i or population i has "slipped" from distribution P_0 to distribution P_1. Hypothesis H_0 represents no slippage. In such a decision problem, the parameter space becomes $\Omega = \{0,\ldots,k\}$ where the parameter value i indicates that hypothesis H_i is true. The action space is taken as $A = \{0,\ldots,k\}$ where action j represents deciding in favor of hypothesis H_j, $j = 0,\ldots,k$. Associated with this slippage problem is a specified loss function (or matrix of losses) $L(i,j) < \infty$, $i, j = 0,\ldots,k$. Finally, let Λ be an Ω-valued (unobservable) random variable which has a priori distribution $G = (g_0,\ldots,g_k)$ on Ω where

$$(1) \qquad g_i = \Pr\{\Lambda=i\} \geqq 0, \quad i = 0,\ldots,k, \quad \sum_{i=0}^{k} g_i = 1 \quad .$$

In such a slippage problem, the statistician's problem is to choose a behaviorial (measurable) decision rule $t(\underset{\sim}{x}) = (t(o|\underset{\sim}{x}),\ldots,t(k|\underset{\sim}{x}))$, where $t(j|\underset{\sim}{x}) = \Pr\{\text{taking action } j|\underset{\sim}{X} = \underset{\sim}{x}\}$ and

$$(2) \qquad 0 \leqq t(j|\underset{\sim}{x}) \leqq 1, \quad \sum_{j=0}^{k} t(j|\underset{\sim}{x}) = 1 \quad \text{a.e. } \mu$$

where μ denotes product measure on $(\mathcal{X}^k, \mathcal{B}^k)$. The risk of such a decision rule when i is the parameter value is

$$(3) \qquad R(i,t) = \sum_{j=0}^{k} L(i,j)E_i[t(j|\underset{\sim}{X})] \quad ,$$

where E_i denotes expectation under H_i. The *Bayes risk* with respect to a priori distribution G is

$$(4) \qquad \begin{aligned} r(G,t) &= \sum_{i=0}^{k} g_i R(i,t) \\ &= \sum_{j=0}^{k} \int t(j|\underset{\sim}{x})[\sum_{i=0}^{k} g_i L(i,j) f_i(\underset{\sim}{x})]d\mu(\underset{\sim}{x}) \quad , \end{aligned}$$

which is minimized by taking $t(j|\underset{\sim}{x}) = t_G(j|\underset{\sim}{x})$, $j = 0,\ldots,k$, where subject to measurability requirements,

$$(5)\quad t_G(j|x) = \begin{cases} 0 & \text{if } \sum_{i=0}^{k} g_i L(i,j) f_i(\underset{\sim}{x}) \\ & \quad > \min_\nu \sum_{i=0}^{k} g_i L(i,\nu) f_i(\underset{\sim}{x}) \\ \gamma_j(\underset{\sim}{x}) & \text{if } \sum_{i=0}^{k} g_i L(i,j) f_i(\underset{\sim}{x}) \\ & \quad = \min \sum_{i=0}^{k} g_i L(i,\nu) f_i(\underset{\sim}{x}) \quad , \end{cases}$$

$0 \leq \gamma_j(\underset{\sim}{x}) \leq 1, j = 0,\ldots,k; \sum_{j=0}^{k} \gamma_j(\underset{\sim}{x}) = 1$ a.e. μ. For later use we shall employ the equivalent form of (5) given by

$$(6)\quad t_G(j|\underset{\sim}{x}) = \begin{cases} 0 & \text{if } \Delta_G(j,\underset{\sim}{x}) > \min_\nu \Delta_G(\nu,x) \\ \gamma_j(\underset{\sim}{x}) & \text{if } \Delta_G(j,\underset{\sim}{x}) = \min_\nu \Delta_G(\nu,\underset{\sim}{x}) \end{cases}$$

$0 \leqq \gamma_j(\underset{\sim}{x}) \leqq 1$, $j = 0,\ldots,k$; $\sum_{j=0}^{k} \gamma_j(\underset{\sim}{x}) = 1$ a.e. μ and where

$$(7)\qquad \Delta_G(j,\underset{\sim}{x}) = \sum_{i=0}^{k} g_i \{L(i,j) - L(i,0)\} f_i(\underset{\sim}{x})$$

The rule $t_G(\underset{\sim}{x}) = (t_G(0|\underset{\sim}{x}),\ldots,t_G(k|\underset{\sim}{x}))$ defined by (5) or (6) and (7) is thus a Bayes rule relative to G, whose risk is

$$(8)\qquad r(G) = r(G,t_G) = \min_t r(G,t) \quad .$$

We shall refer to $r(G)$ as the *Bayes risk functional of* G.

When G is fully known to the statistician, he chooses as optimal a Bayes rule relative to G, t_G, defined by (6) to minimize his risk attaining $r(G)$ in (8). This, however, is usually impossible to do since G is rarely known. The risk $r(G)$ remains the goal to achieve even when G is *unknown* in the empirical Bayes approach.

If one is confronted with a repeated, independent sequence of such slippage problems, then the empirical Bayes approach of Robbins [5] is applicable. Often one can find an empirical Bayes procedure not knowing G which does almost as well as t_G in the $(n+1)$st problem when the number, n, of problems increases. Specifically, let $(\underset{\sim}{X}_1, \Lambda_1)$, $(\underset{\sim}{X}_2, \Lambda_2), \ldots$ be a sequence of mutually independent pairs of random variables where each Λ_ν is distributed as G on Ω and $\underset{\sim}{X}_\nu$ has conditional k-fold product density $f_i(\underset{\sim}{x})$ given $\Lambda_\nu = i$. The empirical Bayes approach attempts to construct a decision procedure concerning Λ_{n+1} (unobservable) at stage $n+1$ based on $\underset{\sim}{X}_1, \ldots, \underset{\sim}{X}_{n+1}$, the data available at stage $n+1$. The $(\Lambda_1, \ldots, \Lambda_n)$ remain unobservable. Therefore, we consider decision rules of the form

$$(9)\qquad \begin{aligned} t_n(\underset{\sim}{x}) &= (t_n(0|\underset{\sim}{x}), \ldots, t_n(k|\underset{\sim}{x})), \\ t_n(j|\underset{\sim}{x}) &= t_n(j|\underset{\sim}{x}_1, \ldots, \underset{\sim}{x}_n; \underset{\sim}{x}), \end{aligned}$$

$j = 0, \ldots, k$ subject to $\sum_{j=0}^{k} t_n(j|\underset{\sim}{x}) = 1$ a.e.μ (for fixed $\underset{\sim}{x}_1, \ldots, \underset{\sim}{x}_n$), and take action j with probability $t_n(j|\underset{\sim}{X}_{n+1})$ at stage $n+1$. The risk at stage $n+1$ is given by

$$(10)\qquad r^*(G, t_n) = \sum_{j=0}^{k} E \int t_n(j|\underset{\sim}{x}) [\sum_{i=0}^{k} L(i,j) f_i(\underset{\sim}{x}) g_i] d\mu(\underset{\sim}{x}),$$

where E denotes expectation with respect to the n independent random variables $\underset{\sim}{X}_1, \ldots, \underset{\sim}{X}_n$ each with common μ-density

$$(11)\qquad f_G(\underset{\sim}{x}) = \sum_{i=0}^{k} g_i f_i(\underset{\sim}{x}) .$$

Note that since the procedure $t_G(\underset{\sim}{x})$ in (5) is Bayes in the (n+1)st decision problem concerning Λ_{n+1},

(12) $$r^*(G,t_n) \geq r(G), \quad n = 1,\ldots$$

Hence, in empirical Bayes theory the non-negative difference $r^*(G,t_n) - r(G)$ is used as a measure of near optimality of the sequence of procedures $\{t_n\}$ and we say:

Definition 1. (Robbins [5].) *The sequence of procedures* $\{t_n\}$ *is said to be asymptotically optimal* (a.o.) *relative to* G *if* $r^*(G,t_n) - r(G) = o(1)$ *as* $n \to \infty$.

Definition 2. *The sequence of procedures* $\{t_n\}$ *is said to be asymptotically optimal of order* α_n *relative to* G *if* $r^*(G,t_n) - r(G) = O(\alpha_n)$ *as* $n \to \infty$, *where* $\lim_{n\to\infty}\alpha_n = 0$.

In the remainder of the paper, we shall construct empirical Bayes rules for certain slippage problems. We shall do this by giving functions $\Delta_{j,n}(\underset{\sim}{x}) = \Delta_{j,n}(\underset{\sim}{x}_1,\ldots,\underset{\sim}{x}_n;\underset{\sim}{x})$ such that a.e. μ,

(13) $$\Delta_{j,n}(\underset{\sim}{x}) \xrightarrow{P} \Delta_G(j,\underset{\sim}{x}) \quad \text{as} \quad n \to \infty \quad ,$$

where $\xrightarrow{P}$ denotes convergence in probability with respect to the sequence of random variables $\{\underset{\sim}{X}_n\}$. The procedure $t_n(\underset{\sim}{x}) = (t_n(0|\underset{\sim}{x}),\ldots,t_n(k|\underset{\sim}{x}))$ is then defined by setting $\Delta_{o,n}(\underset{\sim}{x}) \equiv 0$ and taking

(14) $$t_n(j|\underset{\sim}{x}) = \begin{cases} 0 & \text{if } \Delta_{j,n}(\underset{\sim}{x}) > \min_\nu \Delta_{\nu,n}(\underset{\sim}{x}) \\ \\ \gamma_{j,n}(\underset{\sim}{x}) & \text{if } \Delta_{j,n}(\underset{\sim}{x}) = \min_\nu \Delta_{\nu,n}(\underset{\sim}{x}) \end{cases}$$

where the $\gamma_{j,n}(\underset{\sim}{x}) = \gamma_{j,n}(\underset{\sim}{x}_1,\ldots,\underset{\sim}{x}_n;\underset{\sim}{x})$ and $\sum_{j=1}^k \gamma_{j,n}(\underset{\sim}{x}) = 1$, $\gamma_{j,n}(\underset{\sim}{x}) \geq 0$ a.e. μ.

We shall propose and study various sequences $\{t_n\}$ in what follows.

3. *The case of known distributions.* Assume that the distributions P_i (and hence densities $f_i(x)$), $i = 0,1$ are completely specified. The component slippage problem then becomes the multiple hypothesis test between the simple hypotheses:

$$H_0: \quad X_j \sim P_0 \ , \ j = 1,\ldots,k$$

$$H_i: \quad X_j \sim P_0 \ , \ j \neq i, \ X_i \sim P_1 \ .$$

To construct empirical Bayes rules at stage $n+1$ for $\underset{\sim}{X}_{n+1} = (X_{1,n+1},\ldots,X_{k,n+1})$ based on the past n observation $\underset{\sim}{X}_\nu = (X_{1\nu},\ldots,X_{k\nu})$, it suffices to find functions $\Delta_{j,n}(\underset{\sim}{x})$ satisfying the consistency requirement (13). From (7) and (13) we see that this problem reduces to finding consistent estimates $\hat{g}_i$ of g_i, $i = 0,\ldots,k$. To do this suppose there exists a real-valued measurable function $\xi(x)$ on $\mathcal{X}$, such that

$$E^{(\theta)}\xi(X) = \int \xi(x) f_\theta(x) d\mu^*(x) = \theta, \ \theta = 0,1. \tag{15}$$

Now define,

$$\begin{aligned} \hat{g}_i &= \frac{1}{n} \sum_{\nu=1}^{n} \xi(X_{i\nu}), \ i = 1,\ldots,k \\ \hat{g}_0 &= 1 - \sum_{i=1}^{k} \hat{g}_i \ . \end{aligned} \tag{16}$$

Observe that if E_i denotes expectation under H_i, $i = 0,\ldots,k$ and if δ_{ij} is the Kronecker delta, then from (15) we have

$$E[\xi(X_{i\nu})] = \sum_{j=0}^{k} g_j E_j[\xi(X_{i\nu})]$$
$$= \sum_{j=0}^{k} g_j E^{(\delta_{ij})}[\xi(X)]$$
$$= g_i .$$

Hence, from (16) it follows that since $\sum_{i=0}^{k} g_i = 1$, we have

(17) $$E(\hat{g}_i) = g_i, \quad i = 0,\ldots,k.$$

Also by the law of large numbers, we see that

(18) $$\hat{g}_i \xrightarrow{P} g_i, \; i = 0,\ldots,k \quad .$$

Let us now define the functions $\Delta_{j,n}(\underset{\sim}{x})$ for $j=1,\ldots,k$ by

(19) $$\Delta_{j,n}(\underset{\sim}{x}) = \sum_{i=0}^{k} \hat{g}_i\{L(i,j) - L(i,0)\}f_i(\underset{\sim}{x}).$$

We can now state and prove the following theorem, part (i) of which is a direct consequence of Robbins [5, Corollary 1].

Theorem 1. *Let* $\{t_n\}=\{t_n(\underset{\sim}{X}_{n+1})\}=\{(t_n(0|\underset{\sim}{X}_{n+1}),\ldots,t_n(k|\underset{\sim}{X}_{n+1}))\}$ *be a sequence of empirical Bayes slippage tests defined via* (14), (16) *and* (19).

i) *If* $\xi(x)$ *is such that* (15) *holds, then the sequence* $\{t_n\}$ *is asymptotically optimal relative to any prior distribution* G.

ii) *If, in addition,*

(20) $$E^{(\theta)}\xi^2(X) = \int \xi^2(x)f_\theta(x)d\mu^*(x) < \infty \quad \text{for} \quad \theta = 0,1,$$

then the sequence $\{t_n\}$ *is asymptotically optimal of order* $n^{-1/2}$ *relative to any prior distribution* G.

Proof. To prove ii), consider the conditional risk of the

procedure $t_n(\underset{\sim}{X}_{n+1})$ at stage $n+1$ given the previous n observations $\underset{\sim}{X}_1,\ldots,\underset{\sim}{X}_n$. The risk is (see (4))

$$r(G,t_n) = \sum_{j=0}^{k} \int t_n(j|\underset{\sim}{x})[\sum_{i=0}^{k} g_i L(i,j) f_i(\underset{\sim}{x})]\,d\mu(\underset{\sim}{x}).$$

Since $t_G(\underset{\sim}{X}_{n+1})$ in (5) is Bayes against G in the $(n+1)$st problem, we have with probability one, $r(G,t_n) \geqq r(G)$. Furthermore, we shall show that with probability one,

$$(21) \qquad 0 \leqq r(G,t_n)-r(G) \leqq \sum_{j=1}^{k} \int |\Delta_{j,n}(\underset{\sim}{x})-\Delta_G(j,\underset{\sim}{x})|\,d\mu(\underset{\sim}{x}).$$

Inequality (21) follows by the following series of statements all holding with probability one with respect to the joint distribution of $\underset{\sim}{X}_1,\ldots,\underset{\sim}{X}_n$.

$$\begin{aligned} r(G,t_n)-r(G) &= \sum_{j=1}^{k}\int \{t_n(j|\underset{\sim}{x})-t_G(j|\underset{\sim}{x})\}\Delta_G(j,\underset{\sim}{x})\,d\mu(\underset{\sim}{x}) \\ &= \sum_{j=1}^{k}\int \{t_n(j|\underset{\sim}{x})-t_G(j|\underset{\sim}{x})\{\Delta_G(j,\underset{\sim}{x})-\Delta_{j,n}(\underset{\sim}{x})\}\,d\mu(\underset{\sim}{x}) \\ &\quad + \sum_{j=1}^{k}\int \{t_n(j|\underset{\sim}{x})-t_G(j|\underset{\sim}{x})\}\Delta_{j,n}(\underset{\sim}{x})\,d\mu(\underset{\sim}{x}) \\ &\leqq \sum_{j=1}^{k}\int |\Delta_{j,n}(\underset{\sim}{x})-\Delta_G(j,\underset{\sim}{x})|\,d\mu(\underset{\sim}{x}) \;, \end{aligned}$$

where the last inequality follows from the fact that the definition of $t_n(j|\underset{\sim}{x})$ and $t_G(j|\underset{\sim}{x})$ imply that

$$\begin{aligned} \sum_{j=1}^{k} t_n(j|\underset{\sim}{x})\Delta_{j,n}(\underset{\sim}{x}) &= \min_{0\leqq j\leqq k} \{\Delta_{j,n}(\underset{\sim}{x})\} \\ &= \sum_{j=0}^{k} t_G(j|\underset{\sim}{x}) \min_{0\leqq j\leqq k} \{\Delta_{j,n}(\underset{\sim}{x})\} \\ &\leqq \sum_{j=0}^{k} t_G(j|\underset{\sim}{x})\Delta_{j,n}(\underset{\sim}{x}) \\ &= \sum_{j=1}^{k} t_G(j|\underset{\sim}{x})\Delta_{j,n}(\underset{\sim}{x}) \quad . \end{aligned}$$

Taking expectations in (21) with respect to $X_1,\dots,X_n$, we have

$$(22) \qquad 0 \leqq r^*(G,t_n)-r(G) \leqq \sum_{j=1}^{k}\int E|\Delta_{j,n}(\underset{\sim}{x})-\Delta_G(j,\underset{\sim}{x})|\,d\mu(\underset{\sim}{x}).$$

But, from (7), (16), and (19) and the fact that $\int f_i(\underset{\sim}{x})d\mu(\underset{\sim}{x}) = 1$, we have with $c_{ij} = |L(i,j)-L(i,0)| + |L(0,j) - L(0,0)|$,

$$\int E|\Delta_{j,n}(\underset{\sim}{x})-\Delta_G(j,\underset{\sim}{x})|\,d\mu(\underset{\sim}{x}) \leqq \sum_{i=1}^{k} c_{ij}E|\hat{g}_i-g_i|$$

$$\leqq \sum_{i=1}^{k} c_{ij}\{E(\hat{g}_i-g_i)^2\}^{1/2}$$

$$= n^{-1/2}\sum_{i=1}^{k} c_{ij}\{\mathrm{Var}(\xi(X_{i1}))\}^{1/2} .$$

From this result, (21) yields $r^*(G,t_n) - r(G) \leqq Cn^{-1/2}$ where $C < \infty$ by (20) since

$$C = \sum_{j=1}^{k}\sum_{i=1}^{k} c_{ij}\{(1-g_i)E^{(0)}[\xi^2(X)]+g_iE^{(1)}[\xi^2(X)]-g_i^{\,2}\}^{1/2}.$$

We now state and prove.

Theorem 2. *Let*

$$\{t_n\} = \{t_n(\underset{\sim}{X}_{n+1})\} = \{(t_n(0|\underset{\sim}{X}_{n+1}),\dots,t_n(k|\underset{\sim}{X}_{n+1}))\}$$

be a sequence of empirical Bayes slippage tests defined via (14), (16) *and* (19). *If* $\xi(x)$ *is such that* (15) *holds and for all* $u\varepsilon(-\infty,+\infty)$, $\theta=0,1$,

$$(23) \qquad m_\theta(u) = E^{(\theta)}e^{u\xi(X)} = \int e^{u\xi(x)}f_\theta(x)\,d\mu^*(x) < \infty$$

then for every $\varepsilon > 0$ *there exists* $K = K(\varepsilon)$ *such that for all* G,

(24) $$P\{r(G,t_n) - r(G) \geqq \varepsilon\} \leqq (2k)e^{-nK} \quad .$$

Proof. From inequality (21), we have with probability one,

$$\begin{aligned} r(G,t_n)-r(G) &\leqq \textstyle\sum_{j=1}^{k} \int |\Delta_{j,n}(\underset{\sim}{x})-\Delta_G(j,\underset{\sim}{x})|\,d\mu(\underset{\sim}{x}) \\ &\leqq \textstyle\sum_{j=1}^{k} \sum_{i=0}^{k} |\hat{g}_i-g_i|\,|L(i,j)-L(i,0)| \\ &\leqq \textstyle\sum_{i=1}^{k} c_i|\hat{g}_i-g_i| \ , \end{aligned}$$

where $c_i = \sum_{j=1}^{k}\{|L(i,j)-L(i,0)|+|L(0,j)-L(0,0)|\}$. Hence with $\varepsilon_i = (c_i k)^{-1}\varepsilon$, we have

$$P\{r(G,t_n)-r(G) \geqq \varepsilon\} \leqq \textstyle\sum_{i=1}^{k} P\{|\hat{g}_i-g_i| \geqq \varepsilon_i\} \ .$$

We observe that $\hat{g}_i-g_i$ is an average of i.i.d. random variables $\xi(X_{\nu i})-g_i$, $\nu=1,\ldots,n$, with mean zero and finite moment generating function under condition (23). Therefore a result of Chernoff [1] states that there exists a $0 < \rho_i < 1$ such that $P\{\hat{g}_i-g_i \geqq \varepsilon_i\} \leqq \rho_i^{\,n}$. A similar result states that $P\{\hat{g}_i-g_i \leqq -\varepsilon_i\} \leqq (\rho_i^*)^n$ for some $0 < \rho_i^* < 1$. The result (24) now follows from (25) by taking $K = -\log\,[\max_i\{\max(\rho_i,\rho_i^*)\}]$.

Exponential convergence of the type given in Theorem 2 for empirical Bayes problems was first considered by Hudimoto [3] for a classification problem. In speaking of empirical Bayes rules $\{t_n\}$ satisfying (24) for some G we shall say the rules are *exponentially close* to optimality relative to G.

Note that the empirical Bayes slippage tests take on a

slightly simpler form if we divide the defining inequalities in (6) by $f_0(\underset{\sim}{x}) = \Pi_{i=1}^{k} f_0(x_i) > 0$ a.e. μ and if we randomize equally on the boundary in (6). Then (6) becomes

$$
(26) \quad t_G(j|\underset{\sim}{x}) = \begin{cases} 0 \text{ if } \sum_{i=0}^{k} g_i [L(i,j)-L(i,\nu)] \dfrac{f_1(x_i)}{f_0(x_i)} > 0 \\ \quad \text{for some } \nu \neq j \\ \dfrac{1}{r} \text{ if } \sum_{i=0}^{k} g_i [L(i,j)-L(i,\nu)] \dfrac{f_1(x_i)}{f_0(x_i)} = 0 \\ \quad \text{for } r \text{ of the } \nu\text{'s.} \end{cases}
$$

Hence, we could define $t_n(j|\underset{\sim}{x})$ in (14) more simply by replacing g_i by $\hat{g}_i$ in (26). Theorems 1 and 2 for such empirical Bayes slippage tests of course still hold.

Also, the rules simplify even more in the case of the usual zero-one loss function, that is, when $L(i,j) = 1-\delta_{ij}$. Then, (26) simplifies to

$$
(27) \quad t_G(j|\underset{\sim}{x}) = \begin{cases} 0 \text{ if } g_\nu \dfrac{f_1(x_\nu)}{f_0(x_\nu)} > g_j \dfrac{f_1(x_j)}{f_0(x_j)} \text{ for some } \nu \neq j \\ \dfrac{1}{r} \text{ if } g_\nu \dfrac{f_1(x_\nu)}{f_0(x_\nu)} = g_j \dfrac{f_1(x_j)}{f_0(x_j)} \text{ for } r \text{ of the } \nu\text{'s.} \end{cases}
$$

Examples.

i) The normal distribution

Let $f_\theta(x) = \dfrac{1}{\sqrt{2\pi}\sigma} \exp\{-1/2(\frac{x-\mu_\theta}{\sigma})^2\}, -\infty < x < +\infty, \theta=0,1, \mu_0 \neq \mu_1$.

Since σ^2 is known, we can without loss of generality take $\sigma^2 = 1$. Then,

$$
(28) \qquad \frac{f_1(x)}{f_0(x)} = \exp\{x(\mu_1-\mu_0) - \tfrac{1}{2}(\mu_1^2 - \mu_0^2)\} \quad .
$$

To construct the estimates $\hat{g}_i$, $i = 0,\ldots,k$, from the observations $\underset{\sim}{X}_\nu = (X_{1\nu},\ldots,X_{k\nu})$, $\nu=1,\ldots,n$ we define $\xi(x) = (\mu_1-\mu_0)^{-1}(x-\mu_0)$. Clearly (15) and (20) are satisfied. Hence, Theorem 2 gives asymptotic optimality of order $n^{-1/2}$ for the empirical Bayes slippage tests defined by (14) and (19) with

$$\hat{g}_i = \frac{\overline{X}_{i\cdot}-\mu_0}{\mu_1-\mu_0}, \quad \overline{X}_{i\cdot} = \frac{1}{n}\sum_{\nu=1}^{n} X_{i\nu} \quad .$$

Alternatively, we could define $\{t_n\}$ by (26) with $\hat{g}_i$ replacing g_i and using (28). Note that since (23) also holds, the empirical Bayes slippage tests given here are exponentially close to optimality relative to any prior distribution G.

ii) The binomial distribution.

Let $f_\theta(x)=\binom{m}{x}p_\theta{}^x(1-p_\theta)^{m-x}$, $x = 0,\ldots,m$. Then,

$$\left(\frac{f_1(x)}{f_0(x)}\right) = \left(\frac{p_1(1-p_0)}{p_0(1-p_1)}\right)^x \left(\frac{1-p_1}{1-p_0}\right)^m \quad .$$

To construct the estimates $\hat{g}_i$, $i = 1,\ldots,k$, take $\xi(x) = (x-mp_0)\{m(p_1-p_0)\}^{-1}$. Then we have

$$g_i = (\overline{X}_{i\cdot} - mp_0)\{m(p_1-p_0)\}^{-1}, \ \overline{X}_{i\cdot} = n^{-1}\sum_{\nu=1}^{n} X_{i\nu} \ .$$

Again conditions (15) and (20) of Theorem 1 and condition (23) of Theorem 2 hold. Thus the empirical Bayes slippage tests so defined via (14) and (19) or (26) with g_i replaced by $\hat{g}_i$ are asymptotically optimal of order $n^{-1/2}$ and exponentially close to optimality for any unknown prior distribution.

Remark. Note that for two distinct known distributions $f_0(x)$ and $f_1(x)$ we may always construct a *bounded* function $\xi(x)$ satisfying (15) and a fortiori (20) and (23). To do this pick the measure $\mu^* = P_0 + P_1$ and define $\xi(x) = (c_{11}c_{00} - c_{01}^2)^{-1}[c_{00}f_1(x) - c_{01}f_0(x)]$, $c_{ij} = \int f_i(x)f_j(x)d\mu^*(x)$, $i,j = 0,1$. Hence, for two known distributions one may always define empirical Bayes slippage tests which are asymptotically optimal of order $n^{-1/2}$ as well as exponentially close to optimality relative to any prior distribution G.

4. *The case of a location parameter.* We consider now the case where the component slippage problem can be stated as follows. Let $f_0(x) = f(x-\theta)$ and $f_1(x) = f(x-\theta-\Delta)$, $\Delta>0$ a known quantity, θ an unknown location parameter and $f(x)$ a known density. The component slippage test is then between the $k+1$ composite hypotheses:

$$\text{(29)}\quad \begin{aligned} &H_0: \quad X_j \sim f(x-\theta), \quad j = 1,\ldots,k \\ &H_i: \quad X_j \sim f(x-\theta),\ j\neq i \quad \text{and} \quad X_i \sim f(x-\theta-\Delta). \end{aligned}$$

One way of treating this problem from the viewpoint of empirical Bayes theory would be to construct consistent estimates $\hat{g}_i$ of g_i, $i = 0,\ldots,k$ and a consistent estimate of θ from the past n observations and substitute these estimated values into the corresponding Bayes rule $t_G(\underset{\sim}{x})$ in (6) and (7), (26) or (27). This will be done for the normal case in Section 5.

However, in this section we shall treat the problem using invariance theory. Note that the component slippage problem is invariant under location change. That is, the composite hypotheses H_i, $i = 0,\ldots,k$ are unchanged under location change. Hence, we shall impose upon the component problem slippage tests that they be invariant under change in location. That is, assume

$$t(j|\underset{\sim}{x}) = t(j|x_1,\ldots,x_k) = t(j|x_1+c,\ldots,x_k+c) \quad \text{for all } c > 0 . \tag{30}$$

To find procedures $t(j|\underset{\sim}{x})$ satisfying (30), we consider rules that are functions of the maximal invariant $Y_1,\ldots,Y_{k-1}$, where $Y_i = X_i - X_k$, $i = 1,\ldots,k-1$. In order to obtain the joint distribution of $Y_1,\ldots,Y_{k-1}$, we make the additional assumption that either (i)μ^* is Lebesque measure on the real line or (ii)μ^* is counting measure on the integers.

The joint density of $Y_i = X_i - X_k$, $i = 1,\ldots,k-1$ is obtained from the joint density of $X_1,\ldots,X_k$ by first obtaining the joint density of $Y_i = X_i - X_k$, $i=1,\ldots,k-1$ and $U = X_k$. This density under H_i, $i = 0,\ldots,k$ is given by

$$f_i'(y_1,\ldots,y_{k-1},u) = \Pi_{j=1}^{k} f(y_j+u-\theta-\delta_{ij}\Delta) .$$

Hence, the joint density of $Y_1,\ldots,Y_{k-1}$ under H_i, $i = 0,\ldots,k$ becomes

$$\begin{aligned} f_i^*(y_1,\ldots,y_{k-1}) &= \int\{\Pi_{j=1}^{k} f(y_j+u-\theta-\delta_{ij}\Delta)\}d\mu^*(u) \\ &= \int\{\Pi_{j=1}^{k} f(y_j+t-\delta_{ij} \quad)\}d\mu^*(t) . \end{aligned} \tag{31}$$

For example, in the case of the normal density where $f(t) = \psi(t) = (2\pi)^{-1/2}\exp\{-\frac{1}{2}t^2\}$, we have (see Ferguson [2,

p. 304]) the density in (31) for $i = 1,\ldots,k$ becoming

$$f_i^*(y_1,\ldots,y_{k-1}) = \left(\frac{1}{k(2\pi)^{k-1}}\right)^{1/2}\exp\{-\tfrac{1}{2}\textstyle\sum_{i=1}^{k}(y_i-\bar{y})^2 - \frac{\Delta^2(k-1)}{2k} + \Delta(y_i-\bar{y})\} \tag{32}$$

where $y_k = 0$. Under H_0 the density is given by (32) with $\Delta = 0$.

The Bayes rule for the problem based on the maximal invariant and satisfying (30) becomes

$$t_G(j|\underset{\sim}{x}) = \begin{cases} 0 & \text{if } \Delta_G(j,\underset{\sim}{y}) > \min_\nu \Delta_G(\nu,\underset{\sim}{y}) \\ \gamma_j(\underset{\sim}{y}) & \text{if } \Delta_G(j,\underset{\sim}{y}) = \min_\nu \Delta_G(\nu,\underset{\sim}{y}) \end{cases} \tag{33}$$

where $0 \leq \gamma_j(\underset{\sim}{y}) \leq 1$, $j = 0,\ldots,k$, $\sum_{j=1}^{k}\gamma_j(\underset{\sim}{y}) = 1$ and for $j = 0,\ldots,k$

$$\Delta_G(j,\underset{\sim}{y}) = \textstyle\sum_{i=0}^{k} g_i[L(i,j)-L(i,0)]f_i^*(y_1,\ldots,y_{k-1}). \tag{34}$$

The problem now reduces to finding estimates $\hat{g}_i$ of g_i, $i = 0,\ldots,k$ and defining the rules

$$t_n(j|\underset{\sim}{x}) = \begin{cases} 0 & \text{if } \Delta_n(j,\underset{\sim}{y}) > \min_\nu \Delta_n(\nu,\underset{\sim}{y}) \\ \gamma_{j,n}(\underset{\sim}{y}) & \text{if } \Delta_n(j,\underset{\sim}{y}) = \min_\nu \Delta_n(j,\underset{\sim}{y}) \end{cases} \tag{35}$$

where $0 \leq \gamma_{j,n}(\underset{\sim}{y}) = \gamma_{j,n}(\underset{\sim}{x}_1,\ldots,\underset{\sim}{x}_n;\underset{\sim}{y}) \leq 1$, $j = 0,\ldots,k$, $\sum_{j=0}^{k}\gamma_{j,n}(\underset{\sim}{y}) = 1$ and for $j = 0,\ldots,k$,

$$\Delta_n(j,\underset{\sim}{y}) = \textstyle\sum_{i=0}^{k}\hat{g}_i[L(i,j)-L(i,0)]f_i^*(y_1,\ldots,y_{k-1}). \tag{36}$$

To do this, suppose there exist functions $H_j(\underset{\sim}{x})$ such that

$$(37) \qquad E_i\{H_j(\underset{\sim}{X})\} = \int H_j(\underset{\sim}{x}) f_i(\underset{\sim}{x}) d\mu(\underset{\sim}{x}) = \delta_{ij}$$

$i,j=0,\ldots,k$, with δ_{ij} the Kronecker delta. Then define

$$(38) \qquad \hat{g}_j = \frac{1}{n} \sum_{\nu=1}^{n} H_j(\underset{\sim}{X}_\nu) \quad .$$

Observe that by (37) and the law of large numbers, for $j = 0,\ldots,k$

$$(39) \qquad E(\hat{g}_j) = \sum_{i=0}^{k} g_i E_i\{H_j(\underset{\sim}{X})\} = g_j \, , \quad \text{and}$$

$$\hat{g}_j \xrightarrow{P} g_j \quad \text{as} \quad n \to \infty \quad .$$

We can now state the following theorem whose proof is similar to the proofs of Theorems 1 and 2 and is thus omitted.

Theorem 3. *Let* $\{t_n(\underset{\sim}{X}_{n+1})\} = \{t_n(0|\underset{\sim}{X}_{n+1}),\ldots,t_n(k|\underset{\sim}{X}_{n+1})\}$ *be a sequence of empirical Bayes slippage tests defined by* (35), (36) *and* (38). *Let* $H_j(\underset{\sim}{x})$, $j = 0,\ldots,k$ *be such that* (37) *holds.*

i) *Then the sequence* $\{t_n\}$ *is asymptotically optimal relative to any prior distribution* G.

ii) *If for* $i,j = 0,\ldots,k$

$$E_i H_j^2(\underset{\sim}{X}) = \int H_j^2(\underset{\sim}{x}) f_i(\underset{\sim}{x}) d\mu(\underset{\sim}{x}) < \infty \, ,$$

then the sequence $\{t_n\}$ *is asymptotically optimal of order* $n^{-1/2}$ *relative to any prior distribution* G.

iii) *If for* $i,j = 0,\ldots,k$, $u \varepsilon (-\infty, +\infty)$,

$$(40) \qquad m_{ij}(u) = E_i e^{uH_j(\underset{\sim}{X})} = \int e^{uH_j(\underset{\sim}{x})} f_i(\underset{\sim}{x}) d\mu(\underset{\sim}{x}) < \infty \, ,$$

then for every $\varepsilon > 0$, *there exists a* $K = K(\varepsilon) > 0$, *such that for all* G,

$$P\{r(G,t_n) - r(G) \geqq \varepsilon\} \leqq (2k)e^{-nK} .$$

Constructing estimates $\hat{g}_i$, $i = 0,\ldots,k$.

i) *Known variance case.* Let $\underset{\sim}{X} = (X_1,\ldots,X_k)$ be a random variable distributed under H_i with density $f_i(\underset{\sim}{x}) = \Pi_{j=1}^k f(x_j - \theta - \delta_{ij}\Delta)$. Observe that

$$\sigma^2 = \int x^2 f(x)d\mu^*(x) = \int (x-\theta)^2 f(x-\theta)d\mu^*(x)$$

is independent of θ for a location parameter family. In what follows, we assume $\sigma^2 < \infty$ and known.

Define, for $j = 1,\ldots,k$

$$(41) \qquad H_j(\underset{\sim}{x}) = \frac{1}{2(k-1)} \sum_{t \neq j} \left[\frac{(x_j - x_t)^2 - 2\sigma^2}{\Delta^2} + \frac{(x_j - x_t)}{\Delta} \right]$$

and, $H_0(\underset{\sim}{x}) = 1 - \sum_{j=1}^k H_j(\underset{\sim}{x})$.

Note that if E_i denotes expectation under hypothesis H_i, we have for $i = 0,\ldots,k$, $j \neq t$

$$(42) \qquad E_i(X_j - X_t)^2 = 2\sigma^2 + (\delta_{ij} - \delta_{it})^2 \Delta^2$$

and

$$(43) \qquad E_i(X_j - X_t) = (\delta_{ij} - \delta_{it}) \Delta$$

Therefore, for $i = 0,\ldots,k$; $j = 1,\ldots,k$,

$$(44) \qquad E_i[H_j(\underset{\sim}{X})] = \frac{1}{2(k-1)} \sum_{t \neq j} \{(\delta_{ij} - \delta_{it})^2 + (\delta_{ij} - \delta_{it})\} = \delta_{ij}$$

and for $i = 0,\ldots,k$

$$E_i[H_0(\underset{\sim}{X})] = 1-\sum_{j=1}^{k}\delta_{ij} = \delta_{i0} .$$

Thus, we have shown that with known variance σ^2, the set of functions $H_j(\underset{\sim}{x})$ required in Theorem 3 satisfying (37) are easily constructable. Hence, we may state:

Conclusion ii) *of Theorem* 3, *asymptotic optimality of order* $n^{-1/2}$, *holds for the location parameter family with known variance* $\sigma^2 < \infty$ *when* $\{t_n\}$ *is defined by* (35), (36), (38) *and* (41). *Furthermore, if* $m(u) = \int e^{ux}f(x)d\mu^*(x) < \infty$ *for* $u\varepsilon(-\infty,+\infty)$, *then* $\{t_n\}$ *so defined is exponentially close to optimality for all* G.

For example, in the case of the normal distribution, where $f(x) = (2\pi\sigma^2)^{-1/2}\exp\{-(2\sigma^2)^{-1}x^2\}$, $\{t_n\}$ defined by (35), (36), (38) and (41) is both asymptotically optimal of order $n^{-1/2}$ and exponentially close to optimality for all G.

ii) *General Case.* In general, one can *always* construct the functions $H_j(\underset{\sim}{x})$ satisfying (37). To see this, observe that the functions $f_i(\underset{\sim}{x})$, $i = 0,\ldots,k$ are linearly independent in the space of μ integrable functions, $L_1(\mu)$. This, in turn, can be shown to imply that the functions $f_i{}^*(\underset{\sim}{y})$, $i = 0,\ldots,k$ are linearly independent in $L_1(\mu')$, μ' the k-1 fold product measure of μ^*. Under these conditions a set of functions $H_j(\underset{\sim}{x})$ satisfying (37) are given by

$$\begin{pmatrix} H_0(\underset{\sim}{x}) \\ \vdots \\ H_k(\underset{\sim}{x}) \end{pmatrix} = A \begin{pmatrix} f_0^*(\underset{\sim}{y}) \\ \vdots \\ f_k^*(\underset{\sim}{y}) \end{pmatrix}$$

where $A = B^{-1}$ with B the $(k+1) \times (k+1)$ matrix whose (i,j)th element is $b_{ij} = \int f_i^*(\underset{\sim}{y}) f_j^*(\underset{\sim}{y}) d\mu'(\underset{\sim}{y})$. For details of this matrix form see Van Ryzin [6, Section 4, Remark 1]. See Robbins [5, Section 7] for a general discussion of estimation of priors in the finite parameter case. The g_j would then be defined by (38) with $H_j(\underset{\sim}{x}) = \sum_{t=0}^{k} a_{jt} f_t^*(\underset{\sim}{y})$.

Although such a set of functions $H_j(\underset{\sim}{x})$ are always constructable by the above procedure, it is often times possible to find a simpler set of functions $H_j(\underset{\sim}{x})$ such as those given in (i).

5. *The case of the normal distribution.* Consider the case where the component slippage problem may be stated as the following multiple hypothesis testing problem.

$$(45) \quad \begin{aligned} &H_0: \; X_j \sim N(\mu,\sigma^2), \; j = 1,\ldots,k \\ &H_i: \; X_j \sim N(\mu,\sigma^2), \; j \neq i \;\text{ and }\; X_i \sim N(\mu+\Delta,\sigma^2), \end{aligned}$$

where $\Delta > 0$ is assumed known.

Case 1. μ *unknown*, σ^2 *known*. This case has already been treated in Section 4 by using procedures in (35) based on the component problem maximal invariant with the $\hat{g}_j$, $j=0,\ldots,k$ given by (38) and (41). A second way of treating this problem is as follows.

With $\underset{\sim}{X} = (X_1,\ldots,X_k)$ as the generic random variable for the component problem, observe that

$$(46) \quad E(X_j) = \sum_{i=0}^{k} g_i E_i(X_j) = \sum_{i=0}^{k} g_i(\mu+\delta_{ij}\Delta) = \mu+g_j\Delta.$$

Also by (37) we have

(47) $$E(X_j - \Delta H_j(\underset{\sim}{X})) = \mu .$$

Therefore, by defining

(48) $$\hat{\mu} = \frac{1}{nk} \sum_{j=1}^{k} \sum_{\nu=1}^{n} \{X_{j\nu} - \Delta H_j(\underset{\sim}{X}_\nu)\}$$

we have that (47) and the law of large numbers imply

(49) $$E(\hat{\mu}) = \mu \quad \text{and} \quad \hat{\mu} \xrightarrow{P} \mu \quad \text{as} \quad n \to \infty .$$

Now, construct the sequence of procedures

$$\{t_n(\underset{\sim}{X}_{n+1})\} = \{t_n(0|\underset{\sim}{X}_{n+1}), \ldots, t_n(k|\underset{\sim}{X}_{n+1})\},$$

where

(50) $$t_n(j|\underset{\sim}{x}) = \begin{cases} 0 & \text{if } \Delta_n(j,\underset{\sim}{x}) > \min_\nu \Delta_n(\nu,\underset{\sim}{x}) \\ \gamma_{j,n}(\underset{\sim}{x}) & \text{if } \Delta_n(j,\underset{\sim}{x}) = \min_\nu \Delta_n(\nu,\underset{\sim}{x}), \end{cases}$$

$0 \leqq \gamma_{j,n}(\underset{\sim}{x}) \leqq 1, j=0,\ldots,k, \sum_{j=0}^{k} \gamma_{j,n}(\underset{\sim}{x}) = 1$, and for $j=0,\ldots,k$

(51) $$\Delta_n(j|\underset{\sim}{x}) = \sum_{i=0}^{k} \hat{g}_i [L(i,j) - L(i,0)] \{\Pi_{j=1}^{k} \psi(\frac{x_\nu - \hat{\mu} - \delta_{j\nu}\Delta}{\sigma})\}$$

with $\psi(t) = (2\pi)^{-1/2} \exp\{-t^2/2\}$.

Equation (38) together with (49) and continuity of $\psi(t)$ implies from (51) that

(52) $$\Delta_n(j,\underset{\sim}{x}) \xrightarrow{P} \Delta_G(j,\underset{\sim}{x}) \quad \text{as} \quad n \to \infty, \ j=0,\ldots,k.$$

Hence by using Corollary 1 of Robbins [5], we may state:

In case 1, the sequence of empirical Bayes slippage tests $\{t_n\}$ *defined by* (50), (51), (38), (41) *and* (48) *is asymptotically optimal relative to any* G.

Case 2. μ *known,* σ^2 *unknown.* Define for $j = 1,\ldots,k$,

(53) $$g_j^* = \frac{1}{\Delta}(\bar{X}_{j\cdot} - \mu), \quad \bar{X}_{j\cdot} = \frac{1}{n}\sum_{\nu=1}^{n} X_{j\nu} .$$

Then, by (46) and the law of large numbers, we have

(54) $$E(g_j^*) = g_j, \; g_j^* \xrightarrow{P} g_j \quad \text{as} \quad n \to \infty, \; j=1,\ldots,k.$$

Furthermore, for generic $\underset{\sim}{X} = (X_1,\ldots,X_k)$ observe that

(55) $$\begin{aligned} E(X_j - \mu)^2 &= \sum_{i=0}^{k} g_i \{E_i\,(X_j - \mu - \delta_{ij}\Delta)^2 + \delta_{ij}\Delta^2\} \\ &= \sigma^2 + g_j\Delta^2 . \end{aligned}$$

Next using the method of moments, define with $a^+ = \max(0,a)$,

(56) $$(\sigma^*)^2 = \frac{1}{k}\sum_{j=1}^{k}\{[\frac{1}{n}\sum_{\nu=1}^{n}(X_{j\nu} - \mu)^2] - g_j^* \Delta^2\}^+$$

and note that (54), (55) and the law of large numbers implies

(57) $$(\sigma^*)^2 \xrightarrow{P} \sigma^2 \quad \text{as} \quad n \to \infty.$$

Finally, by taking

(58) $$\Delta_n(j,\underset{\sim}{x}) = \sum_{i=0}^{k} g_i^* \,[L(i,j) - L(i,0)]\prod_{\nu=1}^{k}\{\psi(\frac{x_\nu - \mu - \delta_{i\nu}\Delta}{\max(\sigma^*, n^{-1})})\}$$

we see that (52) is again satisfied. Corollary 1 of Robbins [5] allows us to now state:

In Case 2, the sequence of empirical Bayes slippage tests $\{t_n\}$ *defined by* (50), (58), (53) *and* (56) *is asymptotically optimal relative to any* G.

Case 3. μ *and* σ^2 *unknown.* Observe that by (42), we have

(59) $$E(X_j - X_t)^2 = 2\sigma^2 + (g_j + g_t)\Delta^2, \; j \neq t, j,t=1,\ldots,k.$$

Hence by defining

$$S^2 = \frac{1}{n}\sum_{\nu=1}^{n} S_\nu{}^2,\quad S_\nu{}^2 = \frac{1}{2k(k-1)}\sum_{\substack{j\neq t\\ j,t\neq 0}} (X_{j\nu}-X_{t\nu})^2$$

we have from (59) and the law of large numbers,

$$\begin{aligned} &E(S^2) = E(S_1{}^2) = \sigma^2+k^{-1}(1-g_0)\Delta^2 \\ (60)\quad & \\ &\text{and}\quad S^2 \xrightarrow{P} \sigma^2+k^{-1}(1-g_0)\Delta^2 \quad \text{as}\quad n\to\infty\ . \end{aligned}$$

Next observe that for $j \neq t$, $j, t = 1,\ldots,k$

$$\begin{aligned} E(X_jX_t) &= \sum_{i=0}^{k} g_i E_i(X_jX_t) \\ (61)\qquad &= \sum_{i=0}^{k} g_i(\mu+\delta_{ij}\Delta)(\mu+\delta_{it}\Delta) \\ &= \mu^2+(g_j+g_t)(\Delta\mu). \end{aligned}$$

Therefore by defining

$$T = \frac{1}{n}\sum_{\nu=1}^{n} T_\nu,\quad T_\nu = \frac{1}{k(k-1)}\sum_{\substack{j\neq t\\ j,t\neq 0}} X_{j\nu}X_{t\nu}$$

we see from (61) and the law of large numbers

$$\begin{aligned} &E(T) = E(T_1) = \mu^2+k^{-1}(1-g_0)(2\Delta\mu) \\ (62)\quad & \\ &\text{and}\quad T \xrightarrow{P} \mu^2+k^{-1}(1-g_0)(2\Delta\mu) \quad \text{as}\quad n\to\infty\ . \end{aligned}$$

Next, with $\overline{X}_{..} = n^{-1}\sum_{\nu=1}^{n}\overline{X}_{.\nu}, \overline{X}_{.\nu} = k^{-1}\sum_{j=1}^{k} X_{j\nu}$, we see that (46) and the law of large numbers imply

$$\begin{aligned} &E(\overline{X}_{..}) = k^{-1}\sum_{j=1}^{k} E(\overline{X}_{j.}) = \mu+k^{-1}(1-g_0)\Delta \\ (63)\quad & \\ &\text{and}\quad \overline{X}_{..} \xrightarrow{P} \mu+k^{-1}(1-g_0)\Delta \quad \text{as}\quad n\to\infty\ . \end{aligned}$$

Finally, with $\overline{X}_{j.} = n^{-1}\sum_{\nu=1}^{n} X_{j\nu}$, (46) and the law of large numbers imply for $j = 1,\ldots,k$

(64) $$E(\overline{X}_{j.}) = \mu+g_j\Delta \quad \text{and} \quad \overline{X}_{j.} \xrightarrow{P} \mu+g_j\Delta \quad \text{as} \quad n\to\infty \ .$$

Employing the method of moments in equations (60), (62), (63) and (64), we form the system of equations

$$\begin{aligned} S^2 &= \sigma^2+k^{-1}(1-g_0)\Delta^2 \\ T &= \mu^2+k^{-1}(1-g_0)(2\Delta\mu) \\ \overline{X}_{..} &= \mu+k^{-1}(1-g_0)\Delta \\ \overline{X}_{j.} &= \mu+g_j\Delta, \quad j=1,\ldots,k. \end{aligned}$$

Solving this system of equations for real-valued estimators, we obtain

(65)
$$\begin{aligned} \tilde{\mu} &= \overline{X}_{..} - \{(\overline{X}^2_{..} - T)^+\}^{1/2} \xrightarrow{P} \mu \quad \text{as} \quad n\to\infty \ , \\ \tilde{g}_j &= \Delta^{-1}(\overline{X}_{j.} - \tilde{\mu}) \xrightarrow{P} g_j \quad \text{as} \quad n\to\infty,\ j=1,\ldots,k, \\ \tilde{g}_0 &= 1-\Delta^{-1}k(\overline{X}_{..} - \tilde{\mu}) \xrightarrow{P} g_0 \quad \text{as} \quad n\to\infty, \end{aligned}$$

and

$$\tilde{\sigma}^2 = \{S^2 - \Delta(\overline{X}_{..} - \tilde{\mu})\}^+ \xrightarrow{P} \sigma^2 \quad \text{as} \quad n\to\infty \ .$$

The consistency of these estimates is an immediate consequence of (60), (62), (63), (64) and Slutsky's theorem.

Therefore, by taking

(66) $$\Delta_n(j,\underset{\sim}{x}) = \sum_{i=0}^{k}\tilde{g}_i[L(i,j)-L(i,0)]\{\Pi_{\nu=1}^{k}\psi(\frac{x_j-\tilde{\mu}-\delta_{i\nu}\Delta}{\max(\tilde{\sigma},n^{-1})})\}$$

it follows from (65) that (50) holds. As before, Corollary 1 of Robbins [5] implies:

In Case 3, *the sequence of empirical Bayes slippage tests* $\{t_n\}$ *defined by* (50), (66) *and* (65) *is asymptotically optimal relative to any* G.

References

1. Chernoff, Herman (1952). A measure of asymptotic efficiency for tests of a hypothesis based on the sum of observations. *Ann. Math. Statist.*, 23, 493-507.

2. Ferguson, T. (1967). *Mathematical statistics: A decision theoretic approach*, Academic Press, New York.

3. Hudimoto, H. (1968). On the empirical Bayes procedure I. *Ann. Inst. Statist. Math.*, 20, 169-185.

4. Robbins, H. (1955). An empirical Bayes approach to statistics. *Proc. 3rd Berkeley Symp. Math. Statist. Prob.*, Univ. of Calif. Press, 155-163.

5. Robbins, H. (1964). The empirical Bayes approach to statistical decision problems. *Ann. Math. Statist.*, 35, 1-20.

6. Van Ryzin, J. (1970). Empirical Bayes procedures for multiple decision problems. Tech. Report No. 249, Department of Statistics, Univ. of Wisconsin. (Submitted to *Ann. Inst. Statist. Math.*).

ANALOGUES OF LINEAR COMBINATIONS OF ORDER STATISTICS IN THE LINEAR MODEL

By P. J. Bickel
University of California, Berkeley
and Princeton University*

My intention in what follows is to give an intuitive presentation of the procedures of the title and to state some results. Proofs and details will appear elsewhere ([1]).

Consider the problem of estimating the regression parameters of a linear model as the number of observations becomes large and the number of regression parameters remains fixed. That is, we want to estimate $\underset{\sim}{\beta} = (\beta_1, \ldots, \beta_p)$ when we observe $\underset{\sim}{X} = (X_1, \ldots, X_n)$ where

$$\underset{\sim}{X} = \underset{\sim}{\beta} C + \underset{\sim}{E}$$

where $\underset{\sim}{E} = (E_1, \ldots, E_n)$ is a vector of errors and $C = ||c_{ij}||$ is a matrix of known regression constants of rank p. The errors are independent and identically distributed symmetric about 0 with c.d.f. F and density f. If $p = 1 = c_{1j}$, $1 \leq j \leq n$ we are in the extensively studied location submodel. Two classes of procedures have attracted particular attention in this problem (M) (maximum likelihood type) estimates and linear combinations of order statistics. A

*This work was supported, in part, by a grant to the author from the John Simon Guggenheim Memorial Foundation and in part by Grant N00014-67-A0114-0004 from the Office of Naval Research.

third class, estimates based on rank tests, will not be dealt with here. A comparative review of these procedures may be found in [5]. Briefly, (M) estimates, $\hat{\beta}$, are defined as solutions of equations of the form,

$$\sum_{j=1}^{n} \psi(X_j - \hat{\beta}) = 0 \quad . \tag{1}$$

Under suitable regularity conditions ([3],[4]) they are asymptotically normal with mean β and variance $\frac{K(\psi,F)}{n}$ where,

$$K(\psi,F) = \frac{\int_{-\infty}^{\infty} \psi^2(t)\,dF(t)}{\left(\int_{-\infty}^{\infty} \psi'(t)\,dF(t)\right)^2} \quad . \tag{2}$$

If $X_{(1)} < \ldots < X_{(n)}$ are the ordered $X_1,\ldots,X_n$ and $\lambda_1,\ldots,\lambda_n$ are constants then a linear combination of order statistics is any estimate $\hat{\beta}$ of the form,

$$\hat{\beta} = \sum_{j=1}^{n} \lambda_j X_{(j)} \quad . \tag{3}$$

If the measures Λ_n assigning mass λ_j to $\frac{j}{n+1}$, $1 \leq j \leq n$, tend suitably to some signed measure of mass 1 such that $\int_0^1 F^{-1}(t)\,d\Lambda(t) = 0$ and various other regularity conditions are satisfied (see [2], for example) then $\hat{\beta}$ is asymptotically normal with mean β and variance $\frac{V(\Lambda,F)}{n}$ where

$$V(\Lambda,F) = \int_0^1 \int_0^1 \frac{(\min(s,t) - st)}{f(F^{-1}(s))f(F^{-1}(t))}\,d\Lambda(s)\,d\Lambda(t) \quad . \tag{4}$$

It is well known that both of these classes may be drawn on for efficient estimates if F is known and for robust procedures if F is not known. It was recently noted by Huber and Relles that (M) estimates generalize readily to the regression model, being defined as solutions $\hat{\underset{\sim}{\beta}}$ of systems of equations,

$$\sum_{j=1}^{n} c_{ij}\psi(X_j - \sum_{k=1}^{p} c_{kj}\hat{\beta}_k) = 0, \ i = 1,\ldots,p.$$

Furthermore, under regularity conditions, $\hat{\underset{\sim}{\beta}}$ is asymptotically normal with mean $\underset{\sim}{\beta}$ and variance covariance matrix $K(\psi,F)[CC']^{-1}$. Thus the relative performance of such estimates is essentially independent of the design matrix. This suggests our goal in defining analogues of linear combinations of order statistics: Given a signed measure Λ of mass 1 on [0,1] to define estimates $\hat{\underset{\sim}{\beta}}$ by a procedure which,

(i) Yields linear combinations of order statistics in the usual sense for the location submodel.

(ii) Makes the resulting $\hat{\underset{\sim}{\beta}}$ approximately normal with mean $\underset{\sim}{\beta}$ and variance $V(\Lambda,F)[CC']^{-1}$ for n large.

For simplicity suppose that

(5) $$\frac{1}{n} CC' \to A = C_0C_0'$$

which is positive definite.

(6) $$\max \frac{|c_{ij}|}{\sqrt{n}} \to 0 \quad .$$

To simplify matters further suppose for the moment that all c_{ij} are ≥ 0. Let,

(7) $$Y_j(\underset{\sim}{t}) = X_j - \sum_{i=1}^{p} c_{ij}t_i$$

for $\underset{\sim}{t} = (t_1,\ldots,t_p)$ and define for $i = 1,\ldots,p$,

(8) $$Q_{ni}(s,\underset{\sim}{t}) = \frac{1}{\sum_{j=1}^{n} c_{ij}} \sum_{j=1}^{n} c_{ij} I[Y_j(\underset{\sim}{t}) \leq s] \quad .$$

For fixed $\underset{\sim}{t}$ let $Q_{ni}^{-1}(\cdot,\underset{\sim}{t})$ be the usual inverse on (0,1) of the c.d.f. $Q_{ni}(\cdot,\underset{\sim}{t})$. Basic to what follows is,

Lemma 1: *Suppose that in addition to the given conditions*

f *is uniformly continuous positive and bounded. Then for every* $M < \infty$, $0 < \alpha < 1$,

$$\frac{1}{\sqrt{n}} \sup \{ | [(Q_{ni}^{-1}(w,\underset{\sim}{t}) - F^{-1}(w)) + (Q_{ni}(F^{-1}(w),\underset{\sim}{0}) - w)/q(w)] \tag{9}$$
$$[\textstyle\sum_{j=1}^{n} c_{ij}] + \sum_{k=1}^{p} \sum_{j=1}^{n} c_{ij} c_{kj} t_k | : |\underset{\sim}{t}| \leq \frac{M}{\sqrt{n}} ,$$
$$\alpha \leq w \leq 1-\alpha \} \to 0$$

in $P_{\underset{\sim}{0}}$ *probability where*

$$q(w) = f(F^{-1}(w)) \quad . \tag{10}$$

The subscript on P indicates what parameter value we assume is true. This "linear expansion" for Q_{ni}^{-1} is proved by using the methods of [7] and [8]. Now suppose that we are given an estimate $\underset{\sim}{\beta}^*$ such that,

$$\underset{\sim}{\beta}^*(\underset{\sim}{x} + \underset{\sim}{t}C) = \underset{\sim}{\beta}^*(\underset{\sim}{x}) + \underset{\sim}{t} \tag{11}$$

for all $\underset{\sim}{x}$, $\underset{\sim}{t}$ and,

$$\lim\sup_{M\to\infty} \lim\sup_n P_{\underset{\sim}{\beta}}[\sqrt{n}|\underset{\sim}{\beta}^* - \underset{\sim}{\beta}| > M] = 0 \tag{12}$$

where $|\cdot|$ is a norm on R^p. If F has a second moment we can use the least squares estimate as $\underset{\sim}{\beta}^*$. Under the conditions of Lemma 1 it follows that,

$$\frac{1}{\sqrt{n}} \{ [(Q_{ni}^{-1}(w,\underset{\sim}{\beta}^*) - F^{-1}(w)) + (Q_{ni}(F^{-1}(w),0) - w)/q(w)] \tag{13}$$
$$[\textstyle\sum_{j=1}^{n} c_{ij}] + \sum_{k=1}^{p} \sum_{j=1}^{n} c_{ij} c_{kj} \beta_k^* \} \to 0$$

in $P_{\underset{\sim}{0}}$ probability. Now, under $P_{\underset{\sim}{0}}$,

$$\frac{1}{\sqrt{n}} \{ (Q_{ni}(F^{-1}(w),0) - w)/q(w) \} [\textstyle\sum_{j=1}^{n} c_{ij}]$$

behaves asymptotically like $a_{ii} \frac{Z(w)}{q(w)}$ where $Z(w)$ is a Brownian bridge on $[0,1]$ and thus the

$$\frac{1}{n}\{[Q_{ni}^{-1}(w,\beta^*)][\sum_{j=1}^{n} c_{ij}] + \sum_{k=1}^{p} c_{ij}c_{kj}\beta^*_k\}$$

behave like the $[wn]$th order statistics of a sample from F. This suggests the following definition. Given Λ on $[0,1]$ $\hat{\underset{\sim}{\beta}}$ is the type 1 (L) estimate (linear combination of order statistics) corresponding to Λ if $\hat{\beta} = (\hat{\beta}_1,\ldots,\hat{\beta}_p)$ satisfies the equations,

$$(14)\qquad [\sum_{j=1}^{n} c_{ij}]\int_0^1 Q_{ni}^{-1}(w,\underset{\sim}{\beta}^*)\Lambda(dw) = \sum_{k=1}^{p}(\hat{\beta}_k-\beta_k^*)[\sum_{j=1}^{n} c_{ij}c_{kj}] \quad i = 1,\ldots,p.$$

Equivalently if,

$$(15)\qquad \underset{\sim}{L} = ([\sum_{j=1}^{n} c_{1j}]\int_0^1 Q_{n1}^{-1}(w,\underset{\sim}{\beta}^*)\Lambda(dw),\ldots, [\sum_{j=1}^{n} c_{pj}]\int_0^1 Q_{np}^{-1}(w,\underset{\sim}{\beta}^*)\Lambda(dw))$$

then

$$(16)\qquad \hat{\underset{\sim}{\beta}} = \underset{\sim}{\beta}^* + \underset{\sim}{L}[CC']^{-1}\quad .$$

From our remarks so far it is easy to prove,

Theorem 1: *If* Λ *is a finite signed measure of total mass* 1 *concentrating on* $[\alpha,1-\alpha]$, $0 < \alpha < 1$, $\int_0^1 F^{-1}(w)\Lambda(dw) = 0$, *the conditions stated so far hold,* $\hat{\underset{\sim}{\beta}}$ *is defined by* (16) *and* $\underset{\sim}{\beta}$ *is true, then* $\sqrt{n}(\hat{\underset{\sim}{\beta}} - \underset{\sim}{\beta})$ *is asymptotically normal with mean* $\underset{\sim}{0}$ *and variance covariance matrix* $V(\Lambda,F)A^{-1}$.

Thus, (ii) holds. To see that (i) does also let us describe $\underset{\sim}{L}$ explicitly. Let $Y_{(1)} < \ldots < Y_{(n)}$ be the order statistics of $Y_1(\underset{\sim}{\beta}^*), \ldots, Y_n(\underset{\sim}{\beta}^*)$.

Let $(D_1, \ldots, D_n)$ be the permutation of $(1, \ldots, n)$ defined by,

(17) $$Y_{(j)} = Y_{D_j}(\underset{\sim}{\beta}^*).$$

Let,

(18) $$W_{ij} = \frac{\sum_{r=1}^{j} c_{iD_r}}{\sum_{r=1}^{n} c_{ij}} \quad 1 \le i \le p,\ 1 \le j \le n \quad .$$

Then it is easy to see that,

(19) $$\int_0^1 Q_{ni}^{-1}(w, \underset{\sim}{\beta}^*)\Lambda(dw) = \sum_{r=1}^{n} \Lambda[W_{i(r-1)}, W_{ir}](X_{D_r} - \sum_{i=1}^{p} \beta_i^* c_{ir}) \quad .$$

If $p = 1$, $c_{ij} \equiv 1$, $W_{1r} = \frac{r}{n}$, $X_{D_r} = X_{(r)}$ whatever be β^* and,

(20) $$\hat{\beta} = \sum_{r=1}^{n} \Lambda\left(\frac{(r-1)}{n}, \frac{r}{n}\right] X_{(r)}$$

independent of β^*.

If Λ has a density λ it is natural to approximate the coefficients in (19) by $\frac{c_{iD_r}}{\sum_{j=1}^{n} c_{ij}} \lambda(W_{ir})$. Further natural manipulations suggest that given λ one defines $\hat{\underset{\sim}{\beta}}$, an (L) estimate of type 2, corresponding to λ as the solution of the equations,

(21) $$\sum_{j=1}^{n} c_{iD_j} \lambda(W_{ij}) X_{D_j} = \sum_{k=1}^{p} \hat{\beta}_k \left(\sum_{j=1}^{n} c_{iD_j} c_{kD_j}\right) \lambda(W_{ij}) \quad .$$

It is easy to prove,

Theorem 2: *If* λ *vanishes off* $[\alpha, 1-\alpha]$, $0 < \alpha < 1$, *satisfies a first order Lipschitz condition on* $[\alpha, 1-\alpha]$ $\int_0^1 \lambda(t)\,dt = 1$, $\int_0^1 F^{-1}(t)\lambda(t)\,dt = 0$, *our previous conditions hold, and* $\hat{\underset{\sim}{\beta}}$ *is the type 2 estimate corresponding to* λ *then* $\sqrt{n}\,(\hat{\underset{\sim}{\beta}} - \underset{\sim}{\beta})$ *is asymptotically normal with mean* $\underset{\sim}{0}$ *and variance* $V(\Lambda, F)\underset{\sim}{A}^{-1}$ *where* $\Lambda(t) = \int_0^t \lambda(s)\,ds$.

$$\text{If} \quad \lambda(t) = \begin{cases} \dfrac{1}{(1-2\alpha)} & \text{if} \quad \alpha < t < 1-\alpha \\ 0 & \text{otherwise} \end{cases}$$

we have the analogues of the α trimmed means. For type 2 (regression through the origin), $p = 1$, the estimation procedure is describable as follows. "Order the residuals $Y_j(\beta^*)$, $j = 1, \ldots, n$. Associate with residual $Y_{(r)}$ a position index W_{1r} (for location, $W_{1r} = \frac{r}{n}$). Trim off all observations with $W_r \leq \alpha$ or $W_r \geq 1-\alpha$. Form the usual least squares estimate of β_1 with the remaining observations." For $p > 1$ one trims the p normal equations separately.

Type 1 trimmed means are of course also well defined as is the type 1 "median" which corresponds to Λ placing all its mass at $w = \frac{1}{2}$. Let m be such that $W_{1(m-1)} < \frac{1}{2} < W_{1m}$. If $p = 1$ the (type 1) "median" is then given by,

$$\hat{\beta} = \beta^* + \frac{\sum_{j=1}^{n} c_{ij}}{\sum_{j=1}^{n} c_{1j}^2}\,(X_{D_m} - \beta^* c_{1m}) \qquad (22)$$

There is a natural temptation to pass to the limit in (21) as $\alpha \to \frac{1}{2}$ and, for example, if $p = 1$, to think of $\frac{X_{D_m}}{c_{1D_m}}$

as the "median". This estimate is unfortunately in general not even asymptotically normal.

If all the c_{ij} are not of the same sign definition of our estimates becomes somewhat more awkward. There are at least two ways out. The one we describe is due to J. W. Tukey. Another is given in [1]. Let,

$$Y^*_{ij}(\underset{\sim}{t}) = \operatorname{sgn} c_{ij} Y_j(\underset{\sim}{t}) \quad . \tag{23}$$

Let,

$$Q^*_{ni}(s,\underset{\sim}{t}) = \frac{1}{\sum_{j=1}^n |c_{ij}|} \sum_{j=1}^n |c_{ij}| I_{[Y^*_{ij}(\underset{\sim}{t}) \leq s]} \quad , \tag{24}$$

and define $[Q^*_{ni}]^{-1}$ appropriately. Then the type 1' estimate corresponding to Λ is by definition

$$\hat{\underset{\sim}{\beta}} = \underset{\sim}{\beta}^* + \underset{\sim}{L}^*[CC']^{-1} \tag{25}$$

where

$$\begin{aligned} \underset{\sim}{L}^* = ([\textstyle\sum_{j=1}^n |c_{1j}|] \int_0^1 [Q^*_{n1}]^{-1}(w,\underset{\sim}{\beta}^*)\Lambda(dw), \ldots, \\ [\textstyle\sum_{j=1}^n |c_{pj}|] \int_0^1 [Q^*_{np}]^{-1}(w,\underset{\sim}{\beta}^*)\Lambda(dw)) \quad . \end{aligned} \tag{26}$$

Then the asymptotic theory of Theorem 1 goes through if we require that in addition to the assumptions of Theorem 1 that Λ is symmetric about $\frac{1}{2}$, i.e., $\Lambda(t-) = 1-\Lambda(1-t)$ for all t. This is of course natural for our problem. To define type 2' estimates we need to consider $Y^*_{i(1)} < \ldots < Y^*_{i(n)}$, the order statistics of $Y^*_{i1}(\underset{\sim}{\beta}^*), \ldots, Y^*_{in}(\underset{\sim}{\beta}^*)$, define D^*_{ij} by

$$Y^*_{iD^*_{ij}}(\underset{\sim}{\beta}^*) = Y^*_{i(j)} \quad , \tag{27}$$

and

(28) $$W^*_{ij} = \frac{\sum_{r=1}^{j} |c_{iD^*_{ir}}|}{\sum_{r=1}^{n} |c_{ir}|} \quad .$$

Then the type 2' estimate corresponding to λ is defined as the solution of the equations,

(29) $$\sum_{j=1}^{n} X_{D^*_{ij}} c_{iD^*_{ij}} \lambda(W^*_{ij}) = \sum_{k=1}^{p} \hat{\beta}_k \left(\sum_{j=1}^{n} c_{iD^*_{ij}} c_{kD^*_{kj}} \lambda(W^*_{ij})\right) \quad .$$

Here are some interesting open questions.

1) To what extent do the relatively weak conditions for the asymptotic theory of linear combinations or order statistics suffice in this more general case. Some results to this effect slightly stronger than those of [6] (for location) appear in [1].

2) The most natural analogues $\hat{\underset{\sim}{\beta}}$ are presumably those which are fixed points under the operations we have described. Such fixed points do exist. For instance if $\lambda(t) \equiv 1$ and $\underset{\sim}{\beta}^*$ is the least squares estimate the resulting $\hat{\underset{\sim}{\beta}} = \underset{\sim}{\beta}^*$. Another interesting example is provided by the (M) estimate for $\psi(t) = \text{sgn } t$. When we apply the operation of "forming the median" this estimate is left invariant. Whether such fixed points exist in general and whether the asymptotic theory goes through for them as it does in the above two cases is unknown to me.

3) In an as yet unpublished manuscript Huber obtains expansions for the asymptotic variance of (M) estimates as $p,n \to \infty$ in terms of $\frac{p}{n}$. (If $\frac{p}{n} \not\to 0$ even least squares estimates need not be asymptotically normal.) A similar

development for the procedures of this paper would be of interest.

References

1. Bickel, P.J. (1971). On some analogues of linear combinations of order statistics in the linear model. Submitted to *Ann. Math. Statist.*

2. Chernoff, H., Gastwirth, J., Johns, M.V. (1967). Asymptotic distribution of linear combinations of order statistics. *Ann. Math. Statist.* 38, 52-72.

3. Huber, P.J. (1964). Robust estimation of a location parameter. *Ann. Math. Statist.* 35, 73-101.

4. Huber, P.J. (1965). The behaviour of maximum likelihood estimates under non standard conditions. *Proc. Vth Berk. Symp.* 1, 221-233.

5. Jaeckel, L.B. (1970). Robust estimation of location: Symmetry and asymmetric contamination. To appear in *Ann. Math. Statist.*

6. Moore, D. (1968). An elementary proof of asymptotic normality of linear functions of order statistics. *Ann. Math. Statist.* 39, 263-265.

7. Koul, H.L. (1969). Asymptotic behaviour of Wilcoxon type confidence regions in multiple linear regression. *Ann. Math. Statist.* 40, 1950-1979.

8. Pyke, R. and Shorack, G. (1968). Weak convergence of a two sample empirical process and a new approach to Chernoff-Savage Theorems. *Ann. Math. Statist.* 39, 755-771.

A THEOREM ON EXPONENTIALLY BOUNDED STOPPING TIME OF INVARIANT SPRT'S WITH APPLICATIONS

By R. A. Wijsman
University of Illinois, Urbana

Let $Z_1, Z_2, \ldots$ be iid random variables with common distribution P. The joint distribution of the Z's will also be denoted P. With *the model* we shall mean a specified family of distributions $\mathcal{P} = \{P_\theta : \theta \in \Theta\}$ where Θ is some index set, also called the parameter space. It is important to keep in mind throughout that P may or may not be a member of $\mathcal{P}$.

Suppose Θ_1 and Θ_2 are two disjoint subsets of Θ (not assuming their union is Θ) and suppose it is desired to test sequentially the hypothesis H_1 versus H_2, where $H_j : \theta \in \Theta_j$, $j = 1,2$. If the H_j are both simple, say corresponding to densities p_j with respect to some sigma-finite measure, Wald [6] proposed his sequential probability ratio test (SPRT) under which sampling continues as long as

$$\ell_1 < L_n < \ell_2 \tag{1}$$

in which

$$L_n = \sum_{i=1}^{n} \log\,(p_2(Z_i)/p_1(Z_i)),\ n = 1,2,\ldots \tag{2}$$

and the stopping bounds ℓ_1, ℓ_2 are chosen so that the test has the desired error probabilities. The first $n \geq 1$ at which (1) is violated is the random sample size N, also called *stopping time*. Wald [5] showed

(3) $$P\{N < \infty\} = 1$$

and Stein [4] proved the much stronger result

(4) $$P\{N > n\} < c\,\rho^n, \quad n = 1,2,\ldots$$

for some $c < \infty, \rho < 1$, both (3) and (4) holding for any P whatever with the only exception of such P for which

(5) $$P\{\log(p_2(Z_1)/p_1(Z_1)) = 0\} = 1.$$

The property (4) will be described by saying that N is *exponentially bounded* (under P). It is obviously a desirable property, at least for reasonable values of c and ρ, since it ensures that the distribution of N does not have a "long tail". The reason (4) can be proved with relative ease is that L_n in (2) is a sum of iid random variables, so that $\{L_n, n = 1,2,\ldots\}$ is a random walk on the real line, starting at 0. Thus, N is the termination time of the random walk by absorption at ℓ_1 or ℓ_2 and the only case where N is not exponentially bounded is when the steps in the random walk are zero with probability one, i.e. when (5) holds.

The situation is much harder when the H_j are composite. The usual way to arrive at a sequential test with prescribed error probabilities is to reduce the composite H_j to simple ones, employing either of two methods: adopting priors on the Θ_j, or making an invariance reduction. We shall only be concerned with the latter method. It is applicable whenever there is a group G of invariance transformations such that G is transitive on both Θ_j. Restricting the test to be invariant under G, the two hypotheses now become simple and a SPRT can again be formulated by letting L_n

in (1) be the log probability ratio (at the nth stage) of a maximal invariant. Such a test will be called an *invariant SPRT*. Examples are the sequential t-test, sequential F-test, etc. For a bibliography see [8]. An invariant SPRT shares with Wald's SPRT the pleasant property that the stopping bounds ℓ_1, ℓ_2 in (1) depend in a simple way (at least approximately) on the prescribed error probabilities of the test. However, L_n does no longer have the simple structure (2), i.e. is not a sum of iid random variables and consequently $\{L_n\}$ is no longer a random walk. This makes the study of the stopping time N much harder.

A priori there is no reason why Stein's result (4) for Wald's SPRT could not also be valid for invariant SPRT's. However, as a result of the difficulty of the problem, the beginnings of the investigation of N for invariant SPRT's were very modest, with the establishment of (3) rather than (4), and only for P a member of the model (for a more detailed account of the history of the subject see [8]). Consideration of (4) and of P outside the model came much later. Then, in order to make the proof of (4) possible, certain rather strong restrictions had to be placed on P. An exception was a result of Sethuraman [3] (utilizing an earlier result of Savage and Sethuraman [2]) who proved (4) in a nonparametric problem, excluding only a small class of P's that exhibit a certain degeneracy, comparable to (5) (Sethuraman's result was obtained in 1967, even though publication was delayed until 1970).

In all parametric problems it has been necessary, until recently, to put a certain moment condition on P in order to obtain (4). In order to state this condition more explicitly, suppose we restrict P to be an exponential family. Then there is a function s on the range of Z_1 into Euclidean k-space (for some $k \geq 1$) such that, with the notation $X_i = s(Z_i)$, $\overline{X}_n = (1/n)\sum_1^n X_i$ is a sufficient statistic for the family of distributions of $(Z_1,\ldots,Z_n)$ determined by P. Note that under any P the X_i are iid since the Z_i are. The moment condition on P referred to above is: each component of X_1 should have a finite moment generating function (m.g.f.) in some interval about 0. This is a minimal condition that has been assumed in [7] and by Berk [1] in order to obtain (4).

In 1970 the first two examples were discovered of invariant SPRT's in parametric problems where (4) could be proved without the moment condition on P. These findings were presented at the Sixth Berkeley Symposium on Mathematical Statistics and Probability and will be published in [8]. Also presented was an example of an invariant SPRT where (4) could be demonstrated to be false for a certain family of P's. We shall call such a P for which (4) fails for some choice of ℓ_1, ℓ_2 in (1): *obstructive*. The last mentioned example is as follows: Under the model the common distribution of the Z's is $N(\zeta,\sigma^2)$, ζ unknown, and the two hypotheses are $H_j: \sigma = \sigma_j$, with $\sigma_1 \neq \sigma_2$ specified. It is shown in [8] that P is obstructive if

$$(6) \qquad P\{Z_1 = \zeta \pm a\} = \frac{1}{2}$$

for any $-\infty < \zeta < \infty$ and with $a > 0$ given by

$$(7) \qquad a^2 = (\log \sigma_2 - \log \sigma_1)/((2\sigma_1{}^2)^{-1} - (2\sigma_2{}^2)^{-1})$$

(in [8] only the case $a = 1$ is treated, but the extension to arbitrary $a > 0$ is trivial). It is not shown in [8] that P is obstructive only if (6) holds. Now, however, it will be possible to conclude the validity of this "only if" part as a result of an application of the main theorem below. We shall here present only statements of results. Details of proofs will appear elsewhere [9].

Theorem. N *is exponentially bounded, i.e.* (4) *is valid for any choice of* ℓ_1, ℓ_2 *in* (1), *under the following conditions:*
(i) *for all components* X_{1j} $(j = 1,\ldots,k)$ *of* X_1 *we have* $E_P \exp[t X_{1j}] < \infty$ *for* t *in some interval about* 0 *(the "moment condition"); this implies* $E_P X_1 = \xi$ *is finite;*
(ii) *there exists a neighborhood* V *of* ξ *and a real valued continuous function* Φ *on* V *and a finite constant* B *such that*

$$(8) \qquad |L_n - n\Phi(\overline{X}_n)| < B \quad \text{if} \quad \overline{X}_n \in V, \quad n = 1,2,\ldots,$$

(iii) Φ *has continuous first partial derivatives on* V; *let* $\Delta = \text{grad}\,\Phi$ *evaluated at* ξ, *then*

$$(9) \qquad P\{\Delta'(X_1 - \xi) = 0\} < 1.$$

Condition (iii) *is not needed if* $\Phi(\xi) \neq 0$. *If the moment condition is dropped but* $E_P X_1 = \xi$ *finite retained then the weaker result* (3) *is valid.*

Application 1. In the problem of sequentially testing $\sigma = \sigma_1$ versus $\sigma = \sigma_2$ in a normal population with unknown mean ζ the transformations $Z_i \to Z_i + b$ $(i = 1,2,\ldots)$, $\zeta \to \zeta + b$, $\sigma \to \sigma$, $-\infty < b < \infty$, leave the problem invariant. It is shown in [8] section 4 that, apart from an unimportant multiplicative constant $\neq 0$,

$$(10) \qquad L_n = \sum_{i=1}^{n} (Z_i - \overline{Z}_n)^2 - (n-1)\,a^2$$

in which $\overline{Z}_n = (1/n)\sum_1^n Z_i$ and a^2 is given by (7). In order to prove (4) we distinguish two cases: P unbounded and P bounded. In the former case a simple direct proof of of (4) can be given, based on a study of the behavior of $L_{n+1} - L_n$ (see [9]). In the latter case -- P bounded -- the theorem can be applied. We may take the function s as $s(z) = (z^2, z)$ and Φ as $\Phi(x_1, x_2) = x_1 - x_2^2 - a^2$. Then condition (i) of the theorem is obviously satisfied since P is bounded, and (ii) is true for any $B > a^2$ and any V. Condition (iii) has to be checked only if $\Phi(\xi) = 0$. It turns out that the only P's for which $\Phi(\xi) = 0$ and (9) is violated are the distributions (6). For all other distributions P the theorem concludes that N is exponentially bounded.

Application 2 (sequential t-test). Let the Z's and the function s be as in Application 1. Put $\gamma = \zeta/\sigma$ and test $\gamma = \gamma_1$ against $\gamma = \gamma_2$. The problem is invariant under the transformations $Z_i \to c\, Z_i\, (i = 1,2,\ldots)$, $\zeta \to c\zeta$, $\sigma \to c\sigma$, $c > 0$. With suitably chosen Φ an application of the theorem yields the result that N is exponentially bounded if P satisfies the following two conditions: Z_1^2 has finite m.g.f. in some interval about zero, and P is not one of the two-point distributions defined by

$$P\{Z_1 = (\sigma^2+\zeta^2)^{\frac{1}{2}} \zeta^{-1}((\sigma^2+\zeta^2)^{\frac{1}{2}} \pm \sigma)\} = \tfrac{1}{2}[1 \mp \sigma(\sigma^2+\zeta^2)^{-\frac{1}{2}}], \qquad \sigma > 0,\ \zeta \neq 0. \tag{11}$$

The reader is referred to [9] for the details. Exponential boundedness of N if Z_1^2 has finite m.g.f. was obtained earlier by Berk [1] as an application of a general theorem of his. However, in order to apply that theorem to the sequential t-test a family — different from the one defined by (11) — of two-point distributions had to be excluded.

Suggestions For Further Work. It is not unreasonable to conjecture that exponential boundedness of N is as universal a phenomenon in invariant SPRT's as it is in Wald's SPRT, the obstructive distributions (taking the place of (5)) constituting a small class. In particular, it may be conjectured that the moment condition is never necessary for (4). The results obtained to-date are in that respect encouraging but still very meager. There is only one example (Application 1 in this paper) where a complete classification of P's into those for which N is exponentially bounded and those that are obstructive has been obtained. There is one nonparametric example [3] and two more parametric examples [8] where exponential boundedness of N has been proved without the moment condition, but in these examples there is no complete description of the obstructive P's. More importantly, in none of the more interesting invariant SPRT's for parametric problems, such as the sequential t-test, has exponential boundedness been proved without the moment condition. This is therefore at the present one of the most pressing and interesting problems, either in special cases or, if at all possible, in some generality. Another interesting problem is the evaluation of ρ in (4).

References

1. Berk, R. H. (1970). Stopping time of SPRTS based on exchangeable models. *Ann. Math. Statist.* 41, 979-990.

2. Savage, I. R. and Sethuraman, J. (1966). Stopping time of a rank-order sequential probability ratio test based on Lehmann alternatives. *Ann. Math. Statist.* 37, 1154-1160.

Savage, I. R. and Sethuraman, J. (1967). Corrections to: Stopping time of a rank-order sequential probability ratio test based on Lehmann alternatives. *Ann. Math. Statist.* 38, 1309.

3. Sethuraman, J. (1970). Stopping time of a rank-order sequential probability ratio test based on Lehmann alternatives - II. *Ann. Math. Statist.* 41, 1322-1333.

4. Stein, C. (1946). A note on cumulative sums. *Ann. Math. Statist.* 17, 498-499.

5. Wald, A. (1944). On cumulative sums of random variables. *Ann. Math. Statist.* 15, 283-296.

6. Wald, A. (1945). Sequential tests of statistical hypotheses. *Ann. Math. Statist.* 14, 117-186.

7. Wijsman, R. A. (1968). Bounds on the sample size distribution for a class of invariant sequential probability ratio tests. *Ann. Math. Statist.* 39, 1048-1056.

8. Wijsman, R. A. Examples of exponentially bounded stopping time of invariant sequential probability ratio tests when the model may be false. *Proc. Sixth Berkeley Symp. Math. Statist. and Prob.*

9. Wijsman, R. A. Exponentially bounded stopping time of invariant sequential probability ratio tests.

SOME ASPECTS OF SEARCH STRATEGIES FOR WIENER PROCESSES

By E. M. Klimko and James Yackel*
Purdue University

1. *Introduction.* The problem we wish to consider here is the same search problem considered by Posner and Rumsey, [2]. Our purpose here is to point out some serious errors in their optimality arguments and to discuss some aspects of the search problem which they did not consider.

A brief description of the search problem follows. Let $y_1(t), \ldots, y_n(t)$ be n Wiener processes each with variance $\sigma^2 t$; $n-1$ of them have zero drift and the remaining process has drift μt where μ is known. Our problem is to locate the process with drift μt with probability $1-\varepsilon$ of correct selection. In addition, we are given a prior distribution $p_1, p_2, \ldots, p_n$ where p_i is the probability that the ith process is the correct one.

In Section 2 we discuss specifically the difficulty with Posner and Rumsey's argument for optimality. They used weak limits of the class of lattice time strategies for which they claimed optimality and weak limits of another class of strategies called δ perturbed strategies, for which computations were more tractable, to determine the "optimal expected

*Research of both authors was supported by the National Science Foundation under Grant No. 7631.

search time". We show that neither the class of lattice time nor the class of δ perturbed strategies are tight and hence weak limits do not exist.

The δ perturbed strategies are defined as follows. Observe the process corresponding to the largest prior probability until for the first time the posterior probability has decreased by δ/n, then observe the process with the maximum posterior probability at that time. We call the process which is being searched the *target* and the act of changing targets a *switch*.

Section 3 discusses the expected search time and the expected number of switches of another class of strategies called τ strategies. These strategies are shown to have the same limiting expected search time as the δ-perturbed strategies.

Section 4 discusses the merits of the two types of strategies and points out the simplicity of the τ strategy.

2. *Lack of tightness.* In this section we consider the two classes of strategies which were considered by Posner and Rumsey. We show that it is not possible to consider the weak limits of strategies in these classes which Posner and Rumsey studied since these limits do not exist.

It is necessary to begin with some definitions and structure for the problem. Basic to the situation is a probability space (Ω,A,P) on which are defined the n Wiener processes $y_1(t),\ldots, y_n(t)$ for $t \geq 0$, discussed in Section 1. The strategies which we discuss are functionals of $y_1(t),\ldots, y_n(t)$ whose value at any time t denotes the subscript of that Wiener process which is observed at time t. For example, the discrete time strategy $i_d(\cdot)$ is a functional which is constant over intervals $[kd, (k+1)d)$, $k = 0,1,2,\ldots$.

To study these strategies we choose to use the space $D[0,1]$ of all right continuous real valued functions on $[0,1]$ which have only discontinuities of the first kind. That will be our space of sample functions, the probability measures which we consider on $D[0,1]$ will be those induced by (Ω,A,P) through the functionals i.e. $[i_d(t_0) = k]$ is an event in $D[0,1]$ and also determines an event in Ω whose P probability we assign to that event. Consideration of the strategies as determined for $t \in [0,1]$ is sufficient for our purposes. Since the space $D[0,1]$ contains functions whose discontinuities are only of the first kind we will refer to a discontinuity as a *jump*.

We will show that the sequences of strategies considered by Posner and Rumsey do not converge in the Skorohod D topology, (see [1], p. 109 ff.). Since this topology gives a complete separable metric on the space $D[0,1]$, tightness of the measures is a necessary and sufficient condition for weak convergence (Prohorov's theorem).

Let $\tau_n = (0=t_{0n} < t_{1n} < \ldots < 1)$ be a sequence of partitions of the real line with the time increment going to zero (for simplicity, we assume that each partition is a refinement of its predecessor). We choose the sequence $t_n = t_{1n} \to 0$ (the number 0 plays no special role here). The following lemma reduces our problem to calculating the probability of the set of paths whose first discontinuity is at time t_n.

Lemma 2.1. *Let* $t_n \to 0$ *and let* A_n *be the collection of sample paths which are* 0 *for* $t < t_n$ *and which have jumps on* $[t_n, t_{n-1})$. *Let* P_n *be a sequence of probability measures on* $D[0,1]$ *for which* $P_n(A_n) \geq c > 0$ *for* $n \geq N$. *Then the sequence* P_n *is not tight.*

Before proving the lemma, we introduce some concepts and notations of the D topology. These particulars may be found e.g. in [1] p. 109 ff. Let $i(t)$ denote the sample functions of $D[0,1]$. We define a modulus similar to the modulus of continuity. For $0 < \delta < 1$,

$$w_i'(\delta) = \inf_{\{t_k\}} \max_{0<k<r} \sup_{s,t} \{|i(s)-i(t)| \; s,t\in[t_{i-1},t_k)\}$$

where the infimum extends over all finite sets $\{t_k\}$ of points satisfying the condition

$$0 = t_0 < t_1 < \ldots < t_r = 1$$
$$t_k - t_{k-1} > \delta \qquad k = 1,2,\ldots,r \quad .$$

The following are necessary and sufficient conditions for tightness (cf. [1] p. 125):

(i) for each $\eta > 0$, there is an a such that

$$P_n\{i: \sup_t |i(t)| > a\} \leq \eta \qquad n \geq 1$$

(ii) for each positive ε and η, there exists δ, $0 < \delta < 1$ and an integer n_0 such that

$$P_n\{i: w_i'(\delta) \geq \varepsilon\} \leq \eta \qquad n \geq n_0.$$

Proof of the lemma. Condition (i) is always satisfied since there are only a finite number of processes being searched. We show that (ii) fails. Indeed, for each sample path i belonging to A_n, an easy computation shows that $w_i'(\delta) \geq 1$ for $\delta > t_n$. Therefore, for any $\delta > 0$ and $n \geq \max(N,1/\delta)$ we have $P_n\{w_i'(\delta) \geq 1\} \geq c$ which contradicts (ii).

To show that the sequence i_{τ_n} is not tight, it remains to show that $P_n(A_n) \geq c$. This is the content of the next lemma.

Lemma 2.2. *Under the hypotheses of* Lemma 2.1, $\lim_n P_n(A_n) = 1/2$.

Proof. The probability of a jump at t_n may be computed from the posterior distribution of j being correct given j is being searched.

$$p_j(t_n) = \frac{p_j(0)}{p_j(0) + (1-p_j(0))\exp(\frac{\mu}{2\sigma^2}(\mu t_n - 2y(t)))} .$$

The rule of searching the most likely process at t_n translates (see Posner [2]) into the rule that a switch occurs at time t_n if and only if the likelihood ratio

$$Z(t_n) = \log \frac{p_j(t_n)}{1 - p_j(t_n)} \geq Z(0) \quad ,$$

which is equivalent to

$$-\frac{\mu}{2\sigma^2}(\mu t_n - 2y(t_n)) \geq 0$$

and focuses our attention to the boundary where

$$y(t_n) = 2\mu t_n \quad .$$

The above process at t_n is a normal random variable with mean $(\mu^2/2\sigma^2)t_n$ if j is correct and mean $-(\mu^2/2\sigma^2)t_n$ if j is not correct. In either case, the variance is $\mu^2 t_n/\sigma^2$. The probability of switching at time t_n is

$$p(\text{switch}|j \text{ correct})\ p(j \text{ correct}) + p(\text{switch}|j \text{ not correct})\ p\ (j \text{ not correct})$$

which equals

$$\Phi\left(- \frac{(\mu^2/2\sigma^2)t_n}{\mu\sqrt{t_n}/\sigma}\right) p_j(0) + \Phi\left(\frac{(\mu^2/2\sigma^2)t_n}{\mu\sqrt{t_n}/\sigma}\right) (1-p_j(0))$$

$$= p_j(0) + \Phi\left(\frac{\mu\sqrt{t_n}}{2\sigma}\right) - 2p_j(0) \quad \Phi\left(\frac{\mu\sqrt{t_n}}{2\sigma}\right)$$

where $\Phi(x)$ is the cdf of a normal distribution with mean zero and variance one. Therefore,

$$\lim_{t_n \to 0} \quad p(\text{switch at } t_n) = p_j(0) + \frac{1}{2} - p_j(0) = \frac{1}{2} \quad .$$

We note that this is independent of whether j is the correct process or not.

We now turn our attention to the δ perturbed strategies, as defined in [2].

Lemma 2.3. *The δ perturbed strategies are not tight.*

Proof. Let P_n denote the measure on D determined by δ_n. We will produce a sequence δ_n and a corresponding sequence of times t_n such that $P_n(A_n) \geq c$ where A_n is the set of sample paths which are 0 for $t < t_n$ and different from 0 for $t_n \leq t < t_{n-1}$. Lack of tightness will then follow from Lemma 2.1. For simplicity, we omit the subscript 0 from $p_0(t)$.

The strategy i_δ switches if and only if the posterior probability has decreased by an amount $\delta/n = \delta'$ (assume $\delta < 1$). We will compute the probability of the event

$$\{P(t) > P(0) - \delta',\ 0 \leq t \leq (\delta')^4;\ P(s) < P(0) - \delta',$$

$$\text{for some } s \text{ such that } (\delta')^4 \leq s \leq (\delta')^2\}$$

i.e. the probability of a switch between times $(\delta')^4$ and

$(\delta')^2$. For $P(t) < P(0) - \delta'$ we must have

$$\frac{P(0)}{P(0) + (1-P(0))\exp\left[\frac{\mu}{2\sigma^2}(\mu t - 2y(t))\right]} < P(0) - \delta'$$

or equivalently, the target $y(t)$ must satisfy

$$(1) \qquad y(t) > -\frac{\mu t}{2} + \frac{2\sigma^2}{\mu}\log\left(1 + \frac{\delta'}{[1-P(0)][P(0)-\delta']}\right).$$

Thus the desired probability is that of the first crossing of the boundary in (1) occurring between times $(\delta')^4$ and $(\delta')^2$.

By the result of Shepp [3, p.348] this probability for a target with zero drift is

$$(2) \qquad \begin{aligned} &\Phi\left(-\frac{\mu}{2\sigma}(\delta')^2 + \frac{2\sigma}{\mu(\delta')^2}c(\delta')\right) - e^{c(\delta')}\Phi\left(-\frac{\mu}{2\sigma}(\delta')^2 - \frac{2\sigma}{\mu}\frac{c(\delta')}{(\delta')^2}\right) \\ &-\Phi\left(-\frac{\mu}{2\sigma}\delta' + \frac{2\sigma}{\mu\delta'}c(\delta')\right) + e^{c(\delta')}\Phi\left(-\frac{\mu}{2\sigma}\delta' - \frac{2\sigma}{\mu}\frac{c(\delta')}{\delta'}\right) \end{aligned}$$

where $c(\delta') = \log\left[1 + \frac{\delta'}{(1-P(0))(P(0)-\delta')}\right]$.

Since $c(\delta') = 0(\delta')$ this probability is bounded away from zero as $\delta \to 0$.

Now if δ is any positive number less than 1 and we define the sequence

$$(3) \qquad \delta_1' = \delta'; \qquad \delta_n' = (\delta_{n-1}')^2 \qquad \text{for } n \geq 2$$

then the events

$$A_n = \{P(t) > P(0)-\delta'_n \quad \text{for} \quad 0 \le t \le (\delta'_n)^4 \quad \text{and}$$

$$\text{(4)} \qquad P(s) < P(0)-\delta' \quad \text{for some} \quad s \quad \text{such that}$$

$$(\delta'_n)^4 \le s \le (\delta'_n)^2\}$$

are pairwise disjoint and have P_n measure bounded away from zero. Similarly if the target has drift μt we can generate the same sequence of sets.

Next we see that the Prokoroff distance cannot go to zero as the necessary and sufficient conditions of Billingsley are violated as shown in Lemma 2.1 by this sequence of times in (3) and subsets A_n found in (4)

3. τ *Strategies*. We deal with a search strategy i_τ which chooses the target with the highest posterior probability at each switching time and which does not allow for switching (selecting a different target) before a specified elapsed time τ. We will define the strategy only for the case of a uniform prior distribution. The results obtained in that case clearly indicate what happens with a non-uniform prior.

This strategy should not be confused with the discrete time strategies considered by Posner and Rumsey. Note that after time τ has elapsed this strategy has random switching times determined by boundary crossing times.

Specifically this strategy is described as follows. Let S' be a switching time or time 0. If no posterior probability is $\ge 1 - \varepsilon$ then we select at random a target, set all posterior probabilities equal to $1/n$. The next possible switching time S'' is determined by the rule:

$$S'' = \begin{cases} S' + \tau & \text{if the target has posterior probability } \leq 1/n. \\ s & \text{where } s = \inf\{t : t > S' + \tau \text{ and the target has posterior } \leq 1/n \text{ or } \geq 1 - \varepsilon\}. \end{cases}$$

Thus the strategy i_τ requires at least time τ to switch.

We can easily compute the expected time $E(S'' - S')$, that is, the expected time the strategy i_τ searches the same target before switching or terminating the search. Let $a = \ell n(\frac{1-\varepsilon}{\varepsilon})(n-1)$, and $\lambda = \mu^2/2\sigma^2$, for the process with drift, we find

$$E_c(S''-S') = \tau + \int_0^a M(x)\, dP$$

where $M(x)$ is the expected time for the Wiener process to either reach the switching boundary or the terminating boundary from the point x. More explicitly this expression is

$$E_c(S''-S') = \tau - \frac{1}{\lambda(1-e^{-a})}\{a\psi(-) - (1-e^{-a})(\frac{\lambda\tau}{2}\psi(-) + \sqrt{\frac{\lambda\tau}{2\Pi}}\,[e^{-\frac{\lambda\tau}{8}} - e^{-\frac{(a-\frac{\lambda\tau}{2})^2}{2\lambda\tau}}] - a\psi(+)\}$$

wherein

$$\psi(-) = \Phi(\frac{a-\frac{\lambda\tau}{2}}{\sqrt{\lambda\tau}}) - \Phi(-\frac{\sqrt{\lambda\tau}}{2}),$$

$$\psi(+) = \Phi(\frac{a+\frac{\lambda\tau}{2}}{\sqrt{\lambda\tau}}) - \Phi(\frac{\sqrt{\lambda\tau}}{2}),$$

Φ is the standard normal c.d.f. and $\lambda = \frac{\mu^2}{\sigma^2}$.

When the target process has zero drift this is

$$E_{inc}(S''-S') = \tau - \frac{1}{\lambda(1-e^{a})} \{a(\psi(+)-\psi(-)) - (1-e^{a})(-\frac{\lambda\tau}{2}\psi(+) + \sqrt{\frac{\lambda\tau}{2\Pi}}[e^{-\frac{\lambda\tau}{8}} - e^{-\frac{(a+\frac{\lambda\tau}{2})^2}{2\lambda\tau}}])\}.$$

Similarly the probability of switching before stopping is

$$q_c = \int_{-\infty}^{0} \frac{\phi(\frac{x-\frac{\lambda\tau}{2}}{\sqrt{\lambda\tau}})}{\sqrt{\lambda\tau}} dx + \int_0^a \frac{(e^x - e^{-a})}{(1-e^{-a})} \frac{\phi(\frac{x-\frac{\lambda\tau}{2}}{\sqrt{\lambda\tau}})}{\sqrt{\lambda\tau}} dx$$

for the process with drift and for any process wwth zero drift

$$q_{inc} = \int_{-\infty}^{0} \frac{\phi(\frac{x+\frac{\lambda\tau}{2}}{\sqrt{\lambda\tau}})}{\sqrt{\lambda\tau}} dx + \int_0^a \frac{(e^x - e^{a})}{(1-e^{-a})} \frac{\phi(\frac{x-\frac{\lambda\tau}{2}}{\sqrt{\lambda\tau}})}{\sqrt{\lambda\tau}} dx .$$

From these expressions, the expected search time M and the expected number of switches S must satisfy the relations respectively

$$M = \frac{1}{n} E_c(S'' - S') + \frac{n-1}{n} E_{inc}(S'' - S') + qM$$

and

$$S = 1 + qS = 1 + \frac{1}{n} q_c + \frac{n-1}{n} q_{inc}$$

so that both M and S are found in closed form.

Proposition: *As* $\tau \to 0$ *the expected search time of the* τ *strategy is* $\frac{1}{\lambda}\{(1-2\varepsilon)\ell n(\frac{1-\varepsilon}{\varepsilon})(n-1) + (n-2)(\frac{n-1-\varepsilon n}{n-1})\}$ *and the expected number of switches* $S \sim \frac{c}{\sqrt{\tau}}$ *as* $\tau \to 0$.

Proof: Note that all three expressions $E_c(S''-S')$, $E_{inc}(S''-S')$ and $1 - q$ approach zero at the rate $\sqrt{\tau}$ when $\tau \to 0$.

L'Hospital's rule applied to the expression for M gives its limiting value as $\tau \to 0$ and the equation $S = \frac{1}{1-q}$ immediately shows the limit behavior of S.

4. *Comparison of δ perturbed and τ strategies.* An important advantage of the strategy i_τ is its inherent simplicity in implementation. This simplicity results from the fact that one need never compute posterior probabilities. Each switching time is determined by a pair of linear stopping boundaries for the target process and these boundaries remain unchanged throughout the search. For a given ε, n they are simply:

$$\ell(t) = \frac{\mu t}{2} \quad \text{and} \quad u(t) = \frac{\mu t}{2} + \frac{a\sigma^2}{\mu}$$

for the lower and upper boundaries respectively.

As noted by the proposition of Section 3 the strategy i_τ has the same limiting expected search time when $\tau \to 0$ as the strategy i_δ as $\delta \to 0$, c.f. [2]. This is not completely obvious since the strategy i_τ switches targets "infinitely often as $\tau \to 0$" and hence disregards the actual posteriors "infinitely often as $\tau \to 0$".

The question of switching is an important one which has not been previously considered. We now compare the switching behavior of these two strategies.

Proposition: *Let S_τ and S_δ be the expected number of switches for the two strategies i_τ and i_δ respectively. Then for $\delta = \sqrt{\tau}$*

$$\lim_{n \to \infty} \quad \lim_{\delta,\tau \to 0} \quad \frac{S_\delta}{S_\tau} = \frac{1}{\varepsilon}\sqrt{\frac{\lambda}{2\Pi}} \quad .$$

Proof: An expression for S_δ can be obtained by considering the possible events until a first return to the uniform distribution i.e.

$$S_\delta = 1 + q_1(1 + q_2(\ldots + q_n S_\delta)$$

where $q_1, q_2, \ldots, q_n$ are the probabilities of switching the 1st time, 2nd time, etc. Thus

$$S_\delta = 1 + q_1 + q_1 q_2 + \ldots + q_1 q_2 \ldots q_n S_\delta$$

but each of these terms $q_i = 1 - \frac{n\delta\varepsilon}{(n-1)(n-1-n\varepsilon)} + o(\delta)$, [2], so that we can say

$$S_\delta = \frac{1 - q^n}{(1-q)(1-q^n)} + o(\delta)$$

$$= \frac{1}{\frac{n\delta\varepsilon}{(n-1)(n-1-n\varepsilon)}} + o(\delta) \quad .$$

We have previously seen that $S_\tau = \sqrt{\frac{2\Pi}{\lambda}} \; \frac{(n-1)(1-\varepsilon)}{\sqrt{\tau}} \pm o(\sqrt{\tau})$ and the result follows.

For the sake of comparing some explicit expected search times and expected number of switches, Table I below gives some representative values. Note that appropriate comparison values are for $\delta = \sqrt{\tau}$.

Acknowledgment. The authors wish to thank Professor Joseph Gastwirth for some conversations they had with him regarding this paper.

References

1. Billingsley, P. (1968). *Convergence of Probability Measures.* Wiley, New York.

2. Posner, E.C. and Rumsey, H. (1966). Continuous sequential decision in the presence of a finite number of hypotheses. *Proc. Int. Symp. Inf. Theory,* Los Angeles, Calif. Special issue of *IEEE Trans. Information Theory,* IT-12, 248-255.

3. Shepp, L.A.(1966). Radon-Nikodym derivatives of Gaussian measures, *Annals of Math. Stat.*, 37, pp. 321-354.

Table 1

Comparisons of δ and τ Strategies

Epsilon = .100 Delta = .0010 N = 10 TN(1-ε) = 10.6267

Delta	Expected Time	Expected Switches	Tau	Expected Time	Expected Switches
.0010	10.63	35985.95	.000016	10.65	4981.22
.0020	10.63	17985.95	.00002	10.66	3521.96
.0030	10.63	11985.95	.00003	10.67	2875.49
.0040	10.63	8985.95	.00004	10.68	2490.12
.0050	10.63	7185.95	.00005	10.68	2227.12
.0060	10.63	5985.95	.00006	10.69	2032.99
.0070	10.63	5128.81	.00007	10.69	1882.11
.0080	10.63	4485.95	.00008	10.70	1760.49
.0090	10.63	3985.95	.00009	10.70	1659.75
.0100	10.63	3585.95	.0001	10.71	1574.53
.0200	10.63	1785.96	.0002	10.74	1113.08
.0300	10.64	1185.98	.0003	10.76	908.65
.0400	10.64	885.99	.0004	10.79	786.78
.0500	10.65	706.00	.0005	10.80	703.62
.0600	10.66	586.01	.0006	10.82	642.23
.0700	10.66	500.30	.0007	10.84	594.52
.0800	10.67	436.03	.0008	10.85	556.07
.0900	10.68	386.04	.0009	10.87	524.21
.1000	10.69	346.05	.0010	10.88	497.26
.2000	10.82	166.15	.0020	10.98	351.35
.3000	11.03	106.25	.0030	11.07	286.72
.4000	11.34	76.35	.0040	11.13	248.19
.5000	11.80	58.45	.0050	11.20	221.90
			.0060	11.25	202.50
			.0070	11.30	187.42
			.0080	11.35	175.27
			.0100	11.44	156.68
			.0400	12.30	78.04
			.0900	13.22	51.91
			.1600	14.20	38.91
			.2500	15.25	31.17

OPTIMAL PARI-MUTUEL WAGERING

By James N. Arvesen and Bernard Rosner*
Purdue University and Harvard University

A procedure is proposed to enable a bettor to optimally place a bet on a pari-mutuel event. The problem is essentially one of multivariate classification given data on each contestant. It is shown that one can always decide optimally among the alternatives, (1) bet on any one horse and (2) do not bet at all.

1. *Introduction.* Perhaps the first explicit solution to a non-linear programming problem was presented in Isaacs [1953]. His algorithm enabled one with the prescience of *a priori* probabilities to wager optimally on a pari-mutuel event. His optimal solution determines which contestants should be played, and the amount to be wagered on them. Unfortunately, the result had little practical relevance since obtaining valid *a priori* probabilities remained a problem. Also involved are possible computational difficulties in actually implementing the algorithm. Also his technique was essentially a no data problem. What follows is an attempt to treat pari-mutuel wagering as a problem in statistical

---

Acknowledgment. The authors are indebted to Professor Peter O. Anderson for several helpful discussions.

*This research was supported in part by the NIH Training Grant 5T01-GM-00024 at Purdue University.

decision theory. However, first let us digress to explain pari-mutuel wagering.

2. *Pari-Mutuel Wagering*. Approximately half of the fifty states have legalized pari-mutuel wagering on thoroughbred racing. In addition, several states permit pari-mutuel wagering on harness racing, greyhound racing and quarter-horse racing, while Florida includes jai-alai. In what follows attention will be focused on thoroughbred horse racing, however, the technique is applicable to all pari-mutuel events.

The essence of pari-mutuel wagering is that a number of bettors place bets on various horses, the "house" deducts a fixed proportion of the betting pool, and distributes the balance among the winners. The deducted proportion is typically between .14 and .16. Assume there is a total of S dollars wagered in a race, and Y_j dollars wagered on a horse of interest. Let r denote the proportion withheld by the "house". The odds, o_j, on this horse are given by

$$o_j = B[(1-r)S/(B\,Y_j)] - 1 \qquad (2.1)$$

where $[x]$ denotes the greatest integer in x, and B is called the "breakage". Typically, $B = \$0.10$. We will subsequently be interested in J discrete odds levels.

The above description is for win pari-mutuel wagering. For a discussion of place pari-mutuel wagering, and another betting algorithm, see Willis [1964].

3. *The Classification Problem*. Data on pari-mutuel wagering for thoroughbred horses is almost as plentiful as data for the stock market. In fact there is so much data that one must reduce it to some manageable statistic to make

one's decisions. Most serious handicappers do this in a highly subjective fashion, one they claim was learned by years of experience (and presumably years of financial losses too). The following is perhaps a more objective way to obtain a decision on wagering.

Excluding the possibility of a tie (called a dead-heat), every race of k horses has one winner and $(k-1)$ losers. The problem then is to classify each of the k horses as a potential winner or a potential loser. In fact let us assume that we are using p quantitative handicapping factors to classify the horse. Let X_i, $i = 1,\ldots, k$ be $p \times 1$ vectors denoting the observations on these p factors for horses $1,\ldots, k$. Furthermore, let Z be a $pk \times 1$ vector, $Z' = (X_1, X_2,\ldots, X_k)'$. While selection of these p factors is outside the scope of the present paper, one could use such factors as speed, class, or other commonly used factors (see Epstein [1967], da Silva and Dorcus [1961]).

Next let us assume we are interested in horses of odds at J levels, say $o_1,\ldots, o_J$. Actually one would probably pool several odds levels so that J would not be too large. Order the odds so that $o_1 < o_2 < \ldots < o_J$.

Then there are k states of nature $S_1,\ldots, S_k$, S_i indicating that the ith horse wins. Let us restrict ourselves to strategies which bet at most one horse, and exactly one dollar on each selected horse (never mind the fact that no race track allows less than a two dollar bet!). Then we have $k + 1$ possible actions $a_1,\ldots, a_k, a_{k+1}$, with a_i denoting betting one dollar on the ith horse, and a_{k+1} denoting placing no bet. Then the <u>loss</u> function can be described as follows: $L(a_i|S_i) = -o_{j_i}$, $i = 1,\ldots, k$ where

o_{j_i} are the odds on the ith horse, $L(a_i|S_{i^*}) = 1$, $i \neq i^*$, $1 \leq i, i^* \leq k$, and $L(a_{k+1}|S_i) = 0$, $i = 1,\ldots, k$. That is, one loses one dollar betting on a loser, loses $-o_{j_i}$ dollars (gains o_{j_i} dollars) betting on the ith horse if he is a winner, and loses nothing if no bet is made. The loss table summarizing the above is given in Table I.

Let $q_1,\ldots, q_k$ be the prior probabilities for $S_1,\ldots,S_k$. Then any decision procedure based on Z can be expressed in terms of $\phi(a_1|Z),\ldots, \phi(a_k|Z)$, $\phi(a_{k+1}|Z)$, where $\phi(a_i|Z)$ is defined to be the conditional probability of taking action a_i having observed Z, $i = 1,\ldots, k+1$. Also, let $F(z|S_i)$, $i = 1,\ldots,k$ be the (absolutely continuous) cumulative distribution function of Z if S_i is the state of nature (possible dependence of F on $o_{j_1},\ldots, o_{j_k}$ has been temporarily suppressed). Let $f(z|S_i)$ denote the density function associated with $F(z|S_i)$.

Theorem 1. *Assume the loss table as in* Table I, *and prior probabilities* $q_1,\ldots, q_k$ *for* $S_1,\ldots, S_k$. *Then the Bayes procedure is given by: Let* $\phi(a_i|Z) = 1$, $1 \leq i \leq k$ *if the following two conditions hold,*

$$\text{I.} \quad y_i \equiv -o_{j_i} q_i f(Z|S_i) + \sum_{\substack{i^*=1 \\ i^* \neq i}}^{k} q_{i^*} f(Z|S_{i^*}) < 0,$$

(3.1) and

$$\text{II.} \quad y_i \leq y_{i^*} \qquad \text{for all } i^* \neq 1.$$

If I. *fails to hold for some* $1 \leq i \leq k$, *let* $\phi(a_{k+1}|Z)=1$.

Proof. Let $q = (q_1,\ldots, q_k)$ denote the priors, and ϕ the decision rule. Then the Bayes risk is given by

$$(3.2)\quad \rho(q,\phi) = \sum_{i=1}^{k} q_i \int \Big(-o_{j_i}\,\phi(a_i|z) + \sum_{\substack{i^*=1 \\ i^* \neq i}}^{k} \phi(a_{i^*}|z)\Big)\, dF(z|S_i)$$

where the integral is over the pk dimensional space of Z. Noting that the odds are finite, condition II follows after exchanging the integration and summation. Condition I follows since the Bayes risk using a_{k+1} is zero.

Note that Theorem 1 could also include the discrete case for Z, except the Bayes procedure may not be unique (this is irrelevant, since if there is more than one, a bettor can achieve the same Bayes risk selecting any one of the procedures).

We note that Theorem 1 generalizes a result of Blackwell and Girschick [1954], Section 6.4. They considered the case $k = 2$, $o_{j_1} = o_{j_2} = 1$, $q_1 = q_2 = 1/2$.

One might have difficulty applying (3.1) without the following two seemingly reasonable assumptions.

Assumption 1. $f(Z|S_i) = \Pi_{\ell=1}^{k} f_{o_{j_\ell}}(X_\ell|S_i)$, $i = 1,\ldots,k$, *that is, the observations on the* k *horses are independent given the state of nature.*

Also, $f_{o_{j_\ell}}(\cdot|\cdot)$ indicates the possible dependence on the odds. It appears as if most handicapping factors do depend on the odds of the horse.

Assumption 2. $f_{o_{j_\ell}}(X_\ell|S_{\ell^*}) = f_{o_{j_\ell}}(X_\ell|S_\ell^c)$, $\ell = 1,\ldots,k$, $\ell^* \neq \ell$ *where* S_ℓ^c *indicates the state of nature is not* S_ℓ.

In other words, the observations on the ℓth horse only depend on whether the ℓth horse wins or loses, and not on which other horse won. With this assumption, we can let

$f_{o_{j_\ell}}(X_\ell|S_\ell) \equiv f_{o_{j_\ell}}(X_\ell|W)$, and $f_{o_{j_\ell}}(X_\ell|S_{\ell^*}) \equiv f_{o_{j_\ell}}(X_\ell|L)$, $\ell = 1,\ldots, k$, $\ell^* \neq \ell$ where W and L denote the horse is a winner or loser respectively.

Theorem 2. *Let* $\lambda_i = \dfrac{f_{o_{j_i}}(X_i|W)}{f_{o_{j_i}}(X_i|L)}$, *and the assumptions of* Theorem 1, Assumption 1, *and* Assumption 2 hold. *Then the Bayes procedure is given by: Let* $\phi(a_i|Z) = 1$, $1 \leq i \leq k$ *if the following two conditions hold,*

$$\text{I.}\quad -o_{j_i}q_i\lambda_i + \sum_{\substack{i^*=1\\ i^*\neq i}}^{k} q_{i^*}\lambda_{i^*} < 0,$$

(3.3) *and*

$$\text{II.}\quad \lambda_{i^*}/\lambda_i \leq \left((o_{j_i} + 1)q_i\right)/\left((o_{j_{i^*}} + 1)q_{i^*}\right)$$

for all $i^* \neq i$. *If* I *fails to hold for some* $1 \leq i \leq k$, *let* $\phi(a_{k+1}|Z) = 1$.

Proof. From (3.1) and Assumption 1,

$$y_i = -o_{j_i}q_i \prod_{\ell=1}^{k} f_{o_{j_\ell}}(X_\ell|S_i) + \sum_{\substack{i^*=1\\ i^*\neq i}}^{k} q_{i^*}\prod_{\ell=1}^{k} f_{o_{j_\ell}}(X_\ell|S_{i^*})$$

$$= -o_{j_i}q_i\lambda_i\prod_{\ell=1}^{k} f_{o_{j_\ell}}(X_\ell|L) + \sum_{\substack{i^*=1\\ i^*\neq i}}^{k} q_{i^*}\lambda_{i^*}\prod_{\ell=1}^{k} f_{o_{j_\ell}}(X_\ell|L)$$

using Assumption 2 and the definition of λ_i. Hence,

$$y_i = \Big(-o_{j_i}q_i\lambda_i + \sum_{\substack{i^*=1\\ i^*\neq i}}^{k} q_{i^*}\lambda_{i^*}\Big) \prod_{\ell=1}^{k} f_{o_{j_\ell}}(X_\ell|L) \quad ,$$

and since the last coefficient is positive (we are tacitly assuming all densitites have the same support set) Condition I in (3.3) follows from Condition I in (3.1). Condition II of (3.3) follows from Condition II of (3.1) using the above representation for y_i.

Note that Theorem 2 could also include the discrete case for Z, and yield a (non-unique) Bayes procedure. Unfortunately (3.3) still does not have enough structure to enable a bettor to determine how well he is doing, that is to calculate the Bayes risk in (3.2). Let us make the following assumptions concerning the distribution of Z. Recall that we ordered the odds so that $o_1 < o_2 < \cdots < o_J$.

Assumption 3. *Let* X *stand for the* p x 1 *observation vector on a horse of odds* o_j, *then assume*

$$X|W \sim N_p\left(\mu_j^{(1)}, \Sigma\right),$$

$$X|L \sim N_p\left(\mu_j^{(2)}, \Sigma\right), \qquad j = 1, \ldots, J,$$

where N_p *denotes the* p-*variate normal distribution, and* Σ *is a positive definite covariance matrix.*

Interestingly enough, Assumption 3 appears a reasonable approximation in practice. Moreover, we felt that this assumption was necessary, and that qualitative classification techniques (see Cochran and Hopkins [1961]) required too large a data base to estimate parameters.

Subsequently we will also use Assumption 4.

$\mu_j^{(1)} - \mu_j^{(2)} = \mu$, $j = 1, \ldots, J$.

That is the difference between the mean vector for winners and losers at each odds level is independent of the odds level. Again this assumption appears reasonable in practice, especially if J is not too large.

Theorem 3. *With the assumptions of* Theorem 2 *and* Assumption 3, *the Bayes procedure is given by: let* $\phi(a_i|Z)=1, 1 \leq i \leq k$

if the following two conditions hold,

$$\text{I.}\quad -o_{j_i} q_i \exp\Big(X_i'\Sigma^{-1}(\mu_{j_i}^{(1)}-\mu_{j_i}^{(2)}) - \tfrac{1}{2}(\mu_{j_i}^{(1)}+\mu_{j_i}^{(2)})'\Sigma^{-1}(\mu_{j_i}^{(1)}-\mu_{j_i}^{(2)})\Big) + \sum_{\substack{i^*=1\\ i^*\neq i}}^{k} q_{i^*}\exp\Big(X_{i^*}'\Sigma^{-1}(\mu_{j_{i^*}}^{(1)}-\mu_{j_{i^*}}^{(2)}) - \tfrac{1}{2}(\mu_{j_{i^*}}^{(1)}+\mu_{j_{i^*}}^{(2)})'\Sigma^{-1}(\mu_{j_{i^*}}^{(1)}-\mu_{j_{i^*}}^{(2)})\Big) < 0,$$

(3.4) and

$$\text{II.}\quad X_{i^*}'\Sigma^{-1}(\mu_{j_{i^*}}^{(1)}-\mu_{j_{i^*}}^{(2)})-\tfrac{1}{2}(\mu_{j_{i^*}}^{(1)}+\mu_{j_{i^*}}^{(2)})'\Sigma^{-1}(\mu_{j_{i^*}}^{(1)}-\mu_{j_{i^*}}^{(2)}) - X_i'\Sigma^{-1}(\mu_{j_i}^{(1)}-\mu_{j_i}^{(2)})+\tfrac{1}{2}(\mu_{j_i}^{(1)}+\mu_{j_i}^{(2)})'\Sigma^{-1}(\mu_{j_i}^{(1)}-\mu_{j_i}^{(2)}) \le \ln\big(((o_{j_i}+1)q_i)/((o_{j_{i^*}}+1)q_{i^*})\big)$$

for all $i^* \neq i$. *If* I *fails to hold for some* $1 \le i \le k$, *let* $\phi(a_{k+1}|Z) = 1$.

Proof. The proof follows immediately after noting that with Assumption 3,

$$\lambda_i = \frac{\exp-\frac{1}{2}(X_i-\mu_{j_i}^{(1)})'\Sigma^{-1}(X_i-\mu_{j_i}^{(1)})}{\exp-\frac{1}{2}(X_i-\mu_{j_i}^{(2)})\,\Sigma^{-1}(X_i-\mu_{j_i}^{(2)})}$$

$$= \exp(X_i'\Sigma^{-1}(\mu_{j_i}^{(1)}-\mu_{j_i}^{(2)})-\tfrac{1}{2}(\mu_{j_i}^{(1)}+\mu_{j_i}^{(2)})\Sigma^{-1}(\mu_{j_i}^{(1)}-\mu_{j_i}^{(2)}) \quad .$$

The following is stated without proof.

Corollary 4. *With the assumptions of* Theorem 3 *and* Assumption 4, *the Bayes procedure is given by: let* $\phi(a_i|Z) = 1$,

$1 \leq i \leq k$ *if the following two conditions hold,*

$$\text{I.} \quad -o_{j_i} q_i \exp\left(X_i'\Sigma^{-1}\mu - \tfrac{1}{2}(\mu_{j_i}^{(1)}+\mu_{j_i}^{(2)})'\Sigma^{-1}\mu\right)$$

$$+ \sum_{\substack{i^*=1 \\ i^* \neq i}}^{k} q_{i^*} \exp\left(X_{i^*}'\Sigma^{-1}\mu - \tfrac{1}{2}(\mu_{j_{i^*}}^{(1)}+\mu_{j_{i^*}}^{(2)})'\Sigma^{-1}\mu\right) < 0 \ ,$$

(3.5) *and*

$$\text{II.} \quad (X_{i^*}-X_i)'\Sigma^{-1}\mu - \tfrac{1}{2}(\mu_{j_{i^*}}^{(1)}+\mu_{j_{i^*}}^{(2)}-\mu_{j_i}^{(1)}-\mu_{j_i}^{(2)})\Sigma^{-1}\mu$$

$$\leq \ln\left(((o_{j_i}+1)q_i)/((o_{j_{i^*}}+1)q_{i^*})\right)$$

for all $i^* \neq i$. *If* I *fails to hold for some* $1 \leq i \leq k$, *let* $\phi(a_{k+1}|Z) = 1$.

Note that Condition II of (3.5) is easy to apply at the race track. The same linear combination of the observation vector is used for all odds, and a table of the other two terms for all $\binom{J}{2}$ odds pairs can be readily made. Unfortunately, Condition I, appears most difficult to implement at the race track. Perhaps a first order expansion of each of the exp functions would be a good approximation.

The problem of obtaining the *a priori* probabilities $q = (q_1,\ldots,q_k)$ still remains. There are two seemingly reasonable choices.

Assumption 5. *Choose as prior odds,* $q_i = (1-r)/(o_{j_i}+1)$, $i=1,\ldots,k$. These prior odds are suggested by (2.1), not taking account of the breakage factor. Note that with this assumption, the right hand side of Condition II in (3.4) and (3.5) becomes zero. Da Silva and Dorcus [1961] show that in large samples of races, these q_i's are close to the actual proportion of horses that win at odds o_{j_i}.

However, the simplication of Condition II with Assumption 5, results in making Condition I even more complicated. Perhaps the following is a better assumption.

Assumption 6. *Choose as prior odds*, $q_i = k^{-1}$, $i = 1,\ldots,k$.

That is, include all possible information in your $p \times 1$ observation vector on each horse so that this is a reasonable prior.

Let us now examine the Bayes risk for (3.5) in a special case. Let $P(a_i|S_\ell)$ denote the conditional probability of taking action a_i when the state of nature is S_ℓ. Furthermore, let us assume there are k horses in a race, each with the same amount of money wagered on them, and that the breakage factor does not enter (2.1). Then $o_{j_1} = \ldots = o_{j_k} = \left((1-r)k-1\right)$, and (3.5) reduces to let $\phi(a_i|Z) = 1$, $1 \le i \le k$ if the following hold,

$$\text{(3.6)}\quad \begin{aligned} &\text{I.}\quad -\left((1-r)k-1\right)e^{U_i} + \sum_{\substack{i^*=1 \\ i^*\neq i}}^{k} e^{U_{i^*}} < 0, \\ &\text{II.}\quad U_{i^*} - U_i < 0 \end{aligned}$$

for all $i^* \neq i$, where $U_i = X_i'\Sigma^{-1}\mu - \frac{1}{2}(\mu^{(1)}+\mu^{(2)})'\Sigma^{-1}\mu$, $i = 1,\ldots, k$, and $\mu^{(1)}, \mu^{(2)}$ are the mean vectors of winners and losers respectively of odds $\left((1-r)k-1\right)$. If I fails to hold for some $1 \le i \le k$, let $\phi(a_{k+1}|Z) = 1$.

Note that $U' = (U_1,\ldots,U_k)'$ has a multivariate normal distribution in k dimensions with mean vector given by $E(U') = (-\alpha/2,\ldots,-\alpha/2,+\alpha/2,-\alpha/2,\ldots,-\alpha/2)$ if S_ℓ the ℓth component, where $\alpha = \mu'\Sigma^{-1}\mu$ is the Mahalanobis distance between winners and losers. The covariance matrix is $\alpha \times I$, where I is the $k \times k$ identity matrix. From Assumptions 1-4, and Anderson [1958], Ch. 6, one can readily obtain this distribution for U.

One can now calculate $P(a_i|S_i)$, and $P(a_i|S_{i^*})$, $i \neq i^*$. First, by the assumption of equal odds, we can let $i = 1$ without loss of generality. Then

$$P(a_1|S_1) = P(\textstyle\sum_{i^*=2}^{k} e^{V_{i^*}} < (1-r)k-1,\ V_2 < 0, \ldots, V_k < 0)$$

where $V_{i^*} = U_{i^*} - U_1$, $i^* = 2, \ldots, k$. Since S_1 is true $V' = (V_2, \ldots, V_k)'$ has a multivariate normal distribution in $(k-1)$ dimensions with mean vector $E(V') = (-\alpha, \ldots, -\alpha)$, and covariance matrix,

$$\mathrm{Cov}(V) = \begin{pmatrix} 2\alpha & \alpha & \cdots & \alpha \\ \alpha & 2\alpha & \cdots & \alpha \\ \vdots & \vdots & & \vdots \\ \alpha & \alpha & \cdots & 2\alpha \end{pmatrix}.$$

After normalization, one obtains

$$(3.7)\quad P(a_1|S_1) = P(\textstyle\sum_{i^*=2}^{k} e^{(2\alpha)^{1/2} W_{i^*}} < ((1-r)k-1)e^{\alpha},$$

$$W_2 < (\alpha/2)^{1/2}, \ldots, W_k < (\alpha/2)^{1/2}) ,$$

where $W_2, \ldots, W_k$ are standard normal with $\mathrm{corr}(W_i, W_j) = 1/2$, $i \neq j$. Also, if S_2 is the state of nature, $E(V') = (\alpha, 0, \ldots, 0)$, with the same covariance matrix as above. Hence after normalization, one obtains

$$P(a_1|S_\ell) = P(a_1|S_2) = P(e^{(2\alpha)^{1/2}W_2+\alpha}$$

$$(3.8) \qquad + \sum_{i^*=3}^{k} e^{(2\alpha)^{1/2}W_3} < (1-r)k-1, W_2 < -(\alpha/2)^{1/2},$$
$$W_3 < 0, \ldots, W_k < 0) ,$$

$\ell \neq 1$, $W' = (W_2, \ldots, W_k)'$ having the same distribution as in (3.7).

Thus in the case of equal odds, k horses, a "take" of r, and a Mahalanobis distance of α, the Bayes risk from (3.2), now denoted by $B(k,r,\alpha)$, is given by

$$(3.9) \qquad B(k,r,\alpha) = k^{-1}k\{-((1-r)k-1)P(a_1|S_1)+(k-1)P(a_1|S_2)\}$$
$$= -((1-r)k-1)P(a_1|S_1)+(k-1)P(a_1|S_2) \quad ,$$

$P(a_1|S_1)$, $P(a_1|S_2)$ as in (3.7), (3.8).

For $k = 2$, (3.7) - (3.9) are easy to calculate. Also, for k arbitrary,

$$(3.10) \qquad P(W_2<w_2,\ldots,W_k<w_k) = \int_{-\infty}^{\infty} [\Pi_{i^*=2}^{k} \Phi(2^{1/2}w_{i^*}-y)]\phi(y)dy$$

where Φ and ϕ are the standard normal c.d.f. and density function respectively. This representation, and similar identities may be found in Gupta [1963]. Expression (3.10) may be evaluated on a computer (see Gupta [1963]). Hence one needs to calculate

$$(3.11) \qquad P\,(\sum_{i^*=2}^{k} e^{(2\alpha)^{1/2}W_{i^*}} < ((1-r)k-1)e^{\alpha},$$
$$W_2<(\alpha/2)^{1/2}, \ldots, W_k<(\alpha/2)^{1/2}),$$

and

$$(3.12) \qquad P\Big(e^{(2\alpha)^{1/2}W_2+\alpha} + \sum_{i^*=3}^{k} e^{(2\alpha)^{1/2}W_{i^*}} > (1-r)k-1, \quad W_2 < -(\alpha/2)^{1/2}, W_3<0,\ldots,W_k<0\Big).$$

Unfortunately, expressions (3.11) and (3.12) could be readily evaluated on a computer only when $k = 3$. In that case, (3.11) becomes

$$(3.13) \qquad \int_a^b \phi(x)\{\Phi\big(((\alpha/2)^{1/2}-x/2)/(3/4)^{1/2}\big) - \Phi\big([(\ell n((2-3r)e^{\alpha}-e^{(2\alpha)^{1/2}x}))/(2\alpha)^{1/2}-x/2]/(3/4)^{1/2}\big)\}dx$$

and (3.12) becomes

$$(3.14) \qquad \int_c^d \phi(x)\{\Phi\big((-x/2)/(3/4)^{1/2}\big) - \Phi\big([(\ell n(2-3r-e^{(2\alpha)^{1/2}x+\alpha}))/(2\alpha)^{1/2}-x/2]/(3/4)^{1/2}\big)\}dx \quad ,$$

where $a = (\alpha/2)^{1/2} + (\ell n(1-3r))/(2\alpha)^{1/2}$, $b = (\alpha/2)^{1/2}$, $c = -(\alpha/2)^{1/2} + (\ell n(1-3r))/(2\alpha)^{1/2}$, $d = -(\alpha/2)^{1/2}$, and where $3r < 1$ for problems of interest.

A table of $B(k,r,\alpha)$ for $k = 2,3$, $r = .15, .16$, and several values of α is given in Table II. Also included are $P(a_1|S_1)$, $(k-1)\,P(a_1|S_2)$, and $P(a_{k+1})$. The calculations were done on the Purdue University CDC 6500 computer.

From Table II it is interesting to conjecture that $B(k,r,\alpha)$ is monotone in all three arguments. Also, one should note that the conditional Bayes risk given that a bet was made, call it $BC(k,r,\alpha)$, is given by

$$BC(k,r,\alpha) = B(k,r,\alpha)/(1-P(a_{k+1})). \tag{3.15}$$

Finally, note that a purist might object to our tacit assumption that "winners" and "losers" comprise two populations. They certainly are not two populations in the standard statistical sense. Nevertheless, we feel that this distinction is only of philosophical importance, for if there is a positive Mahalanobis distance $\alpha = \mu'\Sigma^{-1}\mu$, we are willing to act as if we in fact had two populations.

4. *Discussion*. In discussing our procedure as given in (3.5) with that of Isaacs [1953], two interesting points are noted. First, both procedures can select a null subset to play. Also our procedure selects at most one horse per race to play, while his may possibly select more. We realize that a bettor may eliminate mathematically admissible strategies by playing at most one horse per race. Nevertheless the authors feel that in practice it makes little sense to "bet against oneself" by playing more than one horse per race. Also, the mathematics of (3.5) would become more complicated.

Second, Isaac's procedure has an advantage in that it tells the bettor how much he should wager. We feel this is a small point since one can bet very substantial amounts at the large race tracks without seriously affecting the pari-mutuel odds.

Finally, the authors are currently working on estimation problems involving (3.5). Interesting problems in estimating ordered multivariate parameters arise.

References

1. Anderson, T. W. [1958]. *An Introduction to Multivariate Analysis*, John Wiley and Sons, New York

2. Blackwell, D., and Girshick, M. A. [1954]. *Theory of Games and Statistical Decisions*, John Wiley and Sons, New York.

3. Cochran, W. G., and Hopkins, C. E. [1961]. "Some classification problems with multivariate qualitative data", *Biometrics*, (17), 10-32.

4. da Silva, E. R., and Dorcus, R. M. [1961]. *Science in Betting*, Dolphin Books, Doubleday and Company, Garden City, N.Y.

5. Epstein, R. A. [1967]. *The Theory of Gambling and Statistical Logic*, Academic Press, New York.

6. Gupta, S. S. [1963]. "Probability integrals of multivariate normal and multivariate t", *Ann. Math. Statist.*, 34, 792-828.

7. Isaacs, R. [1953]. "Optimal horse race bets", *Amer. Math. Monthly*, 60, 310-315.

8. Willis, K. E. [1964]. "Optimum no-risk strategy for win-place pari-mutuel betting", *Management Sci.* 10, 574-577.

Table I

LOSS TABLE FOR BETTOR'S ACTIONS

State of Nature \ Action	a_1	a_2	. . .	a_k	a_{k+1}
S_1	$-o_{j_1}$	1	. . .	1	0
S_2	1	$-o_{j_2}$	. . .	1	0
⋮	⋮	⋮			
S_k	1		. . .	$-o_{j_k}$	0

Table II

BAYES RISK

$r = .15$

	k = 2				k = 3			
α	Bayes Risk	$P(a_1\|S_1)$	$P(a_1\|S_2)$	$P(a_3)$	Bayes Risk	$P(a_1\|S_1)$	$2P(a_1\|S_2)$	$P(a_4)$
.05	-. 2	.166	.099	.735	-.05	.213	.284	.504
.10	-.05	.283	.154	.563	-.10	.314	.383	.304
.15	-.07	.353	.178	.470	-.15	.368	.417	.215
.20	-.09	.402	.189	.408	-.20	.405	.430	.165
.25	-.11	.440	.196	.365	-.24	.433	.434	.133
.30	-.13	.471	.198	.331	-.27	.456	.433	.111

$r = .16$

	k = 2				k = 3			
α	Bayes Risk	$P(a_1\|S_1)$	$P(a_1\|S_2)$	$P(a_3)$	Bayes Risk	$P(a_1\|S_1)$	$2P(a_1\|S_2)$	$P(a_4)$
.05	-.01	.144	.084	.772	-.04	.193	.254	.553
.10	-.04	.262	.139	.600	-.09	.299	.359	.342
.15	-.06	.334	.164	.503	-.14	.356	.399	.245
.20	-.08	.385	.172	.443	-.19	.396	.415	.189
.25	-.10	.424	.184	.392	-.23	.425	.422	.153
.30	-.12	.456	.188	.356	-.26	.449	.423	.128

NONPARAMETRIC PROCEDURES FOR SELECTING FIXED-SIZE SUBSETS

By M. M. Desu and Milton Sobel
State University of New York at Buffalo
and University of Minnesota

0. *Introduction and Summary.* There is a collection of k populations $\pi_1, \pi_2, \ldots, \pi_k$ where π_i is associated with the continuous distribution function (d.f.) $F_i(x) = F_i$. A number α such that $0 < \alpha < 1$ and integer t where $1 \leq t \leq k-1$ are given. Earlier Sobel [5] considered the problem of selecting those t of the k populations which have the largest α-quantiles. He developed nonparametric procedures based on n independent observations from each of the k populations. Here we consider the problem of selecting a subset of specified size s, where $t \leq s \leq k-1$, which includes those t populations of the given set which have largest α-quantiles. Thus our goal will reduce to the goal in [5] when $s = t$. The proposed procedure is defined in terms of order statistics which are based on n independent observations from each of the k populations. This procedure can be viewed as a nonparametric analogue of the procedure developed by one of the authors in [3]. Assuming that the functional form of F_i is unknown and that F_i is continuous, we determine the sample size n, which makes the procedure explicit, such that the procedure satisfies the usual probability requirement.

We also consider a related problem where the subset size s is to be determined as a function of n, the common size of an available sample from each population. This type of problem has been discussed by the authors in [1] for parametric family of distributions. Thus we have an alternative approach to the subset selection problem considered in [4], where $t = 1$.

Few tables giving the needed n-values are given, where the quantile of interest is the median, i.e. $\alpha = 1/2$.

1. *The Problem.* Let $x_\alpha(F)$ denote the α-quantile of the distribution F. We shall assume that each F_i has a unique α-quantile. Let $F_{[i]}(x) = F_{[i]}$ denote the d.f. with the i-th smallest α-quantile. The unknown ordering of the k distributions is

$$F_{[1]} \leq F_{[2]} \leq \cdots \leq F_{[k]} \tag{1.1}$$

where $F_{[i]} \leq F_{[j]}$ means that $x_\alpha(F_{[i]}) \leq x_\alpha(F_{[j]})$. It is assumed that no a priori information is available concerning the correct pairing of the F_i and the $F_{[i]}$. We shall not assume that the k distributions have the same supports and we do not require that they differ only in a location parameter.

We shall consider two formulations which are called Formulation 1 and Formulation 2. In each formulation two cases are considered.

Formulation 1. Let $\varepsilon_\gamma^* > 0$ $(\gamma = 1,2)$ be two specified numbers such that $\varepsilon_1^* \leq \alpha \leq 1 - \varepsilon_2^*$. Let $\underline{x}_\beta(F)$ and $\overline{x}_\beta(F)$ stand for the infimum and supremum of the set $\{x: F(x) = \beta\}$. It is to be understood, unless mentioned to the contrary, that the indices i,j will run over the ranges $i=1,2,\ldots,k-t$ and $j=k-t+1, k-t+2,\ldots,k$, respectively. Let $\underline{F} = \underline{F}(x)$ and $\overline{F} = \overline{F}(x)$ denote the min $F_{[i]}(x)$ and the max $F_{[j]}(x)$, respectively. Let us define the interval

$$(1.2) \qquad I = [\overline{x}_{\alpha-\varepsilon_1^*}(\overline{F}), \ \underline{x}_{\alpha+\varepsilon_2^*}(\overline{F})] \quad ,$$

and let $d_{ij} = \inf_{x\varepsilon I}(F_{[i]}(x) - F_{[j]}(x))$.

Let

$$(1.3) \qquad d = \min d_{ij} = \inf_{x\varepsilon I}(\underline{F}(x) - \overline{F}(x)) \quad .$$

d^* and P^* are two specified constants such that $d^* > 0$ and $1 > P^* > \binom{k-t}{s-t} \div \binom{k}{s}$. If $x_\alpha(F_{[k-t]}) < x_\alpha(F_{[k-t+1]})$, we define a correct selection (CS) to mean the selection of a subset of size s, which contains the t populations associated with $F_{[j]}$.

The goal is to find a procedure R such that

$$(1.4) \qquad P\{CS|R\} \geq P^* \quad \text{whenever} \quad d \geq d^* \quad .$$

For $d \geq d^* > 0$, each $F_{[i]}(x)$, $i = 1,2,\ldots,k-t$ must avoid the shaded area of Figure 1. That is, $\underline{F}(x)$ must avoid the shaded area.

We shall assume that the common sample size n from each population is sufficiently large so that $1 \leq (n+1)\alpha \leq n$. If r is the positive integer such that

$$(1.5) \qquad r \leq (n+1)\alpha < r + 1,$$

the proposed procedure is based on $Y_{r,\beta}$, which is the rth order statistic in the sample from $F_\beta(\beta = 1,2,\ldots,k)$.

Procedure R: *Take* n *independent observations from each population and select the* s *populations which give rise to the* s-*largest* Y_r -*values*.

To make R explicit, we have to specify the n-value. Thus the problem reduces to that of finding the smallest integer n for which the procedure R satisfies the probability requirement (1.4).

Formulation 2. Let $\varepsilon_\gamma^* > 0$ $(\gamma = 1,2)$ be specified constants as in formulation 1. Let $d'_{ij} = \underline{x}_{\alpha-\varepsilon_1^*}(F_{[j]}) - \overline{x}_{\alpha+\varepsilon_2^*}(F_{[i]})$

and let $d' = \min d'_{ij} = \underline{x}_{\alpha-\varepsilon_1^*}(\overline{F}) - \overline{x}_{\alpha+\varepsilon_2^*}(\underline{F})$. As before our goal is to find a procedure R such that

$$\text{(1.6)} \qquad P\{CS|R\} \geq P^* \quad \text{for} \quad d' \geq 0 \quad .$$

For $d' \geq 0$, each $F_{[i]}(x)$, $i = 1,2,\ldots,k-t$ must avoid the shaded area of Figure 2. That is, $\underline{F}(x)$ must avoid the shaded area.

The form of the procedure is the same as for Formulation 1. Hence the problem again is to determine the smallest integer n such that (1.6) is satisfied.

The next section deals with some properties of $P\{CS|R\}$ and the lower bounds on $P\{CS|R\}$.

2. *Probability of a Correct Selection:* We shall express $P\{CS|R\}$ as an expectation of an indicator function. This will enable us to observe certain monotone properties of $P\{CS|R\}$, from which we obtain lower bounds on PCS.

Let $Y_{(\beta)} = Y_{r,(\beta)}$ be the rth order statistic in the sample from $F_{[\beta]}$. Its distribution function $H_\beta(\cdot)$ is given by

$$\text{(2.1)} \qquad H_\beta(y) = \sum_{j=r}^{n} \binom{n}{j} F^j_{[\beta]}(y)\{1-F_{[\beta]}(y)\}^{n-j} = G(F_{[\beta]}(y)),$$

where $G(p) \equiv G(p;r, n-r+1)$ is the incomplete beta function defined as

$$G(p; r,n-r+1) = \{n!/(r-1)!\}\int_0^p x^{r-1}(1-x)^{n-r}dx \ . \tag{2.2}$$

The probability of a correct selection under the procedure R is given by

$$\begin{aligned} P\{CS|R\} &= \Pr\{\min Y_{(j)} > (s-t+1)\text{st largest of } Y_{(i)}\} \\ &= E\{\psi(Y_{(1)}, Y_{(2)},\ldots,Y_{(k)}\} \end{aligned} \tag{2.3}$$

where

$$\begin{aligned} \psi(y_{(1)},y_{(2)},\ldots,y_{(k)}) &= 1 \text{ if } \min y_{(j)} > (s-t+1)\text{st} \\ &\qquad\qquad \text{largest of } y_{(i)} \ , \\ &= 0 \text{ otherwise.} \end{aligned}$$

Let us denote the $\min Y_{(j)}$ by ξ and the $(s-t+1)$st largest of $Y_{(i)}$ by η. Since ξ and η are independent, we have

$$\begin{aligned} P\{CS|R\} &= \Pr\{\xi > \eta\} \\ &= \int_{-\infty}^{\infty} U(y)dV(y) = \int_{-\infty}^{\infty} \{1-V(y)\}dU(y) \ . \end{aligned} \tag{2.4}$$

(Note that U and V are the distribution functions of η and ξ, respectively.) In general the expressions for U and V are very complicated since neither $Y_{(i)}$ nor $Y_{(j)}$ have the same distribution. Without knowing the exact expression for $P\{CS|R\}$ in terms of $F_{[1]},F_{[2]},\ldots,F_{[k]}$, it is possible to obtain some monotone properties of $P\{CS|R\}$, which will enable us to find lower bounds. The following lemma will enable us to obtain the monotone properties of

$P\{CS|R\}$.

Lemma 2.1: *Let* $\underset{\sim}{X} = (X_1, X_2, \ldots, X_k)$ *denote a set of independent one-dimensional random variables, such that* F_β *is the distribution function of* X_β, $\beta = 1,2,\ldots,k$. *Let* $\psi(\underset{\sim}{x}) = \psi(x_1, x_2, \ldots, x_k)$ *be a function such that for each* $\beta(\beta = 1,2,\ldots,k)$, *it is a nondecreasing function of* x_β *when all other* $x_\gamma(\gamma \neq \beta)$ *are held fixed. Then for each fixed* $\beta(\beta = 1,2,\ldots,k)$,

$$(2.5) \qquad E\{\psi(\underset{\sim}{x})|F_{10}, F_{20}, \ldots, F_{k0}\} \leq E\{\psi(\underset{\sim}{x})|F_{11}, F_{21}, \ldots, F_{k1}\}$$

when for all x, $F_{\gamma 0}(x) = F_{\gamma 1}(x)$ *if* $\gamma \neq \beta$ *and* $F_{\beta 0}(x) \geq F_{\beta 1}(x)$.

This is a simple generalization of problem 11 on page 112 of Lehmann [2]. The proof is simple and hence omitted. The inequality in (2.5) will be reversed if ψ is a nonincreasing function of x_β, when all other x_γ are held fixed.

Our function ψ appearing in (2.3) is a nondecreasing function in each $y_{(j)}(j = k-t+1, k-t+2, \ldots, k)$, when the remaining y's are held fixed and it is a nonincreasing function in each $y_{(i)}(i = 1,2,\ldots,k-t)$, when the remaining y's are held fixed. Using the lemma, it follows that $P\{CS|R\}$ is a nonincreasing function of $F_{[j]}$ $(j = k-t+1, k-t+1, \ldots, k)$ and it is a nondecreasing function of $F_{[i]}$ $(i = 1,2,\ldots,k-t)$. Thus in our search for the infimum of PCS, we need to confine our attention to the configurations

$$(2.6) \qquad F_{[1]} = \cdots = F_{[k-t]} = \underline{F};\ F_{[k-t+1]} = \cdots = F_{[k]} = \overline{F},$$

which are called generalized least favorable configurations. Let $\overline{\mathcal{F}} = [\underline{F}, \ldots, \underline{F}, \overline{F}, \ldots, \overline{F}]$, where the first $(k-t)$

components are equal to $\underline{F}$ and the remaining t components are equal to F. From (2.4), the PCS at $\overline{F}$ is given by

$$
\begin{aligned}
P\{CS|R,\overline{F}\} &\equiv P(\underline{F},\overline{F}) = \int_{-\infty}^{\infty} \{\underline{U}(y)d\overline{V}(y) \\
&= \int_{-\infty}^{\infty} \{1-\overline{V}(y)\}d\underline{U}(y)
\end{aligned} \tag{2.7}
$$

where

$$\underline{U}(y) = G[\underline{H}(y);k-s,s-t+1],\overline{V}(y) = 1-\{1-\overline{H}(y)\}^{t} \quad . \tag{2.8}$$

In (2.8), $\overline{H}(y)$ and $\underline{H}(y)$ are defined as in (2.1), where $F_{[\beta]}$ is to be replaced by $\overline{F}$ and $\underline{F}$, respectively.

The rest of the section is devoted to the derivation of certain bounds on $P\{CS|R,\overline{F}\}$, which is defined by (2.7). These bounds are used to obtain bounds on $P\{CS|R\}$.

2.1. *Formulation* 1A: From (2.7), we have

$$
\begin{aligned}
P(\underline{F},\overline{F}) &= \int_{I^-} \underline{U}(y)d\overline{V}(y) + \int_{I} \underline{U}(y)d\overline{V}(y) + \int_{I^+} \underline{U}(y)d\overline{V}(y) \\
&\equiv T_1 + T_2 + T_3 ,
\end{aligned} \tag{2.9}
$$

where the intervals I^- and I^+ are the infinite intervals to the left and to the right of I, such that $I^-\cup I\cup I^+$ is the entire real line. Since $\underline{F}(y) \geq \overline{F}(y) + d^*$, for $y \in I$ and since $\overline{H}$ is a nondecreasing function of $\overline{F}$, we get

$$T_2 \geq t \int_I G\{G(\overline{F}(y) + d^*);\ k-s,s-t+1\}[1-\overline{H}(y)]^{t-1}d\overline{H}(y) \quad .$$

Denoting $\overline{F}(y)$ by u, this inequality can be expressed as

$$T_2 \geq t \int_{\alpha-\varepsilon_1^*}^{\alpha+\varepsilon_2^*} G[G(u+d^*);k-s,s-t+1][1-G(u)]^{t-1}dG(u) \quad . \tag{2.10}$$

When $y \in I^+$, we have

$$\underline{F}(y) \geq \underline{F}(\underline{x}_{\alpha+\varepsilon_2^*}(\bar{F})) \geq \underline{F}(\underline{x}_{\alpha+\varepsilon_2^*+d^*}(\underline{F})) \geq \alpha + \varepsilon_2^* + d^* \quad ;$$

and hence

$$(2.11) \qquad \begin{aligned} T_3 &= t\int_{I^+} G[G(\underline{F}(y)); k-s,s-t+1][1-\bar{H}(y)]^{t-1} d\bar{H}(y) \\ &\geq G[G(\alpha+\varepsilon_2^*+d^*);k-s,s-t+1]\{1-G(\alpha+\varepsilon_2^*)\}^t . \end{aligned}$$

If $\mathcal{F} = (F_1,\ldots,F_k)$ be any set of admissible distributions such that $d \geq d^*$ and if $\bar{\mathcal{F}}$ is the corresponding generalized least favorable configuration, we have

$$(2.12) \qquad \begin{aligned} P\{CS|R,\mathcal{F}\} &\geq P\{CS|R,\bar{\mathcal{F}}\} \geq T_2 + T_3 \\ &\geq t\int_{\alpha-\varepsilon_1^*}^{\alpha+\varepsilon_2^*} G[G(u+d^*); k-s,s-t+1][1-G(u)]^{t-1} dG(u) \\ &+ G[G(\alpha+\varepsilon_2^*+d^*);k-s,s-t+1][1-G(\alpha+\varepsilon_2^*)]^t . \end{aligned}$$

Using integration by parts, from (2.12) we obtain

$$(2.13) \qquad \begin{aligned} P\{CS|R,\mathcal{F}\} &\geq [1-G(\alpha-\varepsilon_1^*)]^t G[G(\alpha-\varepsilon_1^*+d^*);k-s,s-t+1] \\ &+ \binom{k-t}{k-s}\int_{\alpha-\varepsilon_1^*+d^*}^{\alpha+\varepsilon_2^*+d^*} [1-G(u-d^*)]^t [1-G(u)]^{s-t} d[G^{k-s}(u)]. \end{aligned}$$

This expression for the bound is useful for computational purposes. When $s = t$, the bounds given in (2.12) and (2.13) coincide respectively with (2.9) and (2.10) of Sobel [5].

2.2. *Formulation* 1B: A slightly different lower bound for PCS is obtained on the assumption that $\underline{F}$ and $\overline{F}$ cannot cross each other. Since $\underline{F}(x) \geq \overline{F}(x) + d^*$ for $x \in I$, the assumption of no cross over implies that for all x

$$\underline{F}(x) \geq \overline{F}(x) \quad . \tag{2.14}$$

Now we derive a lower bound for PCS by rewriting (2.9) as

$$\begin{aligned} P(\underline{F},\overline{F}) &= \int_{I^-} \underline{U}(y)\,d\overline{V}(y) + \int_{I} \underline{U}(y)\,d\overline{V}(y) + \int_{I_1^+} \underline{U}(y)\,d\overline{V}(y) \\ &\quad + \int_{I_2^+} \underline{U}(y)\,d\overline{V}(y) \\ &\equiv T_1 + T_2 + T_{31} + T_{32} \ , \end{aligned} \tag{2.15}$$

where I_1^+ is the interval $(\underline{x}_{\alpha+\varepsilon_2^*}(\overline{F}), \overline{x}_{\alpha+\varepsilon_2^*+d^*}(\overline{F}))$ and I_2^+ is the infinite interval to the right of I_1^+. Now

$$\begin{aligned} T_1 &= t\int_{I^-} G[\underline{H}(y);k-s,s-t+1]\{1-\overline{H}(y)\}^{t-1}d\overline{H}(y) \\ &\geq t\int_{I^-} G[\overline{H}(y);k-s,s-t+1]\{1-\overline{H}(y)\}^{t-1}d\overline{H}(y) \ ; \end{aligned}$$

denoting $\overline{F}(y)$ by u, this can be expressed as

$$T_1 \geq t\int_0^{\alpha-\varepsilon_1^*} G[G(u);k-s,s-t+1]\{1-G(u)\}^{t-1}dG(u) \quad . \tag{2.16a}$$

Since $\underline{F}(y) \geq \alpha + \varepsilon_2^* + d^*$ for $y \in I_1^+$, we have

$$\begin{aligned} T_{31} \geq G[G(\alpha+\varepsilon_2^*+d^*);k-s,s-t+1]\,[\{1-G(\alpha+\varepsilon_2^*)\}^t \\ - \{1-G(\alpha+\varepsilon_2^*+d^*)\}^t] \quad . \end{aligned} \tag{2.16b}$$

Using (2.14), it is clear that

$$T_{32} \geq t\int_{\alpha+\varepsilon_2^*+d^*}^{1} G[G(u);k-s,s-t+1]\{1-G(u)\}^{t-1}dG(u) \quad . \tag{2.16c}$$

From (2.10), (2.16a), (2.16b) and (2.16c), it follows that for any $\mathcal{F} = (F_1, F_2, \ldots, F_k)$ such that $d \geq d^*$ and $\underline{F}(x) \geq \overline{F}(x)$,

$$\begin{aligned} P\{CS|R,\mathcal{F}\} &\geq P\{CS|R,\overline{\mathcal{F}}\} \\ &\geq t\int_{0}^{\alpha-\varepsilon_1^*} G\{G(u);k-s,s-t+1\}\{1-G(u)\}^{t-1}dG(u) \\ &+ t\int_{\alpha-\varepsilon_1^*}^{\alpha+\varepsilon_2^*} G\{G(u+d^*);k-s,s-t+1\}\{1-G(u)\}^{t-1}dG(u) \\ &+ G\{G(\alpha+\varepsilon_2^*+d^*);k-s,s-t+1\}[\{1-G(\alpha+\varepsilon_2^*)\}^{t} \\ &\qquad - \{1-G(\alpha+\varepsilon_2^*+d^*)\}^{t}] \\ &+ t\int_{\alpha+\varepsilon_2^*+d^*}^{1} G\{G(u);k-s,s-t+1\}\{1-G(u)\}^{t-1}dG(u) \quad . \end{aligned} \tag{2.17}$$

This bound can be viewed as $P(\underline{F}^{(1)},\overline{F})$ where

$$\underline{F}^{(1)}(x) = \begin{cases} \overline{F}(x) & \text{for } x < \overline{x}_{\alpha-\varepsilon_1^*}(\overline{F}) \\ \overline{F}(x) + d^* & \text{for } x \in I \\ \alpha+\varepsilon_2^*+d^* & \text{for } \underline{x}_{\alpha+\varepsilon_2^*}(\overline{F}) < x \leq \overline{x}_{\alpha+\varepsilon_2^*+d^*}(\overline{F}) \\ \overline{F}(x) & \text{for } x > \overline{x}_{\alpha+\varepsilon_2^*+d^*}(\overline{F}) \quad . \end{cases} \tag{2.18}$$

We note that the bound in (2.17) tends to $\binom{k-t}{k-s}/\binom{k}{s}$ as $d^* \to 0$, for any fixed n and any pair $\varepsilon_1^* \geq 0$ and $\varepsilon_2^* \geq 0$.

The bound obtained in (2.13) is smaller than the bound in (2.17). If $\Omega_2(d^*)$ is the collection of all pairs $(\underline{F},\overline{F})$ such that $d \geq d^*$, from our earlier discussion it follows that

$$\inf_{d \geq d^*} P\{CS|R,F\} = \inf_{\Omega_2(d^*)} P(\underline{F},\overline{F}) .$$

Also for fixed $\overline{F}$, one can show that

$$\inf_{\Omega_2(d^*)} P(\underline{F},\overline{F}) = P(\underline{F}^{(1)}\overline{F}) ,$$

under our assumption of no cross over. Since $P(\underline{F}^{(1)},\overline{F})$ does not depend on $\overline{F}$, we have

$$\inf_{d \geq d^*} P\{CS|R,F\} = P(\underline{F}^{(1)},\overline{F}) . \tag{2.19}$$

2.3. *Formulation* 2A: Starting from (2.7) we have

$$P\{CS|R,F\} \geq P(\underline{F},\overline{F}) \geq \int_{\underline{x}_{\alpha-\varepsilon_1^*}(\overline{F})}^{\infty} \underline{U}(y)d[1-\{1-\overline{H}(y)\}^t] ,$$

for any F such that $d' > 0$. This results in the following lower bound

$$P\{CS|R,F\} \geq G[G(\alpha+\varepsilon_2^*);k-s,s-t+1]\{1-G(\alpha-\varepsilon_1^*)\}^t . \tag{2.20}$$

It may be noted that for $\alpha = 1/2$, $\varepsilon_1^* = \varepsilon_2^* = \varepsilon^*$ and $s = t$ this bound is $G^k(\alpha+\varepsilon^*)$, which does not depend on t.

2.4. *Formulation* 2B: As in Formulation 1B here we make the assumption that $\overline{F}$ and $\underline{F}$ do not cross each other. Using techniques similar to those used in Formulation 1B, we obtain

$$P\{CS|R,F\} \geq t\int_0^{\alpha-\varepsilon_1^*} G[G(u);k-s,s-t+1]\{1-G(u)\}^{t-1}dG(u)$$

$$(2.21) \qquad + G[G(\alpha+\varepsilon_2^*);k-s,s-t+1]\{[1-G(\alpha-\varepsilon_1^*)]^t - [1-G(\alpha+\varepsilon_2^*)]^t\}$$

$$+ t\int_{\alpha+\varepsilon_2^*}^{1} G[G(u);k-s,s-t+1]\{1-G(u)\}^{t-1}dG(u),$$

for any F such that $d' \geq 0$. The right side of (2.21) reduces to $\binom{k-t}{k-s} / \binom{k}{s}$ when $\varepsilon_1^* = \varepsilon_2^* = 0$.

The lower bound in (2.21) can be viewed as $P(\underline{F}^{(2)},\overline{F})$, where

$$(2.22) \qquad \underline{F}^{(2)}(x) = \begin{cases} \overline{F}(x) & x < \overline{x}_{\alpha-\varepsilon_1^*}(\overline{F}) \\ \alpha+\varepsilon_2^* & x \in I \\ \overline{F}(x) & x > \underline{x}_{\alpha+\varepsilon_2^*}(\overline{F}) \end{cases}$$

As in Formulation 1B, we can show that

$$(2.23) \qquad \inf_{d' \geq 0} P\{CS|R,F\} = P(\underline{F}^{(2)},\overline{F}) \quad .$$

This lower bound is larger than the lower bound in Formulation 2A.

2.5. *A Monotone Property of the Lower Bounds on PCS:* Let $Q_1(s,t|n)$, $Q_2(s,t|n)$, $Q_3(s,t|n)$ and $Q_4(s,t|n)$ denote the lower bounds on PCS given by (2.13), (2.17), (2.20) and (2.21), respectively. One can show that, for fixed n, k, t, d^*, ε_1^*, ε_2^* and P^* ,

(2.24a) $\quad Q_i(s,t|n) > Q_i(s-1,t|n)$, $i = 1,2,3,4$

when $s-1 \geq t$. In particular, for fixed n, k, t, d^*, ε_1^*, ε_2^* and P^*,

(2.24b) $\quad Q_i(s,t|n) > Q_i(t,t|n)$ for $s > t$.

This is a consequence of the fact that, for all $0 \leq v \leq 1$,

$$G(v;\tau,n-\tau+1) \leq G(v;\tau-1,n-\tau)$$

where τ and n are integers such that $n > \tau-1 \geq 0$. The inequality (2.24b) relates the lower bounds given here with the corresponding lower bounds for the problem considered by Sobel [5].

For each formulation considered, we obtain the required value of the common sample size as the smallest integer value of n for which the lower bound on PCS, obtained under that formulation, is at least P^*.

From (2.24b), it follows that whenever the required n-value for the problem considered by Sobel [5] exists for a given set of specifications, then the required n-value for our problem, with the same set of specifications, exists.

3. *Tables*. Tables giving the required n-values for the case $\alpha = 1/2$ have been given at the end. In preparing these tables, we restricted ourselves to Formulation 1A with $\varepsilon_1^* = \varepsilon_2^* = d^*$ and Formulation 2A with $\varepsilon_1^* = \varepsilon_2^*$. The range for k is from 2 to 6. For each k all (s,t) combinations with $t < s$ are considered. Under Formulation 2A with $k \geq 3$ and $\alpha = 1/2$ the n-values required by

procedure R, when $s = t \geq 2$ and $\varepsilon_1^* = \varepsilon_2^*$, are the same as the n-values when $s = t = 1$ and hence they are omitted; they are also omitted for formulation 1A. Since the population median is the quantile of interest, we determine n as the smallest *odd* integer for which the lower bound on PCS is at least P^*.

4. *A Related Problem:* A problem related to the one considered is that of selecting a subset of smallest possible fixed size s that will contain the t best (those t having the largest α-quantiles) of k populations ($t \leq s \leq k$), based on any given common sample size from each of the k populations. We want a procedure which would satisfy the probability requirement (1.4) or (1.6). For this purpose we could use the procedure R defined earlier, by choosing s suitably. The choice of s can be made as follows. In order to use the procedure R for the original problem let $n_1(s)$, $n_2(s)$, $n_3(s)$ and $n_4(s)$ be the minimum sample size needed; these are, respectively, obtained from the bounds (2.13), (2.17), (2.20) and (2.21). Suppose we have a table of these values for various combinations of k, t, d^*, ε_1^*, ε_2^* and P^*. To fix our ideas, let us assume that we have adopted formulation 1A. Now from the table of n_1-values, it is possible to find the (smallest) integer s^* such that the common size of the available sample n^* satisfies the relation

$$n_1(s^* - 1) > n^* \geq n_1(s^*). \tag{4.1}$$

Then s^* is the required value of s when one is using the Procedure R. Similar remarks hold for other formulations.

The monotone property of $n_i(s)$ used in (4.1) follows from the result (2.24a).

We shall illustrate the use of tables of section 3, for the problem of this section.

Example: Suppose we are concerned with the above problem when $k = 5$, $t = 2, \alpha = 1/2$, $P^* = 0.95$ and $\varepsilon_1^* = \varepsilon_2^* = 0.15$. If $N^* = 55$ and if we have adopted formulation 2A, from Table 3 our s value is 3. If $t = 3$ and other specifications are the same as above, then we need to take s to be 4.

5. *Property of Unbiasedness:* Let p_β denote the probability that $F_{[\beta]}$ is included in the subset selected by the procedure R.

Theorem. *Let* γ *and* δ *be two integers between* 1 *and* k *and let the distribution functions* $F_{[\gamma]}(\cdot)$ *and* $F_{[\delta]}(\cdot)$ *satisfy the inequality* $F_{[\gamma]}(x) \geq F_{[\delta]}(x)$, *for all* x. *Then*

$$P_\gamma \leq P_\delta \quad .$$

Proof: Let ζ be the $(s-1)$st largest of $\{Y_{(\beta)}: \beta = 1,2,\ldots,k, \beta\neq\gamma, \beta\neq\delta\}$ and let $B(\cdot)$ be its d.f. Now

$$\begin{aligned} P_\gamma - P_\delta &= P\{F_{[\gamma]} \text{ is retained but } F_{[\delta]} \text{ is not retained}\} \\ &\quad - P\{F_{[\delta]} \text{ is retained but } F_{[\gamma]} \text{ is not retained}\} \\ &= P\{Y_{(\delta)} < \zeta < Y_{(\gamma)}\} - P\{Y_{(\gamma)} < \zeta < Y_{(\delta)}\} \\ &= \int_{-\infty}^{\infty} H_\delta(y)[1-H_\gamma(y)]dB(y) - \int_{-\infty}^{\infty} H_\gamma(y)[1-H_\delta(y)]dB(y) \end{aligned}$$

(5.1) i.e., $$P_\gamma - P_\delta = \int_{-\infty}^{\infty} [H_\delta(y) - H_\gamma(y)]\,dB(y) \quad .$$

Since $H_\beta(y)$ is an increasing function of $F_{[\beta]}(y)$ and $F_{[\gamma]}(y) \geq F_{[\delta]}(y)$, the required result follows from (5.1).

Thus under the no-cross over assumption of section 2.2, our procedure R is unbiased. In other words, for each fixed $j(j = k-t+1,\ldots,k)$ the probability of $F_{[j]}$ being included in the subset selected by R is not smaller the probability of $F_{[i]}$ being retained in the subset selected by R for each $i(i = 1,\ldots,k-t)$.

6. *Acknowledgement:* The authors wish to thank Mr. Leo May of University of Minnesota for his help with the preparation of the tables.

References

1. Desu, M. M. and Sobel, M. (1968). A fixed subset-size approach to the selection problem. *Biometrika*, 55, 401-410.

2. Lehmann, E. L. (1959). *Testing statistical hypothesis*, John Wiley and Sons, New York.

3. Mahamunulu, D. M. (1967). Some fixed-sample ranking and selection problems, *Ann. Math. Statist.*, 38, 1079-1091.

4. Rizvi, M. H. and Sobel, M. (1967). Nonparametric procedures for selecting a subset containing the population with the largest α-quantile, *Ann. Math. Statist.*, 38, 1788-1803.

5. Sobel, M. (1967). Nonparametric procedures for selecting the t populations with the largest α-quantiles, *Ann. Math. Statist.*, 38, 1804-1816.

Figure for Formulation 1

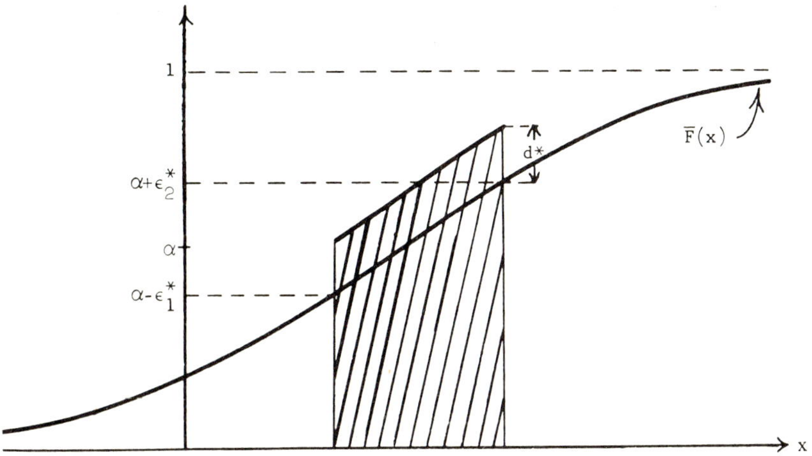

Figure 1

Figure for Formulation 2

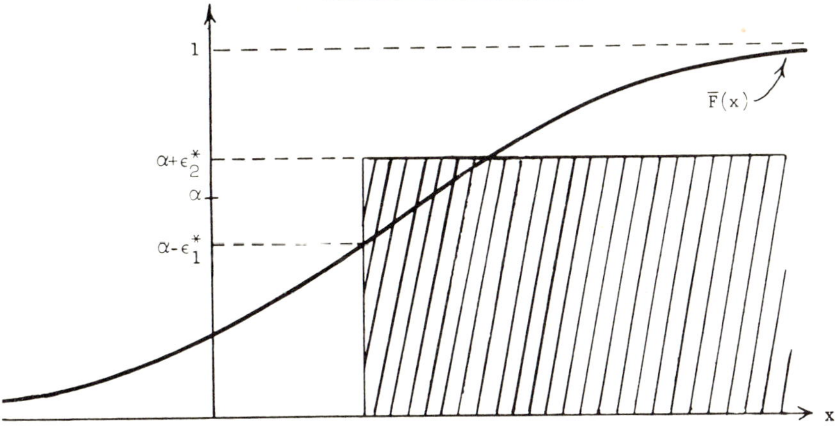

Figure 2

Table 1: n values required by Procedure R under formulation 1A when $\alpha = \frac{1}{2}$ $(d^* = \varepsilon_1^* = \varepsilon_2^* = 0.15)$

k	t	s	.75	.80	.85	.90	.95	.975	.99
			P*						
2	1	1	15	19	27	39	61	85	119
3	1	1	23	31	41	55	81	107	143
3	1	2	7	11	15	23	37	51	73
4	1	1	31	39	51	67	93	121	159
4	1	2	11	15	21	29	47	63	85
4	1	3	7	9	13	19	31	45	61
4	2	3	17	21	27	35	51	67	89
5	1	1	37	47	57	75	103	131	169
5	1	2	15	19	27	37	55	73	93
5	1	3	7	11	15	23	37	51	71
5	1	4	5	9	13	19	31	43	59
5	2	3	23	27	35	45	63	81	105
5	2	4	15	19	23	31	45	57	77
5	3	4	23	29	35	43	59	77	99
6	1	1	43	51	63	81	109	139	177
6	1	2	19	25	31	43	63	79	99
6	1	3	9	13	19	27	41	57	79
6	1	4	7	9	13	19	33	45	61
6	1	5	5	9	13	19	29	41	59
6	2	3	27	35	41	53	73	93	115
6	2	4	17	21	27	35	49	65	87
6	2	5	13	17	23	29	43	55	75
6	3	4	29	35	43	53	73	91	117
6	3	5	21	25	31	39	51	65	87
6	4	5	29	33	39	49	65	83	107

Table 2: n values required by Procedure R under formulation 1A when $\alpha = \frac{1}{2}$ $(d^* = \varepsilon_1^* = \varepsilon_2^* = 0.20)$

k	t	s	.75	.80	.85	.90	.95	.975	.99
			P*						
2	1	1	7	11	15	21	35	47	67
3	1	1	13	17	23	31	45	61	79
3	1	2	5	7	9	13	21	29	39
4	1	1	17	21	29	37	51	67	89
4	1	2	7	9	11	17	25	35	49
4	1	3	3	5	7	11	17	25	35
4	2	3	9	11	15	19	27	37	49
5	1	1	21	25	33	41	57	73	93
5	1	2	9	11	15	21	31	41	55
5	1	3	5	7	9	13	19	27	39
5	1	4	3	5	7	11	17	23	33
5	2	3	13	15	19	25	35	45	59
5	2	4	9	11	13	17	25	31	41
5	3	4	13	15	19	23	33	41	55
6	1	1	23	29	35	45	61	77	99
6	1	2	11	13	17	25	35	47	63
6	1	3	5	7	11	15	23	31	43
6	1	4	3	5	7	11	17	25	35
6	1	5	3	5	7	11	17	23	31
6	2	3	15	19	23	29	41	51	
6	2	4	9	11	15	19	27	35	47
6	2	5	7	9	13	17	23	31	39
6	3	4	17	19	23	29	41	51	65
6	3	5	11	13	17	21	29	35	47
6	4	5	15	19	21	27	35	45	57

Table 3: n values required by Procedure R under formulation 2A when $\alpha = \frac{1}{2}$ $(\varepsilon_1^* = \varepsilon_2^* = 0.15)$

			p*						
k	t	s	.75	.80	.85	.90	.95	.975	.99
2	1	1	13	17	21	29	41	53	71
3	1	1	19	23	29	35	49	61	79
3	1	]	7	9	13	19	29	41	59
4	1	1	23	27	33	41	53	67	83
4	1	2	9	11	15	21	31	43	59
4	1	3	5	9	13	19	29	41	57
4	2	3	15	17	23	29	41	53	71
5	1	1	27	31	37	45	57	71	89
5	1	2	11	15	17	23	33	43	59
5	1	3	7	9	13	19	29	41	57
5	1	4	5	9	11	17	29	41	57
5	2	3	15	19	23	29	41	53	71
5	2	4	13	17	21	29	41	53	71
5	3	4	19	23	29	35	49	61	79
6	1	1	31	35	41	47	61	75	91
6	1	2	13	17	19	25	35	45	59
6	1	3	7	11	13	19	29	41	57
6	1	4	5	9	13	17	29	41	57
6	1	5	5	9	11	17	29	41	57
6	2	3	17	21	25	31	43	55	71
6	2	4	13	17	21	29	41	53	71
6	2	5	13	17	21	29	41	53	71
6	3	4	21	25	29	37	49	61	79
6	3	5	19	23	29	35	49	61	79
6	4	5	23	29	33	41	53	67	83

Table 4: n values required by Procedure R under formulation 2A when $\alpha = \frac{1}{2}$ $(\varepsilon_1^* = \varepsilon_2^* = 0.20)$

			p*						
k	t	s	.75	.80	.85	.90	.95	.975	.99
2	1	1	7	9	13	15	23	29	39
3	1	1	11	13	15	19	27	33	43
3	1	2	5	5	7	11	17	23	31
4	1	1	13	15	19	23	29	37	45
4	1	2	5	7	9	11	17	23	31
4	1	3	3	5	7	9	17	23	31
4	2	3	7	9	13	15	23	29	39
5	1	1	15	17	21	25	31	39	47
5	1	2	7	7	9	13	17	23	33
5	1	3	3	5	7	11	17	23	31
5	1	4	3	5	7	9	17	23	31
5	2	3	9	11	13	17	23	29	39
5	2	4	7	9	13	15	23	29	39
5	3	4	11	13	15	19	27	33	43
6	1	1	17	19	21	27	33	41	49
6	1	2	7	9	11	13	19	25	33
6	1	3	5	5	7	11	17	23	31
6	1	4	3	5	7	9	17	23	31
6	1	5	3	5	7	9	17	23	31
6	2	3	9	11	13	17	23	29	39
6	2	4	7	9	13	15	23	29	39
6	2	5	7	9	13	15	23	29	39
6	3	4	11	13	15	19	27	33	43
6	3	5	11	13	15	19	27	33	43
6	4	5	13	15	19	23	29	37	45

ON A SUBSET SELECTION PROCEDURE FOR THE MOST PROBABLE EVENT IN A MULTINOMIAL DISTRIBUTION*

By S. Panchapakesan
Southern Illinois University

1. *Introduction.* Let $p_1, p_2, \ldots, p_k$ be the unknown cell-probabilities in the multinomial distribution with $\sum_{i=1}^{k} p_i = 1$. The ordered values of the cell-probabilities are denoted by

$$\phi_1 \leq \phi_2 \leq \cdots \leq \phi_k \tag{1.1}$$

and the cell associated with ϕ_i is denoted by $\Pi_{(i)}$, $i = 1,2,\ldots,k$. It is assumed that there is no prior information available about the correct pairing of the ordered and the unordered cell-probabilities. The goal of the experimenter is to select a subset containing the cell with the largest probability which will be called the best cell. In the case of a tie, one of the cells with the largest probability will be considered to be tagged as the best. A correct selection (CS) is defined as the selection of any subset which includes the best cell. Under the subset selection approach used in this paper, we seek a procedure R such that

$$P(CS|R) \geq P^* \tag{1.2}$$

where $P(CS|R)$ denotes the probability of a correct selection using the procedure R and $P^*(\frac{1}{k} < P^* < 1)$ is a

*This research was supported in part by the Office of Naval Research Contract N00014-67-A-0226-00014 and the Aerospace Research Laboratories Contract AF33(615)67C1244 at Purdue University. Reproduction in whole or in part is permitted for any purposes of the United States Government.

specified probability level.

The problem of selecting the particular one of the k multinomial cells with the highest probability was first studied under the so-called indifference zone formulation by Bechhofer, Elmaghraby and Morse [2] who proposed a fixed sample procedure. Under the same formulation, Cacoullos and Sobel [3] inspired by the Banach match-box problem investigated an inverse sampling procedure. A multistage variant of this has been recently studied by Alam, Seo and Thompson [1]. A fixed sample procedure for selecting a subset containing the cell with the largest probability was proposed by Gupta and Nagel [4]. In the present paper we investigate an inverse sampling procedure for the same problem. The procedure R is defined in Section 2 and the expression for the $P(CS|R)$ is derived. Section 3 discusses the infimum of the $P(CS|R)$. It is shown that the infimum is attained for a configuration of the type $(0,\ldots,0,\frac{1}{r},\ldots,\frac{1}{r})$ where $r \geq 2$ is the number of non-zero cell-probabilities. Some asymptotic results for the $P(CS|R)$ are obtained in the next section. It is shown that asymptotically the infimum is attained when all the k cell-probabilities are equal. Exact and asymptotic results for $E(n)$, the expected number of observations required to reach a decision, form the content of Section 5. A brief discussion on the expected subset size follows in the subsequent section. The last two sections are concerned respectively with the binomial case $(k = 2)$ and some remarks on comparing the inverse sampling procedure and the fixed sample procedure of Gupta and Nagel.

2. *The Inverse Sampling Procedure* R *and the* $P(CS|R)$. Observations are taken one at a time from the multinomial

distribution until the count in any one of the cells reaches M. Let $x_1,\ldots,x_k$ be the cell counts at termination of sampling. Of course, one of the x_i is equal to M. The procedure R is defined as follows.

R: Select the cell with the count x_i iff

$$x_i \geq M - D \tag{2.1}$$

where D is an integer such that $0 \leq D \leq M$ and the constants must be chosen so as to satisfy the basic probability requirement (1.2).

Let ν_i be the count in the cell $\Pi_{(i)}$, $i = 1,\ldots,k$ and $M' = M - D$. Then

$$P(CS|R) = 1 - \sum_{\alpha=1}^{k-1} L_\alpha \tag{2.2}$$

where L_α is the probability that the sampling terminates with cell count M in $\Pi_{(i)}$ and $\Pi_{(k)}$ is not included in the selected subset. It is easy to see that

$$L_\alpha = \sum M \frac{(\nu_1+\ldots+\nu_k-1)!}{\nu_1! \ldots \nu_k!} \phi_1^{\nu_1} \ldots \phi_k^{\nu_k} \tag{2.3}$$

where the right hand side is a multiple sum over the set of values of $\nu_1,\ldots,\nu_k$ such that $\nu_\alpha = M$, $0 \leq \nu_k \leq M'-1$ and $0 \leq \nu_\beta \leq M-1$, $\beta = 1,\ldots,k-1$; $\beta \neq \alpha$. This multiple sum can be written as a Dirichlet integral using a theorem of Olkin and Sobel [6] which is restated below as a lemma.

Lemma 2.1. *If* $s_1,s_2,\ldots,s_m$ *are positive integers,* $s > 0$, $\phi_i \geq 0$, $i = 1,\ldots,m$ *and* $\phi_0 = \phi_1+\ldots+\phi_m < 1$, *then*

$$(1-\phi_0)^s \sum_{x_1=0}^{s_1-1} \cdots \sum_{x_m=0}^{s_m-1} \frac{\Gamma(x_0+s)}{\Gamma(s)} \prod_{i=1}^{m} \frac{\phi_i^{x_i}}{x_i!}$$

(2.4)
$$= \frac{\Gamma(s+s_0)}{\Gamma(s)\prod_{i=1}^{m}\Gamma(s_i)} \int_{\phi_1^*} \cdots \int_{\phi_m^*} \frac{\prod_{i=1}^{m}[y_i^{s_i-1}\, dy_i]}{(1+y_0)^{s+s_0}}$$

where $x_0 = \sum_{i=1}^{m} x_i$, $y_0 = \sum_{i=1}^{m} y_i$, $s_0 = \sum_{i=1}^{m} s_i$ *and* $\phi_i^* = \frac{\phi_i}{1-\phi_0}$.

Using the above lemma, we can write

$$L_\alpha = \frac{\Gamma((k-1)M+M')}{[\Gamma(M)]^{k-1}\Gamma(M')} \int_{\frac{\phi_1}{\phi_\alpha}} \cdots \int_{\frac{\phi_k}{\phi_\alpha}}$$

(2.5)
$$\frac{\left(\prod_{i=1}^{k-2} y_i^{M-1}\right) y_{k-1}^{M'-1}}{(1+y_1+\cdots+y_{k-1})^{(k-1)M+M'}}\, dy_1 \cdots dy_{k-1}$$

$$= \frac{1}{B_k(M,\ldots,M')}\, T_\alpha$$

where

(2.6)
$$B_m(a_1,\ldots,a_m) = \frac{\Gamma(a_1)\ldots(a_m)}{\Gamma(a_1+\cdots+a_m)}$$

and T_α denotes the integral on the r.h.s. of (2.5).

3. *The Infimum of the* $P(CS|R)$. To start with, let us define

$$f_k(y_1,\ldots,y_k;\ m_1,\ldots,m_k;\ M;\ \alpha_0;\ \alpha_1,\ldots,\alpha_k)$$

(3.1)
$$= \frac{\prod_{i=1}^{k} y_i^{m_i-1}}{(\alpha_0+\alpha_1 y_1+\ldots+\alpha_k y_k)^{m_1+\ldots+m_k+M}}$$

and

$$F_k(b_1,\ldots,b_k;\ m_1,\ldots,m_k;\ M;\ \alpha_0;\ \alpha_1,\ldots,\alpha_k)$$

(3.2)
$$= \int_{b_1}^{\infty}\cdots\int_{b_k}^{\infty} f_k(y_1,\ldots,y_k;m_1,\ldots,m_k;M;\alpha_0;\alpha_1,\ldots,\alpha_k)\, dy_1\ldots dy_k\ .$$

Then we have from the preceeding section

(3.3)
$$P(CS|R) = 1 - \frac{1}{B_k(M,\ldots,M')}\sum_{\alpha=1}^{k-1} T_\alpha$$

where

(3.4)
$$T_\alpha = F_{k-1}\left(\frac{\phi_1}{\phi_\alpha},\ldots,\frac{\phi_k}{\phi_\alpha};\ M,\ldots,M';\ M;\ 1;\ 1,\ldots,1\right).$$

Our need to use (3.1) and (3.2) will be in situations where $m_1 = \ldots = m_k = m$ or $m_1 = \ldots = m_{k-1} = m$, $m_k = m'$ Consequently we abbreviate the notation in these cases by writing $\underset{\sim}{m}_k$ and $\underset{\sim}{m}_{k-1}, m'$ respectively. Further $\underset{\sim}{\alpha}_k$ will indicate that $\alpha_1 = \ldots = \alpha_k = \alpha$. Hence we write

(3.5)
$$T = F_{k-1}\left(\frac{\phi_1}{\phi_\alpha},\ldots,\frac{\phi_k}{\phi_\alpha};\ \underset{\sim}{M}_{k-2}, M';\ M;\ 1; \underset{\sim}{1}_{k-1}\right).$$

In order to find the infimum of the $P(CS|R)$ over all

configurations of the vector $\underline{\phi} = (\phi_1,\ldots,\phi_k)$ we use a method similar to one of Kesten and Morse [5]. For $1 \le i < j \le k$, we set $\phi_i + \phi_j$ = a constant and minimize the r.h.s. of (3.3) as a function of ϕ_j. Obviously, two cases arise, namely, (1) $1 \le i < j < k$ and (2) $1 \le i < j = k$.

Case (1): $1 \le i < j < k$. For convenience, we will first consider $i = 1$. We have

$$\frac{\partial T_1}{\partial \phi_j} = - \phi_j^{M-1}\phi_1^{-M} F_{k-2}\left(\frac{\phi_2}{\phi_1},\ldots,\frac{\phi_{j-1}}{\phi_1},\frac{\phi_{j+1}}{\phi_1},\ldots,\frac{\phi_k}{\phi_1};\ \underline{M}_{k-3},\ M';\ 2M;\ 1+\frac{\phi_j}{\phi_1};\ \underline{1}_{k-2}\right)$$

$$= - \phi_j^{M-1}\phi_1^{(k-2)M+M'} F_{k-2}\left(\frac{\phi_2}{\phi_1},\ldots,\frac{\phi_{j-1}}{\phi_1},\frac{\phi_{j+1}}{\phi_1},\ldots,\frac{\phi_k}{\phi_1};\ \underline{M}_{k-3}, M';\ 2M;\ \phi_1 + \phi_j;\ \phi_1,\ldots,\phi_1\right).$$

Making the transformation $z_i = \phi_i y_i\ (i = 1,\ldots,k-2)$ we obtain

$$\frac{\partial T_1}{\partial \phi_j} = -\phi_j^{M-1}\ \phi_1^{M}\ F_{k-2}(\underline{\phi}^{(1,j)};\ \underline{M}_{k-3}, M';\ 2M; \phi_1+\phi_j; \underline{1}_{k-2}) \tag{3.6}$$

where $\underline{\phi}^{(\alpha,\beta)}$ denotes $\phi_1,\ldots,\phi_k$ in that order leaving out ϕ_α and ϕ_β. Similarly we can obtain

$$\begin{aligned}\frac{\partial T_1}{\partial \phi_1} = &\sum_{r=2}^{k-1} \phi_r^{M}\phi_1^{M-1} F_{k-2}(\underline{\phi}^{(1,r)}; \underline{M}_{k-3}, M'; 2M; \phi_1+\phi_r; \underline{1}_{k-2}) \\ &+ \phi_k^{M'}\phi_1^{M-1} F_{k-2}(\underline{\phi}^{(1,k)}; \underline{M}_{k-2}; M+M'; \phi_1+\phi_k; \underline{1}_{k-2}) \ .\end{aligned} \tag{3.7}$$

Using (3.6) and (3.7) and defining for sake of brevity

$$G_{k-2}(\underline{\phi}^{(\alpha,\beta)};m_1,\ldots,m_k;M) = F_{k-2}(\underline{\phi}^{(\alpha,\beta)};m_1,\ldots,m_k; M;\phi_\alpha + \phi_\beta ; \underline{1}_{k-2}) , \tag{3.8}$$

we have

$$\begin{aligned} \frac{dT_1}{d\phi_j} = &- \phi_j^{M-1} \phi_1^M G_{k-2}(\underline{\phi}^{(1,j)}; \underline{M}_{k-3},M';2M) \\ &- \sum_{\substack{r=1\\ r\neq 1}}^{k-1} \phi_r^M \phi_1^{M-1} G_{k-2}(\underline{\phi}^{(1,r)};\underline{M}_{k-3},M'; 2M) \\ &+ \phi_k^{M'} \phi_1^{M-1} G_{k-2}(\underline{\phi}^{(1,k)};\underline{M}_{k-2}; M+M') . \end{aligned} \tag{3.9}$$

Similar calculations yield

$$\begin{aligned} \frac{dT_j}{d\phi_j} = &\sum_{\substack{r=1\\ r\neq j}}^{k} \phi_r^M \phi_j^{M-1} G_{k-2}(\underline{\phi}^{(j,r)};\underline{M}_{k-3},M';2M) \\ &+ \phi_k^{M'} \phi_j^{M-1} G_{k-2}(\underline{\phi}^{(j,k)};\underline{M}_{k-2},M+M') \\ &+ \phi_1^{M-1} \phi_j^M G_{k-2}(\underline{\phi}^{(1,j)}; \underline{M}_{k-3},M';2M) \end{aligned} \tag{3.10}$$

and for $\alpha = 2,\ldots,k-1;\alpha \neq j$,

$$\begin{aligned} \frac{dT_\alpha}{d\phi_j} = &- \phi_j^{M-1} \phi_\alpha^M G_{k-2}(\underline{\phi}^{(\alpha,j)};\underline{M}_{k-3},M'; 2M) \\ &+ \phi_1^{M-1} \phi_\alpha^M G_{k-2}(\underline{\phi}^{(1,\alpha)};\underline{M}_{k-3},M'; 2M) . \end{aligned} \tag{3.11}$$

Hence, letting $T = \sum_{\alpha=1}^{k-1} T_\alpha$ and using (3.9), (3.10) and (3.11) we have after some easy simplifications

$$\begin{aligned} \frac{dT}{d\phi_j} = &\phi_k^{M'} \phi_j^{M-1} G_{k-2}(\underline{\phi}^{(j,k)};\underline{M}_{k-2}; M+M') \\ &- \phi_k^{M'} \phi_1^{M-1} G_{k-2}(\underline{\phi}^{(1,k)}; \underline{M}_{k-2}; M+M') . \end{aligned} \tag{3.12}$$

Now,

$$G_{k-2}(\underline{\phi}^{(j,k)};\ \underline{M}_{k-2};\ M+M')$$

$$= F_{k-2}(\phi_1,\ldots,\phi_{j-1},\phi_{j+1},\ldots,\phi_{k-1};\underline{M}_{k-2};\ M+M';\ \phi_j+\phi_k;\ 1,\ldots,1)$$

$$=\int_{\phi_1}^{\infty}\cdots\int_{\phi_{j-1}}^{\infty}\int_{\phi_{j+1}}^{\infty}\cdots\int_{\phi_{k-1}}^{\infty} f_{k-2}(y_1,\ldots,y_{k-2};\ \underline{M}_{k-2};\ M+M';\ \phi_j+\phi_k;\ 1,\ldots,1)\,dy_1\ldots dy_{k-2}\ .$$

Since the integrand is symmetric in $y_1,\ldots,y_{k-2}$, by changing the order of integration and relabeling the variables, we can write

$$G_{k-2}(\underline{\phi}^{(j,k)};\ \underline{M}_{k-2}, M+M')$$

$$= F_{k-2}(\phi_2,\ldots,\phi_{j-1},\phi_1,\phi_{j+1},\ldots,\phi_{k-1};\ \underline{M}_{k-2};\ M+M';\ \underline{1}_{k-2})\ . \tag{3.13}$$

The variables on the r.h.s. of (3.13) are $y_1,\ldots,y_{k-2}$ with $\phi_2,\ldots,\phi_{j-1},\phi_1,\phi_{j+1},\ldots,\phi_{k-1}$ as the lower limits of integration respectively. Transforming the variables by setting

$$\begin{cases} z_1 = y_1,\ldots,z_{j-2} = y_{j-2}, z_{j-1} = y_{j-1}+\phi_j-\phi_1,\ z_j = y_j,\ldots \\ z_{k-2} = y_{k-2}\ , \end{cases} \tag{3.14}$$

we get

$$G_{k-2}(\underline{\phi}^{(j,k)};\ \underline{M}_{k-2};\ M+M')$$

$$=\int_{\phi_2}^{\infty}\cdots\int_{\phi_{k-1}}^{\infty} \frac{z_1^{M-1}\cdots z_{j-2}^{M-1}(z_{j-1}+\phi_1-\phi_j)^{M-1}z_j^{M-1}\cdots z_{k-2}^{M-1}}{(\phi_k+\phi_1+z_1+\ldots+z_{k-2})^{(k-1)M+M'}}\,dz_1\ldots dz_{k-2}\ . \tag{3.15}$$

Thus, from (3.12) and (3.15)

$$\frac{dT}{d\phi_j} = \phi_k^{M'} A \quad , \tag{3.16}$$

where

$$A = \int_{\phi_2}^{\infty} \cdots \int_{\phi_{k-1}}^{\infty} \frac{\left(\prod_{\substack{r=1 \\ r \neq j}}^{k-1} z_{r-1}^{M-1}\right)\left[\phi_j^{M-1}(z_{j-1}+\phi_1-\phi_j)^{M-1} - \phi_1^{M-1} z_{j-1}^{M-1}\right]}{(\phi_1+\phi_k+z_1+\ldots+z_{k-2})^{(k-1)M+M'}} dz_1 \ldots dz_{k-2} \quad . \tag{3.17}$$

Since $\phi_j - \phi_1 \geq 0$ and $z_{j-1} \geq \phi_j$ we have $Z_{j-1}(\phi_j - \phi_1) \geq \phi_j(\phi_j - \phi_1)$, that is, $\phi_j(z_{j-1} - \phi_j + \phi_1) \geq \phi_1 z_{j-1}$ which implies that $A \geq 0$. Thus, when $\phi_1 + \phi_j$ = const, $\frac{dT}{d\phi_j} \geq 0$. This is true for $1 \leq i < j < k$, though we showed for $i = 1$.

The above results and their consequence are summarized in the following lemma.

Lemma 3.1. *Keeping the sum* $\phi_i + \phi_j (1 \leq i < j < k)$ *constant,* $P(CS|R)$ *decreases as we pass from the configuration* $(\phi_1, \ldots, \phi_i, \ldots, \phi_j, \ldots, \phi_k)$ *to* $(\phi_1, \ldots, \phi_i - \varepsilon, \ldots, \phi_j + \varepsilon, \ldots, \phi_k)$ *where* $0 < \varepsilon < \phi$.

Now we consider Case (2): $1 \leq i < j=k$. Again to be specific we will consider $i = 1$; the results are similar for any $i < k$. Calculations similar to those in Case (1) yield

$$\frac{\partial T_1}{\partial \phi_1} = \sum_{r=2}^{k-1} \phi_r^M \phi_1^{M-1} G_{k-2}(\underline{\phi}^{(1,r)}; \underline{M}_{k-3}, M'; 2M) + \phi_k^{M'} \phi_1^{M-1} G_{k-2}(\underline{\phi}^{(1,k)}; \underline{M}_{k-2}, M+M') \tag{3.18}$$

and for $\alpha = 2, \ldots, k-1$, we have

$$\frac{\partial T_\alpha}{\partial \phi_1} = -\phi_1^{M-1} \phi_\alpha^M G_{k-2}(\underline{\phi}^{1,\alpha)}; \underline{M}_{k-3}; M'; 2M) \tag{3.19}$$

and

$$\frac{\partial T_\alpha}{\partial \phi_k} = -\phi_k^{M'-1}\phi_\alpha^M G_{k-2}(\underline{\phi}^{(k,\alpha)};\underline{M}_{k-2};\ M+M') \quad . \tag{3.20}$$

Therefore, when $\phi_1 + \phi_k$ = constant,

$$\begin{aligned}\frac{dT}{d\phi_k} &= -\sum_{\alpha=1}^{k-1} \phi_k^{M'-1}\phi_\alpha^M G_{k-2}(\underline{\phi}^{(k,\alpha)};\underline{M}_{k-2};M+M') \\ &\quad - \phi_k^{M'}\phi_1^{M-1}G_{k-2}(\underline{\phi}^{(1,k)};\underline{M}_{k-2};\ M+M') \\ &< 0 \ .\end{aligned} \tag{3.21}$$

Thus we have the following lemma.

Lemma 3.2. *Keeping the sum* $\phi_i + \phi_k (1 \le i < k)$ *constant,* $P(CS|R)$ *decreases as we pass from the configuration* $(\phi_1,\ldots,\phi_i,\ldots,\phi_k)$ *to* $(\phi_1,\ldots,\phi_i+\varepsilon,\ldots,\phi_k-\varepsilon)$ *where* $0 < \varepsilon \le \phi_k$.

It is to be noted that the results of Lemmas 3.1 and 3.2 are valid even if the order is disturbed in the new configuration. Since we are looking for the least favorable configuration for $P(CS|R)$, the above lemmas throw light on the type of configuration we look for. It has to be a configuration from which we cannot pass to one of smaller probability by the procedures of the two lemmas. Gupta and Nagel [4] have proved the statements of the two lemmas for their fixed sample procedure. We state without proof the following theorem of Gupta and Nagel, which is a simple consequence of Lemmas 3.1 and 3.2.

Theorem 3.1. *Let* α *be the smallest integer such that* $\phi_\alpha > 0$ *and* β *be the largest integer such that* $\phi_\beta < \phi_k$. *For a configuration minimizing* $P(CS|R)$, $\alpha \ge \beta$. *In addition, if* $\alpha = k-1$, *then* $\alpha > \beta$.

From the above theorem, the least favorable configuration is one of the type $(0,\ldots,0,s,p,\ldots,p)$, $0 < s \leq p$. Let r be the number of positive cell-probabilities. Thus

$$\inf_{\Omega} P(CS|R) = \min_{r=2,\ldots,k} \Big(\min_{\frac{1}{r} \leq p < \frac{1}{r-1}} F(k,M,D;\ (0,\ldots,0,s,p,\ldots,p)\Big) \tag{3.22}$$

where Ω is the space of all configurations of the cell-probabilities and $F(k,M,D;\ (0,\ldots,0,s,p,\ldots,p))$ denotes the probability of a correct selection for the configuration $(0,\ldots,0,s,p,\ldots,p)$ and is given by

$$1 - F(k,M,D;\ (0,\ldots,0,s,p,\ldots,p))$$

$$= \sum_{\alpha=k-r+1}^{k-1} \sum M \frac{(\nu_{k-r+1}+\ldots+\nu_k-1)!}{\nu_{k-r+1}!\ \ldots \nu_k!}\ s^{\nu_{k-r+1}} p^{\nu_{k-r+2}+\ \ldots\ +\ \nu_k} \tag{3.23}$$

where the second summation is over the set of ν's such that $\nu_\alpha = M$, $0 \leq \nu_k \leq M'-1$, $0 \leq \nu_\beta \leq M-1$; $\beta \neq \alpha,k$. Using Lemma 2.1 we can write (3.23) as

$$\begin{aligned} &1 - F(k,M,D;\ (0,\ldots,0,s,p,\ldots,p)) \\ &= B_r(M,\ldots,M')[T_1 + (r-1)T_2] \end{aligned} \tag{3.24}$$

where

$$T_1 = F_{r-1}(\tfrac{p}{s},\ldots,\tfrac{p}{s};\ \underline{M}_{r-2},M';\ M;\ \mathbf{1};\ \underline{1}_{r-1}) \tag{3.25}$$

and

$$T_2 = F_{r-1}(\tfrac{s}{p},1,\ldots,1;\ \underline{M}_{r-2},M';\ M;\ 1;\ \underline{1}_{r-1})\ . \tag{3.26}$$

Letting $\psi = p/s$,

$$(3.27)\quad \begin{aligned}\frac{dT_1}{d\psi} &= -(r-1)\psi^{M-1}F_{r-2}(\psi,\ldots,\psi;\underline{M}_{r-3},M';2M;1+\psi;\underline{1}_{r-2}) \\ &\quad -\psi^{M'-1}F_{r-2}(\psi,\ldots,\psi;\ \underline{M}_{r-2};M+M';1+\psi;\ \underline{1}_{r-2})\end{aligned}$$

and

$$(3.28)\quad \begin{aligned}\frac{dT_2}{d\psi} &= \frac{1}{\psi^{M+1}} F_{r-2}(1,\ldots,1;\ \underline{M}_{r-3},M';2M;1+\frac{1}{\psi};\underline{1}_{r-2}) \\ &= \psi^{M-1}\ F_{r-2}(\psi,\ldots,\psi;\ \underline{M}_{r-3},M';2M;1+\ \psi;\underline{1}_{r-2})\end{aligned}$$

by the obvious transformation of the variables. From (3.27) and (3.28), setting $T = T_1 + (r-1)T_2$ and noting that $s + (r-1)p = 1$, we get after some simplifications

$$(3.29)\quad \begin{aligned}\frac{dT}{d\psi} &= -\frac{\psi^{M'-1}}{s^2} F_{r-2}(\psi,\ldots,\psi;\underline{M}_{r-2};M+M';1+\psi;\underline{1}_{r-2}) \\ &< 0 .\end{aligned}$$

Thus $P(CS|R)$ increases in p and

$$(3.30)\quad \inf_{\Omega}\ P(CS|R) = \min_{r=2,\ldots,k} F_r(k,M,D)$$

where $F_r(k,M,D)$ denotes the probability of a correct selection for the configuration $(0,\ldots,0,\frac{1}{r},\ldots,\ \frac{1}{r})$.

Remark. We have no result on the monotonic behavior if any of $F_r(k,M,D)$ in r when we use the exact distribution theory. However, in the asymptotic case discussed in the next section, it will be shown that $F_r(k,M,D)$ decreases in r and hence the overall infimum of the $P(CS|R)$ is given by the configuration $(\frac{1}{k},\ldots,\frac{1}{k})$. For small values of M, if $F_r(k,M,D)$ is to be tabulated we need consider only the case $r = k$, because the value for $r < k$ is the same as $F_r(r,M,D)$, in other words, the table value for a smaller k.

4. *Asymptotic Theory.* Let $\underline{Y} = (Y_1, \ldots, Y_m)$ be a random vector with the Dirichlet density

$$(4.1) \quad f(y_1, \ldots, y_m) = \frac{\Gamma(s+s_0)}{\Gamma(s) \prod_{i=1}^{m} \Gamma(s_i)} \frac{\prod_{i=1}^{m} y_i^{s_i - 1}}{(1+y_0)^{s+s_0}} ; \; y_1, \ldots, y_m \geq 0.$$

where s and the s_i are any positive numbers and $s_0 = s_1 + \ldots + s_m$. $E(Y_i)$ exists for $s > 1$ and $Cov(Y_i, Y_j)$ exists for $s > 2$. We briefly list below as a theorem a few known results. For the details one can see [3].

Theorem 4.1. (i) *If* s *and the* $s_i (i = 1, \ldots, m) \to \infty$ *in such a way that* $\frac{s_i}{N} \to 1$ *and*

$$(4.2) \quad \frac{s_i}{s} \to \lambda_i \quad (i = 1, \ldots, m)$$

where the λ_i *are positive, finite limits, then*

$$(4.3) \quad \begin{cases} E(Y_i) = s_i / (s-1) \sim \lambda_i (i = 1, \ldots, m), \\ V(Y_i) = \dfrac{s_i (s_i + s - 1)}{(s-1)^2 (s-2)} \sim \dfrac{\lambda_i (1+\lambda_i)}{N} \quad (i = 1, \ldots, m), \\ \rho(Y_i, Y_j) = \left[\dfrac{s_i s_j}{(s_i + s - 1)(s_j + s - 1)}\right]^{1/2} \sim \left[\dfrac{\lambda_i \lambda_j}{(1+\lambda_i)(1+\lambda_j)}\right]^{1/2}, \\ \qquad j \neq i. \end{cases}$$

(ii) *If the limits* λ_i *in* (4.2) *are positive and finite, then the asymptotic distribution of the variables*

$$(4.4) \quad Z_i' = \left[\frac{N}{\lambda_i (1+\lambda_i)}\right]^{1/2} (Y_i - \lambda_i) \quad (i = 1, \ldots, m)$$

is a joint distribution with zero means, unit variances and correlation matrix $\Lambda = \{\rho_{ij}\}$ *with* $\rho_{ij} = \rho(Y_i, Y_j)$ *given by* (4.3).

We are interested in the case where $N = M = s = s_1 = \ldots = s_{m-1}$ and $s_m = M'$ and $\frac{M'}{M} \to \lambda (0 < \lambda < 1)$. Then

$$(4.5)\begin{cases} E(Y_m) = \lambda, \; E(Y_i) = 1 \quad (i = 1, \ldots, m-1), \\ V(Y_m) = \frac{\lambda(1+\lambda)}{M}, \quad V(Y_i) = \frac{2}{M} \quad (i = 1, \ldots, m-1), \\ \rho(Y_i, Y_m) = [\frac{\lambda}{2(1+\lambda)}]^{1/2} \quad (i = 1, \ldots, m-1), \\ \rho(Y_i, Y_j) = \frac{1}{2} \quad (i,j = 1, \ldots, m-1; \; i \neq j) \quad . \end{cases}$$

Lemma 4.1. *Let* $X_1, \ldots, X_m$ *be standard normal variables with* $\rho(X_i, X_j) = \rho (i,j = 1, \ldots, m-1; \; i \neq j)$ *and* $\rho(X_i, X_m) = \rho_1$ $(i = 1, \ldots, m-1)$. *Then, if* $0 < \rho_1 \leq \rho < 1$, *we can set*

$$(4.6)\begin{cases} X_i = \sqrt{1-\rho}\, Z_i + \sqrt{\rho}\, Z_0 \quad (i = 1, \ldots, m-1), \\ X_m = \sqrt{\frac{\rho - \rho_1^2}{\rho}}\, Z_m + \frac{\rho_1}{\sqrt{\rho}}\, Z_0 \end{cases}$$

where the Z_i *and* Z_0 *are all independent standard normal variables.*

The proof is easy and hence, omitted. The case $\rho_1 = \rho$ is well-known.

Theorem 4.2. *If* $M \to \infty$ *and* $\frac{M'}{M} \to \lambda \; (0 < \lambda < 1)$, $F_r(k,M,D)$ *defined in* (3.30) *decreases in* r *and hence*

$$(4.7) \qquad \inf_{\Omega} P(CS|R) = F_k(k,M,D) \; .$$

Proof. We know that

$$F_r(k,M,D) = 1 - (r-1)\, P\{Y_i \geq 1,\ i = 1,\ldots, r-1\} \tag{4.8}$$

where $\underline{Y} = (Y_1,\ldots,Y_{r-1})$ is a random vector with the Dirichlet density (4.1) with $m = r-1$, $s_1 = \ldots = s_{r-2} = M$ and $s_{r-1} = M'$. Using Theorem 4.1, we can write

$$F_r(k,M,D) = 1 - (r-1)P\{X_{r-1} \geq \sqrt{\frac{M}{\lambda(1+\lambda)}}\,(1-\lambda) \quad \text{and} \quad X_i \geq 0,\ i = 1,\ldots, r-2\} \tag{4.9}$$

where the X_i are standard normal variables with correlation matrix

$$\Lambda = \begin{pmatrix} 1 & 1/2 & \ldots & 1/2 & \rho \\ 1/2 & 1 & \ldots & 1/2 & \rho_1 \\ \ldots & \ldots & \ldots & \ldots & \ldots \\ 1/2 & 1/2 & \ldots & 1 & \rho_1 \\ \rho_1 & \rho_1 & \ldots & \rho_1 & 1 \end{pmatrix} \tag{4.10}$$

where $\rho_1 = \sqrt{\frac{\lambda}{2(1+\lambda)}} < \frac{1}{2}$. Now, using Lemma 4.1, we have

$$\begin{aligned} F_r(k,M,D) &= 1-(r-1)P\begin{bmatrix} Z_i + Z_0 \geq 0,\ i = 1,\ldots, r-2 \quad \text{and} \\ \sqrt{1-2\rho_1^2}\,Z_{r-1} + \sqrt{2}\rho_1 Z_0 \geq \sqrt{\frac{M}{\lambda(1+\lambda)}}(1-\lambda) \end{bmatrix} \\ &= 1-(r-1)\int_{-\infty}^{\infty} \Phi^{r-2}(x)\,\Phi\left(\frac{\sqrt{2}\rho_1 x - H}{1-2\rho_1^2}\right)\phi(x)\,dx \end{aligned} \tag{4.11}$$

where $H = \sqrt{\frac{M}{\lambda(1+\lambda)}}\,(1-\lambda)$ and, $\phi(x)$ and $\Phi(x)$ are the density and cdf of the standard normal variable. Substituting the value of ρ_1 in (4.11) we obtain

$$F_r(k,M,D) = 1-(r-1)\int_{-\infty}^{\infty} \Phi^{r-2}(x)\,\Phi(\sqrt{\lambda}x - \sqrt{1+\lambda}H)\,\phi(x)\,dx. \tag{4.12}$$

It is easy to see that, for positive integer m and a > 0,

$$(4.13)\quad \int_{-\infty}^{\infty} \Phi^m(x)\Phi(ax+b)\phi(x)dx = \frac{1}{m+1} - \frac{1}{m+1}\int_{-\infty}^{\infty} \Phi^{m+1}(\frac{y-b}{a})d\Phi(y).$$

Using (4.13), we can rewrite (4.12) as

$$(4.14)\qquad F_r(k,M,D) = \int_{-\infty}^{\infty} \Phi^{r-1}(\frac{x+\sqrt{1+\lambda}H}{\sqrt{\lambda}})\ d\Phi(x) \quad .$$

It is clear from (4.14) that $F_r(k,M,D)$ decreases in r and thus we obtain (4.7). This proves the theorem.

Corollary 4.1. *If* $M \to \infty$ *and* $\frac{M'}{M} \to \lambda$ $(0 < \lambda < 1)$, *the values of* M *and* λ *consistent with the basic probability requirement* (1.2) *satisfy*

$$(4.15)\qquad \int_{-\infty}^{\infty} \Phi^{k-1}(\frac{\sqrt{\lambda}x+\sqrt{M}(1-\lambda)}{\lambda})\ d\Phi(x) = P^* .$$

It is possible to get a better normal approximation by transforming the Dirichlet variables $Y_1,\ldots,Y_m$ by a logarithmic transformation. It is known (see [3]) that, if the limits λ_i in (4.2) are positive and finite, then the asymptotic distribution $(N \to \infty)$ of the random variables

$$(4.16)\qquad W_i = (\frac{N\lambda_i}{1+\lambda_i})^{1/2} \log\ (\frac{Y_i}{\lambda_i})\ ,\ i = 1,\ldots,m\ ,$$

is a joint normal distribution with zero means, unit variances and the same correlation matrix $\Lambda = \{\rho_{ij}\}$ given by $\rho_{ij} = \rho(Y_i,Y_j)$ in (4.3). In our problem, corresponding to (4.9) we will have

$$(4.17)\qquad \begin{aligned} F_r(k,M,D) = 1 - (r-1)P\{W_{r-1} \geq -\sqrt{\frac{M\lambda}{1+\lambda}}\log\lambda \text{ and} \\ W_i \geq 0,\ i = 1,\ldots, r-2\} \end{aligned}$$

where $W_1,\ldots,W_{r-1}$ are standard normal variables with $\rho(W_i,W_j) = \frac{1}{2}$ for $i,j = 1,\ldots, r-2$; $i \neq j$; and $\rho(W_i,W_{r-1}) = \sqrt{\frac{\lambda}{2(1+\lambda)}} = \rho_1$ for $i = 1,\ldots, r-2$. It is easily seen using Lemma 4.1, that corresponding to (4.12) we get

$$F_r(k,M,D) = 1 - (r-1)\int_{-\infty}^{\infty} \Phi^{r-2}(x)\Phi(\sqrt{\lambda}x-\sqrt{1+\lambda}H')d\Phi(x) \tag{4.18}$$

where $H' = -\sqrt{\frac{M\lambda}{1+\lambda}}\log\lambda$ and this can be rewritten as

$$F_r(k,M,D) = \int_{-\infty}^{\infty} \Phi^{r-1}\left(\frac{x+\sqrt{1+\lambda}H'}{\sqrt{\lambda}}\right) d\Phi(x) . \tag{4.19}$$

Thus the values of M and λ subject to the probability requirement (1.2) satisfy

$$\int_{-\infty}^{\infty} \Phi^{k-1}\left(\frac{x-\sqrt{M\lambda}\log\lambda}{\sqrt{\lambda}}\right) d\Phi(x) = P^* . \tag{4.20}$$

5. *Exact and Asymptotic Evaluation of* $E(n)$. The average sample size $E(n)$ for the procedure R is given by

$$E(n) = M + \sum_{\alpha=1}^{k} P(E_{(\alpha)})\Big[\sum_{\substack{\beta=1\\ \beta\neq\alpha}}^{k} E(X_{(\beta)}|E_{(\alpha)})\Big] , \tag{5.1}$$

where $E_{(\alpha)}$ is the event that the count in the cell $\Pi_{(\alpha)}$ reaches M first and $E(X_{(\beta)}|E_{(\alpha)})$ is the conditional expection of the count in cell $\Pi_{(\beta)}$ given that $E_{(\alpha)}$ occurred. It is to be noted that the expressions for $E(n)$ obtained in [3] for several configurations of the cell-probabilities are directly valid here because it depends only on the sampling scheme and not the procedure used. We are mainly interested in the configuration $\phi_1 = \ldots = \phi_k = \frac{1}{k}$. In this case

$$E(n) = M+(k-1) \sum_{0\le\nu_2,\ldots,\nu_k\le M-1} \nu_2 \frac{(M+\nu_2+\ldots+\nu_k-1)!}{2(M-1)!\nu_2!\ldots\nu_k!} \left(\frac{1}{k}\right)^{M+\nu_2+\ldots+\nu_k} \tag{5.2}$$

Using a result from [3] this can be written as

$$E(n) = M + M(k-1)k\left[1 - \frac{k}{2} b_{2M}(M,\tfrac{1}{2}) I\right] \tag{5.3}$$

where

$$b_{2M}(M,\tfrac{1}{2}) = \binom{2M}{M}\left(\frac{1}{2}\right)^{2M} \tag{5.4}$$

and

$$I = B_{k-1}(2M,M,\ldots,M)F_{k-2}(\tfrac{1}{2},\ldots,\tfrac{1}{2};\underset{\sim}{M}_{k-2};2M;1;\underset{\sim}{1}_{k-2}) . \tag{5.5}$$

For $k = 2$, this reduces to

$$\begin{aligned} E(n) &= M + 2MI_{1/2}(M+1, M-1) \\ &= 2M\left[1 - \binom{2M}{M}\left(\frac{1}{2}\right)^{2M}\right] . \end{aligned} \tag{5.6}$$

Asymptotically, as $M \to \infty$, we can obtain (see [3])

$$E(n) \sim kM\left[1 - \frac{k}{2(M\pi)^{1/2}} \int_{-\infty}^{\infty} \Phi^{k-1}\left(\frac{x}{\sqrt{2}}\right) d\Phi(x)\right] . \tag{5.7}$$

The special case of $k = 2$ is discussed in a subsequent section.

6. *Expected Subset Size.* Let S denote the number of cells included in the selected subset. Then

$$k - E(S) = \sum_{\alpha=1}^{k} Q_\alpha \tag{6.1}$$

where Q_α is the probability that the cell $\Pi_{(\alpha)}$ is not included in the selected subset. We can write

$$Q_\alpha = \frac{1}{B_k(M,\ldots,M')} \sum_{\substack{i=1 \\ i\neq\alpha}}^{k} L_{\alpha,i} \tag{6.2}$$

where

$$L_{\alpha,i} = F_{k-1}\left(\frac{\phi_1}{\phi_i},\ldots,\frac{\phi_k}{\phi_i};\ (M,M')_\alpha; M; 1; \underline{1}_{k-1}\right) \tag{6.3}$$

where $(M,M')_\alpha$ indicates that the variable in the Dirichlet density whose lower limit of integration is $\frac{\phi_\alpha}{\phi_i}$ has the index $(M'-1)$ and the others have $(M-1)$. Thus

$$\begin{aligned} (k-E(S))B_k(M,\ldots,M') &= \sum_{\alpha=1}^{k} \sum_{\substack{i=1 \\ i\neq\alpha}}^{k} L_{\alpha,i} \\ &= \sum_{i=1}^{k} \sum_{\substack{\alpha=1 \\ \alpha\neq i}}^{k} L_{\alpha,i} = \sum_{i=1}^{k} A_i \end{aligned} \tag{6.4}$$

where $A_i = \sum_{\substack{\alpha=1 \\ \alpha\neq i}}^{k} F_{k-1}\left(\frac{\phi_1}{\phi_i},\ldots,\frac{\phi_k}{\phi_i};\ (M,M')_\alpha;\ M;\ 1;\ \underline{1}_{k-1}\right)$. We have a partial result (not proved here) that $E(S)$ decreases in ϕ_k, when $\phi_1 + \phi_k$ is **constant.** However, for $k = 2$, we have shown in Section 7 that the supremum of $E(S)$ is attained when $\phi_1 = \phi_2 = \frac{1}{2}$.

7. *The Binomial Case* $(k = 2)$. In this case we have

$$\begin{aligned} P(CS|R) &= 1 - \sum_{\nu_2=0}^{M'-1} \frac{(M+\nu_2-1)!}{\nu_2!(M-1)!} \phi_1^M \phi_2^{\nu_2} \\ &= 1 - \frac{1}{B_2(M,M')} \int_{\frac{\phi_2}{\phi_1}}^{\infty} \frac{y^{M'-1}}{(1+y)^{M+M'}}\, dy \quad . \end{aligned} \tag{7.1}$$

By changing the variable by the transformation $t = \frac{y}{1+y}$ we can write (7.1) as

$$P(CS|R) = 1 - I_{\phi_2}(M',M) \tag{7.2}$$

where $I_x(a,b)$ is the incomplete beta function defined by

$$I_x(a,b) = \frac{1}{B(a,b)} \int_0^x t^{a-1}(1-t)^{b-1}dt, \quad a,b > 0 \quad . \tag{7.3}$$

Thus, M and M' should satisfy

$$\inf_{\Omega} I_{\phi_2}(M',M) \geq P^* \quad . \tag{7.4}$$

It is obvious that the infimum on the left side of (7.4) is attained for $\phi_1 = \phi_2 = \frac{1}{2}$ and thus we have

$$I_{1/2}(M',M) \geq P^* \quad . \tag{7.5}$$

Further, it is also easily seen that

$$E(S) = I_{\phi_1}(M',M) + I_{\phi_2}(M',M) \tag{7.6}$$

and

$$\frac{dE(S)}{d\phi_2} = \frac{1}{B(M,M')} [\phi_2^{M'-1}\phi_1^{M-1} - \phi_1^{M'-1}\phi_2^{M-1}]$$

$$= \frac{\phi_1^{M+M'-2}}{B(M,M')} [(\frac{\phi_2}{\phi_1})^{M'-1} - (\frac{\phi_2}{\phi_1})^{M-1}] \tag{7.7}$$

$$\leq 0 \ .$$

Thus

$$\sup_{\Omega} E(S) = 2I_{1/2}(M',M) \quad . \tag{7.8}$$

We can obtain $E(n)$ for any general configuration of $\phi_1 \leq \phi_2$. We see that

$$E(n) = M + \sum_{r=0}^{M-1} r\binom{m+r-1}{r} \phi_1^r \phi_2^M +$$

(7.9)
$$\sum_{r=0}^{M-1} r\binom{m+r-1}{r} \phi_2^r \phi_1^M$$

$$= M + I_1 + I_2, \quad \text{say.}$$

Then

$$I_1 = \sum_{r=1}^{M-1} \frac{(M+r-1)!}{(r-1)!\,(M-1)!} \phi_1^r \phi_2^M$$

(7.10)
$$= \sum_{r=0}^{M-2} \frac{(M+r)!}{r!\,(M-1)!} \phi_1^{r+1} \phi_2^M$$

$$= \frac{M\phi_1}{\phi_2} I_{\phi_2}(M+1,M-1) \quad ,$$

using the well-known result

(7.11)
$$\sum_{s=0}^{a-1} \binom{n+s-1}{s} p^n(1-p)^s = I_p(n,a), \quad 0 < p < 1.$$

Similarly,

(7.12)
$$I_2 = M \frac{\phi_2}{\phi_1} I_{\phi_1}(M+1,M-1) \quad .$$

Thus

(7.13)
$$E(n) = M[1 + \frac{\phi_1}{\phi_2} I_{\phi_2}(M+1,M-1) + \frac{\phi_2}{\phi_1} I_{\phi_1}(M+1,M-1)] \quad .$$

Differentiating w.r.t. ϕ_2, we have

$$\frac{1}{M}\frac{dE(n)}{d\phi_2} = -\frac{1}{\phi_2^2} I_{\phi_2}(M+1,M-1) + \frac{1}{\phi_1^2} I_{\phi_1}(M+1,M-1)$$

$$= \frac{1}{\phi_1^2\phi_2^2}\sum_{t=M+1}^{2M-1}\binom{2M-1}{t}\phi_1^t\phi_2^t \tag{7.14}$$

$$\left(\phi_2^{2M+1-2t} - \phi_1^{2M+1-2t}\right)$$

$$< 0 \quad ,$$

since $2t > 2M+1$.

Thus $E(n)$ is maximized for $\phi_1 = \phi_2 = \frac{1}{2}$ and

$$\sup_{\Omega} E(n) = M + 2M\, I_{1/2}(M+1,M-1) \tag{7.15}$$

$$= 2M\left[1-\binom{2M}{M}\left(\tfrac{1}{2}\right)^{2M}\right] \quad .$$

Asymptotically, using the well-known result

$$\int_{-\infty}^{\infty} \Phi(\alpha x+\beta)\, d\Phi(x) = \Phi\left(\frac{\beta}{\sqrt{1+\alpha^2}}\right) \quad , \tag{7.16}$$

we get respectively from (4.15) and (5.7)

$$(1-\lambda)\sqrt{\frac{M}{\lambda(1+\lambda)}} = \Phi^{-1}(P^*) \tag{7.17}$$

and

$$E(n) = 2M\left[1 - \frac{1}{2\sqrt{M\pi}}\right] \quad . \tag{7.18}$$

8. *Concluding Remarks.* For $k > 2$, some aspects of this investigation are not complete. Further in the general case, the results of this paper regarding the least favorable configuration for the probability of a correct selection are a little different from those of Gupta and Nagel

[4]. Their fixed sample procedure R_o takes N observations and include the cell with count x_i iff

$$(8.1) \qquad x_i \geq \max(x_1,\ldots,x_k) - D_o$$

where D_o is a non-negative integer $\leq N$. It is shown that the worst configuration for $P(CS|R_o)$ is of the type $(0,\ldots,0,s,p,\ldots,p)$, $s \leq p$. If r is the number of non-zero cell-probabilities, $s + (r-1)p = 1$. Their numerical computations showed that the infimum is attained when $p = \frac{1}{r-1}$ or $\frac{1}{r}$ and in one case in the interior of $(\frac{1}{r}, \frac{1}{r-1})$. For $k=2$, R and R_o both have the least favorable configuration $\phi_1 = \phi_2 = \frac{1}{2}$ and $\sup E(S)$ is attained for the same configuration. We do not have a theoretical comparison of N and $E(n)$ for the same level of the probability of a correct selection. There is the possibility of several choices of N and D_o in the case R_o and, M and D in the case of R leading to the same probability of a correct selection. It is proposed by the author to make a detailed study on the basis of numerical computations.

References

1. Alam, K., Seo, K. and Thompson, J.R. (1970). A sequential sampling rule for selecting the most probable multinomial event. Tech. Report No. 46, Department of Mathematics, Clemson University, Clemson, South Carolina.

2. Bechhofer, R.E., Elmaghraby, S. and Morse, N. (1959). A single-sample multiple-decision procedure for selecting multinomial event which has the highest probability. *Ann. Math. Statist.* 30, 102-119.

3. Cacoullos, T. and Sobel, M. (1966). An inverse-sampling procedure for selecting the most probable event in a multinomial distribution. *Multivariate Analysis* (Ed. P.R. Krishnaiah), Academic Press, N.Y., pp. 423-455.

4. Gupta, S.S. and Nagel, K. (1967). On selection and ranking procedures and order statistics from the multinomial distributions. *Sankhyā Ser. B*, 29, 1-34.

5. Kesten, H. and Morse, N. (1959). A property of the multinomial distribution. *Ann. Math. Statist.* 30, 120-127.

6. Olkin, I. and Sobel, M. (1965). Integral expressions for tail probabilities of the multinomial and negative multinomial distribution. *Biometrika* 52, 167-179.

ON APPROXIMATING CONSTANTS REQUIRED TO IMPLEMENT A SELECTION PROCEDURE BASED ON RANKS

By Gary C. McDonald
General Motors Research Laboratories

1. *Introduction.* Two methods of approximating the constants required to implement a ranking and selection procedure based on joint ranks (Gupta and McDonald [5]) are compared with each other and with some available exact results. One of the methods is based on a result of Dudewicz [1] and requires only a slide rule to actually apply. The other method derives from a result given in [5] and requires the use of an auxiliary table such as in Gupta [4]. Other applications for these types of approximations can be found in [1] and Dudewicz and Zaino [2], with special reference given to Bechhofer-type selection procedures and selection from a multivariate normal population. The particular subset selection procedure to which these approximations will be applied will be discussed first.

2. *A Subset Selection Procedure Based on Ranks.* Let $\pi_1, \pi_2, \ldots, \pi_k$ be $k \geq 2$ independent populations. The associated random variables X_{ij}, $j = 1, \ldots, n$; $i = 1, \ldots, k$, are assumed independent and to have a continuous distribution $F_{\theta_i}(x)$ where the θ_i belong to some interval Θ on the real line. Suppose $F_\theta(x)$ is a stochastically increasing (SI) family of distributions; i.e., if θ_1 is less

than θ_2, then $F_{\theta_1}(x)$ and $F_{\theta_2}(x)$ are distinct and $F_{\theta_2}(x) \leq F_{\theta_1}(x)$ for all x. Examples of such families of distributions are: 1) any location parameter family, i.e., $F_\theta(x) = F(x-\theta)$; 2) any scale parameter family, i.e., $F_\theta(x) = F(x/\theta)$, $x > 0$, $\theta > 0$; 3) any family of distribution functions whose densities possess the monotone likelihood ratio (or TP_2) property. Let R_{ij} denote the rank of observation x_{ij} in the combined sample; i.e., if there are exactly r observations less than x_{ij}, then $R_{ij} = r + 1$. These ranks are well-defined with probability one, since the random variables are assumed to have a continuous distribution. With each of the random variables X_{ij} associate the integer R_{ij} and define the rank sums

(2.1) $$T_i = \sum_{j=1}^{n} R_{ij}, \quad i = 1, \ldots, k.$$

Using the quantities T_i, a procedure will be defined for selecting a subset of the k populations. Letting $\theta_{[i]}$ denote the ith smallest unknown parameter, we have

(2.2) $$F_{\theta_{[1]}}(x) \geq F_{\theta_{[2]}}(x) \geq \ldots \geq F_{\theta_{[k]}}(x), \quad \forall x .$$

The population whose associated random variables have the distribution $F_{\theta_{[k]}}(x)$ will be called the best population. In case several populations possess the largest parameter value $\theta_{[k]}$, one of them is tagged at random and called the best. In the usual subset selection problem one wishes to select a subset such that the probability is at least equal to a preassigned constant $P^*(k^{-1} < P^* < 1)$ that the selected subset includes the best population. A "correct selection" (CS) is said to occur if and only if the best population is included in the selected subset. Formally, for a given selection rule R, we desire

$$\inf_{\Omega} P(CS|R) \geq P^* , \tag{2.3}$$

where

$$\Omega = \{\underline{\theta} = (\theta_1, \ldots, \theta_k) : \theta_i \in \Theta, \quad i = 1,2,\ldots,k\} . \tag{2.4}$$

The subset selection rule of interest in this paper is as follows:

$$\text{R: Select } \pi_i \text{ iff } T_i \geq \max_{1 \leq j \leq k} T_j - m, \; i = 1,\ldots,k, \; m \geq 0. \tag{2.5}$$

All the populations possessing rank sums "sufficiently close" to the maximum rank sum are put in the selected subset. This selection rule has been studied (as a member of a class of selection procedures) in Gupta and McDonald [5] and the results given below can also be obtained for this class. As shown in [5], the infimum over Ω of the probability of a correct selection is actually attained when all the populations are identical (i.e., when $\theta_1 = \theta_2 = \ldots = \theta_k$) *if* Ω represents a *slippage* parameter space. Thus, if

$$\Omega' = \{\underline{\theta} = (\theta_1, \ldots, \theta_k) : \theta_{[1]} = \ldots = \theta_{[k-1]} \leq \theta_{[k]}\}, \tag{2.6}$$

then

$$\inf_{\Omega'} P(CS|R) = P_0(CS|R) = P_0(T_k \geq \max_{1 \leq j \leq k} T_j - m), \tag{2.7}$$

where P_0 indicates that the probability is calculated under the assumption that the random variables X_{ij} are independent and identically distributed. Note that the probability in (2.7) does not depend on the common underlying distribution. All subsequent probabilities will be computed assuming independent identically distributed (IID) populations and P will be used rather than P_0. The problem now is: For a given constant $P^*(k^{-1} < P^* < 1)$ find m such that

(2.8) $$P(T_k \geq \max_{1 \leq j \leq k} T_j - m) = P^* \quad .$$

Due to IID conditions,

(2.9) $$P(T_i \geq \max_{1 \leq j \leq k} T_j - m) = P(T_k \geq \max_{1 \leq j \leq k} T_j - m)$$

for any $i(1 \leq i \leq k)$. Also, since $\max_{1 \leq j \leq k} T_j - T_i$ assumes only a finite number of non-negative integer values, an m-solution to equation (2.8) exists for only a finite number of values of P^*; hence the problem is modified to be: find the smallest integer m such that

(2.10) $$P(T_k \geq \max_{1 \leq j \leq k} T_j - m) \geq P^* \quad .$$

For $k = 2$ an exact solution can be obtained by the use of the Mann-Whitney U-statistic tables. For $k = 3$, $n = 2(1)5$ exact solutions are available in Table I of [5]. Exact solutions for other k and n configurations are, at best, very expensive to obtain; thus good approximations become a practical necessity, and two such methods are compared in this paper. The application of these approximating methods will be justified by noting that the limiting joint distribution of the statistics involved, namely the rank sums, is multivariate normal. Hence these methods would apply to other selection rules where the relevant statistics have the same asymptotic behavior.

3. *An Approximation Which is Asymptotic with Respect to Sample Size.* Now consider the probability $P[T_k \geq \max_{1 \leq j \leq k} T_j - m]$. An asymptotic $(n \to \infty)$ expression for this quantity is (see Gupta and McDonald [5])

$$\text{(3.1)} \qquad P[T_k \leq \max_{1 \leq j \leq k} T_j - m] \approx \int_{-\infty}^{\infty} [\Phi(x+m/z)]^{k-1} \phi(x)dx, \quad m \geq 0,$$

where $\Phi(\cdot)$ and $\phi(\cdot)$ are the cumulative distribution function and probability density function of a standard normal random variable, respectively, and

$$\text{(3.2)} \qquad z = z(n,k) = n[k(nk + 1)/12]^{1/2} .$$

The calculation of this approximation is carried out with the aid of tables given in Gupta [4].

We now give an alternate expression for the probability of interest; this will be used in Section 4. The asymptotic joint distribution of the rank sums T_i is a multivariate normal distribution, the moments of which are well-known. We can write

$$\text{(3.3)} \qquad P[T_k \geq \max_{1 \leq j \leq k} T_j - m] = P[\bigcap_{i=1}^{k-1} \{T_k - T_i \geq -m\}],$$

$$= P[\min_{1 \leq i \leq k-1} Y_i \geq -m],$$

where

$$\text{(3.4)} \qquad Y_i = T_k - T_i, \qquad i = 1,\ldots,k-1.$$

Using Equation (3.4) and the moments for rank sums, it is easily seen that

$$\text{(3.5)} \qquad E(Y_i) = 0, \qquad i = 1,\ldots,k-1,$$

$$\text{(3.6)} \qquad \operatorname{Var}(Y_i) = 2 \operatorname{Var}(T_k) - 2 \operatorname{Cov}(T_1, T_k) = n^2 k(nk + 1)/6,$$

$$i = 1,\ldots,k-1,$$

(3.7) $$\mathrm{Cov}(Y_i, Y_j) = \mathrm{Var}(T_k) - \mathrm{Cov}(T_1, T_k) = n^2k(nk+1)/12,$$
$$1 \le i,\ j \le k,\ i \ne j.$$

Thus,

(3.8) $$W_i = [n^2k(nk+1)/6]^{-1/2} Y_i, \quad i = 1, \ldots, k-1 ,$$

has an asymptotic multivariate normal distribution with zero means, unit variances and a covariance matrix with off-diagonal elements 1/2. In light of Equation (3.3) we now have

(3.9) $$P[T_k \ge \max_{1 \le j \le k} T_j - m] = P\{\min_{1 \le i \le k-1} W_i \ge -m[n^2k(nk+1)/6]^{-1/2}\}.$$

4. *Dudewicz's Theorem and Its Application to Rule R.* Let $f(\underline{x}|\Sigma)$ be the probability density function of a $(k-1)$-dimensional normal distribution with zero means, unit variances and correlation matrix Σ. For $\delta > 0$ consider the integral

(4.1) $$P^*(\delta) = \int_{-\delta}^{\infty} \cdots \int_{-\delta}^{\infty} f(x|\Sigma)\, dx_1 \ldots dx_{k-1} .$$

Assume no element of Σ is a function of δ. Note that $P^*(\delta)$ is an increasing function of δ and $P^*(\delta) \to 1$ as $\delta \to \infty$. Theorem 4.1 is due to E. J. Dudewicz [1]. Throughout this paper, all logarithms are taken to the base e.

Theorem 4.1: *For large* P^* (near 1), *an approximation to* δ *which satisfies* (4.1) *is*

(4.2) $$\delta^2 \approx -2[\log(1 - P^*)] ,$$

i.e., the ratio tends to 1 *as* $P^* \to 1$.

The approximation is independent of k and of the correlation matrix Σ. Let $Z_1, Z_2, \ldots, Z_{k-1}$ be $k-1$ normally distributed random variables with zero means, unit variances and correlation matrix Σ. Then (4.1) can be written as

$$P^*(\delta) = P[\bigcap_{i=1}^{k-1} \{Z_i \geq -\delta\}] = P[\min_{1 \leq i \leq k-1} Z_i \geq -\delta]. \tag{4.3}$$

Using Theorem 4.1 and (3.9) we obtain the approximation

$$m^2 \approx -[n^2 k(nk+1)/3]\log(1-P^*) , \tag{4.4}$$

i.e., the ratio tends to 1 as $P^* \to 1$. The approximation given in Equation (4.4) can also be obtained from the relation (3.1). From Rizvi and Woodworth [6] (see Lemma 2) one has

$$m/z \approx 2^{1/2}\ \Phi^{-1}(P^*) \quad \text{as} \quad P^* \to 1. \tag{4.5}$$

Thus,

$$m^2 \approx 2z^2(\Phi^{-1}(P^*))^2 \approx -n^2[k(nk+1)/3]\log(1-P^*) , \tag{4.6}$$

which is (4.4). In (4.6) use was made of the well-known relation

$$\Phi^{-1}(P^*) \approx [-2\log(1-P^*)]^{1/2} \quad \text{as} \quad P^* \to 1. \tag{4.7}$$

5. *Comparisons of the Two Approximations*. For $P^* = .99$, the approximations for the smallest integral value of m satisfying $P[T_k > \max_{1 \leq j \leq k} T_j - m] \geq P^* = .99$ are computed using the previously described two methods. The value obtained via (3.1) is denoted by $\tilde{m}_1$ and that obtained from (4.4) by $\tilde{m}_2$. Table I gives $L(\tilde{m}_1)$ and $L(\tilde{m}_2)$, where $L(x)$ is the smallest integer greater than or equal to x, for $k = 2(1)5$, $n = 5(5)25$; the difference $L(\tilde{m}_2)-L(\tilde{m}_1)$ and ratio $L(\tilde{m}_1)/L(\tilde{m}_2)$ are also included in this table, along with some exact results.

TABLE I

P* = .99		Exact m	$L(\tilde{m}_1)$	$L(\tilde{m}_2)$	$L(\tilde{m}_2)-L(\tilde{m}_1)$	$L(\tilde{m}_1)/L(\tilde{m}_2)$
	n=5	21	23	30	7	.77
	10	60	62	81	19	.77
k=2	15	111	113	147	34	.77
	20	170	172	225	53	.76
	25		240	313	73	.77
	n=5	35	37	43	6	.86
	10		101	120	19	.84
k=3	15		185	219	34	.84
	20		283	336	53	.84
	25		395	468	73	.84
	n=5		51	57	6	.89
	10		141	159	18	.89
k=4	15		257	291	34	.88
	20		395	447	52	.88
	25		551	623	72	.88
	n=5		65	71	6	.92
	10		181	198	17	.91
k=5	15		331	363	32	.91
	20		509	557	48	.91
	25		711	778	67	.91

Several empirical points should be noted in regard to this table:

1. The difference $\tilde{m}_2 - \tilde{m}_1$ is a nondecreasing function of n for a fixed k, and a nonincreasing function of k for a fixed n.
2. The ratio $\tilde{m}_1/\tilde{m}_2$ is nondecreasing function of k for a fixed n, and is a constant for a fixed k over the various n values.
3. Where the exact m values are given, the approximations are "conservative", $\tilde{m}_2$ being more so than $\tilde{m}_1$;

however, the values $\tilde{m}_2$ are more easily calculated than the corresponding $\tilde{m}_1$.

In the case $k = 2$, the approximations are

$$\tilde{m}_1 = n((2n+1)/3)^{1/2}\ \Phi^{-1}(P^*) \ , \tag{5.1}$$

$$\tilde{m}_2 = n((2n+1)/3)^{1/2}(-2\log(1-P^*))^{1/2} \ . \tag{5.2}$$

The above three remarks can now be established for this case.

Theorem 5.1: *For* $1/2 < P^* < 1$ *and* $k = 2$,

(i) *the difference* $\tilde{m}_2 - \tilde{m}_1$ *is positive and an increasing function of* n, *and*

(ii) *the ratio* $\tilde{m}_2/\tilde{m}_1$ *is independent of* n.

Proof: Part (ii) is immediate. For (i) we have

$$\tilde{m}_2 - \tilde{m}_1 = n((2n+1)/3)^{1/2}[(-2\log(1-P^*))^{1/2} - \Phi^{-1}(P^*)], \tag{5.3}$$

which is clearly increasing in n if the difference in the brackets is positive. To show the difference is positive it suffices to show that $P^* < \Phi[(-2\log(1-P^*))^{1/2}]$. Using the relation (see Feller [2], p.166)

$$1 - \Phi(x) < (2\pi)^{-1/2}\ e^{-x^2/2}\ x^{-1}, \quad x > 0 \ , \tag{5.4}$$

it follows that

$$\begin{aligned} 1 - \Phi[(-2\log(1-P^*))^{1/2}] & \\ &< (2\pi)^{-1/2} e^{\log(1-P^*)}(-2\log(1-P^*))^{-1/2} \\ &= [-4\pi\log(1-P^*)]^{-1/2}(1-P^*) \\ &\le 1 - P^* \ . \end{aligned} \tag{5.5}$$

This completes the proof.

More generally,

Theorem 5.2: *For* $k^{-1} < P^* < 1$ *and* $k = 2,3,\ldots,$ *the ratio* $\tilde{m}_2/\tilde{m}_1$ *is a constant with respect to* n *for a fixed* k.

Proof: From the relation

$$\int_{-\infty}^{\infty} [\Phi(x + \tilde{m}_1/z)]^{k-1} \phi(x)dx = P^* \tag{5.6}$$

it is clear that the ratio $\tilde{m}_1/z$ is a function of k and P* only, i.e., $\tilde{m}_1/z = h(k,P^*)$. From (4.4) and (3.2),

$$\tilde{m}_2 = 2z[-\log(1-P^*)]^{1/2} \quad . \tag{5.7}$$

Thus,

$$\tilde{m}_2/\tilde{m}_1 = 2[-\log(1-P^*)]^{1/2}/h(k,P^*) \quad , \tag{5.8}$$

independent of n.

The difference $\tilde{m}_2 - \tilde{m}_1$ does not always remain non-negative for $k^{-1} < P^* < 1$, $k = 3,4,\ldots,$. Hence, $\tilde{m}_2$ is not, in general, more "conservative" than $\tilde{m}_1$. To show that $\tilde{m}_2 < \tilde{m}_1$ for k sufficiently large, it suffices to show that for a fixed P*

$$\int_{-\infty}^{\infty} [\Phi(x + \tilde{m}_2/z)]^{k-1} \phi(x)dx < P^* \quad , \tag{5.9}$$

since $\tilde{m}_1$ is determined as the smallest integer greater than or equal to the m-solution of

$$\int_{-\infty}^{\infty} [\Phi(x + m/z)]^{k-1}\phi(x)dx = P^* \quad . \tag{5.10}$$

Using (5.7), equation (5.9) may be written as

$$\int_{-\infty}^{\infty} [\Phi(x + c)]^{k-1} \phi(x)dx < P^* \quad , \tag{5.11}$$

where $c = 2[-\log(1-P^*)]^{1/2}$ is a positive constant with respect to k. Choose $M > \Phi^{-1}(1-P^*)$. Then

$$\begin{aligned}
\int_{-\infty}^{\infty} [\Phi(x+c)]^{k-1}\phi(x)dx &= \int_{-M}^{M} [\Phi(x+c)]^{k-1}\phi(x)dx \\
&+ \int_{-\infty}^{-M} [\Phi(x+c)]^{k-1}\phi(x)dx + \int_{M}^{\infty} [\Phi(x+c)]^{k-1}\phi(x)dx \\
&< \int_{-M}^{M} [\Phi(x+c)]^{k-1}\phi(x)dx + [\Phi(-M+c)]^{k-1} + [1-\Phi(M)] \\
&< \int_{-M}^{M} [\Phi(x+c)]^{k-1}\phi(x)dx + [\Phi(-M+c)]^{k-1} + P^* \quad .
\end{aligned} \tag{5.12}$$

By the bounded Convergence Theorem,

$$\lim_{k\to\infty} \int_{-M}^{M} [\Phi(x+c)]^{k-1}\phi(x)dx = 0 \quad , \tag{5.13}$$

and since $0 < \Phi(-M+c) < 1$,

$$\lim_{k\to\infty} [\Phi(-M+c)]^{k-1} = 0 \quad . \tag{5.14}$$

Thus,

$$\lim_{k\to\infty} \int_{-\infty}^{\infty} [\Phi(x+c)]^{k-1}\phi(x)dx < P^* \quad ,$$

and (5.9) is established.

It follows from (5.11) that for each value of P^* there exists an appropriate number of populations $k(P^*)$ such that for all values of n,

$$(5.15)\qquad \begin{cases} \tilde{m}_2 - \tilde{m}_1 \geq 0 & \text{if } k \leq k(P^*) \\ \tilde{m}_2 - \tilde{m}_1 < 0 & \text{if } k > k(P^*) \end{cases} .$$

It is interesting to note from Table II that $k(P^*) = 11$ for $P^* = .99, .975, .95, .90,$ and $.75$.

TABLE II

P^*	$\tilde{m}_2[2^{1/2}z(n,k)]^{-1}$ k=2,3,...	$\tilde{m}_1[2^{1/2}z(n,k)]^{-1}$ k=11	$\tilde{m}_1[2^{1/2}z(n,k)]^{-1}$ k=12
.99	3.035	3.031	3.057
.975	2.716	2.716	2.743
.95	2.448	2.448	2.477
.90	2.146	2.142	2.172
.75	1.665	1.636	1.667

6. *Conclusions*. Two methods for approximating the constants required to actually implement a particular selection procedure have been discussed. As a general rule, $\tilde{m}_1$, computed with the assistance of tables given in Gupta [4], is recommended for use rather than $\tilde{m}_2$. However, one may prefer to use $\tilde{m}_2$ because it is easy to compute for *all* values of k, n, and P^*; whereas $\tilde{m}_1$ (using [4]) can be determined for $k = 2(1)51$; $P^* = .99, .975, .95, .90, .75$ and all values of n. For low values of $k(\leq 11)$ both approximations appear to yield (see Tables I, II, III) conservative values, $\tilde{m}_2$ being the larger value. Hence, $\tilde{m}_1$ would be the preferred value to use. Table III gives the m value determined from a Monte Carlo simulation with 2000 repetitions, along with the approximations under consideration,

for $k = 11$ and 15, $n = 5$, and $P^* = .99, .975, .95, .90$, and $.75$. For the larger value of k, $\tilde{m}_2$ is now less than $\tilde{m}_1$; however, it is also less than the m value as determined from the Monte Carlo simulations, and one might then prefer to use the larger value, $\tilde{m}_1$, even though this value might also be too small. In cases where *exact* P^* conditions must be maintained (rather than be achieved approximately), the bounds given in Gupta and McDonald [5] are recommended. These bounds will lead to non-trivial m values which are conservative, but do guarantee a given P^* level.

TABLE III

For $n = 5$, the upper entry corresponds to $k = 11$, the lower to $k = 15$

P^*	Monte Carlo m	$L(\tilde{m}_2)$	$L(\tilde{m}_1)$
.99	147 215	154 210	154 216
.975	133 189	138 188	138 194
.95	119 171	125 169	125 176
.90	107 154	109 148	109 155
.75	83 124	85 115	83 121

References

1. Dudewicz, E. J. (1969). An Approximation to the Sample Size in Selection Problems, *Ann. Math. Statist.* 40, 492-497.

2. Dudewicz, E. J. and Zaino, N. A. (1971). Sample Size for Selection, this volume.

3. Feller, W. (1957). *An Introduction to Probability Theory and Its Applications, Vol. I.* John Wiley, New York.

4. Gupta, S. S. (1963). Probability Integrals of Multivariate Normal and Multivariate t, *Ann. Math. Statist.* 34, 792-828.

5. Gupta, S. S. and McDonald, G. C. (1970). On Some Classes of Selection Procedures Based on Ranks. *Nonparametric Techniques in Statistical Inference*, edited by M. L. Puri, Cambridge University Press, 491-514.

6. Rizvi, M. H. and Woodworth, G. G. (1970). On Selection Procedures Based on Ranks: Counterexamples Concerning Least Favorable Configurations, *Ann. Math. Statist.* 41, 1942-1951.

SELECTION PROCEDURES WITH RESPECT TO MEASURES OF ASSOCIATION

By Z. Govindarajulu and Anil P. Gore
University of Kentucky

1. *Summary*. This paper is concerned with selecting a single or a subset of p-variate populations having the highest "association" from amongst a set of c populations. Asymptotic results are worked out in detail, for the case of bivariate populations. Extensions to multivariate case are obtained. In the bivariate problem, the procedures are based on the rank correlation coefficient τ, and the product moment correlation coefficient. Analogous procedures can be developed by considering different scoring functions. Asymptotic efficiency of procedures based on τ relative to the normal theory procedures is found to be equal to the asymptotic relative efficiency of the corresponding tests of independence.

2. *Introduction and Notation*. Let $F_i(x,y)$ denote the continuous distribution function of $\pi_i (i = 1,\ldots,c)$, a set of c bivariate populations. We may be interested in ranking these populations according to some measure of association, for instance, in multiple regression one has to select predictor variables which have high (or low) association with the response variable. Also, one might like to choose from a group of tranquilizers, the one which has minimum

association between its main effect and the undesirable side effect, namely, drop in blood pressure. Let $\tau_i(\rho_i)$ denote the rank correlation coefficient (product-moment correlation coefficient) for population $\Pi_i (i = 1,\ldots,c)$. Let $\tau_{[1]},\ldots,\tau_{[c]}$ $(\rho_{[1]},\ldots,\rho_{[c]})$ be the ordered values of $\tau_i(\rho_i)(i = 1,\ldots,c)$. Then the problem is to identify the population (or a subset of populations) associated with $\tau_{[c]}(\rho_{[c]})$ (that includes the population associated with $\tau_{[c]}(\rho_{[c]})$). The problem concerning $\tau_{[1]}(\rho_{[1]})$ is analogous. Without loss of generality, let us, throughout, assume that Π_i has the ith smallest $\tau_i(\rho_i)$ $(i = 1,\ldots,c)$. That is, $\tau_1 < \tau_2 \ldots < \tau_c$ $(\rho_1 < \rho_2 < \ldots < \rho_c)$.

Let $(X_{i,j}, Y_{i,j})$ $j = 1,\ldots,n$ and $i = 1,\ldots,c$ denote n independent observations from each of the c populations. Let $R_{i,1},\ldots, R_{i,n}$ denote the ranks of the $Y_{i,j}(j=1,\ldots,n)$ when the $X_{i,j}(j=1,2,\ldots,n)$ are such that $X_{i1} < X_{i2} < \ldots < X_{in}$. Then the rank-correlation coefficient is defined by

$$T_i = \binom{n}{2}^{-1} \sum_{j}^{n} \sum_{< k}^{n} \mathrm{sign}(R_{ij} - R_{ik}),\ i = 1,\ldots,c, \tag{2.1}$$

and let r_i denote the product moment correlation coefficient based on the sample drawn from Π_i $(i = 1,\ldots,c)$.

3. *Selection Procedures*. In this section we shall provide the various procedures for selection from among the c bivariate populations. In the indifference zone formulation (see, for instance, Bechhofer et al (1954)) it is assumed that a minimum probability of correct selection (to be abbreviated as P(CS)) P^* and also d^* the lower bound for $\tau_c - \tau_{c-1}$ (d, the lower bound for $\rho_c - \rho_{c-1}$) that one is

interested in detecting are specified. In the subset formulation, (see, Gupta (1956)) one specifies P^* and the common sample size n such that populations having τ_i (ρ_i) within h of $\tau_c(\rho_c)$ can be included in the subset where h is determined by the procedure. First let us study the procedure based on r_i wherein it is assumed that $F_i(x,y)$ is bivariate normal, having ρ_i for the correlation coefficient $(i = 1,\ldots,c)$.

3.1. *Normal Theory Procedure.* For the indifference zone (I.Z.) formulation, select the population which gave rise to the largest r_i.

For the subset formulation (S.F.) include Π_i in the subset if

(3.1) $$r_i \geq \max_i r_i - h,\ i = 1,\ldots,c.$$

It is well known that r_i is asymptotically normal with mean ρ and variance $((1 - \rho^2)^2)/n$. Then we have the following results, the proofs of which are elementary and hence are omitted.

Result 3.1.1. *For sufficiently large* n, *one obtains*

(3.2) $$P(CS|I.Z.) \geq P(U_i \leq \sqrt{n}\ \delta/\sqrt{2},\ i = 1,\ldots, c-1)\ ,$$

and

(3.3) $$P(CS|S.F.) \geq P(U_i \leq \sqrt{n}\ h/\sqrt{2},\ i = 1,\ldots, c-1)\ ,$$

where U_i *have a multi-variate normal distribution with*

(3.4) $$EU_i = 0,\ \mathrm{Var}\ U_i = 1,\ E(U_iU_j) = \frac{1}{2},\ i \neq j$$

and

(3.5) $$\delta \leq (\rho_c - \rho_{c-1})\ .$$

Remark 3.1.1.1. It should be noted that the joint

distribution of $U_i (i = 1,\ldots,c-1)$ (a multivariate normal with known covariance matrix (see (3.4))) is well tabulated by Gupta (1963).

Consider the following modified subset selection procedure. Include Π_i in the subset if $S_i > \max_j S_j - h$ where $S_i = (1/2)\log\{(1+r_i)/(1-r_i)\}$ $i = 1,\ldots,c$ and h satisfies

$$P(U_i < h\sqrt{n/2},\ i = 1,\ldots,c-1) = P^* \quad ,$$

U_i being defined by (3.4), and let Ω_c be the configuration such that $\rho_c - \rho_i \geq \delta$. Then if $\rho_1 = \ldots = \rho_{c-1} = \rho_c - \delta$, for given $0 < \varepsilon < c-1$ the required sample size can be determined from the following result.

Result 3.1.2. *For sufficiently large* n, *we have*

$$E(\text{subset size} | \rho_c - \rho_i = \delta,\ i = 1,\ldots,c-1) \leq$$

$$P(U_i \leq (h+\delta)\sqrt{n/2},\quad i = 1,\ldots,c-1) +$$

$$(c-1)\ P(U_i \leq h\sqrt{n/2},\quad i = 1,\ldots,c-1) = 1 + \varepsilon.$$

Proof: The proof can be completed after noting that S_i is asymptotically normal with mean $(1/2)\log\{(1+\rho_i)/(1-\rho_i)\}$ and variance $1/n$, and that

$$ES_i - ES_j = (\rho_i - \rho_j)/(1+\rho_i)(1+\rho_j) + 0(\rho_j^2) \ .$$

Remark 3.1.2.1. It should be noted that the procedures based on r_i are identical to those based on S_i which are obtained by logarithmically transforming the r_i since S_i is a monotonic increasing function of r_i $(i = 1,\ldots,c)$.

Sometimes we may be interested in ranking bivariate normal populations by the absolute values of correlations. A modified I.Z. procedure for this problem would be, select the population Π_j if $|r_j| \geq |r_i|$, $i = 1,\ldots,c$. A modified

S.F. procedure, similarly is, include Π_i in the subset if $|r_i| > \max |r_j| - h$. Regarding the probabilities of correct selection, we have the following result.

Result 3.1.3: *For sufficiently large* n, *one obtains*

$$P(CS|I.Z.) \geq P(U_i \leq \sqrt{n}\,\delta/\sqrt{2},\ i = 1,\ldots,c-1),\ \textit{and}$$
$$P(CS|S.F.) \geq P(U_i \leq \sqrt{n}\,h/\sqrt{2},\ i = 1,\ldots,c-1),$$

where $\max_i|\rho_i| - |\rho_j| \geq \delta$, *provided* $\rho_i \neq 0$ $(i = 1,\ldots,c)$.

Proof. The proof will be identical to the one that would be employed in Result 3.1.1 after noting that $|r_i|$ is asymptotically normal with mean $|\rho_i|$ and variance $((1 - \rho_i^2)^2)/n$.

3.2. *The Procedure based on the rank correlation.* The procedure is given as follows. For I.Z. formulation, select the population associated with the largest T_i and for the S.F. formulation, include Π_i in the subset if

$$T_i \geq \max_i T_i - h,\ i = 1,\ldots,c, \tag{3.6}$$

where the T_i are given by (3.1).

Towards evaluating the probabilities of correct selection for the above procedures let us assume that

$$X_{ij} = X^*_{ij} + \sqrt{\Delta_i}\, Z_{ij},\quad Y_{ij} = Y^*_{ij} + \sqrt{\Delta_i}\, Z_{ij},\quad j=1,2,\ldots,n \text{ and } i = 1,\ldots,c \tag{3.7}$$

where X^*_{ij}, Y^*_{ij} and Z_{ij} are mutually independent and unobservable random variables having F, G and H for their respective distribution functions. Further assume that Δ_i are positive and small, for instance, $0 < \Delta_i < 1$. So, from the structure of X_{ij} and Y_{ij} we infer that the correlation between any two X's is always nonnegative. If the correlation between X_{ij} and Y_{ij} is negative, then write

$Y_{ij} = Y^*_{ij} - \sqrt{\Delta_i}\, Z_{ij}$ and X_{ij} as in (3.7). It is well known (see, for instance, Hoeffding (1947) or Noether (1967) p.70) that T_i is asymptotically normal with mean $2\theta_i - 1$ and variance $16(\theta_{ii} - \theta_i^2)/n$ where

$$\begin{aligned} \theta_i &= P((X_{i1}, Y_{i1}) \text{ is concordant with } (X_{i2}, Y_{i2})) \\ &= P[X_{i1} > X_{i2},\ Y_{i1} > Y_{i2}] \\ &\quad + P[X_{i1} < X_{i2},\ Y_{i1} < Y_{i2}],\ i = 1,\ldots,c \end{aligned} \tag{3.8}$$

and

$$\theta_{ii} = P((X_{i1}, Y_{i1}) \text{ is concordant with } (X_{i2}, Y_{i2}) \text{ and } (X_{i3}, Y_{i3}))$$

$$\begin{aligned} &= P[(X_{i1}, Y_{i1}) < (X_{i2}, Y_{i2}) \text{ and } (X_{i3}, Y_{i3}) \text{ or} \\ &\quad (X_{i1}, Y_{i1}) > (X_{i2}, Y_{i2}) \text{ and } (X_{i3}, Y_{i3}) \text{ or} \\ &\quad (X_{i3}, Y_{i3}) < (X_{i1}, Y_{i1}) < (X_{i2}, Y_{i2}) \text{ or } (X_{i2}, Y_{i2}) \\ &\quad < (X_{i1}, Y_{i1}) < (X_{i3}, Y_{i3})],\quad i = 1,\ldots,c. \end{aligned} \tag{3.9}$$

Result 3.2.1. *Let* F *and* G *be absolutely continuous such that*

(i) $\int |f|^3\, dx < \infty$, $\int |g|^3\, dx < \infty$,

(ii) $f^2(x) \to 0$, $g^2(x) \to 0$ as $|x| \to \infty$,

(iii) f',g' *exist, are continuous and are uniformly integrable with respect to* F *and* G *respectively, and*

(iv) Var Z < ∞,

then for small Δ_i *we have*

$$\theta_i = \frac{1}{2} + 4\Delta_i(\text{Var } Z)\left(\int f^2 dx\right)\left(\int g^2 dx\right) + o(\Delta_i) \tag{3.10}$$

and

$$\theta_{ii}-\theta_i^2 = \frac{1}{36} + 6\Delta_i(\text{Var } Z)[(\int f^2dx)(\int g^2dx)$$
$$- 2(\int(1-F)f^2dx)(\int g^2Gdx)$$
$$- 2(\int F\ f^2dx)(\int(1-G)g^2dx)] + o(\Delta_i). \tag{3.11}$$

Proof. $\theta_i = 2P(X^*_{i1}+\sqrt{\Delta_i}Z_{i1} \leq X^*_{i2}+\sqrt{\Delta_i}Z_{i2}$ and

$Y^*_{i1}+\sqrt{\Delta_i}Z_{i1} < Y^*_{i2}+\sqrt{\Delta_i}Z_{i2})$

$$= 2\int_{z_1}\int_{z_2} [\int F(x+(z_2-z_1)\sqrt{\Delta_i})dF]\cdot$$
$$[\int G(y+(z_2-z_1)\sqrt{\Delta_i})dG]dH(z_1)dH(z_2) .$$

Now expanding $F(x+(z_2-z_1)\sqrt{\Delta_i})$ and $G(y+(\ ))$ around x and y respectively and noting that

$$\int f'dF = \int f\ df = \frac{1}{2}\int df^2 = 0 \quad \text{and} \quad \int g'dG = 0$$

we obtain the approximate expression for θ_i.

Next consider

$$P(X_{i1} < X_{i2}, X_{i1} < X_{i3}, Y_{i1} < Y_{i2}, Y_{i1} < Y_{i3})$$
$$= \int_{z_1}\int_{z_2}\int_{z_3} [\{1-F(x+\sqrt{\Delta_i}(z_1-z_2))\}\cdot$$
$$\cdot\{1-F(x+\sqrt{\Delta_i}(z_1-z_3))\}\{1-G(y+\sqrt{\Delta_i}(z_1-z_2))\}\cdot$$
$$\cdot\{1-G(y+\sqrt{\Delta_i}(z_1-z_3))\}]\{dH(z_1)dH(z_2)dH(z_3) . \tag{3.12}$$

Expanding the product within the square brackets around $\Delta_i = 0$ and integrating we obtain: left side of (3.12) equals

$$\frac{1}{9} + 2(\text{Var } Z)\Delta_i[2(\int f^2(1-F)dx)(\int g^2(1-G)dx)$$

$$- \frac{1}{3}\int(1-F)f' \, dF - \frac{1}{3}\int(1-G)g' \, dG]$$

$$+ (\text{Var } Z)\Delta_i[\frac{1}{3}\int f^3 dx + \frac{1}{3}\int g^3 dy$$

$$+ 2\{\int f^2(1-F)dx\}\{\int g^2(1-G)dy\}] + o(\Delta_i)$$

$$(3.13) = \frac{1}{9} + 6\Delta_i(\text{Var } Z)[\{\int f^2(1-F)dx\}\{\int g^2(1-G)dy\}] + o(\Delta_i)$$

after noting that

$$2\int(1-F)f'(x)f(x)dx = \int(1-F)d(f^2) = \int f^3 dx$$

and

$$2\int(1-G)g'g \, dy = \int g^3 dy \; .$$

Analogously, one can obtain

$$(3.14) \quad \begin{aligned} &P(X_{i1} > X_{i2}, X_{i1} > X_{i3}, Y_{i1} > Y_{i2}, Y_{i1} > Y_{i3}) \\ &= \frac{1}{9} + 6\Delta_i(\text{Var } Z)[\{\int f^2 F dx\}\{\int g^2 G dy\}] + o(\Delta_i) \; . \end{aligned}$$

Similar computations yield

$$P(X_{i1} > X_{i2}, X_{i1} < X_{i3}, Y_{i1} > Y_{i2}, Y_{i1} < Y_{i3})$$

$$= P(X_{i1} < X_{i2}, X_{i1} > X_{i3}, Y_{i1} < Y_{i2}, Y_{i1} > Y_{i3})$$

$$(3.15) \quad = \frac{1}{36} + \Delta_i(\text{Var } Z)[2\{\int(1-F)f^2 dx\}\{\int(1-G)g^2 dy\}$$

$$+ 2\{\int F \, f^2 dx\}\{\int G \, g^2 dy\} - \{\int(1-F)f^2 dx\}\{\int G \, g^2 dy\}$$

$$- \{\int F \, f^2 dx\}\{\int(1-G)g^2 dy\}] + o(\Delta_i) \; .$$

Hence

$$\theta_{ii} = \frac{5}{18} + \Delta_i(\text{Var } Z)[24\{\int f^2 F\, dx\}\{\int g^2 G\, dy\}$$

$$(3.16) \qquad + 10\{\int f^2 dx\}\{\int g^2 dy\} - 12\{\int f^2 dx\}\{\int G\, g^2 dy\}$$

$$- 12\{\int g^2 dy\}\{\int F\, f^2 dx\}] + o(\Delta_i) \quad .$$

the desired result follows from (3.16) and (3.10).

Corollary 3.2.1.1. *One can write*

$$(3.17) \qquad \theta_{ii} - \theta_i^2 = \frac{1}{36} + 6\Delta_i(\text{Var } Z)[\int(2F-1)f^2 dx][\int(2G-1)g^2 dy] + o(\Delta_i) \quad .$$

Proof. In (3.11) write $\int f^2 = \int(1-F+F)f^2$, and $\int g^2 = \int(1-G+G)g^2$.

Remark 3.2.1.1. *Let* $B = [\int(2F-1)f^2][\int(2G-1)g^2]$. Then $B = 0$ if F or G is symmetric about zero. Also $B > 0$ if $F = G$. $B > 0$ if f and g are negative exponential densities with different location or scale parameters or if f and g are Weibull densities with different shape parameters. However $B < 0$ if

$$(3.18) \qquad \begin{cases} f(x) = x^{\theta_1}, \; 0 < x < 1, \; 0 < \theta_1 < 1 & \text{and} \\ G(x) = x^{\theta_2}, \; 0 < x < 1, \; \theta_2 > 1 & . \end{cases}$$

Then, we are led to the following results.

Result 3.2.2. *We have, for sufficiently small* $\Delta_i\,(i=1,\ldots,c)$ *and large* n,

$$P(CS|I.Z.) \geq P(U_i \leq \sqrt{n}\,\frac{2(\text{Var } Z)(\int f^2dx)(\int g^2dy)d}{4\sqrt{2/36}},\ i \neq c)$$

$$\text{if} \quad B \leq 0$$

$$(3.19) \qquad \geq P(U_i \leq \sqrt{n}\,\frac{2(\text{Var } Z)(\int f^2dx)(\int g^2dy)d}{4\sqrt{\frac{2}{36} + 12(\int f^2dx)(\int g^2dy)}},\ i \neq c)$$

$$\text{if} \quad B > 0$$

where $d \leq (\Delta_c - \Delta_{c-1})$ *and* $\Delta_c > \Delta_{c-1} > \ldots > \Delta_1$ *and* B *is as defined in* Remark 3.2.1.1.

Proof. Noting the asymptotic normality of T_i when suitably standardized, and using Result 3.2.1 we obtain

$$P(CS|I.Z.) \geq P(U_{i'} \leq \frac{2(\text{Var } Z)(\int f^2dx)(\int g^2dy)(\Delta_c - \Delta_{c-1})}{4\sqrt{\frac{2}{36} + 12(\text{Var } Z)B}},$$

$$i \neq c)$$

since

$$(3.20) \qquad \tau_c - \tau_i = E(T_c) - E(T_i) = 2(\Delta_c - \Delta_i)\text{Var } Z\cdot\{\int f^2\}\{\int g^2\} + o(\Delta_c)$$

Now use (3.11) and note that $\Delta_c \leq 1$.

Result 3.2.3. *For sufficiently small* $\Delta_i (i = 1,\ldots,c)$ *and large* n *we have*

$$P(CS|SF) \geq P(U_i \leq \sqrt{n}\,h/4(\sqrt{2/36}), i=1,\ldots,c-1) \text{ if } B \leq 0$$

$$(3.21) \qquad \geq P(U_i \leq \frac{\sqrt{n}\ h}{4\sqrt{\frac{2}{36} + 12(\int f^2)(\int g^2)}}, i=1,\ldots,c-1)$$

$$\text{if } B > 0 .$$

Result 3.2.4. *Let* Ω_c^* *be the configuration such that* $\Delta_c - \Delta_i = d$, $i \neq c$. *Then for given* d,

$$E(\text{subset size} \mid \Delta_c - \Delta_i = d,\ i \neq c)$$

$$\le P\left[U_i \le \frac{\sqrt{n}[h+2(\text{Var } Z)(\int f^2)(\int g^2)d]}{4\sqrt{\frac{2}{36} - 24[\{\int(1-F)f^2dx\}\{\int Gg^2dy\} + \{\int(1-G)g^2dy\}\{\int Ff^2dx\}]}},\ i=1,\ldots,c-1\right] \tag{3.22}$$

$$+ (c-1)P(U_i \le \sqrt{n}\, h/4(\sqrt{2/36}),\ i \neq c), \quad \text{if} \quad B \le 0,$$

and

$$E(\text{subset size} \mid \Delta_c - \Delta_i = d,\ i \neq c)$$

$$\le P\left(U_i \le \frac{\sqrt{n}\{h+2(\text{Var } Z)(\int f^2)(\int g^2)d\}}{4\sqrt{2/36}},\ i = 1,\ldots,c-1\right)$$

$$+ (c-1)\ P\left(U_i \le \frac{\sqrt{n}\ h}{4\sqrt{2/36}}\quad i = 1,\ldots,c-1\right), \text{ if } \quad B > 0.$$

Recall that in order to carry out the procedure, we need to know only $\int f^2$, $\int g^2$ and Var Z, when Δ_i are fairly small. However, it is possible that f and g are unknown. Then one can estimate $\int f^2$ and $\int g^2$ from the sample data. If the Δ_i are going to zero as $n \to \infty$, the samples X_{ij}, $i = 1,2,\ldots,c$ and $j = 1,2,\ldots,n$ behave like data from F(x). Then define the estimate

$$\widehat{\int f^2 dx} = \frac{B_n}{(nc)^2} \sum_{\ell=1}^{nc} \sum_{m=1}^{nc} K(B_n(Y_\ell - Y_m)) \tag{3.23}$$

where $B_n \ge 0$, and Y_ℓ are the X_{ij} written in a vector form and K is some weight function.

Result 3.2.4. *If* $B_n/n \to 0$ as $n \to \infty$ *and the weight function* $K(\omega)$ *is such that*

(i) $K(\omega) \geq 0$, $K(\omega) = K(-\omega)$, *for every* ω,

(ii) $\lim_{|\omega| \to \infty} \omega K(\omega) = 0$, *and*

(iii) $\int_{-\infty}^{\infty} K(\omega) d\omega = 1$,

then, the estimate given by (3.23) *is consistent provided* $\Delta_i \to 0$ *as* $n \to \infty$.

Proof: Using Parzen's (1962) theorem we infer that

$$\widehat{\int f^2 dx} = \frac{B_n}{c^2 n} K(0) + \frac{B_n}{c^2 n^2} \sum_{\ell \neq m} \sum K(B_n(Y_\ell - Y_m))$$

$$\to \frac{1}{nc} \sum_{\ell=1}^{nc} f(Y_\ell) = \int_{-\infty}^{\infty} f(x) d\, F_{nc}(x)$$

where $F_{nc}(x)$ is the empirical distribution based on a sample of size nc. Now

$$\int f\, dF_{nc}(x) \to \int f\, dF = \int f^2 dx \quad \text{in probability.}$$

An analogous estimate and a result will be available for $\int g^2 dy$.

Remark 3.2.4.1. In a similar fashion one obtains consistent estimates of $\int Ff^2$ and $\int Gg^2$.

3.3. In this section we consider the case when the structure of X_i and Y_i and $F_i(x,y)$ are unknown. Also, some of the τ_i may be positive and some negative. For the I.Z. formulation, we propose a two-stage procedure which is in the spirit of the one proposed by Bechhofer et al (1954) for selecting the normal population having the largest mean when the population variances are equal but unknown.

Procedure (I.Z.): Draw an initial sample of size m from each of the c bivariate populations. Compute

$$(3.24)\qquad T_i = \binom{m}{2}^{-1} \sum_{k > j}^{m} \sum^{m} \operatorname{sign}(X_{ik}-X_{ij})\operatorname{sign}(Y_{ik}-Y_{ij}), \quad i = 1\ 2,\ldots,c.$$

Let

$$(3.25)\qquad \begin{aligned} \phi^{(i)}(j;k) &= 1, \text{ if } (X_{ij},Y_{ij}) \text{ is concordant with } (X_{ik}, Y_{ik}) \\ &= 0, \text{ otherwise.} \end{aligned}$$

Also let

$$(3.26)\qquad \begin{aligned} \phi^{(i)}(j;k,\ell) &= 1 \text{ if } (X_{ij},Y_{ij}) \text{ is concordant with } (X_{ik},Y_{ik}) \text{ and } (X_{i\ell},Y_{i\ell}) \\ &= 0, \text{ otherwise,} \end{aligned}$$

where concordance between two pairs of observations and three pairs of observations are as defined in (3.8) and (3.9) respectively. Then, define

$$(3.27)\qquad \hat{\theta}_i = \sum_{j \neq k}^{m} \sum^{m} \phi^{(i)}(j;k)/m(m-1),$$

$$(3.28)\qquad \hat{\theta}_{i,i} = \sum_{j \neq k \neq \ell}^{m} \sum^{m} \sum^{m} \phi^{(i)}(j;k,\ell)/m(m-1)(m-2),$$

and

$$(3.29)\qquad \hat{A}_i = \hat{\theta}_{i,i} - \hat{\theta}_i^2 \quad \text{where } A_i = \theta_{ii}-\theta_i^2,\ i=1,\ldots,c.$$

Notice that $\hat{\theta}_i$ is linearly related to T_i given by (2.1) and hence is asymptotically normal with mean θ_i and variance $4(\theta_{ii}-\theta_i^2)/n$. Thus $\hat{\theta}_i$ and $\hat{\theta}_i^2$ are consistent estimators of θ_i and θ_i^2 respectively. One can also write $\hat{\theta}_{ii}$ as

$$\hat{\theta}_{ii} = \binom{m}{3}^{-1} \sum_{j} \sum_{<k<} \sum_{\ell}^{m} \phi^{(i)*}(j,k,\ell) \text{ where}$$

$$\phi^{(i)*}(j,k,\ell) = \frac{1}{3}[\phi^{(i)}(j;k,\ell) + \phi^{(i)}(k;\ell,j) + \phi^{(i)}(\ell;j,k)] ,$$

which is a U-statistic with symmetric kernel $\phi^{(i)*}(j,k,\ell)$. So, from Hoeffding's (1948) Theorem 7.1 it follows that $\hat{\theta}_{ii}$ is asymptotically normal with mean θ_{ii} and variance $9[E\{\phi^{(i)*}(j,k,\ell)\phi^{(i)*}(j,k,r)\} - \phi_{ii}^2]/n$ which is bounded above by $81/n$. Hence $\hat{\theta}_{ii}$ consistently estimates ϕ_{ii}. Consequently $\hat{A}_i$ is a consistent estimator of A_i. Also, let

(3.30) $\hat{A} = \max(\hat{A}_1,\ldots,\hat{A}_c)$, and $A = \max(A_1,\ldots,A_c)$.

For given $P^* = P(CS)$ find η such that

(3.31) $P(U_i \le \eta,\ i = 1,\ldots,c-1) = P^*$

where U_i are as defined in (3.4). Also, let

(3.32) $\delta^* \le (\tau_c - \tau_{c-1})$ where $\tau_c > \tau_{c-1} > \ldots > \tau_1$.

Now, draw an additional sample of size $n-m$ where

(3.33) $n = \max(m,\ 32\hat{A}\eta^2/\delta^{*2})$,

and compute $T_1,\ldots,T_c$ that are based on samples of size n from each of the c bivariate populations. Identify the population as best that yielded the largest T_i.

The justification for the above two-stage procedure would be clear from the following considerations.

Lemma 3.3.1. *If the random variables* $Z_1,\ldots,Z_c$ *are mutually independent and* Z_i *converges to* μ_i *in probability then* $W = \max_i Z_i$ *converges to* $\max_i \mu_i$ *in probability (or*

$W^* = \min_i Z_i$ *converges to* $\min_i \mu_i$ *in probability*).

Proof. Without loss of generality let $\mu_c = \max_i \mu_i$. Then consider

$$P(|W-\mu_c| \geq \varepsilon) = P(Z_i > \mu_c+\varepsilon, \text{ for some } i) + \prod_{i=1}^{c} P(Z_i \leq \mu_c-\varepsilon) \leq \sum_{i=1}^{c} P(Z_i > \mu_c + \varepsilon) + P(Z_c \leq \mu_c - \varepsilon) \ .$$

An analogous proof holds for W^* converging to $\min_i \mu_i$ in probability.

Corollary 3.3.1.1. It follows from Lemma 3.3.1 that $\hat{A}$ converges to A in probability. Now, one can arrive at

$$P(CS|\delta^*, IZ) = P\left(U_i \leq \frac{(\tau_c-\tau_i)\sqrt{n}}{4\sqrt{A_c^2+A_i^2}}, \ i = 1,\ldots,c-1\right) \tag{3.34}$$
$$\geq P\left(U_i \leq \frac{\delta^*\sqrt{n}}{4\sqrt{2A}}, \ i = 1,\ldots,c-1\right) .$$

So, comparing (3.31) and (3.34) we have

$$\delta^*\sqrt{n}/4\sqrt{2A} > \eta \quad \text{or} \quad n > 32\, A\eta^2/\delta^{*2} \ . \tag{3.35}$$

Since A is unknown we estimate it by $\hat{A}$. Further by using Cramér's Lemma (1966) p. 254, one can write (3.44) as

$$P(CS|\delta^*) \geq P(U_i \leq \delta^*\sqrt{n}/4\sqrt{2\hat{A}}, \ i = 1,\ldots,c-1),$$

and obtain $$n > 32\,\hat{A}\,\eta^2/\delta^{*2} \ .$$

Procedure for S.F.

Draw n observations from population Π_i and compute the statistics $T_i (i = 1,\ldots,c)$. Include Π_j in the subset if $T_j > \max T_i - h$ for some $-1 \leq h \leq 1$. Then the problem is to determine h for given n and P^*. Towards this we have the following result.

Result 3.3.1. *For given* P^* *and* n *(sufficiently large) we have*

$$h \doteq 4\sqrt{2\hat{A}}\ \eta/\sqrt{n} ,$$

where η *is defined by* (3.31) *and* $\hat{A}$ *is given by* (3.30).

Proof.

$$P(CS) = P\left(\frac{T_j-\tau_j-(T_c-\tau_c)}{\sqrt{\widehat{\mathrm{Var}}\ T_j + \widehat{\mathrm{Var}}\ T_c}} \leq \frac{h+\tau_c-\tau_j}{\sqrt{\widehat{\mathrm{Var}}\ T_c + \widehat{\mathrm{Var}}\ T_j}},\ j \neq c\right)$$

(3.36)

$$\geq P(U_i \leq h\sqrt{n}/4\sqrt{2\hat{A}},\ i = 1,\ldots,c-1) = P^*.$$

Comparing (3.31) and (3.36) we get the approximate expression for h. Towards the expected subset size we have the following result.

Result 3.3.2. *Let* $\tilde{\Omega}_c$ *be the configuration such that* $\tau_c-\tau_i \geq \delta^*$. *Then, the probability of correct selection is minimized for sufficiently large* n *if* $\tau_1=\ldots=\tau_{c-1}=\tau_c-\delta^*$. *Furthermore,*

$$E\,(\text{subset}\ |\tau_c-\tau_i=\delta^*,\ i\neq c) \leq P(U_i\leq(h+\delta)\sqrt{n}/4\sqrt{2D},\ i = 1,\ldots,c-1)$$
$$+(c-1)P(U_i\leq h\sqrt{n}/4\sqrt{2D},\ i = 1,\ldots,c-1)$$

where

$$D = \min\,(A_1,\ldots,A_c)\ .$$

Remark 3.3.2.1. Since D is unknown, we can use $\hat{D} = \min\,(\hat{A}_1,\ldots,\hat{A}_c)$ in order to get an approximate upper bound for $E(\text{subset}\ |\tau_c-\tau_i=\delta^*,\ i\neq c)$ for given h, δ^* and n.

4. *Asymptotic Efficiencies of the Various Procedures.* Since the results pertaining to the properties of the procedures are based on large samples, it is of interest to compare the various procedures for sufficiently large sample sizes. Let us assume that $F_i(x,y)$ is bivariate normal with correlation $\rho_i (i = 1,\dots,c)$. Then we have the following lemma.

Lemma 4.1. *If* $F_i(x,y)$ *is bivariate normal with correlation* ρ_i *then*

$$\theta_i = \frac{1}{2} + \frac{\rho_i}{\pi} + o(\rho_i), \quad i = 1,\dots,c. \tag{4.1}$$

Proof. Without loss of generality let us assume that the bivariate normal distribution has zero means and unit variances. Then

$$\theta_i = 2P(X_{i1} < X_{i2}, Y_{i1} < Y_{i2})$$

$$= 2 \int\int\int\int_{x_1<x_2,\, y_1<y_2} f_i(x_1,y_1) f_i(x_2,y_2) dx_1 dx_2 dy_1 dy_2$$

where $f_i(x,y) = f(x,y;\rho_i)$. Expanding the integrand around $\rho_i = 0$ and performing integration we obtain the desired result.

Remark 4.1.1. We have

$$\tau_c - \tau_i = 2(\theta_c - 1) - 2(\theta_i - 1) = \frac{2(\rho_c - \rho_i)}{\pi} + o(\rho_c) \ . \tag{4.2}$$

Remark 4.1.2. If f,g are standard normal and Z is normal with zero mean and variance σ^2 then we have,

$$(\Delta_c - \Delta_i)(\text{Var } Z) = \frac{\rho_c - \rho_i}{(1-\rho_c)(1-\rho_i)} \geq (\rho_c - \rho_i) \ . \tag{4.3}$$

Thus, we have the following result.

Result 4.1. *For sufficiently small* ρ_i, *(say* $= \rho_i = \xi_i / n^{\frac{1}{4} - \beta}$, $\frac{1}{4} > \beta > 0$*) the asymptotic efficiency of the procedure based on the rank correlation coefficient relative to the one based on product-moment correlation coefficient is* $9/\pi^2$ *when the underlying populations are bivariate normal.*

Proof. For the procedure based on the rank correlation coefficient based on a sample of size n

$$P(CS) = P^* = P\left(U_i \le \frac{\sqrt{n}(2/\pi)\cdot(\rho_c - \rho_{c-1}) + o(\rho_c)\sqrt{n}}{4\sqrt{2A}}, \quad i = 1, \ldots, c-1\right) \tag{4.4}$$

where $A = 1/36$ and for the procedure based on the product-moment correlation coefficient computed from a sample of size n^*

$$P^* \doteq P(U_i \le \sqrt{n^*}\,(\rho_c - \rho_{c-1})/\sqrt{2},\ i = 1, \ldots, c-1). \tag{4.5}$$

Furthermore, for the procedure based on rank correlation when the structure of the variables is given by (3.7),

$$P^* \doteq P\left(U_i \le \frac{8(\mathrm{Var}\ Z)(\Delta_k - \Delta_i)(\int f^2)(\int g^2)\sqrt{n}}{4\sqrt{2/36}}, i = 1, \ldots, c-1\right). \tag{4.6}$$

That is,

$$P^* \doteq P\left(U_i \le \frac{\sqrt{n}(\rho_c - \rho_{c-1})}{2\pi\sqrt{2/36}}, \quad i = 1, \ldots, c-1\right)$$

if f and g are standard normal. So, by equating the upper limits for U_i and solving for n^*/n we get the desired result.

Corollary 4.1.1. *When the structure of the variables is given by (3.7), the asymptotic efficiency of the procedure based on rank correlation coefficient relative to the one based on ordinary correlation is* $144(\int f^2dx)^2(\int g^2dx)^2$.

5. *Nonparametric Selection Procedures based on other Criteria of Dependence.* Any distribution-free test-criteria designed to test for independence of a set of variables can be employed for selection procedures. For instance, let

$$T_i = F_{i,n}(x,y) - F_{i,n}(x)G_{i,n}(y),\ i=1,\ldots,c \tag{5.1}$$

where $F_{i,n}(x,y)$, $F_{i,n}(x)$ and $G_{i,n}(y)$ denote the empirical distribution functions based on the bivariate sample, the first uni-variate sample and the second uni-variate sample respectively. Also, $F_i(x,y)$, $F_i(x)$ and $G_i(y)$ denote respectively the bivariate and marginal distribution functions of the ith population. Then, one can formulate selection procedures for the indifference zone approach as well as the subset approach based on the T_i's. Large value of T_i might indicate more dependence of the variables in the ith population. Also rank tests for independence proposed by Bhuchongkul (1964) and, Hájek and Šidák (1968) are based on

$$T_i = \sum_{j=1}^{n} a_n(R_{ij},f)a_n(Q_{ij},g) \tag{5.2}$$

where $R_{ij}(Q_{ij})$ is the rank of $X_{ij}(Y_{ij})$ among $X_{i1},\ldots,X_{in}(Y_{i1},\ldots,Y_{in})$ and $a_n(j,f)(a_n(j,g))$ are some scores based on the density $f(g)$. For standard logistic f and g, the T_i in (5.2) are proportional to rank correlation coefficients and for standard normal f and g, $a_N(j,f)$ becomes the expected value of the jth smallest normal order statistic in a sample of size n. For Φ denoting the standard normal distribution function, let

$$T_i = \sum_{j=1}^{n} \Phi^{-1}(R_{ij}/(n+1))\Phi^{-1}(Q_{ij}/(n+1)) , \tag{5.3}$$

using Bhuchongkul's (1964) asymptotic results it is possible to show that the asymptotic efficiency of the selection procedure based on the T_i given by (5.3) relative to the selection procedure based on the product-moment correlation coefficients defined by (2.2) is unity when the underlying populations are bivariate normal.

6. *Multivariate Case.* It is of interest to extend results of sections 3 and 4 to the p-variate case. Recently Gnanadesikan and Gupta (1970) have proposed a subset selection procedure for multivariate normal populations in terms of generalized variances. A slightly different version of their procedure in terms of determinants of the correlations matrices may be appropriate when the interest lies in some measure of association. Gupta and Panchapakesan (1969) have given a subset selection procedure for multivariate normal populations in terms of the multiple correlation coefficient which, however, is not symmetric in all coordinates. Hence, it may not be an appropriate criterion for ranking populations when some overall measure of association is of interest.

6.2. *Procedures based on a p-variate analogue of the rank correlation.* For the p-variate case an appropriate analogue of the bivariate rank correlation coefficient is not available. Moran (1951) proposed a multiple rank correlation by replacing simple correlations in the expression for multiple correlation by corresponding rank correlations. However sampling distribution of this statistic seems to be intractable. We use a simplistic measure of association defined below.

$$\text{We say that } \underline{X}_\ell^{(i)} > \underline{X}_m^{(i)} \text{ if and only if} \tag{6.1}$$
$$X_{j\ell}^{(i)} > X_{jm}^{(i)}, \; j = 1,\ldots,p.$$

Let $\theta_i = P(\underline{X}_\ell^{(i)} > \underline{X}_m^{(i)}$ or $\underline{X}_m^{(i)} > \underline{X}_\ell^{(i)})$. θ_i can be looked upon as probability of concordance for population Π_j, which we take as a measure of association. Define

$$\phi_{\ell,m}^{(i)} = 1 \text{ if } \underline{X}_\ell^{(i)} > \underline{X}_m^{(i)} \text{ or } \underline{X}_m^{(i)} > \underline{X}_\ell^{(i)}, \tag{6.2}$$
$$= 0, \text{ otherwise}$$

and

$$T_i = \binom{n}{2}^{-1} \sum_{\ell < m}\sum \phi_{\ell,m}^{(i)} \quad \ell,m = 1,\ldots,n. \tag{6.3}$$

Then it is easy to see that T_i is a U-statistic and $\sqrt{n}(T_i-\theta_i)$ is asymptotically normal with zero mean and variance $16(\theta_{ii}-\theta_i^2)$ where

$$\theta_{ii} = P(\underline{X}_1^{(i)} \text{ is concordant with } \underline{X}_2^{(i)} \text{ and } \underline{X}_3^{(i)}. \tag{6.4}$$

For the I.Z. formulation in which we seek to select the population with highest probability of concordance, select that population which gave rise to the largest T_i, and for S.F., include Π_i in the subset if $T_i \geq \max_i T_i - h$.

If, for mutually independent $\underline{X}_\ell^*$ and z_ℓ, we assume that

$$\underline{X}_\ell^{(i)} = \underline{X}_\ell^* + \sqrt{\underline{\Delta}^{(i)}}\, Z_\ell, \tag{6.5}$$

where $\underline{X}_\ell^*$ is a vector with independent co-ordinates $X^*_{j\ell}$ with distributions G_j, $j = 1,\ldots,p$, $\underline{\Delta}^{(i)'} = (\Delta_1^{(i)},\ldots,\Delta_p^{(i)})$ and Z_ℓ is a real valued random variable with distribution H, then one can obtain results analogous to those of Section 3.2. If the structure of the multivariate population is unknown we can carry out a two-stage procedure similar to the one proposed in Section 3.3. Details are omitted.

In sections 6.3 and 6.4 we develop new criteria for selection which are symmetric in the p-variables and which are more efficient.

6.3. *Procedures based on sum of bivariate product-moment correlations.* A measure $\nu^{(i)}$ defined by

(6.6.) $$\nu^{(i)} = \sum_{k \neq}^{p} \sum_{\ell}^{p} \rho_{k\ell}^{(i)}/p(p-1)$$

where $\rho_{k\ell}^{(i)}$ is the bivariate product-moment correlation coefficient between kth and ℓth co-ordinate of a vector $\underline{X}$ from the population Π_i, seems to be a reasonable measure of association when F_i is a p-variate normal distribution. In this subsection we study a procedure for ranking c populations in terms of $\nu^{(i)}$'s.

Lemma 6.3.1. *Let* (X_i, Y_i), $i = 1,\ldots,n$ *be independent, identically distributed random vectors, having a bivariate normal distribution, where* $\text{cov}(X_i, Y_i) = \rho$ *and without loss of generality it is assumed that* $E(X_i) = E(Y_i) = 0$,

$\text{Var}(X_i) = \text{Var}(Y_i) = 1$. *Then* $\sqrt{n}(r-\rho)$ *and* $\sqrt{n}[n^{-1} \sum_1^n X_i Y_i - \rho]$

are asymptotically equivalent having the same limiting normal distribution with mean zero and variance $1 + \rho^2$, *where* r *is the sample correlation coefficient.*

Proof. The sample correlation r is given by

$$(6.7) \qquad r = \sum_{i=1}^{n} (X_i - \overline{X})(Y_i - \overline{Y})/n\, S_X S_Y$$

where $\overline{X} = \sum_{1}^{n} X_i/n$, $\overline{Y} = \sum_{1}^{n} Y_i/n$, $S_X^2 = \sum(X_i-\overline{X})^2/n$ and $S_Y^2 = \sum(Y_i-Y)^2/n$. Note that S_X and S_Y converge in probability to 1. Further, because of Chebyshev's inequality $n^{1/2}\overline{X}$ and $n^{1/2}\overline{Y}$ are bounded in probability, so that $\sqrt{n}\ \overline{X}\ \overline{Y}$ converges in probability to zero. Now the asymptotic equivalance of the two statistics follows from Cramér's lemma (1966). Asymptotic normality follows from the classical central limit theorem and noting that
$E\{(XY)^2\} = E(X^2(1-\rho^2+\rho^2X^2)) = 1 + 2\rho^2$. Now define

$$(6.8) \qquad V_i = \sum_{k}^{p} \sum_{\neq\, \ell}^{p} r_{k\ell}^{(i)}/p(p-1)$$

where $r_{k\ell}^{(i)}$ is the sample correlation coefficient between kth and ℓth co-ordinates of vector $X^{(i)}$ from the population Π_i, based on a random sample of size n. V_i is thus the sample analogue of $\nu^{(i)}$ defined in (6.9).

Remark 6.3.1. In view of Lemma 6.3.1, V_i has limiting behaviour identical to V_i^* where

$$(6.9) \qquad V_i^* = (1/n) \sum_{j=1}^{n} [\sum_{k}^{p} \sum_{\neq\, \ell}^{p} X_{kj}^{(i)}\ X_{\ell j}^{(i)}/p(p-1)]\ .$$

Note that V_i^* is the mean of n independent and identically distributed random variables $W_j^{(i)}$ where

$$(6.10) \qquad W_j^{(i)} = \sum_{k} \sum_{\neq\, \ell} X_{kj}^{(i)} \cdot X_{\ell j}^{(i)}\ /p(p-1)\ .$$

Clearly

$$E(W_j^{(i)}) = \sum_{k \neq \ell}^{p} \sum_{\ell}^{p} \rho_{k\ell}^{(i)}/p(p-1) \tag{6.11}$$

and

$$\begin{aligned} E(W_j^{(i)2}) = \frac{1}{p^2(p-1)^2} E[2\sum_{k \neq \ell} \sum_{\ell}^{p} X_{kj}^{(i)^2} \cdot X_{\ell j}^{(i)^2} \\ + 4 \sum_{k \neq \ell \neq r} \sum \sum X_{kj}^{(i)^2} \cdot X_{\ell j}^{(i)} X_{rj}^{(i)} \\ + \sum_{k \neq \ell \neq r \neq s} \sum \sum \sum X_{kj}^{(i)} X_{\ell j}^{(i)} X_{rj}^{(i)} X_{sj}^{(i)}] . \end{aligned} \tag{6.12}$$

For obtaining the explicit value of the right hand expression in (6.12) we prove the following lemmas.

Lemma 6.3.2. *Let* (X,Y,Z) *have a trivariate normal distribution with zero means and unit variances. Then* $E(X^2YZ) = \rho_{ZY} + 2\rho_{ZX}\rho_{XY}$, *with obvious notation.*

Proof. Consider repeated conditional expectations and use Result (5) of Anderson (1958).

Lemma 6.3.3. *If* (X,Y,Z,W) *have a 4-variate normal distribution with zero means, unit variances and the usual covariance matrix, then* E(XYZW) = 0.

Proof: Consider $E(ZW|X,Y)$ and use Result (5) of Anderson (1958). Using lemmas 6.3.2 and 6.3.3 and after some algebraic simplifications we have

$$\begin{aligned} \xi_i = \operatorname{Var}(W_j^{(i)}) = p^{-2}(1-p)^{-2}[2p(p-1) + 2 \sum_{k \neq \ell} \sum \rho_{k\ell}^{(i)^2} \\ + 4(p-2) \sum_{\ell \neq s} \sum \rho_{\ell s}^{(i)} + 4 \sum_{k \neq \ell \neq s} \sum \sum \rho_{k\ell}^{(i)} \rho_{ks}^{(i)} \\ - \sum_{k \neq \ell \neq s \neq r} \sum \sum \sum \rho_{k\ell}^{(i)} \rho_{rs}^{(i)}]. \end{aligned} \tag{6.13}$$

Hence, using the central limit theorem it follows that

$\sqrt{n}(V_i^* - \nu^{(i)})$ (where V_i^* is as defined in (6.9) and $\nu^{(i)}$ is as defined in (6.6)), is asymptotically normal with zero mean and variance ξ_i given by right hand expression of (6.13).

Remark 6.3.2: ξ_i/n, the variance of V_i^* is always less than

$$[4p(p-1)+8p(p-1)(p-2)+p(p-1)(p-2)(p-3)]/np^2(p-1)^2$$
$$= (p+3)(p-3)/np(p-1) .$$

With this background we propose the following selection procedure. For the IZ formulation, select the population which gave rise to the largest V_i. For the SF formulation include Π_i in the subset if $V_i \geq \max_i V_i - h$, where h is a constant given by the procedure for fixed values of n, P^* and p.

Result 6.3.1: *We have, for sufficiently large* n,

$$\text{(6.14)} \quad P(CS|IZ) \geq P[U_i \leq \sqrt{n}\, d(2(p+3)(p-3)/p(p-1))^{-1/2}, \; i = 1,\dots,c-1]$$

where

$$\nu^{(c)} - \nu^{(i)} \geq d, \; i = 1,\dots,c-1$$

and

$$\text{(6.15)} \quad P(CS|SF) \geq P(U_i \leq \sqrt{n}\, h(2(p+3)(p-3)/p(p-1))^{-1/2}, \; i = 1,\dots,c-1)$$

where U_i, $i = 1,\dots,c-1$ *are as defined in* (3.4).

Proof: In view of the asymptotic normality of V_i^*, and remarks 6.3.1 and 6.3.2, the desired result can easily be proved.

6.4. *Procedures based on sum of bivariate rank correlation coefficients.* Analogous to $\nu^{(i)}$ we may define a non-parametric measure of association. Let $\tau_{jk}^{(i)}$ denote the population (bivariate) rank correlation between the jth and the kth co-ordinates of $\underline{X}^{(i)}$ where $\underline{X}^{(i)}$ has c.d.f. F_i, i = 1,...,c. Then define

$$\tau^{(i)} = \sum_{j}^{p} \underset{\neq}{} \sum_{k}^{p} \tau_{j,k}^{(i)}/p(p-1),\ i = 1,\ldots,c\ .$$

$\tau^{(i)}$ may be regarded as a measure of association in multivariate populations. Let $T^{(i)}$ be the corresponding sample value. Clearly

$$T^{(i)} = \sum_{j}^{p} \underset{\neq}{} \sum_{k}^{p} T_{jk}^{(i)}/p(p-1) = [n(n-1)p(p-1)]^{-1}\cdot$$

(6.16)

$$\cdot \sum_{j}^{p} \underset{\neq}{} \sum_{k}^{p} \sum_{\ell}^{n} \underset{\neq}{} \sum_{m}^{n} [2\phi_{jk}^{(i)}(\ell,m)-1]\quad ,$$

where $\phi_{jk}^{(i)}(\ell,m) = 1$ if $(X_{k\ell}^{(i)}, X_{j\ell}^{(i)})'$ is concordant with, $(X_{km}^{(i)} X_{jm}^{(j)})'$ and, is equal to zero otherwise. Towards the sampling distribution of $T^{(i)}$ we have the following result.

Result 6.4.1: $\sqrt{n}(T^{(i)} - ET^{(i)})$ *is asymptotically normal with zero mean and variance given by*

$$\sigma_i^2 = 4[\sum_{k}^{p} \underset{\neq}{} \sum_{j}^{p} \sum_{h}^{p} \underset{\neq}{} \sum_{r}^{p} \theta_{jkhr}^{(i)} - \tau^{(i)^2}]/p^2(p-1)^2$$

where

$$\theta_{jkhr}^{(i)} = E\ \phi_{jk}^{(i)}(\ell,m)\cdot\phi_{hr}^{(i)}(\ell,m'),\ 1 \leq \ell \neq m \neq m' \leq n.$$

Proof: Note that $T^{(i)}$ can be rewritten as a U-statistic with

$$\sum_{k} \underset{\neq}{} \sum_{j} \{2\phi_{jk}^{(i)}(\ell,m) - 1\}/p(p-1)$$

as its symmetric kernel. Hence, the result follows as a direct application of Theorem 7.1 of Hoeffding (1948).

Again, our objective is to choose the population with highest value of $\tau^{(i)}$, $(i = 1,\ldots,c,)$ say $\tau^{(c)}$. We give a two-stage procedure for the IZ formulation, similar to the one in Section 3.3. In stage 1, draw samples of size n from each population and compute

$$\frac{\hat{\sigma}_i^2}{4} = \Big[\sum_{k \neq j}^{p}\sum^{p}\sum_{h \neq r}^{p}\sum^{p} \hat{\theta}_{kjhr}^{(i)} - \hat{\tau}^{(i)^2}\Big]$$

where

$$\hat{\theta}_{kjhr}^{(i)} = \sum{}^{*}(\phi_{kj}^{(i)}(\ell,m)\phi_{hr}^{(i)}(\ell,m'))/n(n-1)(n-2),$$

and $*$ denotes sum over all possible permutations of triplets (ℓ,m,m'), $\ell \neq m \neq m'$, $\ell,m,m' = 1,\ldots,n$. In stage 2 take $N-n$ more observations from each population, where

$$(6.17)\qquad \begin{aligned} N &= \max\{n,\ 2\hat{\sigma}^2\ \eta^2/d_o^2\}; \\ \hat{\sigma}^2 &= \max_i\ \hat{\sigma}_i^2,\quad \tau^{(c)}-\tau^{(i)} \geq d_o,\ i = 1,\ldots,c, \end{aligned}$$

and η is as defined in (3.31). Now compute $T^{(i)}$, $i = 1,\ldots,c$, using all N observations and select the population that gave rise to the largest value of the $T^{(i)}$. Clearly

$$P(CS|IZ) = P\left(U_i \leq \frac{(\tau^{(c)}-\tau^{(i)})\sqrt{N}}{\sqrt{\sigma_i^2 + \sigma_c^2}},\ i = 1,\ldots,c-1\right).$$

Hence using Cramér's lemma (1966), and noting that $2\hat{\sigma}^2 \geq \hat{\sigma}_i^2 + \hat{\sigma}_c^2$, we have

$$P(CS|IZ) \geq P(U_i \leq d_o\sqrt{N}/\sqrt{2\hat{\sigma}^2},\ i = 1,\ldots,c-1).$$

However because of (6.17) $d_o\sqrt{N}/\sqrt{2\hat{\sigma}^2} > \eta$. Therefore, for large N,

(6.18) $$P(CS|IZ) \geq P(U_i \leq \eta,\ i = 1,\ldots,c-1).$$

Alternatively, putting a crude upper bound on σ_i^2, we can give a single-stage procedure. Note that

$$\sigma_i^2 = 4[\sum_{j \neq k}\sum\ \sum_{h \neq r}\sum \theta_{jkhr}^{(i)} - \tau^{(i)^2}]/p^2(p-1)^2 \leq 4.$$

For IZ, select the population which gave rise to the largest value of the $T^{(i)}$.

For SF, include Π_i in the subset if $T^{(i)} \geq \max_i T^{(i)} - h$.

Then the following result can easily be obtained.

Result 6.4.2. *For the procedures based on* $T^{(i)}$ *we have, for sufficiently large* n

$$P(CS|IZ) \geq P(U_i \leq d_o\sqrt{n}/2\sqrt{2},\ i = 1,\ldots,c-1)$$

and

$$P(CS|SF) \geq P(U_i \leq h\sqrt{n}/2\sqrt{2},\ i = 1,\ldots,c-1)\quad .$$

6.5. *Asymptotic Efficiency for the Procedures Proposed in Sections* 6.3 *and* 6.4. Following Lehmann (1963), we let the bivariate correlations and rank correlations go to zero at a suitable rate so that we can replace the variances in each case by their values computed under the assumption that the variables are pairwise independent. The following lemma gives the required 'null' variance of $T^{(i)}$.

Lemma 6.5.1. *When the* p *variates are pairwise independent, for large* n, *the variance of* $T^{(i)}$ *(defined in* (6.16)) *is given by* $8/9np(p-1)$.

Proof. When the variables are pairwise independent, routine computations yield

$$E(T_{k\ell}^{(i)}) = 0, \quad \text{and}$$

$$E(T_{k\ell}^{(i)}\ T_{kr}^{(i)}) = \begin{cases} 16/36n, & \text{if } \ell = r \\ 0, & \text{if } \ell \neq r. \end{cases} \tag{6.19}$$

This completes the indication of the proof of the lemma.

Using Remark 4.1.1 and Lemma 4.1 we obtain

$$\tau^{(c)} - \tau^{(i)} = 2(\nu^{(c)} - \nu^{(i)})/\pi + o(\nu^{(c)}). \tag{6.20}$$

We have the following extension of Result 4.1 to the p-variate situation.

Result 6.5.1: *For sufficiently small values of* $\rho_{jk}^{(i)}$, $j,k = 1,\ldots,p$, $i = 1,\ldots,c$, *the asymptotic efficiency of the procedure based on sum of all bivariate rank correlation coefficients, relative to the one based on sum of all bivariate product-moment correlation coefficients is* $9/\pi^2$, *when the underlying distributions are normal.*

Proof: For the procedure based on the $T^{(i)}$

$$P(CS) = P^* = P\left(U_i \le \frac{\sqrt{n}(2/\pi)(\nu^{(c)} - \nu^{(i)}) + o(\nu^{(c)})\sqrt{n}}{\sqrt{2\sigma^2}},\right. \tag{6.21}$$

$$\left. i = 1,\ldots,c-1\right).$$

where $\sigma^2 = 8/9p(p-1)$. For the procedure based on the V_i,

$$P(CS) = P\left(U_i \le \frac{\sqrt{n^*}(\nu^{(c)} - \nu^{(i)})}{\sqrt{4/p(p-1)}},\ i = 1,\ldots,c-1\right).$$

Therefore, for any common value of $P(CS)$,

$$\lim_{n^*, n \to \infty} \{n^*/n\} = 9/\pi^2, \tag{6.22}$$

which is the same as the corresponding efficiency for the bivariate case, obtained in Result 4.1. Along similar lines the nonparametric procedure proposed in Section 6.2 may also be compared with the parametric procedure proposed in Section 6.3.

Lemma 6.5.2. *If the populations* $\Pi_i (i = 1,...,c)$ *have p-variate normal distributions with zero means, unit variances and correlation matrices given by* $\underline{C}^{(i)} = ((\rho_{jk}^{(i)}))$, *then*

$$(6.23) \quad \theta_i = \frac{1}{2^{p-1}} + \frac{\sum\sum_{i \neq k} \rho_{jk}^{(i)}}{2^{p-1}\pi} \quad p(p-1) + o(\nu^{(i)}), i=1,...,c.$$

Proof:

$$\theta_i = 2P(X_{j\ell}^{(i)} < X_{jm}^{(i)}, \; j = 1,...,p)$$

$$= \int_{[\underline{x}_\ell < \underline{x}_m]} f_\ell^{(i)}(\underline{x}_\ell) \, f_m^{(i)}(\underline{x}_m) d\underline{x}_\ell d\underline{x}_m \quad .$$

Expanding the integrand as Taylor series with respect to its $p(p-1)$ variables around $\rho_{jk}^{(i)} = 0$, $j, k-1,...,p$, $j \neq k$, and performing integration we obtain the approximate expression for θ_i.

Corollary 6.5.1. *We have*

$$\theta_c - \theta_i = \frac{p(p-1)}{2^{p-1}\pi} [\nu^{(c)} - \nu^{(i)}] + o(\nu^{(c)}).$$

Result 6.5.2. *For normal populations with sufficiently small values of* $\rho_{jk}^{(i)}$, $(j \neq k = 1,...,p, \; i = 1,...,c,)$ *the asymptotic efficiency of the procedure (see Section 6.2) based on the p-variate analogue of rank correlation relative to the procedure (see Section 6.4) based on sum of all product-moment correlation coefficients is*

$$(6.24) \qquad p(p-1)3^p/[2^p(2^p+1)-2\cdot 3^p]\pi^2 \quad .$$

Proof. For the first procedure based on samples of size n (large) we have

$$P(CS) \doteq P\left(U_i \le \frac{\sqrt{n}\,p(p-1)}{2^{p-1}\pi} \frac{(\nu^{(c)}-\nu^{(i)})}{\sqrt{2\sigma^2}} + o(\nu^{(c)}-\nu^{(i)}),\quad i = 1,\ldots,c-1\right)$$

where

$$\sigma^2 = \frac{8}{(12)^p}\left[2^p(2^p+1) - 2\cdot 3^p\right] \quad . \tag{6.25}$$

For the normal theory procedure based on samples of size n^* (large) we have

$$P(CS) = P\left(U_i \le \frac{(\nu^{(c)}-\nu^{(i)})\sqrt{n^*}}{\sqrt{4/p(p-1)}},\ i = 1,\ldots,c-1\right).$$

Equating the corresponding upper limits of U_i's we get $\frac{n^*}{n}$ equals the expression in (6.24).

Remark 6.5.2.1. For $p = 2$, (6.24) reduces to $9/\pi^2$ which is the asymptotic relative efficiency for the bivariate situation.

Corollary 6.5.2.1. *For normal populations with sufficiently small bivariate correlations the asymptotic efficiency of the procedure (see Section 6.2) based on* p-*variate analogue of rank correlation relative to the procedure (see Section 6.4) based on sum of simple rank correlations is*

$$p(p-1)3^{p-2}/[2^p(2^p+1)-2\cdot 3^p] \quad . \tag{6.26}$$

Note that the efficiency given by (6.26) is of the order of $p^2(3/4)^p$ which goes to zero as p tends to infinity. Values of the relative efficiency for different values of p are given in Table 6.5.1.

Table 6.5.1

Showing the relative efficiency

given by (6.26) for selected values of p.

p	2	3	4	5	10	25	50
Rel. Efficiency	1	1	.98	.95	.63	.05	.0002

Remark 6.5.2.2. The loss of efficiency in using the T_i (see (6.3)) appears to be due to the fact that the counter function defined in (6.2) takes the value zero even if there is one discordant element in a pair of observations. In the trivariate case, there is only one possible alternative to concordance namely presence of one discordant element, so that the counter function and hence T_i retains all the information. This explains the value unity for $p = 3$.

References

1. Anderson, T.W. (1958). *An Introduction to Multivariate Statistical Analysis*, John Wiley, New York., p.28.

2. Bartlett, N.S. and Govindarajulu, Z. (1968). Some distribution-free statistics and their application to the selection problem. *Annals of the Institute of Statistical Mathematics*, 20, 79-97.

3. Bechhofer, R.E., Dunnett, C.W. and Sobel, M. (1954). A two-sample multiple decision procedure. *Biometrika*, 41, 170-176.

4. Bhuchongkul, S. (1964). A class of nonparametric tests for independence in bivariate populations. *Ann. Math. Statist.*, 35, 138-149.

5. Cramér, H. (1966). *Mathematical Methods in Statistics*. Princeton University Press, Princeton, N.J. p. 254.

6. Gnanadesikan, M. and Gupta, S.S. (1970). A selection procedure for multi-variate normal distributions in terms of the generalized variances. *Technometrics*, 12, 103-118.

7. Gupta, S.S. (1956). *On a decision rule for a problem in ranking means.* Univ. of North Carolina, Institute of Statistics, Mimeo Series No. 150.

8. Gupta, S.S. (1963). Probability integrals of multi-variate normal and multi-variate t. *Ann. Math. Statist.* 34, 792-828.

9. Gupta, S.S. and Panchapakesan, S. (1969). Some selection and ranking procedures for multivariate normal populations. *Multivariate Analysis-II* (P.R.Krishnaiah,ed.) Academic Press, New York, 475-505.

10. Hájek, J. and Sidák, Z. (1967). *Theory of Rank Tests.* Academic Press, New York, p.111.

11. Hoeffding, W. (1947). On the distribution of the rank correlation coefficient tau when the variables are not independent. *Biometrika,* 36, 183-196.

12. Hoeffding, W. (1948). A class of statistics with asymptotically normal distributions. *Ann. Math. Statist.* 19, 293-325.

13. Kendall, M.G. and Stuart, A. (1963). *The Advanced Theory of Statistics,* London, Griffin Vol. 1, p.390.

14. Kendall, M.G. and Stuart, A. (1967). *The Advanced Theory of Statistics,* Hafner, New York, Vol. II , p.342.

15. Lehmann, E.L. (1963). A class of selection procedures based on ranks. *Math. Annalen,* 150, 268-275.

16. Moran, P.A.P. (1951). Partial and multiple rank correlation. *Biometrika,* 38, 26-32.

17. Noether, G.E. (1967). *Elements of Nonparametric Statistics,* John Wiley and Sons, New York, p. 70.

18. Parzen, E. (1962). On estimation of a probability density function and mode. *Ann. Math. Statist.* 33, 1065-1076.

19. Wilks, S.S. (1962). *Mathematical Statistics,* John Wiley and Sons, New York, p. 276.

SAMPLE SIZE FOR SELECTION

By Edward J. Dudewicz* and Nicholas A. Zaino, Jr.
The University of Rochester

1. *Introduction.* Dudewicz (1969); Ramberg (1969); Bechhofer, Kiefer, and Sobel (BKS) (1968); and Siegmund and Robbins (1968) have given approximations to the sample size $n(k,\lambda^*,P^*)$ needed by the ranking and selection procedure of Bechhofer (1954), under various conditions: $P^* \to 1$ (Dudewicz; BKS), $k \to \infty$ (Siegmund and Robbins). (Some extensions of Dudewicz's results are derived in Section 5.) Several of these approximations also hold for more general problems than that considered by Bechhofer (1954); e.g. that of Dudewicz (1969) holds for selection from a multivariate normal population. All might be used in circumstances other than those for which they were derived, due to lack of tables and as a quick method. In this paper we numerically compare the approximations for various ranges of k,P^* in order to obtain the small-sample ranges of these variables where each of the approximations is best. Some analytic comparisons are also made, but in practical problems these are suspect unless corroborated by small-sample studies. Thus, the numerical comparisons are to be regarded as most

---

*This author's research was supported by ONR contract N00014-68A-0091 and by NSF Grant GP-8958. "This research is supported in whole or in part by the Center for Naval Analyses of the University of Rochester. Such support does not imply endorsement of the content by The Navy."

meaningful for practice, while the analytic comparisons are useful for theory.

2. *Definitions and Notation.* Although these approximations (Ramberg's are more appropriately called bounds) for required sample size apply to many problems (e.g., see BKS (1968), Dudewicz (1969), McDonald (1970), Ramberg (1970), and Tong (1969)), we will discuss them in the terms of Bechhofer (1954):

Given k populations $\pi_1,\ldots,\pi_k$ the observations from which are normally distributed with respective unknown means $\mu_1,\ldots,\mu_k$ and a common known variance σ^2, the problem is to select any one of the (at least one) populations associated with $\mu_{[k]} = \max(\mu_1,\ldots,\mu_k)$. Take N independent observations from each population and choose the population which yields the largest sample mean as being associated with $\mu_{[k]}$. Let $\{\lambda^*,P^*\}$ $(0 < \lambda^* < \infty,\ 1/k < P^* < 1)$ be two specified constants, and denote the ranked means by $\mu_{[1]} \leq \cdots \leq \mu_{[k]}$. Then N is to be set as the smallest sample size which guarantees the following probability requirement: We are to select the population associated with $\mu_{[k]}$, i.e. we are to make a correct selection (CS), with probability $P(CS) \geq P^*$ whenever $\mu_{[k]} - \mu_{[k-1]} \geq \lambda^*\sigma$.

All logarithms in this paper are to the base e unless otherwise noted. $\Phi^{-1}(\cdot)$ is the inverse of the standard normal (univariate) distribution function. The approximations considered are those of

Dudewicz (1969):

$$N_1 = \frac{-4}{(\lambda^*)^2} \log(1-P^*) \quad ;$$

Ramberg (1969, 1970):

$$N_2 = \frac{2}{(\lambda^*)^2}\left[\Phi^{-1}\left(\frac{1-P^*}{k-1}\right)\right]^2 ,$$

$$N_3 = \frac{2}{(\lambda^*)^2}\left[\Phi^{-1}\left((P^*)^{\frac{1}{k-1}}\right)\right]^2 ;$$

Bechhofer-Kiefer-Sobel (1968):

$$N_4 = \frac{1}{(\lambda^*)^2}\left\{4 \log\left\{\frac{k-1}{1-P^*}\right\} - 2 \log \log\left\{\frac{k-1}{1-P^*}\right\} - 2 \log 4\pi\right\}; \text{ and}$$

Siegmund and Robbins (1968):

$$N_5 = \frac{2 \log (k-1)}{(\lambda^*)^2} .$$

The authors of N_1, N_2, N_3, N_4, N_5 have proven the following properties:
$\lim_{P^*\to 1} N_1/N = 1$, $\lim_{P^*\to 1} |N_4 - N| = 0$ (and hence $\lim_{P^*\to 1} N_4/N = 1$), and $\lim_{k\to\infty} N_5/N = 1$. Note that Siegmund and Robbins (1968), p.274, give $(k-1)N_5$ as their approximation; this is in error and their suggested method of derivation of an approximation yields N_5 (this also affects the comparison they give, on p.277, of their procedure with that of Bechhofer (1954)). The small-sample results obtained below were not obvious a priori, but are of obvious practical use; the large-sample results may be useful for theory. It is surprising to note that N_1 does so well in comparison with N_4, since the latter incorporates higher-order terms; in effect, for all k and P^* of practical use with $k \geq 7$, the higher-order terms are insufficient to "cut down" the effect of the $4 \log (k-1)$ term until P^* is very close to 1. (Essentially -- see Section 4 -- N_4 needs to be, for example, multiplied by $a(k,P^*)$ such that $a(k,P^*) \to 1$ as $P^* \to 1$

while $a(k,P^*) \to 1/2$ as $k \to \infty$.)

3. *Numerical Comparisons.* $N_1,\ldots,N_5$ (see Section 2) were used to approximate the sample size N required by the ranking and selection procedure of Bechhofer (1954) for various values of $k \geq 3$ and $\frac{1}{k} \leq P^* < 1$. (For $k = 2$, it can easily be seen that N_2 and N_3 give exact results.) For each (P^*,k) the five approximations were compared to the value of N obtained from Table II of Milton (1963). The approximation numerically closest to N was noted; these results are given in Figure 1. (The comparisons were made with λ^* equal to 1, since the approximation closest to N when $\lambda^* = 1$ is also closest for $\lambda^* \neq 1$.) Values of P^* were selected to correspond to entries in Table II of Milton (1963).

In Figure 1, one finds that: (a) N_2 does not appear as best for any (P^*,k) combination. This phenomenon can be explained by the observation (see Section 4) that N_3 is uniformly better than N_2. (b) N_5 appears in Figure 1 only in isolated spots. Since N_5 does not depend on P^*, its value for any particular value of k will be exactly N for only one value of P^*. (Similarly if one replaces N_5 by N_1, P^* by k, and k by P^*.) This indicates that approximation N_5 will not be useful for the situations we are considering. It may be useful in asymptotic $(k \to \infty)$ theory. (c) For $k \leq 6$, approximations N_3 and N_4 dominate the others with N_3 being best for "small" and "very large" P^* and N_4 being best for "moderate" P^*. For $6 < k \leq 25$, N_1 dominates the others for most values of P^* with N_4 being best for "large" P^*.

In order to take account of situations in which one might want an approximation that is conservative (i.e., greater than or equal to N), another comparison was performed. For various (P^*,k,λ^*), approximations N_1, N_3 and N_4 were rounded up to the next greatest integer and then compared to the rounded up value of N, N^+. The "best" approximation was defined as the one closest to, and greater than or equal to, N^+. The results are given in Figures 2 through 5; since in many instances two or three of the approximations gave the same result, the best approximations are there denoted by:

Symbol	Approximation(s)	Symbol	Approximation(s)
1	N_1	5	N_1 and N_4
2	N_3	6	N_3 and N_4
3	N_1 and N_3	7	N_1 and N_3 and N_4
4	N_4		

Some of the data used to generate Figures 1 through 5 is given in Table 1. From this table one can see the values of the 5 approximations and N for $\lambda^* = 1$ and representative values of k and P^*.

In Figures 2 - 5 one finds that: (a) Symbol 7 dominates for all P^* and all k when λ^* is large (≥ 2). This phenomenon is explained by noting that for large λ^* the values of N, N_1, N_3 and N_4 are all less than 1. When rounded up to the next greatest integer, all the approximations are judged as best. (b) For $\lambda^* < 2$, N_3 and N_4 dominate N_1 for small $k (k \leq 6)$. For moderate k (i.e. $k = 10$), the situation is reversed and N_1 dominates the others. For large $k (k = 25)$, N_3 and N_4 again dominate N_1 except when $P^* \leq 0.15 + 0.20\lambda^*$.

With the difficulty of setting λ^*, P^* to begin with (a difficulty at least comparable to that of setting the level of a test), one may rather just be close to N. In this case use of Figure 1 is indicated, and as a quick method use of approximation N_1 (which requires only a slide-rule) is recommended.

4. *Analytic Comparisons.* For $k = 2$, it can easily be seen that N_2 and N_3 are identical and are equal to N. For $k \geq 3$, N_2 and N_3 are conservative, i.e. both are greater than or equal to N; this can be established using the Bonferroni and Slepian inequalities (see Ramberg (1970)). We will now prove that N_3 is always less than N_2 for $\frac{1}{k} \leq P^* < 1$ and $k \geq 3$, and that thus (in terms still of Bechhofer (1954)) N_3 is uniformly better than N_2. This result is hinted without proof in Ramberg (1970), and we have since learned that a proof different than ours is given by Ramberg (1969), p.94. (Note that on p.95 of Ramberg (1969), the factor "2" in approximations (C.1) and (C.2) should be "$\sqrt{2}$".)

To show $N_3 < N_2$ it suffices to show that for $\frac{1}{k} \leq P < 1$, $k = 3,4,\ldots$

$$(1) \qquad \left[\Phi^{-1}\left(P^{\frac{1}{k-1}}\right)\right]^2 < \left[\Phi^{-1}\left(\frac{1-P}{k-1}\right)\right]^2 .$$

From the nature of the inverse standard normal distribution function it is sufficient to show that

$$(2) \qquad \left|P^{\frac{1}{k-1}} - \frac{1}{2}\right| < \left|\frac{1-P}{k-1} - \frac{1}{2}\right| = \frac{1}{2} - \frac{1-P}{k-1} .$$

First note that, for $0 < P < 1$ and $k \geq 3$, $P^{\frac{1}{k-1}}-1 < \frac{P-1}{k-1}$ (this is simply the fact that $(1-b)^x < 1 - xb$ with $0 < x = (k-1)^{-1} \leq 1/2$ and $1 > b = 1 - P > 0$). Hence,

$$(3) \qquad P^{\frac{1}{k-1}} - \frac{1}{2} < \frac{1}{2} - \frac{1-P}{k-1} \quad .$$

Now, $k < 2^{k-1} \Rightarrow P \geq k^{-1} > 2^{-(k-1)} \Rightarrow P^{(k-1)^{-1}} > 1/2$, and (3) becomes

$$\left| P^{\frac{1}{k-1}} - \frac{1}{2} \right| < \frac{1}{2} - \frac{1-P}{k-1} \quad ;$$

hence (1) is true and $N_3 < N_2$.

<u>$P^* \to 1$</u>. Comparisons of N_5 with N, N_1, N_3, N_4 as $P^* \to 1$ are simple since N_5 is constant while the others each $\to +\infty$. Relationships proven by the authors of N_1, N_4 relate them to N as $P^* \to 1$ (see the end of Section 2). One easily shows (using a change of variable and ℓ'Hospital's rule) that $\lim_{P^* \to 1} N_3/N_1 = 1$. The limits of N_1/N_4, N_3/N_4, N_3/N then follow (e.g. $\lim_{P^*\to 1} N_1/N_4 = (\lim_{P^*\to 1} N_1/N)(\lim_{P^*\to 1} N/N_4)$).

<u>$k \to \infty$</u>. Comparison of N_1 with N, N_3, N_4, N_5 as $k \to \infty$ is simple since N_1 is constant while the others each $\to +\infty$. A relationship proven by Siegmund and Robbins (1968) relates N_5 to N as $k \to \infty$ (see the end of Section 2). One easily shows (by forming the ratio and taking the limit as $k \to \infty$) that $N_4/N_5 \to 2$; hence (using the previously given relation $N_5/N \to 1$) $N_4/N \to 2$. By multiple uses of changes of variable and ℓ'Hospital's rule, one finds $N_3/N_5 \to 2$; hence also $N_3/N \to 2$ and $N_3/N_4 \to 1$.

Although, since N_1 does not depend on k and $N_1/N \to 0$ as $k \to \infty$ one would expect it to be a poor approximation for large k, in the numerical comparisons we saw that for $k = 25$ (the largest k considered here) N_1 was "best" for a large range of values of P^*. The above analytic comparisons are summarized in Table 2.

5. *Extensions of Dudewicz's Results.* Let $f(\underline{x}|P_1)$ be the pdf of a $(k-1)$-dimensional normal distribution with zero means, unit variances, and correlation matrix P_1. Consider the integral, for $\delta > 0$,

$$(4) \qquad \int_{-\delta}^{\infty} \cdots \int_{-\delta}^{\infty} f(\underline{x}|P_1)\,dx_1 \ldots dx_{k-1} = \alpha(\delta), \text{ say.}$$

Assume that no element of P_1 is a function of δ. Note that $\alpha(\delta)$ is an increasing function of δ and $\alpha(\delta) \to 1$ as $\delta \to \infty$. Dudewicz (1969) proved the following

Theorem. *For large* α *(near* 1), *an approximation to* δ, *which satisfies the equation*

$$(5) \qquad \int_{-\delta}^{\infty} \cdots \int_{-\delta}^{\infty} f(\underline{x}|P_1)\,dx_1 \ldots dx_{k-1} = \alpha,$$

is $\delta^2 \sim -2 \log (1-\alpha)$. *The ratio tends to* 1 *as* $\alpha \to 1$. *This approximation is independent of* k.

This theorem was then applied to obtain approximations to sample size for a number of problems.

Let $c_1, \ldots, c_{k-1}$ be any $k-1$ fixed positive numbers. Below we extend theorem (5).

Theorem. *For large* α *(near* 1), *an approximation to* δ, *which satisfies the equation*

$$(6) \qquad \int_{-c_1\delta}^{\infty} \cdots \int_{-c_{k-1}\delta}^{\infty} f(\underline{x}|P_1)\,dx_1 \ldots dx_{k-1} = \alpha,$$

is $\delta^2 \sim (-2\ell n(1-\alpha))/(\min(c_1, \ldots, c_{k-1}))^2$. *The ratio tends to* 1 *as* $\alpha \to 1$. *This approximation depends on* k *only through* $\min(c_1, \ldots, c_{k-1})$.

Proof:

$$(7) \qquad \alpha(\delta) = \int_{-c_1\delta}^{\infty} \cdots \int_{-c_{k-1}\delta}^{\infty} f(\underline{x}|P_1)\,dx_1 \ldots dx_{k-1}$$

$$= P[\bigcap_{i=1}^{k-1} \{Z_i > -c_i\delta\}] = P[\bigcap_i E_i],$$

say. Then,

$$(8) \qquad 1-\alpha(\delta) = P[\bigcup_i \bar{E}_i] \leq (k-1)\Phi(-c_{[1]}\delta).$$

Also,

$$(9) \qquad 1-\alpha(\delta) \geq \Phi(-c_{[1]}\delta).$$

Hence,

$$(10) \quad -2\ell n(k-1)-2\ell n\Phi(-c_{[1]}\delta) \leq -2\ell n(1-\alpha) \leq -2\ell n\Phi(-c_{[1]}\delta);$$

the theorem follows upon dividing (10) by $c_{[1]}^2\delta^2$ and taking the limit as $\alpha \to 1$ (hence $\delta \to \infty$).

This result has implications for ranking and selection; e.g., in Dudewicz (1969), one can go from equation (13) without the lower bound to equation (15) for the sample size N (and not for an upper bound $\bar{N}$ for N).

Note that a constructive proof of theorem (6) can be given along the lines of Dudewicz (1969), but is considerably more complex than the proof given above.

Acknowledgment. The authors wish to thank Dr. Gary C. McDonald and the referee for their comments on preliminary versions of this paper.

References

1. Bechhofer, R. E. (1954). "A single-sample multiple decision procedure for ranking means of normal populations with known variances", *Annals of Mathematical Statistics*, Vol. 25, pp. 16-39.

2. Bechhofer, R. E., Kiefer, J. and Sobel, M. (1968). *Sequential Identification and Ranking Procedures* (with special reference to Koopman-Darmois populations), University of Chicago Press, Chicago, Illinois.

3. Dudewicz, E. J. (1969). "An approximation to the sample size in selection problems", *Annals of Mathematical Statistics*, Vol. 40, pp. 492-497.

4. McDonald, G. C. (1970). "On approximating constants for certain selection procedures", this volume.

5. Milton, R. C. (1963). "Tables of the equally correlated multivariate normal probability integral", Technical Report No. 27, Department of Statistics, University of Minnesota.

6. Ramberg, J. S. (1969). "A multiple-decision approach to the selection of the best set of predictor variates", Technical Report No. 79, Department of Operations Research, Cornell University.

7. Ramberg, J. S. (1970). "Selection sample size approximations", unpublished paper.

8. Robbins, H. and Siegmund, D. (1968). "Iterated logarithm inequalities and related statistical procedures", *Mathematics of the Decision Sciences*, Part 2, edited by G. B. Dantzig and A. F. Veinott, Jr., American Mathematical Society, Providence, Rhode Island, pp. 267-279.

9. Tong, Y. L. (1969). "On partitioning a set of normal populations by their locations with respect to a control", *Annals of Mathematical Statistics*, Vol. 40, pp. 1300-1324.

SAMPLE SIZE FOR SELECTION

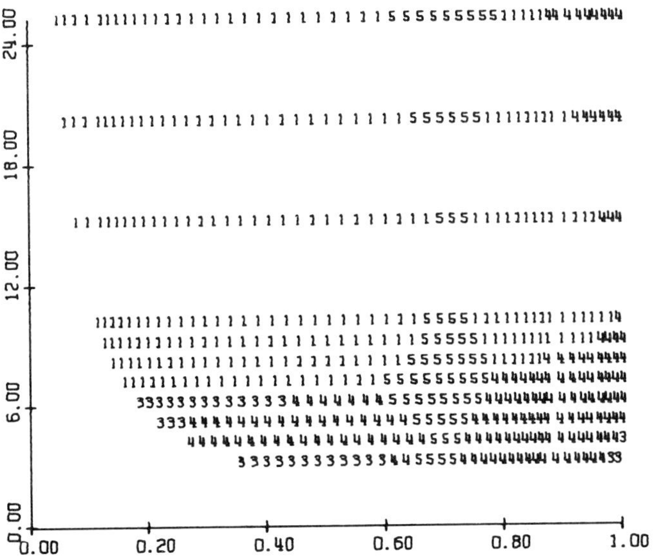

Figure 1

Fig. 1 Best approximation to sample size.

Number of Populations k

Probability Requirement P*

Code

1 for N_1

3 for N_3

4 for N_4

5 for N_5

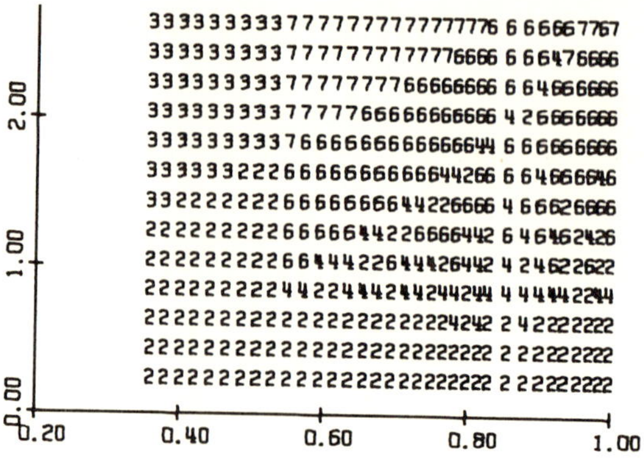

Figure 2

Fig. 2 Best approximation $\geq N^+$ for k = 3.
Indifference Zone λ^*
Probability Requirement P^*

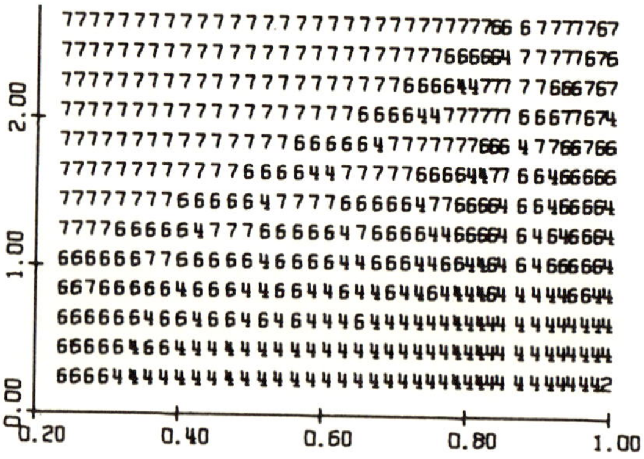

Figure 3

Fig. 3 Best approximation $\geq N^+$ for k = 5.
Indifference Zone λ^*
Probability Requirement P^*

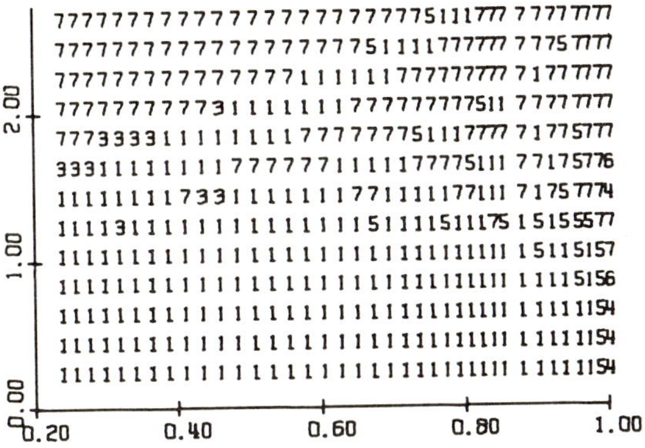

Figure 4

Fig. 4 Best approximation $\geq N^{+}$ for $k = 10$.

Indifference Zone λ^*

Probability Requirement P^*

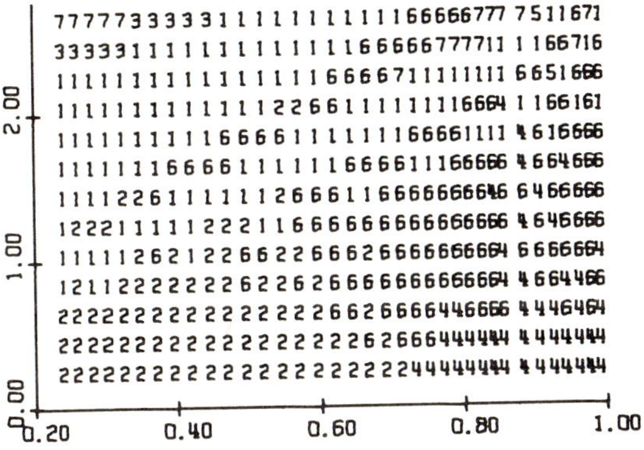

Figure 5

Fig. 5 Best approximation $\geq N^{+}$ for $k = 25$.

Indifference Zone λ^*

Probability Requirement P^*

Table 1

Comparison of Approximations, $\lambda^* = 1$

	p^*	N	N_1	N_2	N_3	N_4	N_5
k = 3	.50282283	0.32000	2.79524	0.92191	0.60667	-0.15564	1.38629
	.61009258	0.84500	3.76738	1.47846	1.20392	0.49465	
	.70922334	1.62000	4.94080	2.23204	2.01342	1.33801	
	.74520359	2.00000	5.46916	2.59362	2.39825	1.73387	
	.80940601	2.88000	6.63044	3.42604	3.27513	2.63150	
	.85024100	3.64500	7.59491	4.14941	4.02847	3.40069	
	.90426581	5.12000	9.77042	5.86050	5.78799	5.19522	
	.94817527	7.22000	11.83955	7.56284	7.51863	6.95897	
	.98241192	11.04500	16.16214	11.27344	11.25792	10.76327	
	.99840838	19.84500	25.77201	19.93882	19.93736	19.55221	1.38629
k = 4	.50376083	0.72000	2.80279	1.89132	1.36557	0.96038	2.19722
	.61499277	1.44500	3.81797	2.57324	2.15552	1.71167	
	.71701484	2.42000	5.04944	3.45615	3.14397	2.66370	
	.75373126	2.88000	5.60533	3.87061	3.59738	3.10519	
	.80352795	3.64500	6.50894	4.56167	4.34190	3.83578	
	.85937624	4.80500	7.84667	5.61758	5.45859	4.94206	
	.90317095	6.12500	9.33923	6.83275	6.72207	6.20452	
	.94861153	8.40500	11.87337	8.96346	8.90373	8.39998	
	.98079491	12.00500	15.81032	12.39215	12.36932	11.90347	
	.99803070	20.48000	24.92031	20.64868	20.64626	20.26912	2.19722
k = 5	.49040918	0.98000	2.69659	2.59363	1.92681	1.73388	2.77259
	.60465162	1.80500	3.71195	3.31895	2.80417	2.51688	
	.71000380	2.88000	4.95155	4.24820	3.87176	3.50514	
	.74798646	3.38000	5.51309	4.68205	4.35502	3.96245	
	.79950493	4.20500	6.42786	5.40320	5.14286	4.71827	
	.85721097	5.44500	7.78555	6.50133	6.31535	5.86112	
	.90231150	6.84500	9.30389	7.76140	7.63348	7.16373	
	.95442865	9.68000	12.35390	10.36954	10.30907	9.84012	
	.98126195	13.00500	15.90880	13.50219	13.47693	13.03269	
	.99846942	22.44500	25.92843	22.64715	22.64502	22.28585	2.77259
k = 6	.51642036	1.44500	2.90616	3.38257	2.67347	2.58500	3.21888
	.60876504	2.20500	3.75379	4.01556	3.45089	3.25896	
	.69498596	3.12500	4.74959	4.78277	4.34767	4.06832	
	.75326523	3.92000	5.59777	5.45305	5.10317	4.77033	
	.80482013	4.80500	6.53533	6.20918	5.93338	5.55787	
	.84908318	5.78000	7.56411	7.05456	6.85148	6.43402	
	.90663723	7.60500	9.48505	8.66921	8.53716	8.09784	
	.95187229	10.12500	12.13559	10.95713	10.88851	10.44043	
	.98029797	13.52000	15.70813	14.12072	14.09226	13.66112	
	.99811668	22.44500	25.09888	22.70566	22.70286	22.34487	3.21888

Table 1, (Cont'd.)

	P*	N	N_1	N_2	N_3	N_4	N_5
k = 10	.50346522	2.20500	2.80041	5.09866	4.20978	4.39968	4.39445
	.59927344	3.12500	3.65790	5.78291	5.09097	5.11441	
	.68905319	4.20500	4.67253	6.60858	6.08645	5.97231	
	.74975003	5.12000	5.54118	7.32733	6.91370	6.71590	
	.80333041	6.12500	6.50492	8.13589	7.81459	7.54946	
	.84914370	7.22000	7.56571	9.03767	8.79315	8.47613	
	.90821425	9.24500	9.55319	10.75521	10.60736	10.23423	
	.95387014	12.00500	12.30518	13.18147	13.10708	12.70663	
	.98179705	15.68000	16.02469	16.52691	16.49731	16.10134	
	.99891694	26.64500	27.31186	26.96685	26.96504	26.63867	4.39445
k = 15	.50118717	2.88000	2.78210	6.50756	5.53197	5.86758	5.27811
	.59884710	3.92000	3.65365	7.22728	6.47708	6.61255	
	.69028677	5.12000	4.68843	8.09439	7.53517	7.50674	
	.75194929	6.12500	5.57649	8.84810	8.40918	8.28156	
	.80618879	7.22000	6.56348	9.69486	9.35714	9.14979	
	.85234378	8.40500	7.65147	10.63806	10.38357	10.11455	
	.90127913	10.12500	9.26184	12.05041	11.88176	11.55542	
	.95051092	13.00500	12.02401	14.51026	14.42603	14.05663	
	.98325005	17.40500	16.35744	18.44153	18.41286	18.03894	
	.99949769	31.20500	30.38517	31.52781	31.52693	31.22766	5.27811
k = 20	.50117245	3.38000	2.78198	7.51901	6.50060	6.91376	5.88888
	.59986910	4.50000	3.66385	8.26083	7.48298	7.67802	
	.69216573	5.78000	4.71277	9.15403	8.57825	8.59550	
	.75427196	6.84500	5.61412	9.92989	9.48045	9.39041	
	.80875579	8.00000	6.61682	10.80100	10.45716	10.28100	
	.85496035	9.24500	7.72299	11.77071	11.51318	11.27038	
	.90370950	11.04500	9.36154	13.22173	13.05254	12.74757	
	.95233861	14.04500	12.17453	15.74661	15.66332	15.31070	
	.98420178	18.60500	16.59143	19.77738	19.74966	19.38912	
	.99566398	23.80500	21.76319	24.57155	24.56387	24.22596	5.88888
k = 25	.51466857	3.92000	2.89169	8.39830	7.38890	7.81941	6.35611
	.61353026	5.12000	3.80281	9.17502	8.41051	8.61702	
	.70513026	6.48000	4.88489	10.10753	9.54670	9.57217	
	.74669685	7.22000	5.49267	10.63561	10.16137	10.11205	
	.80260289	8.40500	6.49015	11.50830	11.14573	11.00284	
	.85015310	9.68000	7.59256	12.82747	12.58230	12.34655	
	.90045483	11.52000	9.22858	13.93712	13.75905	13.47464	
	.95075156	14.58000	12.04351	16.47439	16.38695	16.04815	
	.98373281	19.22000	16.47442	20.25128	22.23304	21.88653	
	.99556561	24.50000	21.67346	25.36055	25.35259	25.02094	6.35611

Table II

Comparison of Approximations, $k\to\infty$, $P^*\to 1$

	N_1	N_3	N_4	N_5
N_3	$\lim_{k\to\infty} \frac{N_1}{N_3} = 0$ $\lim_{P^*\to 1} \frac{N_1}{N_3} = 1$			
N_4	$\lim_{k\to\infty} \frac{N_1}{N_4} = 0$ $\lim_{P^*\to 1} \frac{N_1}{N_4} = 1$	$\lim_{k\to\infty} \frac{N_3}{N_4} = 1$ $\lim_{P^*\to 1} \frac{N_3}{N_4} = 1$		
N_5	$\lim_{k\to\infty} \frac{N_1}{N_5} = 0$ $\lim_{P^*\to 1} \frac{N_1}{N_5} = +\infty$	$\lim_{k\to\infty} \frac{N_3}{N_5} = 2$ $\lim_{P^*\to 1} \frac{N_3}{N_5} = +\infty$	$\lim_{k\to\infty} \frac{N_4}{N_5} = 2$ $\lim_{P^*\to 1} \frac{N_4}{N_5} = +\infty$	
N	$\lim_{k\to\infty} \frac{N_1}{N} = 0$ $\lim_{P^*\to 1} \frac{N_1}{N} = 1$	$\lim_{k\to\infty} \frac{N_3}{N} = 2$ $\lim_{P^*\to 1} \frac{N_3}{N} = 1$	$\lim_{k\to\infty} \frac{N_4}{N} = 2$ $\lim_{P^*\to 1} \frac{N_4}{N} = 1$	$\lim_{k\to\infty} \frac{N_5}{n} = 1$ $\lim_{P^*\to 1} \frac{N_5}{N} = 0$

OPTIMAL CONFIDENCE INTERVALS FOR THE LARGEST LOCATION PARAMETER

By Edward J. Dudewicz[1] and Yung Liang Tong[2]

University of Rochester and University of Nebraska

Summary. Suppose that $\Pi_1, \Pi_2, \ldots, \Pi_k$ are k given populations $(k \geq 1)$ with location parameters $\theta_1, \theta_2, \ldots, \theta_k$, respectively, T is an appropriate statistic with density $g(y,\theta) = g(y-\theta)$, and $t_1, t_2, \ldots, t_k$ is the set of observed T values from $\Pi_1, \Pi_2, \ldots, \Pi_k$, respectively. In this paper we consider an optimal confidence interval of the form $I = (t^*-(L-d), t^*+d)$ for the largest location parameter $\theta^* = \max_{1 \leq i \leq k} \theta_i$ based on $t^* = \max_{1 \leq i \leq k} t_i$. Under certain assumptions on g we have obtained a general least favorable (LF) configuration for I. For a given L (the length of I), we have proved that the d value which maximizes the coverage probability of I under the LF configuration is equal to $\frac{L}{2}$ for $k = 1,2$ and less than $\frac{L}{2}$ for $k > 2$. Tables are given, for normal populations, of this optimal value of d and the corresponding coverage probabilities.

1. *Introduction*. We first introduce some notations. $\mathcal{F} = \{F(x,\theta) = F(x-\theta) : \theta \in \Omega\}$ is a location parameter family where Ω is an interval on the real line. $\Pi_1, \Pi_2, \ldots, \Pi_k$

[1]This author's research was supported by ONR Contract N00014-68A-0091 and by NSF Grant GP-8958.

[2]This author's research was supported by the Nebraska Research Council.

are k populations $(k \geq 1)$ with distributions $F(x,\theta_i) \in \mathcal{F}$ $(i = 1,2,\ldots,k)$. For fixed n let $\{X_j\},\{X_{ij}\}$ $(j = 1,2,\ldots,n)$ be independent random variables with distributions $F(x,\theta)$ and $F(x,\theta_i)$, respectively. Let T be an appropriate statistic and let

$$t = T(X_1,X_2,\ldots,X_n) \ , \tag{1.1}$$

$$t_i = T(X_{i1}, X_{i2},\ldots, X_{in}) \ (i=1,2,\ldots,k). \tag{1.2}$$

We assume that the distribution of t belongs to a location parameter family, and denote the distribution function and the density function of t by $G_n(y,\theta) = G(y-\theta)$ and $g_n(y,\theta) = g(y-\theta)$, respectively.

Let

$$\theta^* = \max_{1\leq i\leq k} \theta_i \tag{1.3}$$

denote the largest location parameter of the k populations. Estimation of θ^* based on $(t_1,t_2,\ldots,t_k)$ has been considered by several authors. Blumenthal and Cohen [1], [2] considered point estimation of θ^* for the case $k = 2$, and investigated the bias and mean squared error of some symmetric and invariant estimators. Construction of two-sided and one-sided confidence intervals for θ^* based on

$$t^* = \max_{1\leq i\leq k} t_i \tag{1.4}$$

was considered by Saxena and Tong [8], Dudewicz [3], [4], Tong [9] and others.

The two-sided confidence intervals for θ^* considered by Saxena and Tong were symmetric in that for fixed $L > 0$ the confidence interval (of length L) has the form

(1.5) $$I' = (t^* - \frac{L}{2},\ t^* + \frac{L}{2}) \ .$$

In most applications t^* is a consistent estimator of θ^*. However, it is known that if $E_\theta t = \theta$, then t^* overestimates θ^* for $k \geq 2$, and the bias increases as k increases ([5]). This suggests that unsymmetric (i.e. not symmetric about t^*) confidence intervals should be considered. If the confidence interval is defined as

(1.6) $$I = (t^* - d_1,\ t^* + d_2) \ ,$$

then under the restriction that $d_1 + d_2 = L$, we can expect I to perform better than I' (in terms of coverage probabilities) when d_2 (or d_1) is chosen properly.

The purpose of this paper is to investigate the behavior of the optimal value of d_2 when the length L of the interval is kept fixed. Under the same conditions imposed on the density function $g(y-\theta)$ by Saxena and Tong, we first obtain a general theorem (Theorem 1) regarding the infimum of the coverage probability over the set of all parameter vectors $\underset{\sim}{\omega}$, where

(1.7) $$\underset{\sim}{\omega} = (\theta_1,\ \theta_2, \ldots,\ \theta_k) \ .$$

(The present theorem covers as special cases the results, for interval estimation of θ^*, regarding least favorable configurations given in [8] and [3].) We then consider the (optimal) value of d_2 which maximizes the infimum of the coverage probability. It is shown (Theorem 3) that this value is $\frac{L}{2}$ when $k = 1$ or 2, and less than $\frac{L}{2}$ for $k \geq 3$. Therefore when $k \geq 3$, the unsymmetric interval I with $d_2 < d_1$ performs better than the symmetric interval I'.

An application of the given method to normal populations is considered in Section 4. The optimal confidence interval, which depends on k and the ratio of L and the common sample standard deviation, is given in Table 1; its corresponding coverage probability is tabulated in Table 2. Comparisons between this optimal confidence interval and the symmetric confidence interval are made; the improvement is significant, especially when k is large.

2. *The Coverage Probability and its Infimum.* We follow the notations of Section 1 and, for the present, assume that d_1, d_2 are arbitrary but fixed with $d_1 + d_2 > 0$. The assumption $d_1 + d_2 = L$ will be made later.

For given $\underset{\sim}{\omega}$ let $\beta_{\underset{\sim}{\omega}}(d_1, d_2)$ denote the probability that I covers θ^*; then

$$\begin{aligned} \beta_{\underset{\sim}{\omega}}(d_1,d_2) &= P_{\underset{\sim}{\omega}}[\theta^* \varepsilon I] \\ &= P_{\underset{\sim}{\omega}}[t^* \le \theta^* + d_1] - P_{\underset{\sim}{\omega}}[t^* \le \theta^* - d_2] \\ &= \prod_{i=1}^{k} G(\delta_i + d_1) - \prod_{i=1}^{k} G(\delta_i - d_2) \end{aligned} \tag{2.1}$$

where

$$\delta_i = \theta^* - \theta_i \quad (i = 1,2,\ldots, k) \tag{2.2}$$

are nonnegative and at least one of the δ_i's is 0. Without loss of generality assume $\delta_k = 0(\theta_k = \theta^*)$. Let $\underset{\sim}{\omega}^o$ be a least favorable (LF) configuration (which depends on d_1 and d_2) satisfying

$$\beta_{\underset{\sim}{\omega}^o}(d_1,d_2) = \inf_{\underset{\sim}{\omega}} \beta_{\underset{\sim}{\omega}}(d_1,d_2) . \tag{2.3}$$

We now state and prove a theorem regarding $\underset{\sim}{\omega}^o$.

Theorem 1. *Suppose that* (a) *the family* $\{g(\underset{\sim}{y},\theta)=g(y-\theta):\theta\varepsilon\Omega\}$ *has monotone likelihood ratio and* (b) $g(y) = g(-y) > 0$ *for all* y. *Then for arbitrary fixed* d_1, d_2 *satisfying* $d_1 + d_2 > 0$ *either*

(2.4) $$\underset{\sim}{\omega}^o = (-\infty, \cdots, -\infty, \theta)$$

or

(2.5) $$\underset{\sim}{\omega}^o = (\theta, \cdots, \theta, \theta),$$

according as $G(d_1) - G(-d_2) <$ *or* $> G^k(d_1) - G^k(-d_2)$; *where* θ *is an arbitrary real number.*

Theorem 1 implies that under the LF configuration $\underset{\sim}{\omega}^o$, the distance between the largest parameter θ^* and the other $k-1$ parameters is either 0 or ∞. To prove this theorem we need the following lemma.

Lemma 1. *Define*

(2.6) $$f(r) = G^r(d_1) - G^r(-d_2) \quad (r = 1,2,\ldots, k).$$

Then under the conditions of Theorem 1, $\min_{1 \leq r \leq k} f(r)$ *is either* $f(1)$ *or* $f(k)$ *or both (but not* $f(r)$ *if* $r \neq 1,k$).

Proof. By symmetry condition (b), $G(y) = 1 - G(-y)$ for every y. Therefore for any $r = 1, 2, \ldots, k-1$,

$$f(r+1) - f(r) = G^r(-d_2)G(d_2) - G^r(d_1)G(-d_1)$$

which is $\begin{matrix} > \\ = \\ < \end{matrix} 0$ according as $\left[\frac{G(-d_2)}{G(d_1)}\right]^r \begin{matrix} > \\ = \\ < \end{matrix} \frac{G(-d_1)}{G(d_2)}$. Since $f(1) = G(d_1) - G(-d_2) > 0$, $\left[\frac{G(-d_2)}{G(d_1)}\right]^r \leq \frac{G(-d_1)}{G(d_2)}$ implies $\left[\frac{G(-d_2)}{G(d_1)}\right]^{r+1} < \frac{G(-d_1)}{G(d_2)}$ and $f(r+1) \leq f(r)$ implies $f(r+2) < f(r+1)$. Hence either $f(1) < f(r)$ for $r = 2,\ldots,k$ or $f(k) < f(r)$ for $r = 1,\ldots,k-1$, hence the lemma.

Proof of the theorem: We give a proof similar to that of Theorem 1 of Saxena and Tong [8]. For $j = 1,\ldots, k-1$

consider

$$\frac{\partial}{\partial\delta_j} \beta_{\underset{\sim}{\omega}}(d_1,d_2) = AG(d_1)g(\delta_j+d_1) - BG(-d_2)g(\delta_j-d_2)$$

$$= AG(d_1)g(\delta_j+d_1)\left[1-\frac{BG(-d_2)}{AG(d_1)}\cdot\frac{g(\delta_j-d_2)}{g(\delta_j+d_1)}\right]$$

$$= AG(d_1)g(\delta_j+d_1)\cdot H(\delta_j), \quad \text{say},$$

where

$$A = \prod_{\substack{i=1\\ i\neq j}}^{k-1} G(\delta_i+d_1), \qquad B = \prod_{\substack{i=1\\ i\neq j}}^{k-1} G(\delta_i-d_2) \quad .$$

Since $-d_1 < d_2$ and the family of densities g has monotone likelihood ratio, $H(\delta_j)$ is a monotonically decreasing function of δ_j. Given d_1 and d_2 we have three possibilities: (1) $H(\delta_j) \geq 0$ for every $\delta_j \geq 0$, (2) $H(\delta_j) \leq 0$ for every $\delta_j \geq 0$ and (3) there exists a δ_j' such that $H(\delta_j) \geq 0$ for $\delta_j \leq \delta_j'$ and $H(\delta_j) \leq 0$ for $\delta_j \geq \delta_j'$. Thus, $\beta_{\underset{\sim}{\omega}}(d_1,d_2)$ is minimized at either $\delta_j = 0$ or $\delta_j = \infty$ given $(\delta_1,\ldots,\delta_{j-1},\delta_{j+1},\ldots,\delta_{k-1})$. The rest of the proof follows from Lemma 1.

We note that (2.5) holds when $d_1 = d_2$, which is the two-sided symmetric interval case considered by Saxena and Tong. If $d_1 = \infty$, then (2.4) holds; this reduces to the one-sided interval case considered by Dudewicz.

We now assume that

$$d_1 + d_2 = L \,, \tag{2.7}$$

where the length of the interval $L > 0$ is predetermined. For simplicity of notation we write $d_2 = d$ and $d_1 = L-d$. Then from Theorem 1 the infimum of the coverage probability is

(2.8) $\beta(d) = \beta_{\underset{\sim}{\omega}^{o}}(d) = \min\{[G(L-d)-G(-d)],[G^k(L-d)-G^k(-d)]\}.$

Theorem 2. *Under the conditions of* Theorem 1, (1) *for every* $k \geq 2$ *there exists a* $d' = d'(k,L)$ *such that*

$$\beta(d) = \begin{cases} G(L-d)-G(-d) & \text{if } d < d', \\ G^k(L-d)-G^k(-d) & \text{if } d > d'; \end{cases} \tag{2.9}$$

and (2) $d' = \frac{L}{2}$ *for* $k=2$ *and* $d' < \frac{L}{2}$ *for* $k > 2$.

Proof. Write

$$G^k(L-d)-G^k(-d) = [G(L-d)-G(-d)]Q(d)$$

where

$$Q(d) = \sum_{j=0}^{k-1} G^{(k-1)-j}(L-d)\, G^j(-d);$$

then

$$G(L-d)-G(-d) \underset{>}{\overset{<}{=}} G^k(L-d)-G^k(-d)$$

according as

$$Q(d) \underset{<}{\overset{>}{=}} 1 .$$

Since $Q(-\infty) = k$, $Q(\infty) = 0$ and $Q(d)$ is monotonically decreasing in d, d' is the unique solution of the equation $Q(d) = 1$. This proves (1). To prove (2) we realize that, by the symmetry of g, $G(L-d) + G(-d) \underset{<}{\overset{>}{=}} 1$ according as $d \underset{>}{\overset{<}{=}} \frac{L}{2}$. Hence the case for $k = 2$ is obvious. For $k > 2$ if $d > \frac{L}{2}$, then $Q(d) < [G(L-d)+G(-d)]^{k-1} < 1$ and $G^k(L-d)-G^k(-d) < G(L-d)-G(-d)$. This completes the proof.

3. *The Optimal Confidence Interval.* We now consider the optimal choice of the two-sided confidence interval for θ^*. For convenience we rewrite I as

$$I = (t^* - (L-d),\ t^* + d) \tag{3.1}$$

where $d \in (-\infty,\infty)$ and the length L of I is fixed. Let $d_0 = d_0(k,L)$ satisfy

$$\beta(d_0) = \sup_d \beta(d)\ ; \tag{3.2}$$

then d_0 is that choice of d which maximizes the infimum (over the product parameter space) of the coverage probability of I. We have the following theorem.

Theorem 3. *Under the conditions of* Theorem 1, $d_0 = \frac{L}{2}$ *for* $k = 1, 2$ *and* $d_0 < \frac{L}{2}$ *for* $k > 2$.

Proof: Since the density g is symmetric and strongly unimodal ([6: p. 34]), the theorem is obvious for $k = 1$. For $k = 2$ it follows from Theorem 2 that

$$\beta(d) = \begin{cases} G(L-d)-G(-d) & \text{for } d \le \frac{L}{2}, \\ G^2(L-d)-G^2(-d) & \text{for } d > \frac{L}{2}, \end{cases}$$

and the supremum of $\beta(d)$ is also achieved at $d = \frac{L}{2}$.

To prove this theorem for $k > 2$ we consider the function $G^k(L-d)-G^k(-d)$ and denote its first derivative by

$$\alpha(d) = k[G^{k-1}(-d)g(-d)-G^{k-1}(L-d)g(L-d)]\ .$$

Clearly $\alpha(d) = 0$ iff

$$\frac{G(L-d)}{G(-d)} = \left[\frac{g(d)}{g(d-L)}\right]^{\frac{1}{k-1}}\ . \tag{3.3}$$

It is easy to see that $\frac{g(d)}{g(d-L)}$ is monotonically decreasing in d and is ≤ 1 for $d \ge \frac{L}{2}$; $\frac{G(L-d)}{G(-d)}$ is monotonically increasing in d (by [7]) and is always greater than 1. Therefore there is a unique $d = d''$ (say) satisfying (3.3),

d'' is less than $\frac{L}{2}$, and the function $G^k(L-d)-G^k(-d)$ is monotonically increasing (decreasing) for $d < (>)\ d''$. Since by Theorem 2

$$\beta(d) = G^k(L-d)-G^k(-d) \quad \text{for } d \geq \frac{L}{2} \quad ,$$

it follows that d_0 (the d which maximizes $\beta(d)$) is $< \frac{L}{2}$.

It is easy to see from the above proof that we can restrict our attention to d' and d'' only, and $d_0 = \max(d',d'')$. (Note that $d' \to -\infty$ as $k \uparrow \infty$, and that $d'(k+1) < d'(k)$ iff $G^k(L-d'(k)) < G(d'(k))$.) Therefore for given k,L and family of distributions $\mathfrak{F}$, d_0 can be computed numerically.

Theorem 3 asserts that the symmetric interval is optimal for $k \leq 2$. For $k > 2$, the unsymmetric interval with $d < \frac{L}{2}$ should be used, and t^* should be greater than the midpoint of the interval. The optimal value d_0 in general depends on k,L and the given family of distributions. We show in Section 4 that for normal populations d_0 can be negative when k is large (which means that the entire interval is to the left of t^*). This is consistent with the result in point estimation that t^* overestimates θ^* and the bias increases as k increases.

4. *The Normal Family.* In this section we consider the optimal confidence interval for the largest normal mean with known variances. The case of unknown variances is under investigation and will appear in a later paper.

Let $\Pi_1,\Pi_2,\ldots,\Pi_k$ denote k normal populations with unknown means $\theta_1,\theta_2,\ldots,\theta_k$ and known variances $\sigma_1^2, \sigma_2^2,\ldots,\sigma_k^2$, respectively. After taking n_i

observations from Π_i let t_i denote the sample mean from $\Pi_i (i = 1,2,\ldots, k)$. Assume that $t_1, t_2, \ldots, t_k$ have a common variance

$$\tau^2 = \frac{\sigma_1^2}{n_1} = \ldots = \frac{\sigma_k^2}{n_k} . \tag{4.1}$$

Let t^* be the largest sample mean and let the confidence interval I for the largest mean be as in (3.1). Then the infimum (over the product parameter space) of the coverage probability of I is

$$\beta(d) = \beta(x) = \min\{[\Phi(c-x)-\Phi(-x)],[\Phi^k(c-x)-\Phi^k(-x)]\} \tag{4.2}$$

where

$$c = \frac{L}{\tau}, \quad x = \frac{d}{\tau}, \quad \text{and} \quad \Phi(y) = \int_{-\infty}^{y} (2\pi)^{-1/2} e^{-0.5u^2} du. \tag{4.3}$$

Let x_0 satisfy

$$\beta(x_0) = \sup_x \beta(x) . \tag{4.4}$$

It follows from the general result given in Section 3 that x_0 is either the root of the equation

$$\Phi(c-x)-\Phi(-x)-[\Phi^k(c-x)-\Phi^k(-x)] = 0 \tag{4.5}$$

or the x value where $\Phi^k(c-x)-\Phi^k(-x)$ achieves its maximum. Those x_0 values for $k = 3(1)6(2)14$ and $c = 1.0(0.1)4.0$ are given in Table 1.

To use Table 1 for a given k and L, we compute $c = \frac{L}{\tau}$. For this (k,c) we find the optimal value x_0 from Table 1 and take the interval I to be

$$I = (t^* - (L - \tau \cdot x_0),\ t^* + \tau \cdot x_0) .$$

We note that for the k,c values given in Table 1 x_0 is the root of Equation (4.5). Therefore for those k,c

values the configurations of (2.4) and (2.5) are simultaneously least favorable under the optimal confidence interval. The coverage probability under those configurations is then

$$\Phi(c-x_0) - \Phi(-x_0) = \Phi^k(c-x_0) - \Phi^k(-x_0), \tag{4.6}$$

which is tabulated in Table 2.

We now compare this optimal interval with the symmetric interval. Let P_1 denote the probability given in (4.6) and P_2 denote the coverage probability of the symmetric interval under the LF configuration, namely $\Phi^k(\frac{c}{2}) - \Phi^k(\frac{-c}{2})$. In the following we give P_1 and P_2 values for several selected k and c for the purpose of illustration:

$k = 3$, $c = 1.6$, $P_1 = 0.5684$, $P_2 = 0.4801$;
$k = 12$, $c = 1.6$, $P_1 = 0.4630$, $P_2 = 0.0574$;
$k = 3$, $c = 2.8$, $P_1 = 0.8327$, $P_2 = 0.7762$;
$k = 12$, $c = 2.8$, $P_1 = 0.7632$, $P_2 = 0.3641$;
$k = 3$, $c = 4.0$, $P_1 = 0.9523$, $P_2 = 0.9333$;
$k = 12$, $c = 4.0$, $P_1 = 0.9273$, $P_2 = 0.7587$.

It appears that as k becomes large, P_1 decreases only slightly for fixed c. Therefore the improvement is more significant for large k.

Acknowledgment. The authors wish to thank the referee for his careful reading of the manuscript.

References

1. Blumenthal, S. and Cohen, A. (1968). "Estimation of the Larger of Two Normal Means", *Journal of the American Statistical Association*, 63, 861-876.

2. __________ (1968). "Estimation of the Larger Translation Parameter", *Annals of Mathematical Statistics*, 39, 502-516.

3. Dudewicz, E. J. (1970). "Confidence Intervals for Ranked Means", *Naval Research Logistics Quarterly*, 17, 69-78.

4. __________ (1970). "Two-Sided Confidence Intervals for Ranked Means", submitted for publication.

5. __________ (1970). "Estimation of Ordered Parameters", submitted for publication.

6. Hájek, J. and Sidák, Z. (1967). *Theory of Rank Tests*, Academic Press, N. Y.

7. Saxena, K.M.L. and Savage, I.R. (1969). "Monotonicity of Rank Order Likelihood Ratio", *Annals of the Institute of Statistical Mathematics*, 21, 265-275.

8. Saxena, K.M.L. and Tong, Y. L. (1969). "Interval Estimation of the Largest Mean of k Normal Populations with Known Variances", *Journal of the American Statistical Association*, 64, 296-299.

9. Tong, Y. L. (1970). "Multi-Stage Interval Estimations of the Largest Mean of k Normal Populations", *Journal of the Royal Statistical Society, Series B*, 32, 272-277.

Table 1

Optimal Values of x for the Normal Family

c \ k	3	4	5	6	8	10	12	14
1.0	0.3087	0.1767	0.0767	-0.0033	-0.1263	-0.2188	-0.2926	-0.3537
1.1	0.3596	0.2285	0.1295	0.0504	-0.0709	-0.1620	-0.2345	-0.2945
1.2	0.4105	0.2804	0.1824	0.1043	-0.0152	-0.1047	-0.1758	-0.2346
1.3	0.4614	0.3325	0.2356	0.1586	0.0410	-0.0469	-0.1167	-0.1743
1.4	0.5125	0.3848	0.2891	0.2132	0.0975	0.0113	-0.0571	-0.1136
1.5	0.5636	0.4372	0.3427	0.2680	0.1544	0.0698	0.0028	-0.0526
1.6	0.6148	0.4897	0.3966	0.3231	0.2115	0.1286	0.0629	0.0087
1.7	0.6661	0.5424	0.4507	0.3784	0.2689	0.1877	0.1234	0.0703
1.8	0.7174	0.5953	0.5049	0.4339	0.3266	0.2470	0.1839	0.1319
1.9	0.7688	0.6482	0.5593	0.4896	0.3844	0.3064	0.2447	0.1937
2.0	0.8203	0.7013	0.6139	0.5454	0.4423	0.3659	0.3054	0.2555
2.1	0.8718	0.7545	0.6686	0.6014	0.5004	0.4256	0.3663	0.3173
2.2	0.9234	0.8078	0.7234	0.6575	0.5585	0.4852	0.4271	0.3791
2.3	0.9751	0.8612	0.7783	0.7137	0.6167	0.5449	0.4879	0.4408
2.4	1.0268	0.9147	0.8333	0.7700	0.6750	0.6046	0.5487	0.5025
2.5	1.0786	0.9682	0.8884	0.8263	0.7332	0.6642	0.6094	0.5641
2.6	1.1305	1.0219	0.9435	0.8827	0.7914	0.7237	0.6700	0.6255
2.7	1.1823	1.0755	0.9987	0.9391	0.8496	0.7832	0.7305	0.6869
2.8	1.2343	1.1293	1.0539	0.9954	0.9077	0.8426	0.7909	0.7481
2.9	1.2862	1.1830	1.1091	1.0518	0.9658	0.9019	0.8512	0.8091
3.0	1.3382	1.2368	1.1643	1.1081	1.0237	0.9611	0.9113	0.8700
3.1	1.3902	1.2906	1.2194	1.1643	1.0816	1.0201	0.9712	0.9307
3.2	1.4423	1.3444	1.2746	1.2206	1.1394	1.0791	1.0310	0.9912
3.3	1.4943	1.3982	1.3297	1.2767	1.1970	1.1378	1.0907	1.0516
3.4	1.5464	1.4520	1.3848	1.3328	1.2546	1.1964	1.1501	1.1117
3.5	1.5985	1.5058	1.4398	1.3888	1.3120	1.2549	1.2094	1.1717
3.6	1.6506	1.5595	1.4948	1.4447	1.3693	1.3132	1.2686	1.2315
3.7	1.7027	1.6132	1.5497	1.5005	1.4265	1.3714	1.3275	1.2910
3.8	1.7548	1.6669	1.6045	1.5562	1.4835	1.4294	1.3863	1.3504
3.9	1.8068	1.7205	1.6592	1.6118	1.5404	1.4872	1.4448	1.4096
4.0	1.8589	1.7741	1.7139	1.6673	1.5972	1.5449	1.5032	1.4686

Table 2

Optimal Coverage Probabilities for the Normal Family

c	3	4	5	6	8	10	12	14
1.0	.376540	.364961	.352646	.340827	.319733	.301936	.286838	.273866
1.1	.410896	.398629	.385613	.373142	.350914	.332177	.316280	.302615
1.2	.444367	.431526	.417935	.404936	.381801	.362312	.345775	.331549
1.3	.476899	.463599	.449561	.436157	.412339	.392287	.375264	.380604
1.4	.508442	.494797	.480438	.466754	.442471	.422036	.404675	.389707
1.5	.538952	.525076	.510518	.496673	.472135	.451489	.433933	.418773
1.6	.568392	.554395	.539758	.525863	.501269	.480573	.462953	.447711
1.7	.596731	.582717	.568112	.554274	.529807	.509210	.491647	.476427
1.8	.623943	.610012	.595542	.581860	.557686	.537322	.519926	.504825
1.9	.650009	.636252	.622014	.608574	.584843	.564833	.547710	.532810
2.0	.674917	.661418	.647496	.634375	.611218	.591669	.574906	.560288
2.1	.698658	.685493	.671961	.659228	.636758	.617761	.601437	.587172
2.2	.721233	.708466	.695388	.683100	.661411	.643045	.627229	.613377
2.3	.742644	.730332	.717762	.705965	.685135	.667465	.652214	.638829
2.4	.762901	.751091	.739071	.727801	.707891	.690970	.676332	.663460
2.5	.782019	.770747	.759310	.748594	.729651	.713519	.699533	.687209
2.6	.800015	.789311	.778479	.768336	.750391	.735077	.721772	.710024
2.7	.816914	.806796	.796583	.787025	.770096	.755620	.743015	.731866
2.8	.832742	.823221	.813634	.804663	.788758	.775126	.763238	.752699
2.9	.847529	.838609	.829647	.821262	.806376	.793593	.782421	.772501
3.0	.861308	.852987	.844643	.836835	.822956	.811015	.800559	.791257
3.1	.874116	.866385	.858645	.851402	.838511	.827397	.817647	.808960
3.2	.885990	.878836	.871684	.864989	.853058	.842754	.833696	.825613
3.3	.896970	.890375	.883791	.877624	.866621	.857098	.848716	.841224
3.4	.907098	.901041	.895000	.889340	.879227	.870459	.862729	.855808
3.5	.916415	.910873	.905349	.900171	.890908	.882864	.875759	.869389
3.6	.924965	.919910	.914877	.910155	.901699	.894343	.887835	.881994
3.7	.932790	.928196	.923624	.919333	.911637	.904934	.898993	.893655
3.8	.939934	.935773	.931633	.927745	.920765	.914674	.909270	.904407
3.9	.946438	.942682	.938945	.935434	.929121	.923606	.918706	.914291
4.0	.952346	.948965	.945602	.942441	.936750	.931771	.927342	.923348

NON-OPTIMALITY OF LIKELIHOOD RATIO TESTS FOR SEQUENTIAL DETECTION OF SIGNALS IN GAUSSIAN NOISE

By Bennett Eisenberg
University of New Mexico

Abstract. This paper is motivated by two papers Selin [1964,1965] on the problem of the sequential detection of signals in normal noise. Selin's problem was to construct a decision procedure with given error probabilities and of minimal expected time for the hypotheses signal present and signal absent.

Here, the behaviour of the likelihood ratio test used by Selin is re-examined. It is shown that this test need not be optimal.

1. *The Structure of the Likelihood Ratio as a Stochastic Process.* Let X be a mean zero Gaussian process (signal absent) and let $X + m$ be a process with mean $m(t)$ (signal present) with corresponding measures on path space μ_X and μ_{X+m}. Let H_T denote the Hilbert space spanned by the random variables x_t for t in the set T with underlying measure μ_X. If $m(t)$ can be expressed as $E_X(x_t\psi)$ for some ψ in H_T then μ_X and μ_{X+m} are mutually absolutely continuous with respect to each other and

$$\frac{d\mu_{X+m}}{d\mu_X}(\omega) = e^{\psi(\omega) - \frac{1}{2}||\psi||^2} \quad \text{where} \quad ||\psi||^2 = E_X(\psi^2) .$$

For an elegant proof, see Hida [1970].

Let $S \subset T$ with $m(u) = E(x_u \psi)$ for u in T. Then for u in $S, m(u) = E[x_u \psi] = E[x_u P_S \psi]$, P_S being the projection onto H_S. Thus the likelihood ratio $\Lambda(s,\omega) = d\mu_{x+m}/d\mu_x$ is given by

$$\Lambda(s,\omega) = e^{P_S\psi - \frac{1}{2}||P_S\psi||^2} .$$

Since $\log \Lambda(s,\omega) = P_S\psi - \frac{1}{2}||P_S||^2$, and uncorrelated Gaussian random variables are independent it follows that $\log \Lambda(s,\omega)$ is a Gaussian process with independent increments relative to both μ_x and μ_{x+m}. According to μ_x

$$E(\log \Lambda(s,\omega)) = -\frac{1}{2}||P_S\psi||^2$$

$$\mathrm{Var}(\log \Lambda(s,\omega)) = ||P_S\psi||^2 ,$$

and according to μ_{x+m}

$$E_{x+m}(\log \Lambda(s,\omega)) = E_{x+m}(P_S\psi) - \frac{1}{2}||P_S\psi||^2$$

$$= E_x[P_S\psi \cdot \psi] - \frac{1}{2}||P_S\psi||^2 = \frac{1}{2}||P_S\psi||^2 .$$

The variance remains $||P_S\psi||^2$.

The key observation is the following:

Proposition 1: *Assume* X *has continuous covariance* R *and that* $m(t) = E(x_t\psi)$ *for* t *in* T. *Then according to* μ_x

$\log \Lambda(s,\omega)$ *is equal in law to* $b(||P_S\psi||^2) - \frac{1}{2}||P_S\psi||^2$,

where b *is Brownian motion. Its sample paths are thus left continuous with right hand limits.*

According to μ_{x+m}

$\log \Lambda(s,\omega)$ *is equal in law to* $b(||P_S\psi||^2) + \frac{1}{2}||P_S\psi||^2$.

To prove this merely note that Gaussian processes are determined by their mean and covariance functions.

This result extends to say that if μ_{x+m} and μ_x are absolutely continuous over every finite observation period $[0,s]$ then

$\log \Lambda(s,\omega)$ is equal in law to $b(g(s)) - \frac{1}{2} g(s)$ under hypothesis signal absent, where $g(s)$ is a non-decreasing left continuous function and b is Brownian motion.

2. *On the Optimality of the Wald Test.* The Wald sequential test is of the form, choose $a > 0 > c$ and observe whether $\log \Lambda(t,\omega)$ takes the value a or c first. If $g(s)$ is continuous and approaches infinity it must hit one of these eventually under either hypothesis by Proposition 1 since $b(g(s)) - \frac{1}{2} g(s) \to -\infty$ as $g(s) \to \infty$ and $b(g(s)) + \frac{1}{2} g(s) \to \infty$ as $g(s) \to \infty$. If it hits a first say H_1; otherwise say H_0. The error probabilities are then $P(a|H_0)$ and $P(c|H_1)$.

Wald showed that if the test consists of making independent observations of a random variable distributed according to one of two distribution functions, then the sequential probability ratio test minimizes the average time G for making a decision among all tests with the given error probabilities. This generalizes to say that if $\log \Lambda(t)$ has stationary independent increments the same optimality exists (Dvoretzky, Kiefer, Wolfowitz, 1953). Thus the test is optimal in the sense of Wald if $g(s) = cs$ but not necessarily so in general. Instead of minimizing the expected time for decision the test minimizes the expectation of a monotone function of that time, so it still is of interest in finding the optimal sequential test.

Assume $\log \Lambda(t) \stackrel{L}{=} b(g(t)) - \frac{g(t)}{2}$ (or $b(g(t)) + \frac{g(t)}{2}$ under H_1), where $g(0) = 0$, $g(t)$ is continuous and $g(t) \to \infty$ as $t \to \infty$. The last condition ensures that a decision is eventually reached using the Wald test and also ensures that a fixed time test exists. The continuity conditions simplify the following work but are not necessary.

Proposition 2: *Let* G *be the first time* $\log \Lambda(t)$ *hits* $\pm a$. *Under the hypotheses above* $E(G < \infty)$ *if and only if*

$$\int_0^{\infty} \exp\left(- \frac{g(t)}{8}\left(1 + \frac{\Pi^2}{a^2}\right)\right) dt < \infty \quad .$$

Proof: Let

$$T_{(-a,a)} = \inf \{t: |b(t)| = a\} \quad .$$

By a formula of Darling and Siegert (1953)

$$P[T_{(-a,a)} > t] = \frac{2}{\Pi} \sum_0^{\infty} \frac{(-1)^j}{(j+\frac{1}{2})} \exp\left(\frac{-(j+\frac{1}{2})^2 \Pi^2 t}{2a^2}\right) \quad .$$

The terms in the sum decrease in absolute value. Thus

$$\frac{4}{\Pi}\left(\exp\left(\frac{-\Pi^2 t}{8a^2}\right) - \frac{1}{3}\exp\left(-\frac{9\Pi^2 t}{8a^2}\right)\right) \le P[T_{(-a,a)} > t]$$

$$\le \frac{4}{\Pi}\exp\left(\frac{-\Pi^2 t}{8a^2}\right) \quad .$$

For t large enough we thus have

$$\frac{2}{\Pi}\exp\left(\frac{-\Pi^2 t}{8a^2}\right) \le P[T_{(-a,a)} > t] \le \frac{4}{\Pi}\exp\left(\frac{-\Pi^2 t}{8a^2}\right) \quad .$$

Now let

$$G = \inf \{t: |b(g(t)) - \frac{g(t)}{2}| = a\} \quad .$$

$$P[G > S] = \int_{\substack{\sup|X(t)| \leq a \\ t \leq S}} d\mu_{b(g(t)) - \frac{g(t)}{2}}$$

$$= \int_{\substack{\sup|X(t)| \leq a \\ t \leq g(S)}} d\mu_{b(t) - t/2}$$

$$= \int_{\substack{\sup|X(t)| \leq a \\ t \leq g(S)}} \exp\left(- \frac{b(g(S))}{2} - \frac{g(S)}{8}\right) d\mu_b$$

Hence

$$e^{-\frac{a}{2}} e^{-\frac{g(S)}{8}} P[T_{(-a,a)} > g(S)] \leq P[G > S]$$

$$\leq e^{\frac{a}{2}} e^{-\frac{g(S)}{8}} P[T_{(-a,a)} > g(S)]$$

and for t large enough

$$\frac{2}{\Pi} e^{-\frac{a}{2}} \exp\left(- \frac{g(S)}{8}\left(1 + \frac{\Pi^2}{a^2}\right)\right) \leq P[G > S]$$

$$\leq \frac{4e^{a/2}}{\Pi} \exp\left(- \frac{g(S)}{8}\left(1 + \frac{\Pi^2}{a^2}\right)\right) .$$

But $E(G < \infty)$ if and only if

$$\int_0^\infty P(G > S)\, dS < \infty. \qquad \text{Q.E.D.}$$

Corollary: *If* $\int_0^\infty \exp\left(- \frac{g(t)}{8}\left(1 + \frac{\Pi^2}{a^2}\right)\right) dt = \infty$ *then the Wald test cannot be optimal.*

Proof: Since $g(t) \to \infty$ a finite test exists. It has finite average duration while the Wald test does not. Q.E.D.

The following curious dividing line exists between tests with finite and infinite expected time.

Assume that for t large, $g = c \log t$. Then $E(G)$ exists if and only if $C > 8/(1 + \frac{\Pi^2}{a^2})$. In particular, if $C \geq 8$ then $E(G) < \infty$ for all $a > 0$. If $0 < C < 8$ then there exists a for which $E(G_a) = \infty$. If $g < c \log t$ for all $c > 0$ and t large enough, then $E(G_a) = \infty$ for all a.

The problem arises of finding the optimal test when the Wald test is not optimal. Although this is as yet unsolved, the following observation reduces the problem to another problem deserving of attention.

Proposition 3: *The problem of minimizing* $E(G)$ *in a sequential test for arbitrary signal in correlated Gaussian noise (i.e., where* $\log \Lambda(t) \overset{L}{=} b(g(t)) - g(t)/2)$ *can be transformed to the problem of minimizing* $E(g^{-1}(G))$, *where* $\log \Lambda(t) \overset{L}{=} b(t) - t/2$.

It follows from results of Weiss (1953) that if there is an optimal test, it would be a generalized sequential probability ratio test. This paper should motivate the problem of finding stopping curves in the case of independent observations of a random variable under one of two hypotheses where the problem is to minimize the expectation of a monotone function of the test duration, rather than the expectation of the time of the test. If a risk approach is used, Chernoff's method reduces the question to a free boundary value problem. However, even qualitative properties of the boundary for simple loss functions are difficult to obtain by this method.

References

1. Chernoff, Herman (1960). Sequential Tests for the Mean of a Normal Distribution, *Fourth Berkeley Symposium*, Vol. 4, p. 79-91.

2. Darling, and Siegert, (1953). The First Passage Problem for a Continuous Markov Process, *Annals of Mathematical Statistics*, Vol. 24, p. 624-639.

3. Dvoretzky, Kiefer and Wolfowitz, (1953). Sequential Decision Problems for Processes with Continuous Time, Testing Hypotheses, *Annals of Mathematical Statistics*, Vol. 24, p. 254-264.

4. Eisenberg, B. (1970). Translating Gaussian Processes, *Annals of Mathematical Statistics*, Vol. 41, p.888-893.

5. Hajek, J. (1962). On linear Statistical Problems in Stochastic Processes, 12(87), *Czechoslovak Mathematical Journal*, p. 404-442.

6. Hida, T., (1970). *Stationary Stochastic Processes*, Princeton University Press, Princeton, New Jersey.

7. Selin, Ivan, (1964). The Sequential Estimation and Detection of Signals and Normal Noise I, *Journal of Information and Control*, Vol. 7, p. 512-534.

8. Selin, Ivan, (1965). The Sequential Estimation and Detection of Signals in Normal Noise II, *Journal of Information and Control*, Vol. 8, p. 1-35.

9. Weiss, L., (1953). Testing One Simple Hypothesis Against Another, *Annals of Mathematical Statistics*, Vol. 24, p. 273-281.